BUSINESS LAW

1

BUSINESS LAW

A. G. King MA, Solicitor (Hons)
Director of Education, Clifford Chance
Formerly Senior Lecturer, College of Law, London

and

J. S. Barlow MA (Cantab), LLM (London), Solicitor
Principal Lecturer and Head of CPE, College of Law, York

 BLACKSTONE PRESS LIMITED

First published in Great Britain 1993 by Blackstone Press Limited, 9-15 Aldine Street, London W12 8AW.
Telephone: 081-740 1173

ISBN: 1 85431 291 X

British Library Cataloguing in Publication Data
A CIP catalogue record for this book is available from the British Library.

Reprinted 1993

Typeset by Montage Studios Ltd, Tonbridge, Kent
Printed by Ashford Colour Press, Gosport, Hampshire

CONTENTS

Preface   ix

Acknowledgment   x

PARTNERSHIPS   1

1 Characteristics of Partnerships   3

1.1 Introduction — 1.2 Relevant law — 1.3 Definition of partnership — 1.4 Nature of partnership — 1.5 Number of partners — 1.6 Capacity — 1.7 Duration of partnership — 1.8 Partnership name and publicity of information

2 Partnership Management and Finance   7

2.1 Introduction — 2.2 Management of the business — 2.3 The legal relationship between the partners (s. 24) — 2.4 The duty of good faith — 2.5 The partnership's finances — 2.6 The distinction between a partner and a lender — 2.7 Division of profits between partners — 2.8 Payment of interest — 2.9 Partnership property

3 Liability of Partners to Outsiders   15

3.1 Introduction — 3.2 Nature of liability — 3.3 Partnership and agency — 3.4 Persons held out as partners — 3.5 Liability of new partners — 3.6 Partners' liability in tort — 3.7 Suing or being sued

4 Partnership Disputes   21

4.1 Introduction — 4.2 Dissolution by the court — 4.3 Appointment of a receiver — 4.4 Arbitration — 4.5 Expulsion of a partner

5 Termination of and Retirement from a Partnership   25

5.1 Introduction — 5.2 Dissolution of partnership — 5.3 Retirement of a partner — 5.4 Death

COMPANIES   33

6 Limited Companies   35

6.1 Introduction — 6.2 Corporations — 6.3 Sources of company law — 6.4 Registration — 6.5 Types of registered company — 6.6 Public and private companies — 6.7 Separate legal personality — 6.8 'Lifting the veil of incorporation'

CONTENTS

7 Formation of a Limited Company   43

7.1 Introduction — 7.2 Steps leading to incorporation — 7.3 The certificate of incorporation — 7.4 Steps necessary after incorporation — 7.5 Methods of incorporation — 7.6 Pre-incorporation contracts — 7.7 Change of name — 7.8 Change of objects

8 Directors   55

8.1 Division of powers within a company — 8.2 Appointment of directors — 8.3 Removal of directors from office — 8.4 Alternate directors — 8.5 Shadow directors — 8.6 Powers of directors — 8.7 Directors' duties — 8.8 Statutory provisions concerning directors — 8.9 Managing directors — 8.10 Removal of directors (s. 303 CA 1985) — 8.11 The directors and protection of outsiders — 8.12 The company secretary

9 Shareholders   69

9.1 Introduction — 9.2 Registration of membership — 9.3 Powers and duties of shareholders — 9.4 Internal disputes – introduction — 9.5 Section 14 Companies Act 1985 — 9.6 *Foss* v *Harbottle* — 9.7 Actions by shareholders – procedure — 9.8 Section 459 Companies Act 1985 — 9.9 Just and equitable winding up — 9.10 Shareholders and profits — 9.11 Procedure for declaring and paying a dividend — 9.12 Restrictions on sources of dividends

10 Company Finance   83

10.1 Introduction — 10.2 Issue of shares — 10.3 Share capital — 10.4 Financial assistance by company for purchase of shares — 10.5 Classes of shares — 10.6 The power to borrow — 10.7 Secured loans — 10.8 Registration of charges — 10.9 Priority of charges — 10.10 Remedies of debenture-holders — 10.11 Receivers — 10.12 Position of debenture-holders — 10.13 Steps to be taken by a lender to a company — 10.14 Alteration to the capital clause

11 Disposal of Shares   97

11.1 Introduction — 11.2 Transfer of shares — 11.3 Transmission by operation of law — 11.4 Financial involvement by the company

12 Company Meetings and Resolutions   103

12.1 Types of general meeting — 12.2 Resolutions — 12.3 Calling a general meeting — 12.4 Notice of meetings — 12.5 Proceedings at meetings — 12.6 Dispensing with meetings — 12.7 Minutes and returns

TAXATION   109

13 The Taxation of the Income Profits and Losses of Sole Traders and Partnerships   111

13.1 Introduction — 13.2 Income profits — 13.3 The basis of assessment for income tax — 13.4 Losses under the income tax system — 13.5 Income tax liability of partnerships

14 The Tax Consequences of Leaving and Joining a Partnership   123

14.1 Introduction — 14.2 The tax consequences of the dissolution of a partnership — 14.3 The tax consequences of the retirement of a partner — 14.4 The tax consequences of death — 14.5 The tax consequences of expulsion from a partnership — 14.6 The tax consequences of admission of a new partner

15 The Corporation Tax System   135

15.1 Introduction — 15.2 Calculation of profits – corporation tax — 15.3 Assessment – corporation tax — 15.4 Loss relief under the corporation tax system — 15.5 Close companies

16   Taxation of Dividends, Debenture Interest and Directors' Fees   141

16.1 Introduction — 16.2 Taxation of distributions — 16.3 Interest on debentures — 16.4 Directors' fees — 16.5 Retained profits — 16.6 Raising the funds to invest in the company — 16.7 Conclusion

17   Capital Allowances   157

17.1 Introduction — 17.2 Plant and machinery — 17.3 Industrial buildings — 17.4 Other expenditure which attracts capital allowances

18   Capital Gains Tax and Inheritance Tax on Business Assets   161

18.1 Introduction — 18.2 Capital gains tax — 18.3 Inheritance tax

19   Retirement Provision   173

19.1 Introduction — 19.2 Retirement provision for directors and employees — 19.3 Retirement provision for sole proprietors and partners

THE EUROPEAN COMMUNITY   179

20   The European Community: the Right of Establishment and the Right to Provide Services   181

20.1 Introduction — 20.2 Establishment and services — 20.3 Limitations on the rights of establishment and provision of services

21   Treaty of Rome Articles 85 and 86   183

21.1 Introduction — 21.2 Article 85 — 21.3 Article 86 — 21.4 Enforcement of competition policy — 21.5 UK competition law

INSOLVENCY   187

22   Bankruptcy   189

22.1 Introduction — 22.2 The bankruptcy procedure — 22.3 The trustee in bankruptcy — 22.4 Effect of the bankruptcy order on the bankrupt personally — 22.5 Assets in the bankrupt's estate — 22.6 Distribution of the bankrupt's assets — 22.7 Duration of the bankruptcy and discharge of the bankrupt — 22.8 Voluntary arrangements

23   Company Insolvency Proceedings   201

23.1 Introduction — 23.2 Administration orders — 23.3 Voluntary arrangements (sections 1 to 7) — 23.4 Receivership — 23.5 Liquidation or winding up — 23.6 Liquidators — 23.7 Collection and distribution of assets in liquidation — 23.8 Order of entitlement to assets — 23.9 Dissolution

24   Liabilities Arising from Insolvency   215

24.1 Wrongful trading (section 214) — 24.2 Transactions at an undervalue and preferences — 24.3 Transactions defrauding creditors — 24.4 Floating charges (section 245)

CONTENTS

SPECIAL TOPICS   219

25   The Partnership Agreement   221

25.1 Introduction — 25.2 Is a written partnership agreement necessary? — 25.3 The clauses of the partnership agreement — 25.4 Issues for an incoming partner

26   The Articles of a Private Company   225

26.1 Table A — 26.2 Provisions concerning shares and membership — 26.3 Provisions concerning meetings of shareholders — 26.4 Provisions concerning directors — 26.5 Alteration of articles

27   A Debenture Document   231

27.1 Introduction — 27.2 Terms relating to repayment and interest — 27.3 Terms relating to security — 27.4 Clauses designed to give the lender further protection

28   Shareholders' Agreements   235

28.1 Introduction — 28.2 The advantages of a shareholders' agreement — 28.3 Drafting a shareholders' agreement — 28.4 Legal limits on the use of shareholders' agreements — 28.5 Enforcing the agreement

29   Making and Interpreting a Company Search and Accounts   239

29.1 Introduction — 29.2 Official notification — 29.3 Company searches — 29.4 The duty to submit accounts — 29.5 Small and medium sized companies — 29.6 Profit and loss account — 29.7 Balance sheet — 29.8 Format of accounts — 29.9 Interpretation of accounts — 29.10 Solvency — 29.11 Profitability

30   Sale of a Business to a Company   251

30.1 Introduction — 30.2 Income tax — 30.3 Capital gains tax — 30.4 VAT — 30.5 Capital tax relief and retained assets — 30.6 Stamp duty — 30.7 Subsidiary matters

31   Choice of Business Medium   261

31.1 Introduction — 31.2 Risk of capital — 31.3 Expense — 31.4 Management — 31.5 Publicity — 31.6 Taxation – trading profits — 31.7 Interest relief — 31.8 Capital gains — 31.9 Inheritance tax — 31.10 Pensions and social security — 31.11 Conclusion

32   Public Companies   269

32.1 Introduction — 32.2 The distinguishing features of a public company — 32.3 Seeking and maintaining a Stock Exchange listing

33   Business Contracts — Distributorship or Marketing Agreements   279

33.1 Introduction — 33.2 An agent or a distributor? — 33.3 Types of distributorship agreement — 33.4 The competition issues — 33.5 The provisions of exclusive distribution agreements

Index   289

PREFACE

This Guide is designed for use in the Legal Practice Course. We have included in it the material for the compulsory head on business law. The first part of the Guide deals with partnership law and practice. The second part deals with company law and practice. In each of these parts we have concentrated on the essential background law which all trainees who are following the LPC will need so as to follow their courses.

The third part of the Guide deals with taxation. This is separated from the substantive law so that trainees may make a comparison between companies and partnerships. Taxation is looked at both from the point of view of the business and from the point of view of the proprietors/investors in the business.

We have also included a short section in the Guide on EC law. In doing so we have chosen two topics of substantive EC law which are likely to be particularly relevant in a business context.

Insolvency (both in relation to individuals and companies) is dealt with in a separate part of the Guide.

The last part of the Guide deals with a number of chapters on what we have described as 'special topics'. These are topics which we believe to be of particular practical significance in the context of a Legal Practice Course. It may be that students at some institutions will not have separate course elements on all of these topics. Nevertheless, we believe that they will all prove useful in putting business law into a practical context.

Once again our thanks go to everyone at Blackstone Press (and especially Mandy Preece) for their patience, support and efficiency.

John Barlow
Anthony King

ACKNOWLEDGMENT

Chapter 33 is based on an article entitled 'Distributorships — Low Risk Expansion into New Markets' by Michael Arnold (a partner in Evershed Wells & Hind) which appeared in *PLC Magazine*, Volume IV, Number 2 (March 1993). The authors would like to thank Michael Arnold and *PLC Magazine* for their help with the chapter.

PARTNERSHIPS

ONE

CHARACTERISTICS OF PARTNERSHIPS

1.1 Introduction

1.1.1 TYPES OF BUSINESS MEDIUM

Trading businesses in this country are run by sole proprietors, partnerships or companies. Unincorporated businesses, such as sole proprietorships and partnerships, tend to be relatively small enterprises (with the notable exceptions of certain professional partnerships). Businesses run through companies range across the whole spectrum in terms of size, from the very small to the huge.

This Guide is principally concerned with the formation, administration and 'termination' of partnerships (and, where relevant, sole proprietorships) and of companies, as well as with the question of whether a company is preferable to a partnership as a means of running a particular business.

In this chapter, we will look at the rules for determining whether a partnership has come into existence as well as the formalities with which businesses which will be run through partnerships must comply. (This Guide will not consider the rules relating to limited partnerships created under the Limited Partnership Act 1907.)

We will not look separately in this chapter, or in the ones which follow, at sole proprietorships. However, many of the formalities to which partnerships are subject (for example, in relation to the choice of a business name) apply equally to sole proprietors.

1.2 Relevant Law

Much of the law relating to partnership is to be found in the Partnership Act (PA) 1890. The Act was mainly declaratory of the law of partnership as it had developed up to 1890. The Act does not provide a complete code of partnership law, and indeed s. 46 specifically provides that: 'The rules of equity and of common law applicable to partnership shall continue in force except so far as they are inconsistent with the express provisions of this Act.'.

1.3 Definition of Partnership

The definition of a partnership is to be found in s. 1(1) PA 1890 which states: 'Partnership is the relation which subsists between persons carrying on a business in common with a view to profit.' (A registered company is specifically excluded from the definition by s. 1(2)). To satisfy the definition two or more persons must be carrying on a business. It follows from this that an agreement to run a business in the future does not constitute an immediate partnership, nor does the taking of preliminary steps to enable a business to be run. 'Business' is defined by s. 45 PA 1890 as including 'every trade, occupation or profession'.

Section 2 PA 1890 lays down certain 'rules for determining the existence of a partnership'. These provide that:

(a) Joint or common ownership of property 'does not of itself create a partnership' even where profits from the property are shared (s. 2(1)).

(b) The sharing of *gross* returns does not of itself create a partnership (s. 2(2)). A person is not, therefore, a partner in a business merely because he receives commission on sales which he has introduced.

(c) The receipt of a share of *profits* is prima facie evidence of partnership (s. 2(3)). This topic is dealt with in **2.6**.

It should be noted that a written partnership agreement is not a pre-requisite for the existence of a partnership. The existence of a partnership is always a question of fact.

1.4 Nature of Partnership

A partnership is, in law, a very different type of institution from a company. The most significant difference is that partners have unlimited liability for the debts of the partnership, whereas the liability of shareholders for company's debts is limited. (The liability of partners to creditors is considered in **Chapter 3**.) Partnerships, unlike companies, are not required to go through any registration process when they are formed and, again unlike companies, they are under no obligation to make their accounts public.

A partnership is not a separate legal entity from its partners (in contrast to companies which are legally distinct from their shareholders). However, to a limited extent in relation to litigation (see **Chapter 3**) and taxation (see **Chapter 13**), the existence of the partnership is recognised as being independent of the individual members.

1.5 Number of Partners

The maximum number of persons who may be members of a particular parnership is usually 20 (s. 716 Companies Act (CA) 1985). However, under s. 716(2) certain professions, including those of solicitors and accountants, are exempt from this limit.

1.6 Capacity

Generally speaking any person including a minor (person under 18) is legally capable of forming a partnership with any other person. Companies as well as individuals can, provided their objects clause gives them the power to do so, enter into a partnership with other companies or with individuals.

1.7 Duration of Partnership

Most partnerships are partnerships 'at will'. This means that no particular period is agreed upon as being the time during which the partnership is to last. A partnership at will can be dissolved by notice by any partner unless there is an agreement to the contrary.

A partnership for a fixed term or for a term defined by reference to some event (e.g., the completion of some particular job) is also possible. Such a partnership cannot generally be dissolved by notice.

There may sometimes be difficulty in deciding when a partnership begins. Because of the way partnership is defined this is essentially a question of fact. The terms of a partnership agreement as to commencement may be evidence (though not conclusive evidence) of when a partnership begins.

1.8 Partnership Name and Publicity of Information

A partnership is entitled (subject to what is said below) to choose any name which it wishes. There is nothing in partnership law corresponding with the requirement that a company should have a corporate name which is registered with the Registrar of Companies (see **7.2.1.1**).

The law relating to partnership names is now contained in the Business Names Act (BNA) 1985. The Act permits the free use of certain names and requires approval for others. In addition it contains rules requiring publicity as to the membership of partnerships in certain circumstances.

1.8.1 AUTOMATICALLY PERMITTED NAMES

If the business of a partnership is carried on under a name which consists of the surnames of all the partners no restrictions apply (s. 1 BNA 1985). This is also the case where the name consists of the partners' surnames together with 'permitted additions' and nothing else. The permitted additions are:

(a) the forenames or initials of the partners;
(b) the addition of an 's' to a surname to signify that there is more than one partner with that name; and/or
(c) a statement that the business is being carried on in succession to the business of a former owner.

Where the name of the partnership does not consist solely of the surnames of the partners, or of the surnames of the partners together with permitted additions, then the disclosure requirements of s. 4 BNA 1985 will apply and in some cases approval of the name is required under ss. 2 and 3.

1.8.2 APPROVAL UNDER ss. 2 AND 3 BNA 1985

Section 2 BNA 1985 makes it an offence to carry on business (without the approval of the Secretary of State) under a name which suggests a connection with the government or a local authority, or which includes a word specified in regulations made under the Act. Section 3 gives the Secretary of State power to make such regulations. Regulations have been made under the Act which specify scores of words for which approval is required.

Partners who are starting a business and who wish to use a business name should consult the regulations. If they find that their name includes a word covered by the regulations they should first write to the government department or other body (if any) which is to be consulted in relation to that word asking it whether it objects. They should then apply to the Secretary of State for approval stating that they have made such a request and enclosing a copy of any reply that they have received from the government department or other body that they have consulted.

1.8.3 DISCLOSURE REQUIREMENTS OF s. 4 BNA 1985

Any partnership which uses a business name (other than one permitted under s. 1 BNA 1985) is required to state the name of each partner (together with an address for service in Great Britain) on:

(a) every business letter;
(b) order for goods or services;
(c) invoice;
(d) receipt; and
(e) written demand for payment of a debt (s. 4(1)(a) BNA 1985).

CHARACTERISTICS OF PARTNERSHIPS

The same information must also be given by a notice in a prominent position at each place of business of the partnership (s. 4(1)(b) BNA 1985). The same information must also be given (in writing) to anyone with whom the partnership has had dealings or negotiations and who asks for the information (s. 4(2) BNA 1985).

The requirement of including names and addresses in letters, etc., does not apply to a partnership with more than 20 members provided that instead of the partners' names, the letter includes a statement of the address of the principal place of business and a statement that the names and addresses of the partners can be inspected there.

TWO

PARTNERSHIP MANAGEMENT AND FINANCE

2.1 Introduction

In this chapter we will look at:

(a) the ways a partnership can be managed;

(b) the relationship of the partners to each other and the obligations which partnerships owe to each other; and

(c) how the finances of a partnership can be handled, both in terms of the raising of capital to finance the business and the distribution of the profits the business makes.

2.2 Management of the Business

The business of a partnership will usually be controlled by all the partners, each of whom will take an active part in management.

Section 24(5) PA 1890 provides that (in the absence of any express or implied agreement to the contrary): 'Every partner may take part in the management of the partnership business'. If the management structure of a particular partnership is to be different from the equality of partners which is presumed by s. 24(5), then ideally express agreement should be made. For example, in a large partnership there may be different grades of partners, major decisions being taken only by the senior grade. Similarly, some partners may be 'sleeping partners', that is partners who have contributed capital but who do not take an active part in management of the partnership business or in decision-making.

2.3 The Legal Relationship between the Partners (s. 24)

Section 24 PA 1890 lays down a number of rules which regulate the relationship between partners. These rules '. . . may be varied by the consent of all the partners, and such consent may be express or inferred from a course of conduct'. Several of the subsections of s. 24 deal with the relationship of the partners in respect of the distribution of profits and losses made by the partnership; these subsections are dealt with in **2.7** below.

2.3.1 DECISIONS OF THE PARTNERS

Among the subsections dealing with this area, perhaps the most important is subsection 8 which says that (subject to contrary agreement, express or implied):

Any differences arising as to ordinary matters connected with the partnership business may be decided by a majority of the partners, but no change may be made in the nature of the partnership business without the consent of all the partners.

In most circumstances, therefore, a simple majority of the partners is required to take a decision. If there is an equality of votes a decision has not been taken and the status quo is preserved.

2.3.2 RESTRICTIONS ON THE MAJORITY

There are three main limitations imposed on the ability of the majority of the partners to bind the whole firm. First, partners are under a fiduciary duty to each other and so must exercise their powers for the benefit of the firm as a whole. For example, in *Blisset* v *Daniel* (1853) 10 Hare 493, a power was given (by the partnership agreement) to the majority of the partners permitting them to expel a partner. The majority exercised this power with a view to obtaining the expelled partner's shares in the partnership cheaply. This was held to be an illegal use of the power to expel as it amounted to a breach of the duty of good faith required of a fiduciary.

Secondly, the majority may not impose their views on the minority without first consulting them (*Const* v *Harris* (1824) T & R 496). However, in the case of a partnership there is no requirement that consultation should take the form of a meeting (unless the partnership agreement so provides).

Thirdly, the following provisions of the Partnership Act limit majority rule:

(a)   Section 24(8) requires unanimity for a change in the partnership business. This is so that a partner who has decided to invest in one particular type of business will not be forced to invest in something else against his wishes.

(b)   Section 24(7) provides that: 'No person may be introduced as a partner without the consent of all the existing partners.' Such a rule is vital to the running of a small partnership where each partner will wish to ensure that his fellow partners cannot force him to go into partnership with someone of whom he disapproves. In a large partnership it may be considered appropriate that s. 24(7) should not apply (so that, for example, the senior partners may be given power to decide who to take on as junior partners and who to promote to senior partnership), in which case the partnership agreement must exclude the requirement of unanimity in this respect.

(c)   Unanimity is required by s. 19 for an alteration to the partnership agreement. The agreement of the partners to an alteration can be inferred from a course of dealings.

(d)   Section 25 prevents expulsion of a partner by a majority of the partners unless all the partners have *expressly* agreed to this.

2.3.3 OTHER PROVISIONS

Other provisions of s. 24 which affect the relationship between the partners are as follows:

(a)   Section 24(2) gives a partner a right to be indemnified by the firm in respect of payments made and personal liabilities incurred 'in the ordinary and proper conduct of the business of the firm or in or about anything necessarily done for the preservation of the business or property of the firm'.

(b)   Section 24(9) gives all the partners a right to inspect and copy the partnership accounts.

2.4   The Duty of Good Faith

2.4.1   EQUITABLE PROVISIONS

The contract of partnership is a contract *uberrimae fidei* (of the utmost good faith), so that a partner is required to disclose all relevant information in his possession to his partners. If he fails to do so his partners may set aside transactions which they have entered into with him as a result of the non-disclosure.

Similarly, a partner owes a fiduciary duty to his fellow partners; that is he owes the duties of good faith to his partners in his dealings with them which a trustee owes to a beneficiary. This duty continues even after the dissolution of the partnership. For example, in *Thompson's Trustee in Bankruptcy* v *Heaton* [1974] 1 WLR 605, a farming partnership was dissolved at a time when it owned a lease. One of the former partners (Heaton) was permitted by the other (Thompson) to continue in occupation of the leasehold property. Heaton then (through a company which he owned) purchased the freehold reversion and sold it for a profit. It was held that the profit belonged to the partners, as it arose out of the ownership of the lease by the partnership. Thompson's estate was, therefore, entitled to an equal share in the profit.

2.4.2 STATUTORY PROVISIONS

The requirement of good faith in dealings between partners is of general application but three particular aspects of the duty are dealt with in ss. 28-30 PA 1890.

2.4.2.1 Duty to disclose information

Section 28 provides that: 'Partners are bound to render true accounts and full information of all things affecting the partnership to any partner or his legal representative.' This is really just a formulation in statutory language of the duty of disclosure imposed by equity. A good illustration of the working of the rule is given by *Law* v *Law* [1905] 1 Ch 140. In that case one partner offered to buy the share of another at a price which seemed fair to the vendor who was not actively engaged in running the business. The purchaser, however, knew of facts which made the vendor's share more valuable than the vendor realised. When the vendor discovered this it was held that he was entitled to rescind the contract of sale on the ground of non-disclosure.

2.4.2.2 Duty to account for secret profits

Section 29 is concerned with secret profits; it states that:

(1) Every partner must account to the firm for any benefit derived by him without the consent of the other partners from any transaction concerning the partnership, or from any use by him of the partnership property, name or business connection.
(2) This section applies also to transactions undertaken after a partnership has been dissolved by the death of a partner, and before the affairs thereof have been completely wound up, either by any surviving partner or by the representative of the deceased partner.

This section imposes the same restrictions and duties on partners as apply to company directors. Any profit made in breach of the section is held on trust for the benefit of the partnership as a whole. The rule applies to transactions entered into by a partner where the opportunity came to him as a result of the partnership, to commissions received on contracts introduced to the partnership, to sales of property to the partnership by a partner and to profits derived from sales of partnership property. A partner may retain any such profit if his partners consent following full disclosure of the circumstances.

2.4.2.3 Duty to account for profits from competing business

Section 30 PA 1890 provides that: 'If a partner, without the consent of the other partners, carries on any business of the same nature as and competing with that of the firm, he must account for and pay over to the firm all profits made by him in that business.' The provisions of s. 30 are quite narrow. In order to succeed under this section the partners must show that the businesses are of the same nature and that they are in fact competing for the same customers. Thus in *Aas* v *Benham* [1891] 2 Ch 244, a partner in a firm of shipbrokers was held not to be accountable for profits he had made from shipbuilding. However, in *Glassington* v *Thwaites* (1823) 1 Sim & St 124, a partner in a morning newspaper who set up an evening newspaper was held to be accountable. It should be noted that there is overlap between s. 30 and s. 29(1) — a partner may be held accountable because he is competing with his partners or because he is using 'the partnership property name or business connection'; often a partner who sets up a new business will be doing both these things.

A partner who sets up a non-competing business and who does not use the partnership property, name or business connection is not liable to his partners in any way under the Act. Many partnership agreements, therefore, provide that the partners are to devote their whole time to the partnership and specify that the partners are not to start any other businesses. With such an agreement the partners may be able to obtain an injunction, damages or dissolution of the partnership against the partner who sets up a new business, even though it does not compete with the firm's business. They will not, however, have any right to make him contribute his profits in the other business to the partnership.

2.5 The Partnership's Finances

2.5.1 SOURCES OF FINANCE

The sources of finance for a partnership are basically the same as those available to any business. A partnership will need assets and cash in order to run its business. Money (or in some cases assets) may be contributed in the form of a permanent investment by the partners or it may be borrowed either from the partners or from outside sources. Once the business of the partnership has started further finance may also be provided by retention of profits.

2.5.2 PARTNERS' CAPITAL

The permanent investment of a partner is described as his 'capital'. The capital of a partner may be contributed by him in the form of cash or property (including, for example, business premises or the goodwill of an existing business). The term capital is somewhat ambiguous. It is often used to mean the actual cash or other assets contributed to the partnership by a partner but is also used to mean the indebtedness of the partnership as a whole to the partner resulting from the contribution which he has made by his investment. A partner's capital in this latter sense should be contrasted with other debts which the firm owes to the partner, as repayment of the capital cannot normally be claimed from the firm until dissolution. Other indebtedness to a partner may be repaid before dissolution.

2.6 The Distinction between a Partner and a Lender

As we saw in **Chapter 1** the essential nature of a partnership is that two or more people are sharing profits of a business. A person who merely lends to a partnership is not a partner. The distinction between a partner and a lender is extremely important as a partner bears unlimited liability for the debts of the partnership whereas the lender only stands to lose the money invested if the business fails (if he has taken security for his loan, his risk of losing even that much may be small). However, if a business is successful a partner stands to earn a great deal of profit whereas a lender will receive only interest on his loan.

Many investors would like to have the best of both worlds, i.e., limited liability and a share of profits. This can be achieved by investing in a company. However, in other cases s. 2(3) PA 1890 effectively restricts this type of investment. Section 2(3) provides that: 'The receipt by a person of a share of profits . . . is prima facie evidence that he is a partner . . . but does not of itself make him a partner . . .'. The subsection then sets out some particular rules which provide that:

(a) A person does not become a partner merely because a debt or other liquidated sum is paid to him by instalments out of profits.

(b) A servant or agent does not become a partner merely because his remuneration varies with profits.

(c) A widow or child of a partner is not a partner merely because a proportion of profits is paid to that person as an annuity.

(d) A lender whose interest varies with profits is not automatically a partner if the contract is in writing and signed by all the parties.

(e) A vendor who receives payment for his business in the form of an annuity varying with profits is not automatically a partner.

Sharing of profits is only prima facie evidence of partnership and particular types of contract are covered by the five rules mentioned above. However, anyone who receives a share of profits *may* be held to be a partner and therefore personally liable for debts. Anyone entering into such an arrangement who does not wish to take on the risk of unlimited liability should take steps to ensure that he or she does not become a partner, e.g., by avoiding any suggestion that he has a right to take part in management and by having a written agreement setting out the terms of his involvement with the firm.

2.7 Division of Profits between Partners

Section 24 PA 1890 lays down a number of rules as to division of profits. *These rules may be varied by an express or implied agreement of the partners.* Section 24 deals with the division of both income and capital profits.

2.7.1 SHARE OF PROFITS AND LOSSES (s. 24(1))

Section 24(1) states:

All the partners are entitled to share equally in the capital and profits of the business, and must contribute equally towards the losses whether of capital or otherwise sustained by the firm.

This rule may be broken down into three parts which will be examined in turn.

2.7.1.1 Sharing of capital

The first rule states that 'all the partners are entitled to share equally in the capital'. On the face of it this means that when a partner leaves the firm or when the firm is dissolved he is entitled to take out a part of the capital corresponding with the total amount of capital divided by the number of partners. However, in practice this is unlikely to be so. All the rules in s. 24 are subject to contrary agreement express or implied. Where the partners have contributed unequally to the capital, there is an implied agreement that they are entitled to withdraw capital unequally. For example, if A contributes £10,000, B £20,000 and C £30,000 those are the sums which each can withdraw on leaving in the absence of any express agreement to the contrary.

2.7.1.2 Sharing of profits

The second part of the rule in s. 24(1) states that 'all the partners are entitled to share equally in the profits of the business'. The provision of capital in unequal shares does not give rise to the implication that *this* rule has been displaced. Thus in the example given above if the profits of the firm were £9,000, A, B, and C would each be entitled to £3,000. If a partner is to receive more than an equal share of profits because of his capital contribution or the work he does, this must be specifically agreed to and should be expressly stated in the partnership agreement.

The rule as to share of profits applies to capital as well as income profits. Thus when the firm in our example is dissolved any capital profit will be shared equally even though the capital was not contributed equally. Thus after A has received £10,000, B £20,000 and C £30,000, any surplus will be divided equally. The partners are, of course, free to agree to the contrary. It may well be decided that capital profits should be divided in the same ratio as capital was provided. The ratio in which capital profits are divided (sometimes called the 'assets surplus ratio') is often different from the income profit sharing ratio.

2.7.1.3 Sharing of losses

The third part of the rule in s. 24(1) states that losses of capital and income are prima facie to be shared equally. However, if the partners share profits unequally (because of an express or implied agreement to do so), then s. 44 PA 1890 says that losses will also be shared unequally unless there is an agreement to the contrary. For the avoidance of doubt the partnership agreement should state how both profits and losses are to be shared even if in fact the agreement follows some or all of the statutory presumptions.

2.7.2 INTEREST ON LOANS

In the absence of contrary agreement a loan by a partner to the partnership carries only 5% interest. It should be noted that this rate of interest is only paid on 'actual payments or advances'. Interest is not payable under s. 24(3) on a share of profits which is simply left in the business. The partners are, of course, free to agree that interest will be paid on undrawn profits if they wish.

2.7.3 INTEREST ON CAPITAL

Section 24(4) provides that: 'A partner is not entitled . . . to interest on capital.' Where capital is contributed unequally it may be considered appropriate to make provision in the partnership agreement for interest on capital to compensate the partner who has contributed more. The agreement should specify the rate of interest or the method by which the rate is to be determined. Interest on capital is not a deductible expense of the business in determining its net'profits. It is merely a preferential appropriation of profits. This means that once the net profit of the partnership has been ascertained the partners' first entitlement will be to interest and then the remaining net profit will be allocated in accordance with the agreed profit-sharing ratio.

2.7.4 REMUNERATION OF PARTNERS

Section 24(6) provides that: 'No partner shall be entitled to remuneration for acting in the partnership business.' In many partnerships the division of work between the partners is unequal, and therefore it will have to be expressly agreed that some of the partners be paid a salary to compensate them for the extra work which they have done. As with interest on capital, a salary payable to a partner is not a deductible expense but is merely a preferential appropriation of profit.

Example In a partnership with three members it might be agreed that:

(a)   the profit-sharing ratio will be D 20%, E 40%, F 40%;
(b)   that interest on capital will be paid at a rate of 10% p.a. (D's capital is £10,000, E's £20,000 and F's £30,000); and
(c)   that D is to have a salary of £20,000 p.a.

·If profits of £100,000 are made they will be divided as follows:

		£	£
Profit			100,000
Interest:	D	1,000	
	E	2,000	
	F	3,000	
			6,000
Salary:	D		20,000
Share of profits:	D(20%)	14,800	
	E(40%)	29,600	
	F(40%)	29,600	
			74,000
			100,000

In some partnerships (particularly professional partnerships) there may be relatively junior partners who are entitled to a salary to the exclusion of any other share of profits. At first sight it is hard to see how such 'salaried partners' can be regarded as partners at all, as partnership requires that the partners are 'carrying on business in common with a view of profit' (s. 1(1) PA 1890). Nevertheless, in *Stekel* v *Ellice* [1973] 1 WLR 191, it was held that a salaried partner could be, in law, a full partner with all the rights and duties which that entails.

2.7.5 DRAWINGS

The amount to which a partner is entitled from the profits in a firm (as salary and interest, if agreed to, and share of profits) will not be known until the profit and loss account has been drawn up after the end of the partnership's financial year. The partnership agreement will, therefore, usually provide that a partner is to have the right to take a specified amount of money on account of his expected profits during the course of the year. Sums taken on account in this way are called 'drawings'. If at the end of the year the partner has taken less than he was entitled to he can draw the balance; if he has taken more than it turns out he was entitled to then the partnership agreement will probably require him to pay back the excess and/or pay interest on it. The partnership agreement may provide that each partner is to leave undrawn in the business a proportion of his entitlement to profit. This is because businesses normally need to retain funds to meet increased costs of trading and to fund any future expansion.

2.8 Payment of Interest

A payment of interest by a partnership to a creditor will usually be a business expense. This is because the interest payment will satisfy the test for deduction of expenses, that is, that the payment is incurred 'wholly and exclusively for the purposes of the trade'. As mentioned above, payment of interest on capital to a partner is not a business expense, it is an allocation of profits to the partner.

Where a partnership receives interest this is treated as income of the partners.

2.9 Partnership Property

2.9.1 DEFINITION

Partnership property is partly defined by s. 20(1) PA 1890 as: 'All property and rights and interests in property originally brought into the partnership stock or acquired, whether by purchase or otherwise, on account of the firm, or for the purposes and in the course of the partnership business . . .' Section 21 deals with a slightly different situation and states: 'Unless the contrary intention appears, property bought with money belonging to the firm is deemed to have been bought on account of the firm.'

2.9.2 THE TEST

Whether property is partnership property or remains the separate property of a partner depends on the intention of the partners, express or implied. Property is not partnership property merely because it is used by the firm. The court does not readily assume therefore, that property introduced by a partner thereby becomes partnership property.

This is illustrated by the leading case of *Miles* v *Clarke* [1953] 1 All ER 779. Clarke carried on a photographic business in premises of which he owned the lease. He and Miles went into partnership and for a time the business was successful. However, eventually a petition for dissolution was presented as the partners were unable to agree. The question arose as to which assets were partnership property and which belonged to the partners individually. Harman J held that in the absence of express agreement he would hold property to be partnership property to the extent necessary to give business efficacy to the agreement. Therefore, the lease of the business premises belonged on dissolution to Clarke alone, each partner was entitled to his own business connection which he had brought into the firm and only the stock in trade (unused films, chemicals, etc.) could be regarded as partnership property.

There is a major reason why it may be important to decide what property is and what is not partnership property. When the firm is dissolved each partner is entitled to retain any property which is his own personal property; property which is partnership property is used first to pay creditors of the firm and then any surplus is distributed among the partners in accordance with the terms of the partnership agreement (equally in the absence of contrary agreement). This is so, once it is decided that an asset is partnership property, even though the asset was introduced by one particular partner and the asset has risen in value thus creating a capital profit for the partnership.

THREE

LIABILITY OF PARTNERS TO OUTSIDERS

3.1 Introduction

In the course of carrying on the partnership's business, the partners will incur debts and other obligations. In this chapter, we look at the nature of the partners' liabilities in these circumstances as well as the extent to which an individual partner can bind the partnership as a whole. We will then go on to look at whether it is possible for individuals who are not partners at the time the debt or obligation was incurred (whether because they have been held out as partners or because they are admitted to the partnership subsequently) to be liable for that debt or obligation.

3.2 Nature of Liability

Partners are liable for the debts and obligations of the partnership without limit (s. 9 PA). Their liability is joint in the case of contractual obligations and joint and several in the case of tortious obligations (see **3.6**). The significance of this distinction was much reduced by the Civil Liability (Contribution) Act 1978 which allows proceedings to be brought successively against persons jointly liable despite an earlier judgment against others.

Where a partnership is unable to pay its debts out of partnership property, the creditor is entitled to obtain payment from the private estates of the partners. Special rules apply in such cases, so as to attempt to do justice both to the creditors of the firm and to the creditors of the individual partners. It is not our intention to deal with these rules in detail. They may be summarised by saying that, in the first instance, the partnership property is used to pay partnership creditors in priority to private creditors and the private property of each partner is used to pay his private creditors in priority to partnership creditors. If the private creditors of a particular partner are paid in full from private property, then partnership creditors may resort to the balance of that partner's private property. If the partnership creditors are paid in full from partnership property then the private creditors of a partner may resort to the balance of his share of the partnership assets.

3.3 Partnership and Agency

3.3.1 INTRODUCTION

The relationship between partnership law and agency is very close. Indeed, most of the rules regulating the relationship between a partnership and the outside world can be explained purely in terms of particular applications of agency principles.

3.3.2 TYPES OF AUTHORITY OF A PARTNER

The partnership as a whole is bound by a partner acting within the scope of his authority. The authority of a partner may arise in three ways:

(a) First, the authority of the partners (or of a particular partner) may be specifically agreed upon by the partners — authority of this type is called 'express actual' authority.

(b) Secondly, authority may be implied either from a course of dealings between the partners (which amounts to an actual agreement) or because the authority is a natural consequence of an authority actually given to the partner — this is normally called 'implied actual' authority.

(c) Thirdly, authority may arise from the fact that a person dealing with a partner is, in certain circumstances, entitled to assume that the partner has authority to bind the firm — this type of authority is generally called 'apparent' or 'ostensible' authority, although terminology in agency law is far from consistent.

3.3.3 EXPRESS AND IMPLIED ACTUAL AUTHORITY

The scope of express and implied authority depends on the agreement between the parties. The partnership agreement may specify what powers the partners individually are to have and may specify that some are to have greater powers than others. The extent of actual authority, whether express or implied, is not, in practical terms, of great significance to a person dealing with a partner. This is because, whether or not there is actual authority, he will be able to rely on apparent authority in most circumstances in relation to most normal types of transaction. The outsider need only rely on actual authority where the partner has done something which the law does not consider to be within the apparent authority of a partner.

A partnership is bound by decisions and actions of its employees acting within the scope of their authority. An outsider seeking to rely on a decision or action of an employee would have to show that the employee had actual authority, had been held out (by the partners) as having actual authority or had been held out (by the partners) to be a partner. An individual partner cannot delegate authority to the employees (this is an application of the well known maxim of agency law *delegatus non potest delegare*).

The Partnership Act 1890 has little to say about a partner's actual authority. However, s. 6 recognises that the firm is bound by 'the acts or instruments' entered into with the authority of the firm.

3.3.4 APPARENT AUTHORITY

3.3.4.1 General principles

The scope of apparent (or ostensible) authority is not always easy to establish or describe. Such authority is sometimes said to result from a type of estoppel whereby the principal (in this case the partnership as a whole) represents, by words or conduct, that the agent (that is the partner who is negotiating with the outsider) has authority to bind the firm. Once such a representation is made and acted upon by the outsider the partnership cannot deny the authority of the individual partner to bind the firm. Alternatively, apparent authority may be said to arise simply from the fact that the partner who is negotiating *appears* to have authority to bind the firm and it is, therefore, reasonable for the outsider to assume such authority. In fact nothing really turns on this distinction, application of either test is likely to produce the same result in most circumstances.

3.3.4.2 Section 5, Partnership Act 1890

It is clear that the liability of the firm may result from the actual holding out of an agent (not necessarily a partner) as having a particular authority. However, in most cases the outsider seeks to rely on an apparent authority resulting from the fact that a person is known to be a partner in a firm. The outsider is then entitled to assume that the partner has the usual authority of a partner to bind his firm. This principle is laid down in s. 5 PA 1890 which says:

> Every partner is an agent for the firm and his other partners for the purposes of the business of the partnership; and the acts of every partner who does any act for carrying on in the usual way the business of the kind carried on by the firm of which he is a member bind the firm and his partners, unless the partner so acting has in fact no authority to act for the firm in the particular matter, and the person with whom he is dealing either knows that he has no authority, or does not know or believe him to be a partner.

The easiest way to understand the scope of the section (and thus of that part of the partner's authority which derives from the usual authority given to partners generally), is to examine each of the qualifications on a partner's authority which the section recognises.

The first qualification is that the partner can only bind the firm 'for the purposes of the business of the partnership'. The section does not say, therefore, that anything which a partner does binds the firm. The partnership agreement may be of some assistance in deciding what is the scope of the partnership business. However, it is not conclusive. In *Mercantile Credit Co. Ltd* v *Garrod* [1962] 3 All ER 1103, Mocatta J held that the test as to whether a type of business is within the scope of the partnership depends on what is apparent to the outside world in general. Consequently a sleeping partner in a garage business whose agreement specifically excluded dealing in cars was held liable on a contract for the sale of a car as this was within the scope of what outsiders would expect the business to include.

The second qualification in s. 5 is that the partnership is only bound if a partner does an act 'for carrying on in the usual way the business of the firm'. This restriction excludes the liability of the firm where the transaction is for the purposes of the business but is itself of an unusual type. For example, in *Niemann* v *Niemann* (1890) 43 ChD 198, a debt was owed to a partnership; one of the partners intended to accept payment of the debt in the form of shares in a company. This was held not to be binding on the other partner in the absence of a specific agreement. Similarly, *Powell* v *Brodhurst* [1901] 2 Ch 160 decided that a partner does not have ostensible authority to accept payment of a debt due to another partner personally rather than to the firm.

The third qualification to s. 5 is that the firm is not bound if the partner has no actual authority and the outsider either knows this or does not know or believe the person with whom he is dealing to be a partner. Clearly in such cases the firm is not bound whether one takes the view that apparent authority depends on estoppel or on appearance of authority. The outsider cannot say that he has relied on any misrepresentation nor can he claim that there appeared to be authority when he knows this to be untrue or does not think he is dealing with an agent at all.

Where, in accordance with normal agency principles, a contract made without authority is ratified by the partnership, it becomes binding on them as well as on the outsider. A partner who makes a contract with an outsider without authority will be personally liable to the outsider for breach of warranty of authority where the partnership as a whole is not made liable on the contract.

Section 8 PA 1890 provides that an outsider is not prejudiced by any restriction placed on the powers of a partner unless he has notice of it.

3.3.5 EXAMPLES OF APPARENT AUTHORITY

The question of what apparent authority a partner has in a particular case is determined by the application of s. 5 to that particular case. This is at least in part a question of fact. However, over the years the courts have decided upon examples of powers which will be assumed to be covered by apparent authority in the case of all partners in the absence of some special circumstance. The court has also recognised certain powers which it will be assumed all partners in a trading partnership have in the absence of some special circumstance. The powers of partners in a trading partnership are more extensive than the powers of partners in general. This is because the court recognises the need of the partners and the persons dealing with them to rely on normal trading practices.

Examples of powers assumed to be available to partners generally include:

(a) power to buy and sell goods (not just stock) used in the business;
(b) power to hire employees;
(c) power to receive payment of debts due to the partnership;
(d) power to pay debts owed by the partnership including a power to draw cheques for this purpose;
(e) power to engage a solicitor to represent the firm.

A partner in a trading partnership will be assumed to have all the above powers and also:

(a) power to grant security for borrowings (this does not, however, include a power to create a legal mortgage);
(b) a wider power than is given to a non-trading partner to deal with cheques and bills of exchange.

3.4 Persons Held Out as Partners

So far we have only considered the liability of actual partners to outsiders. A person who holds himself out as a partner or who 'suffers himself to be represented as a partner' is liable to anyone who 'on the faith of such representation' gives credit to the firm as if he were a partner (s. 14 PA 1890). The commonest example of the application of this rule is where a person allows his name to be used by the partnership (e.g., on notepaper) after he has ceased to be a partner (as to which, see **5.3.3.4(b)**).

A person cannot be held liable under s. 14 unless he has in some way contributed to the mistake made by the person giving credit to the firm, for example by allowing his name to be given as a partner. It is not, however, necessary that he himself should have done anything to inform the person giving credit.

Section 14 only applies where credit is given to the firm. This is construed widely so that, for example, the apparent partner is liable where goods are delivered as well as where cash is lent to the firm.

3.5 Liability of New Partners

Section 17(1) PA 1890 provides that 'a person who is admitted as a partner into an existing firm does not thereby become liable to the creditors of the firm for anything done before he became a partner'. This provision ensures that an incoming partner is not liable to the existing creditors of the firm merely because he has become a partner.

As between himself and the existing partners the incoming partner may agree to pay a share of debts owed to existing creditors. This does not make him liable to the existing creditors as they are not privy to the contract. The new partner may become liable to existing creditors by a novation (that is, a tripartite contract between the old partners, the new partner and an outsider whereby the existing contract between the old partners and the outsider is discharged and replaced by a contract between the new firm, including the new partner, and the outsider). However, this will not be a regular occurrence.

3.6 Partners' Liability in Tort

A partner who himself commits a tort is liable according to general principles of the law of tort. The liability of the firm as a whole is governed by s. 10 PA 1890:

Where, by any wrongful act or omission of any partner acting in the ordinary course of the business of the firm, or with the authority of his co-partners, loss or injury is caused to any person . . . the firm is liable . . . to the same extent as the partner so acting or omitting to act.

It should be noted that the firm (as opposed to the actual tortfeasor) is only liable if either the commission of the tort was authorised by the partners or was committed 'in the ordinary course of business'. A partnership is also liable to the same extent as other employers (under common-law principles of vicarious liability) for torts committed by its employees.

3.7   Suing or Being Sued

A partnership is not a separate legal entity. Nevertheless, the partners may sue or be sued in the firm's name under Ord. 81 of the Rules of the Supreme Court. All the partners at the date when the cause of action accrued are then parties to the action. Where an action is brought against a partnership in the firm's name the writ may be served on any partner, on any person having control or management of the business at the principal place of business or by post to the principal place of business.

A person who has a judgment against a partner for the partner's personal liability may enforce that judgment against the partner's share of partnership property by means of a charging order (s. 23(2) PA 1890). He may not enforce such a judgment against the partnership property by means of execution or garnishee proceedings (s. 23(1)). Where a charging order is made the other partners may discharge it by paying off the judgment debt; if a sale of the property is ordered, they may purchase it. A charging order gives the other partners a right to dissolve the partnership if they wish.

FOUR

PARTNERSHIP DISPUTES

4.1 Introduction

We saw in **Chapter 2** that a decision of the majority of the partners on an 'ordinary matter' is bonding on the minority. The wishes of the majority prevail over those of the minority who object. However, partnership law provides some machinery for protecting the partner who is aggrieved by what the other partners have done.

In this chapter we will look at the remedies available to a partner, which include dissolution of the partnership, appointment of a receiver and remedies available under the terms of the partnership agreement itself.

4.2 Dissolution by the Court

Dissolution of a partnership may occur automatically (e.g., on the death of a partner) by notice (e.g., any partner can give notice dissolving a partnership at will) or by court order (e.g., in the case of permanent incapacity of a partner). The various circumstances in which dissolution takes place will be considered in **Chapter 5**. In this chapter we intend to consider only those types of dissolution which provide a remedy to a partner against his co-partners under s. 35(c), (d) or (f) Partnership Act 1890.

4.2.1 SECTION 35(c): CONDUCT PREJUDICIAL TO THE BUSINESS

Section 35(c) provides that a partner may apply to the court for dissolution 'when a partner, other than the partner suing, has been guilty of such conduct as, in the opinion of the court, regard being had to the nature of the business, is calculated to prejudicially affect the carrying on of the business'. This paragraph may be relied upon even though the prejudicial conduct has nothing directly to do with the partnership. A conviction for dishonesty, for example, would be likely to be regarded as prejudicial conduct in the case of many professional partnerships even though the dishonesty did not relate to the practice as such. The test is an objective one so that it need not be shown that the guilty partner *intended* to affect the business (this is so despite the use of the word 'calculated' in s. 35(c)).

4.2.2 SECTION 35(d): BREACH OF PARTNERSHIP AGREEMENT

Section 35(d) provides that a partner may apply to the court for dissolution 'when a partner, other than the partner suing, wilfully or persistently commits a breach of the partnership agreement, or otherwise so conducts himself in matters relating to the partnership business that it is not reasonably practicable for the other partner or partners to carry on business in partnership with him'. This paragraph contemplates that the trust between partners has broken down. If this breakdown results from persistent breaches of the partnership agreement or conduct in relation to the business (although not conduct in relation to other matters), then the court can order dissolution. Many of the cases under this paragraph have revolved around financial irregularities (such as failure to account for money received on behalf of the partnership or payment of private debts from partnership money).

4.2.3 SECTION 35(f): JUST AND EQUITABLE DISSOLUTION

Section 35(f) provides that a partner may apply to the court for dissolution 'whenever in any case circumstances have arisen which in the opinion of the court render it just and equitable that the partnership be dissolved'. This provision is the equivalent of s. 122(1)(g) Insolvency Act 1986, which is in essentially similar terms but applies only to companies. The cases decided under s. 122(1)(g) (and its predecessors) are relevant also to s. 35(f), especially where the company which was the subject of the petition was intended to be run as if it were a partnership. Deadlock or other irreconcilable differences between partners are the most likely grounds on which a successful petition could be based. Exclusion of a partner from management (contrary to s. 24(5)) would also be grounds for petition, although this case would also probably be covered by s. 35(d).

4.3 Appointment of a Receiver

The court has power to appoint a receiver to run the business of a partnership for the protection of the partners. The receiver's duty is to carry on the business of the partnership for the benefit of the partners generally, not to realise a security, so that his position is quite different from that of a company receiver appointed by a debenture-holder. There is comparatively little authority as to when a receiver will be appointed but it does seem to be an exceptional step and the court is particularly reluctant to make an appointment in the case of a professional partnership (*Floydd* v *Cheney* [1970] 2 WLR 314).

4.4 Arbitration

Disputes may be solved by arbitration if the partners agree to this. It is common to make provision for arbitration in the partnership agreement. As in other types of contract an arbitration clause cannot effectively oust the jurisdiction of the court altogether. If such a clause is so widely drawn as an attempt to oust the jurisdiction of the court entirely it will be held to be void. If an action is commenced despite the presence of an arbitration clause the court has a discretion to stay the proceedings to enable the arbitration to take place.

The court action can continue without there being any question of a stay when, as a matter of construction, the court decides that the dispute which has arisen is not covered by the arbitration clause in the partnership agreement. The clause should expressly say that disputes arising during dissolution may be referred to arbitration and that the clause is binding on assignees of partners.

4.5 Expulsion of a Partner

We have seen in this chapter that it is possible for a partnership to be dissolved by the court as a way of giving the plaintiff partner a remedy against his co-partners. However, the circumstances of the dispute within the partnership may be such that some partners would prefer to get rid of one or more of their co-partners without fully dissolving the partnership.

This is only possible if an appropriate provision is included in the partnership agreement, as s. 25 PA 1890 provides:

> No majority of the partners can expel any partner unless a power to do so has been confirmed by express agreement between the partners.

The question as to whether expulsion should be provided for, and if so by what majority, is one of the issues which must be considered when a partnership agreement is being drafted (see **Chapter 24**).

Where an expulsion clause is included in the agreement it will normally state that specific activities, such as fraud, breaches of certain terms of the partnership agreement, such as that requiring a partner not to compete with the partnership or to devote the whole of his time to the business, will justify expulsion. Bankruptcy is a ground for the automatic dissolution of the whole partnership (s. 33(2) PA 1890) but in order to avoid the consequences of dissolution it is common for the partnership agreement to provide that a bankruptcy will not cause dissolution, rather that it will justify expulsion.

An expulsion clause will generally deal with the manner in which the expulsion is to be effected. It is normal to provide that written notice must be given to the offending partner and that it is to have immediate effect. The partnership agreement will normally distinguish expulsion and retirement in respect of financial arrangements. Thus, if annuities are to be paid the agreement would normally provide that an expelled partner should forfeit his rights.

If an expulsion clause is included in the partnership agreement, then the power must be exercised strictly in accordance with the agreement and in a bona fide manner and for the benefit of the partnership as a whole (*Blissett* v *Daniel* (1853) 10 Hare 493).

FIVE

TERMINATION OF AND RETIREMENT FROM A PARTNERSHIP

5.1 Introduction

An individual may cease to be a partner on the happening of one of the following events:

(a) the dissolution of the partnership;
(b) his retirement; or
(c) expulsion from the partnership.

If the partnership is dissolved, the *partnership* will come to an end, whereas on retirement or expulsion, the former partners can carry on the *business*, albeit through the medium of a newly constituted partnership.

In this chapter we will consider the legal consequences of the occurrence of these events.

The taxation consequences of the events covered in this chapter will be considered in **Chapter 14**.

5.2 Dissolution of Partnership

If an event occurs which causes a partnership to be dissolved, the partnership relationship ceases and the assets of the business must be realised. Under the Partnership Act 1890 certain events result in automatic dissolution unless the partnership agreement provides otherwise. Dissolution is such an extreme step that it is common for partners to provide expressly in their partnership agreement that dissolution is not to occur automatically on the occurrence of the events specified in the Partnership Act.

5.2.1 THE METHODS OF DISSOLVING A PARTNERSHIP

5.2.1.1 Dissolution by notice

Under ss. 26 and 32(c) PA 1890 one or more partners can, at any time, give notice to their fellow partners to dissolve the partnership. This notice takes effect from the date specified in the notice but if the notice is silent on the point, it takes effect from the date when all partners received the notice. Dissolution under ss. 26 and 32(c) can result in an immediate dissolution of the partnership. This could have disastrous consequences for the business.

However, ss. 26 and 32(c) can be overridden if the partnership agreement contains provisions to the contrary. As a result many partnership agreements require a minimum period of notice to be given before the partnership is dissolved.

5.2.1.2 Dissolution by agreement

The partnership agreement can specify circumstances which cause the partnership to be dissolved, such as the occurrence of a particular event. The agreement can also specify the manner in which the partnership will be dissolved.

5.2.1.3 Automatic dissolution

A number of events cause partnerships to dissolve automatically:

(a) *Bankruptcy, death or charge* The death or bankruptcy of a partner causes the partnership to be automatically dissolved, unless the partnership agreement contains provisions to the contrary (s. 33(1) PA 1890). Since dissolution is a serious matter for the other partners, many partnership agreements provide that, instead of causing automatic dissolution, the death of a partner shall give rise to the same consequences as a retirement (see **5.3** below). A bankruptcy is often treated in the same way as an expulsion (see **4.5**). (If a partner allows his share of the partnership property to be charged for his personal debts, the other partners have an *option* to dissolve the partnership (s. 33(2) PA 1890).)

(b) *Illegality* Partnerships formed to carry out an illegal activity or which are contrary to public policy are automatically dissolved. A change of circumstances can subsequently make illegal a partnership initially formed for a legal purpose. This can arise where, for example, a partnership is formed to carry on a particular activity which is subsequently made illegal by a change in the law. In these circumstances, s. 34 PA 1890 provides that the partnership is dissolved on the happening of the event which makes the business unlawful. (In our illustration, on the date the change in the law takes effect.) A provision to the contrary in the partnership agreement will not override s. 34.

(c) *By expiration* Under s. 32(a) and (b) PA 1890, a partnership is dissolved:

(i) if it was entered into for a fixed term, upon the expiration of that term;

(ii) if it was entered into for a single adventure or undertaking, upon the completion of that adventure or undertaking.

A provision to the contrary in the partnership agreement overrides s. 32(a) and (b).

If the agreement is silent and the partnership continues despite the occurrence of the events set out above, s. 27 provides that a partnership at will dissolvable by notice is brought into existence. Such a partnership is subject to the terms of the original agreement to the extent that these do not conflict with the incidents of a partnership at will.

5.2.1.4 Dissolution by the court

Finally, a partner may apply to the court for dissolution of the partnership provided one of the statutory grounds for dissolution by the court exists.

Under s. 96 of the Mental Health Act 1983, the court has power, if satisfied after considering medical evidence that a partner is a mental 'patient', to dissolve or give directions for the dissolution of any partnership of which a 'patient' is a member. A 'patient' is a person incapable, by reason of mental disorder, of managing his own property and affairs.

In addition to s. 96 MHA 1983, s. 35 PA 1890 sets out grounds for dissolution by the court. Those grounds which give the partners a remedy in the event of a dispute (that is to say, s. 35(c), (d) and (f)) have been considered in **4.2**. The full list of s. 35 grounds is as follows:

Section 35(a) Repealed by the predecessor to the Mental Health Act 1983.

Section 35(b)   When a partner, other than the partner suing, becomes permanently incapable of performing his part of the partnership contract.

Whether or not a partner has become *permanently* incapable is a question of fact. Since there may be difficulties in proving either that the partner is incapable or that his incapacity is permanent, and since there will be difficulties in running a partnership where a partner has a long illness, it is common to include a term in the partnership agreement allowing expulsion or insisting on retirement once a partner has been absent through illness for more than a specified time.

Section 35(c)   When a partner, other than the partner suing, has been guilty of such conduct as, in the opinion of the court, regard being had to the nature of the business, is calculated to affect prejudicially the carrying on of the business (see **4.2**).

Section 35(d)   When a partner, other than the partner suing, wilfully or persistently commits a breach of the partnership agreement, or otherwise so conducts himself in matters relating to the partnership business that it is not reasonably practicable for the other partner or partners to carry on the business in partnership with him (see **4.2**).

Section 35(e)   When the business of the partnership can only be carried on at a loss.

This is arguably one of the most important grounds for dissolution. In order for s. 35(e) to be invoked, the circumstances must be such as to make it a practical impossibility for the partnership to make a profit. If the partners who find themselves in this position cannot agree to bring the partnership to an end. This may be a valuable right if a delay in terminating the partnership will increase the amount of the loss, for which all the partners will be personally liable. It is important to note that a partnership is not necessarily insolvent simply because it is making a loss. It may well have valuable assets which, when sold, will discharge all liabilities and provide a surplus for the partners.

Section 35(f)   Whenever, in the opinion of the court, it is just and equitable that the partnership be dissolved (see **4.2**).

5.2.2   THE LEGAL CONSEQUENCES OF DISSOLUTION

5.2.2.1   Continuing authority of partners for purposes of winding up (s. 38 PA 1890)

The occurence of one of the events set out in **5.2.1** above will cause the partnership to be dissolved but there may be various steps which need to be taken to wind up the affairs of the firm. Section 38 provides that, after the dissolution, the authority of each partner to bind the firm (as well as the other rights and obligations of the partners) continues despite the dissolution but only to the extent necessary to wind up the affairs of the partnership, and to complete transactions begun but unfinished at the time of the dissolution. However, where the dissolution is by order of the court, this authority can be terminated by the appointment of a receiver (who will simply wind up the business) or of a receiver and manager (who will continue running the business but only with a view to the beneficial realisation of the assets by means of, for example, a sale of the business as a going concern). Such appointments are likely to be made where there is a likelihood of dispute if the former partners try to wind up the affairs of the partnership.

5.2.2.2   Realisation of partnership property on dissolution

Once the firm has been dissolved, the value of the assets owned by the partnership will be ascertained, as will the extent of the debts and liabilities owed to creditors. In so far as it is necessary, the assets will be sold to raise the funds to discharge the debts. The partners may merely sell the assets used in the business or they may decide to sell the business as a going concern. If the partners decide to adopt the latter course of action, they may be able to sell the business for more than the aggregate market value of the assets used in the business because the sale price may take into account the 'goodwill' attaching to the business. (It should be borne in mind that the purchasers in this instance may well be some of the partners from the dissolved firm who wish to continue the business under a new guise.)

Goodwill has been defined as 'the whole advantage' whatever it may be, of the reputation and connection of the firm' (*Trego* v *Hunt* [1896] AC 7). This 'advantage' can arise as a result of various factors. If the partners have considerable expertise in their chosen field, their customers may return repeatedly. This 'goodwill' may, however, be largely personal to the partners with the result that it would disappear if they ceased trading. Conversely, if the firm is situated in a prime location (such as the main shopping street in the town), the business may be very successful because of the convenience of access for its customers. In this latter case, the goodwill may attach to the premises rather than the partners, and so may be a very valuable asset of the partnership since it can be passed on to successors.

If the firm has saleable goodwill, a value will be attached to it. The valuation of goodwill is somewhat speculative and any formula for determining its value is inevitably rather artificial. A common formula is to ascertain the net profits of the business for a particular year and then for the parties to agree to multiply the period's profits by an agreed number, often two or three.

Where goodwill is sold, the purchasers will want to protect their investment against the loss of custom arising from the former owners setting up in competition in the same vicinity. Accordingly, the purchaser may wish to include a restrictive covenant in the sale agreement to guard against this possibility. If the purchasers are some of the partners of the dissolved partnership, they too should consider including restrictive covenants to protect their interests.

5.2.2.3 Application of the partnership property on dissolution (ss. 39 and 44 PA 1890)

Once the assets and liabilities have been ascertained, s. 39 entitles each partner to have the property of the partnership applied so that the debts and liabilities of the firm are discharged first. Once these liabilities have been met, any surplus is distributed to the partners (after deducting any sums for which each partner is liable to contribute to the firm, such as contributions to make up losses or deficiencies of capital). In order to ensure that the assets of the partnership are not distributed to the partners personally before the outside creditors are paid off, s. 39 goes on to give each partner the right to apply to the court to wind up the business and affairs of the firm in such a way as to ensure that the s. 39 order for application of assets is observed.

Section 44 provides that once the creditors of the firm have been paid, subject to any contrary agreement, the assets of the firm shall be applied in the following order:

(a) in repaying advances received from partners;
(b) in repaying the amounts shown as standing to the credit of each partner on his capital account; and
(c) any balance being divided between the partners in accordance with the profit sharing ratio.

If the partnership has made losses (including losses or deficiencies of capital), these shall be met in the following order:

(a) from profits;
(b) from capital;
(c) from contributions made by the partners in the proportion in which profits are divisible.

Both parts of s. 44 are subject to contrary agreement. In particular the partners may agree to share surplus assets and to contribute to capital losses in a ratio different from the normal profit sharing.

5.2.2.4 Notification of the dissolution

Section 38 gives partners continued authority to bind the firm after dissolution for the purpose of winding up the business (see **5.2.2.1** above). If a partner exceeds this authority, under s. 36(1) PA

1890 outsiders dealing with the firm after a change in the constitution are entitled to treat all apparent members of the firm as still being members until the outsider has notice of the change (see **5.3.3.2** below).

In order to protect themselves from liability for unauthorised debts incurred after the dissolution, the partners in the dissolved firm are entitled publicly to notify the fact of the dissolution (s. 37 PA 1890). To obtain protection from liability on unauthorised debts incurred with *existing* customers, the former partners should give notice personally to the customer. Notice in the *London Gazette* is sufficient to gain protection from liability on debts with *new* customers (this point is considered in more detail in relation to retirement in **5.3.3.2** below).

5.3 Retirement of a Partner

5.3.1 CIRCUMSTANCES WHEN 'RETIREMENT' OCCURS

The term 'retirement' is most frequently applied to mean a person retiring from full-time work having reached the statutory age of retirement. However, in the partnership context 'retirement' simply means leaving the partnership voluntarily irrespective of the age of the partner in question.

5.3.2 RETIREMENT UNDER THE PARTNERSHIP ACT 1890

Partnership agreements can, and should, contain provisions dealing with retirement by partners. This is because the Partnership Act 1890 does not specifically deal with retirement. Under the 1890 Act the only option available to a partner is to give notice under s. 26. If s. 26 notice is given the partnership will be *dissolved* (see **5.2.1.1**); the section does not permit a partner to retire leaving the partnership otherwise unaffected. To avoid this, suitable provisions must be included in the agreement. One common form of wording provides that the partner wishing to retire should give written notice of a specified length (say, six months or one year). On expiry of the notice period, the retiring partner will leave and may be entitled to some financial settlement from his former partners but otherwise the partnership continues unaffected.

Partnership agreements frequently provide that a deceased person is to be treated as having retired. Additional problems relating specifically to death are considered in **5.4** below.

5.3.3 THE LEGAL CONSEQUENCES OF RETIREMENT

5.3.3.1 Debts incurred before retirement

The mere fact that a partner retires does not release him from his obligations in respect of debts incurred while he was a partner. Section 17(2) PA 1890 provides that 'a partner who retires from a firm does not thereby cease to be liable for partnership debts or obligations incurred before his retirement'.

To avoid the problems of having to meet such debts after retirement, the retiring partner should, if possible, ensure that the debts are paid before he leaves. Since this may be difficult in many cases, the partner will be concerned to gain protection in other ways. In some cases it may be agreed that he will be indemnified by his former partners or that he will be released from his obligations by the creditor.

5.3.3.2 Debts incurred after retirement

The general rule is that only partners are liable for debts incurred by the partnership and so ceasing to be a partner prevents the *former* partner becoming liable on future debts. This is because the retirement terminates the agency relationship. However, this general rule is subject to ss. 36 and 14 PA 1890. Under these sections a former partner becomes liable for debts incurred *after* he has left the partnership in certain circumstances.

5.3.3.3 Section 36

Section 36(3) provides that the estate of a partner '. . . who, *not having been known to the person dealing with the firm to be a partner*, retires is not liable for partnership debts contracted after the date of the . . . retirement'.

The date at which knowledge is tested for the purposes of this subsection is the date of retirement. If a creditor does not know at that date of the retiring partner's connection with the firm, the former partner will not be liable; the fact that the creditor may subsequently discover the former membership cannot make the former partner liable.

The subsection was considered in *Tower Cabinet Co. Ltd* v *Ingram* [1949] 2 KB 397. The facts of the case were that A and B were in partnership. A retired and B continued the business under the old name. After A's retirement, the business ordered goods from a new supplier and failed to pay. The supplier sought to enforce judgment against A. The only knowledge the supplier had of A's connection with the firm was that A's name appeared on headed notepaper which, contrary to A's express instructions, had not been destroyed. The court found that, as the customer had no knowledge prior to A's retirement that A was a partner in the firm, A was completely protected by s. 36(3). (A further question arose of A's possible liability under s. 14(1) — see below.)

In cases where creditors know of the partner's connection with the firm before the former partner retires, s. 36(3) is of no assistance. Section 36(1) provides that 'where a person deals with a firm after a change in its constitution, he is entitled to treat all apparent members of the old firm as still being members of the firm until he has notice of the change'. It is necessary to consider what constitutes 'notice' for this purpose; and what makes a former partner an 'apparent' member of the continuing firm.

(a) *Notice*   Section 36(2) provides that in *respect of persons who had no dealings with the firm before the date of the dissolution or change* a notice in the *London Gazette* (where the firm has its principal place of business in England and Wales) will be sufficient notice.

Thus, to protect himself from liability to new customers who knew of his connection with the firm a retiring partner should ensure that a notice is published in the *London Gazette*.

Notice in the *London Gazette* will not be sufficient to relieve the former partner from liability in respect of customers who *did* have dealings with the firm prior to the dissolution or change. If the retiring partner wishes to be absolutely protected from liability for future debts he should give the customers formal notification.

(b) *Apparent membership*   Where persons dealing with the firm know that a person was a partner, that partner will be liable for new debts so long as he is an apparent member of the firm (and until he gives notice). Persons may be 'apparent members' either because a customer has had dealings with them before or because their names appear on the notepaper or on a sign on the door or because the customer has some indirect information about their being partners.

A retiring partner should ensure that his apparent membership of the firm is terminated. He should give actual notice to existing customers and should publish a notice in the *Gazette* to cover the situation where people have not had dealings with the firm but are aware of the partner's connection with the firm.

5.3.3.4 Section 14

Liability for subsequent debts may also arise under s. 14 PA 1890. It will be recalled from **3.4** that s. 14(1) provides that:

Every one who by words spoken or written or by conduct represents himself, or who knowingly suffers himself to be represented, as a partner in a particular firm, is liable as a partner to any one who has on the faith of any such representation given credit to the firm, whether the representation has or has not been made or communicated to the person so giving credit by or with the knowledge of the apparent partner making the representation or suffering it to be made.

Therefore, even if no liability arises under s. 36, the former partner may be liable to any person (whether they had previous dealings with the firm or not) who has given 'credit' to the firm on the faith of a representation that he is still a partner which is made by the former partner or which he has 'knowingly' allowed to be made.

The word 'apparent' in s. 14(1) has the same meaning as in s. 36(1) so that the decision in the *Tower Cabinet* case (see above) is equally relevant in these circumstances. In the case, it was alleged that the former partner had allowed himself to be held out as a partner. However, since the former partner had not authorised the use of the old notepaper, he had not 'knowingly' allowed himself to be held out as an 'apparent' partner and so no liability under s. 14 arose.

A retiring partner should ensure that his name is removed from any signs and that any notepaper is destroyed in order to prevent an accusation that he knowingly allowed himself to be represented as a partner.

5.3.3.5 Compliance with Business Names Act 1985

After the change in the partnership, the notepaper will normally be changed and care should be taken to ensure that it complies with the requirements of the Business Names Act 1985 (which were considered in **1.8**).

5.3.3.6 Dealing with the finances

Once the partner has retired from the firm, the arrangements for severing, or changing the basis of, the financial connection with the firm will be of considerable importance. These matters are generally covered by the partnership agreement and usually relate to the provision for the partner (and for his dependants) for some form of pension (whether paid by the former partners, under an approved annuity contract, or under a consultancy arrangement). In addition, the arrangements will deal with the former partner's entitlement (if any) to payment for his share in the partnership assets (which may include goodwill).

If there is no agreement, the former partner has a right to receive the net value of his share in the partnership property from his former partners.

5.4 Death

5.4.1 INTRODUCTION

As we saw in **5.2.1.3** above, death causes the automatic dissolution of a partnership. In order to avoid inconvenience to the surviving partners it is common to provide in the partnership agreement that instead of causing an automatic dissolution of the partnership, a deceased partner shall be treated as if he had retired.

5.4.2 RIGHT OF ESTATE TO SHARE IN PROFITS AND OBTAIN AMOUNTS DUE

Subject to contrary agreement, s. 42(1) of PA 1890 provides that where any member of a firm has died (or otherwise ceased to be a partner) and the surviving (or continuing) partners carry on the business of the firm without any final settlement of accounts as between the firm and the outgoing partner or his estate, the outgoing partner or his estate is entitled at the option of himself or his personal representatives to claim such share of the profits made since the dissolution as the court may find to be attributable to the use of his share of the partnership assets (or to interest at the rate of 5% p.a. on the amount of his share of the partnership assets). Any amount due from the surviving partners to the deceased partner's personal representatives in respect of his share is a debt accruing at the date of the death (s. 43 PA 1890).

5.4.3 TREATMENT IN THE PARTNERSHIP AGREEMENT

Raising a large capital sum to pay to the estate of a deceased partner may strain the resources of a partnership which is continuing after the death of a partner. This issue is normally dealt with by the partners in the partnership agreement as follows:

(a) By taking out insurance cover.

(b) By providing that on death (and/or retirement) capital sums due should be paid by yearly instalments over a specified period — interest being payable on the amount outstanding.

(c) By providing for a method of calculating the amount due.

(d) By providing that the deceased (or retiring) partner is to be entitled to a fixed amount in lieu of a share of profits. This avoids the need to apportion profits to the date of death (or retirement).

5.4.4 LIABILITY FOR DEBTS

Every partner is jointly liable for debts and obligations of the firm incurred while he is a partner. In addition, s. 9 PA 1890 provides that the estate of a deceased person is severally liable for such debts and obligations so far as they remain unsatisfied *but* subject to the prior payment of the deceased partner's personal debts. A partnership creditor can, therefore, proceed against the estate of a deceased partner in respect of partnership debts (even after obtaining a judgment against the other partners) provided some part of the debt is unsatisfied. However, partnership creditors are postponed to the deceased partner's own creditors.

So far as subsequent debts are concerned, s. 36(3) PA 1890 provides that the deceased partner's estate is not liable for partnership debts contracted after the death. However, if the deceased partner's personal representatives take part in the management of the business they make themselves liable for debts incurred from the time their participation commences.

COMPANIES

SIX

LIMITED COMPANIES

6.1 Introduction

In this chapter we will begin to look at the legal position of limited companies. Very many businesses are run by limited companies. These range from international conglomerates to companies owned by one person running a small business. Before turning to the detailed legal rules about companies we need to see how they fit into the complex pattern of institutions which the law has created. We will also introduce the distinction between private and public companies. Further information about public companies will be found in **Chapter 31**.

6.2 Corporations

A 'company' is in law a corporation, that is, an artificial legal 'person' with rights and obligations distinct from those of its members. Business associations were occasionally made corporations by Royal Charter from about the sixteenth century (for example, the East India Company in 1600), but until the industrial revolution few businesses were incorporated. With the growth of the canal and railway systems incorporations were permitted in increasing numbers under Acts of Parliament. The vast majority of corporations are now companies formed under the Companies Act 1985 or under earlier legislation superseded by that Act.

6.3 Sources of Company Law

6.3.1 COMPANY LEGISLATION

The Companies Act (CA) 1985 is the most important source of company law. The 1985 Act is a consolidating Act which brings together legislation contained in a number of earlier Companies Acts and a few other pieces of legislation dealing with company law. The 1985 Act has been amended in significant respects by the Insolvency Act 1986 and by the Companies Act 1989.

The 1985 Act applies throughout Great Britain although a number of provisions apply only to Scotland or only to England and Wales. Northern Ireland has its own legislation which is substantially the same as the British legislation.

Some of the basic rules concerning companies result from judicial decisions and do not appear in the Act. Of special importance are the rules of equity relating to fiduciary relationships (which play a major part in determining the legal position of company directors) and the rule in *Foss* v *Harbottle*. There are also hundreds of reported cases in which Companies Acts have been interpreted by the courts. Most of these cases were decided before the 1985 Act came into force but continue to be authoritative interpretations of the consolidated legislation.

6.3.2 TAX LEGISLATION

The taxation of companies is largely dealt with in the Income and Corporation Taxes Act 1988 as amended by subsequent Finance Acts. Companies' capital gains are largely dealt with in accordance with the Taxation of Chargeable Gains Act 1992, as amended. Again, many decisions of the courts have interpreted the meaning of this legislation.

6.3.3 THE COMPANY'S OWN REGULATIONS: ARTICLES OF ASSOCIATION

Despite the vast amount of law which applies to companies, a great deal of freedom of choice is given to each individual company as to how it will be administered. This is both desirable and inevitable because of the widely differing circumstances in which each company operates. To provide for its own internal administration each company must have a set of regulations known as *articles of association* (**Chapters 7** and **26**). These may be specially prepared for the company by the draftsman who assists with its formation; however, the Companies Act provides for a model form of articles (Table A) and most of the regulations adopted by a company will follow that model. The provisions of Table A are contained in a statutory instrument (SI 1985 No 805) which came into force with the 1985 Act. Companies formed before the 1985 Act usually have regulations based on earlier versions of Table A.

6.3.4 THE GENERAL LAW

Finally, it is worth pointing out that the general law applies to companies as it applies to individuals, except to the extent that it has been modified by specific rules of company law. The general law of contract, for example, applies to companies with very few modifications, as does the law of tort, conveyancing and so on. This is really just a consequence of the fact that a company is a corporation and, therefore, in law a 'person' with legal rights and obligations.

6.4 Registration

The process by which a company is formed under the Companies Act is called registration. The steps to be taken are considered in **Chapter 7**. For the moment it is sufficient to point out that when the Registrar of Companies issues the certificate of incorporation, '. . . the subscribers of the memorandum, together with such other persons as may from time to time become members of the company, shall be a body corporate by the name contained in the memorandum' (s. 13(3) CA 1985).

The official who is responsible for registering companies in England and Wales is the Registrar of Companies. The Registrar is also responsible for maintaining the records which are required to be sent to him by registered companies. The Companies' Registry is in Cardiff.

6.5 Types of Registered Company

6.5.1 COMPANIES LIMITED BY SHARES

The vast majority of companies registered under the Companies Act are companies 'limited by shares'. This means that the members (or shareholders — the terms are almost interchangeable) have a limited liability to pay the debts of the company. When new shares are issued by a company the person who takes the shares must agree to pay for them. Usually payment will be made immediately but sometimes the shares will be issued 'unpaid' or 'partly-paid', in which case payment must be made later. If the company goes into liquidation and is insolvent the members are liable to pay for their shares in full if they have not already done so. This really means that a member who has paid for his shares stands to lose his shares *but nothing more* on the insolvency of the company; a member who has not paid for his shares in full stands to lose his shares *and* the unpaid amount but nothing more.

6.5.1.1 Comparison with partnership

The position of a shareholder in a limited company is quite different from the position of a member of a partnership. If a partnership business fails each of the partners stands to lose not only what he has invested but also any private wealth which he may have. Limited liability can be an enormous advantage to a businessman, although creditors (particularly those who have lent money to the company) may require personal guarantees of the company's debts from shareholders, thus reducing the advantage.

6.5.2 COMPANIES LIMITED BY GUARANTEE

A small number of companies are limited by guarantee rather than by shares. This means that each member undertakes to pay a specified amount if the company is wound up while he is a member or within a year after he ceases to be a member. Most companies limited by guarantee are charities or other non-trading companies.

6.5.3 UNLIMITED COMPANIES

An unlimited company is one which is registered under the Companies Act but without any limit on the liability of the members. If an unlimited company goes into liquidation the members are liable to contribute the whole of their private wealth (if so much is needed) to the payment of the company's debts. The creditors cannot sue the members direct but must claim in the liquidation. The liquidator then calls for contributions from the members.

6.6 Public and Private Companies (see also Chapter 32)

6.6.1 CLASSIFICATION

Nearly all company law rules apply equally to all companies. There are a small number of rules which distinguish between 'public companies' and 'private companies'. A public company is defined by s. 1 CA 1985 as 'a company limited by shares . . ., being a company:

(a) the memorandum of which states that the company is to be a public company; and
(b) in relation to which the provisions of [the Companies Act] as to the registration or re-registration of a company as a public company have been complied with . .'.

The same section defines a private company as any company which is not a public company. On incorporation the promoters (that is, the people who form the company) will decide whether it is to be a public company or a private company and will draft the memorandum accordingly.

6.6.2 DIFFERENCES

The principal differences between public and private companies are as follows:

(a) *Authorised minimum share capital* A public company cannot commence business until a certificate is issued by the Registrar showing that the authorised minimum share capital has been issued (s. 117 CA 1985). The authorised minimum is currently £50,000 but can be increased by statutory instrument. A private company can commence business as soon as it is incorporated.
(b) *Payment for shares* A public company cannot issue shares unless they are immediately paid for at least to the extent of 25% of the nominal value and the whole of any premium (s. 101 CA 1985) (for the definitions of nominal value and premium see **Chapter 10**. A private company can issue shares without requiring immediate payment for them.

(c) *Issuing shares* A public company can issue shares or debentures to the public (hence the description 'public company'); a private company is prohibited from doing so by the Financial Services Act 1986.

(d) *Name* The name of a public company must end with the words 'Public Limited Company' or its equivalent (equivalents include PLC and, for Welsh companies, Cwmni Cyfyngedig Cyhoeddus or CCC). The names of private limited companies cannot end with these words and must end with 'Limited' or its equivalent (e.g. Ltd, Cyfyngedig or Cyf) unless the company has obtained permission to dispense with the use of the word 'Limited' in its name.

(e) *Directors* A public company must have at least two directors, a private company need only have one (s. 282 CA 1985).

(f) *Miscellaneous* There are a large number of smaller differences between the two types of company — for example, the directors of a private company need not retire at 70, those of a public company must (s. 293 CA 1985: however, this section may be avoided even in the case of a public company); a proxy can speak only at a meeting of a private company; a single resolution at a meeting of a private company may validly elect two or more directors, in the case of a public company each appointment must be voted on separately.

6.6.3   OTHER DEFINITIONS

All companies are public or private but there are a number of other categories of company to which special rules apply:

(a) *Quoted company* A company is in this category if its shares are quoted on a stock exchange. A quoted company must keep a special register of those shareholders with 5% or more of the shares. Because of Stock Exchange rules only public companies can obtain a quotation.

(b) *Close company* This category is relevant only for tax purposes; special tax rules apply to close companies. Virtually all private companies are close and so are some public companies. A company which is not close is sometimes called an 'open company' but 'non-close company' is more correct.

(c) *Small and medium-sized companies* These are companies which because of their relatively small size (in financial terms) are exempt from providing certain information in their accounts.

(d) *Partnership company* This category will be introduced by regulations made under the Companies Act 1989. A partnership company will in most respects be an ordinary private company but with regulations suitable for a company which is owned by its own employees.

(e) *Elective regime company* This category was introduced by the Companies Act 1989. An 'elective regime company' is an ordinary private company which has opted out of certain provisions of the Companies Act. It will only be possible to opt out if the shareholders unanimously agree. Once they have done so the company need not hold an annual general meeting nor a shareholders' meeting to consider accounts. The procedure for calling meetings and issuing shares is also simpler than in the case of other companies.

6.6.4   PROVISION IN ARTICLES

As was explained above, a company is now public if its memorandum says so and it complies with certain other requirements; otherwise it is private. Until the Companies Act 1980 (now consolidated in CA 1985) came into force a company was public unless its *articles* made it private by including provisions which:

(a) restricted the right to transfer shares;
(b) restricted membership to 50;
(c) prevented public issue of shares.

For a considerable time to come many private companies will have articles doing these three things because they were formed at a time when they could not be private companies unless their articles contained such restrictions. It should be noted that modern private companies need not include any of these provisions in their articles, although many do restrict the right to transfer shares and the restriction on public issue is imposed independently of the articles by the Financial Services Act 1986.

6.7 Separate Legal Personality

As we have already seen, a company is a 'body corporate', that is, it is a legal person distinct from its members. A number of consequences flow from this so that a company:

(a) is able to own property;
(b) it is liable for its own debts;
(c) can sue its debtors;
(d) is liable to be sued by its creditors; and
(e) has 'perpetual succession' — this means that the company does not cease to exist just because a member (however many shares he may own) dies or otherwise ceases to be a member.

The leading case of *Salomon* v *A. Salomon and Co. Ltd* [1897] AC 22, illustrates the nature of a company's separate legal personality very clearly. Mr Salomon was a wholesale boot manufacturer with a fairly substantial business. He decided to form a company to buy the business which he valued at £40,000. £30,000 worth of shares were issued, fully paid, to Salomon over a period of time (of these, six were held by his relatives to satisfy the requirement then in force that every company should have a minimum of seven members — two, or in some cases one, is now sufficient). The other £10,000 of the purchase price was left outstanding and was secured by a debenture (i.e., the assets of the company were mortgaged in favour of Salomon). Within a year the company became insolvent because the company lost its main source of income (which was supplying boots to the army). The liquidator of the company claimed that Salomon was liable to indemnify the company personally against the claims of the ordinary creditors because the company was 'a mere alias or agent of the vendor'. This argument was upheld in the High Court and in the Court of Appeal but the House of Lords reversed the decision. Lord Macnaghten explained the position of a registered company in the following way:

> When the memorandum is duly signed and registered, though there be only seven shares taken, the subscribers are a body corporate 'capable forthwith', to use the words of the enactment, 'of exercising all the functions of an incorporated company' . . . I cannot understand how a body corporate thus made capable by statute can lose its individuality by issuing the bulk of its capital to one person, whether he be a subscriber to the memorandum or not. The company is at law a different person altogether from the subscribers to the memorandum; and though it may be that after incorporation the business is precisely the same as it was before, and the same persons are managers, and the same hands receive the profits, the company is not in law the agent of the subscribers or trustee for them. Nor are the subscribers as members liable, in any shape or form, except to the extent and in the manner provided by the Act. . . Any member of a company, acting in good faith, is as much entitled to take and hold the company's debentures as any outside creditor . . . It has become the fashion to call companies of this class 'one man companies'. That is a taking nickname, but it does not help one much in the way of argument. If it is intended to convey the meaning that a company which is under the absolute control of one person is not a company legally incorporated . . . it is inaccurate and misleading . . .

Since Salomon had not acted fraudulently his security was valid even though his valuation of the business at £40,000 was probably excessive. In fact, Salomon assigned the debenture to a third party before the company collapsed so that he did not gain personally from the decision of the House of Lords.

Another rule which is at least in part a consequence of separate legal personality is the rule in *Foss* v *Harbottle* (1843) 2 Hare 461, which prevents a shareholder from suing when a wrong is done to his company. (This rule is considered in **9.6**.)

6.8 'Lifting the Veil of Incorporation'

There are a number of circumstances in which the court is willing to ignore the fact that a company is a separate legal person. Legislation also sometimes ignores the distinction between a company and its members. These circumstances are rather fancifully described as 'lifting the veil of incorporation' because the law looks behind the legal 'veil' which separates the company from its members.

The occasions when the veil of incorporation is lifted are hard to classify and it is probably open to the courts to extend the circumstances in the future. It is, of course, open to Parliament to do so by legislation.

6.8.1 COMPANY LEGISLATION

The Companies Act 1985 and the Insolvency Act 1986 contain a number of rules which depart from the general principle of separate corporate personality; for example:

(a) *Fraudulent trading* Section 213 of the Insolvency Act 1986 provides that any person who is or was knowingly a party to fraudulent trading by a company whose business is being carried on with intent to defraud creditors or other persons, may be liable to pay the debts of the company. This liability arises only if the company is being wound up (although criminal penalties may be imposed for fraudulent trading under s. 458 CA 1985 even if the company is not being wound up).

(b) *Wrongful trading* Section 214 of the Insolvency Act 1986 provides that directors of the company may be personally liable in cases of wrongful trading. This arises where a company becomes insolvent and the directors then fail to take steps to protect creditors. This type of liability only arises if the company is being wound up.

(c) *Group accounts* Where companies are members of a group, group accounts must be produced to reflect that the financial transactions of the subsidiaries are in reality activities of the holding company.

6.8.2 DECISIONS OF THE COURTS

6.8.2.1 Attempts to avoid legal obligations

The courts have occasionally lifted the veil of incorporation by making orders against companies where the proprietors have used a company as a means of avoiding a personal legal obligation. For example in *Jones* v *Lipman* [1962] 1 WLR 832, the defendant had contracted to sell land to the plaintiff and later conveyed it to a company in an attempt to avoid the possibility of an order of specific performance (an order of specific performance cannot normally be made once a third party has acquired rights in the subject-matter of the contract). The company was owned and controlled by the defendant and so an order of specific performance was made against the company as well as the vendor.

6.8.2.2 Agency and trusts

In a few cases the court has held that a company is either an agent for its shareholders or their trustee; however, the exact scope of these decisions is rather unclear and these cases ought to be regarded as providing exceptions rather than general rules. A company will *not* generally be regarded as either an agent for, or trustee of, its members.

6.8.3 TAX LEGISLATION

Tax legislation often imposes tax liability on shareholders to reflect the fact that transactions of their company are in reality transactions conducted on their behalf. It is not proposed to deal with all the rules involved but the following examples should be sufficient to indicate their scope:

(a) The companies in a 'group' of companies (i.e., broadly speaking, a holding company and its subsidiaries) are in many ways treated as one company for corporation tax purposes. Thus the rate of tax depends on the size of the group's profits rather than on the size of each company's profits, losses made by one member of a group can generally be set off against profits made by others, and dividend payments within the group may be ignored for tax purposes.

(b) Gifts made by a close company are treated as made by its members for the purpose of inheritance tax.

(c) The sale of a business to a company in return for shares can usually be ignored for capital gains tax purposes.

SEVEN

FORMATION OF A LIMITED COMPANY

7.1   Introduction

In this chapter we will look at the way in which a limited company is formed and at the documentation which is required to lead to the formation and following the formation.

A solicitor who is advising a client on the formation of a new business or on the possibility of changing an existing business into a company, would first discuss the advisability of incorporation. An informed discussion of this topic requires detailed knowledge of partnership and company law and of the relevant tax considerations. We therefore leave this topic until **Chapter 31**. For the rest of this chapter we will assume that these discussions have taken place and that the client has decided that he wishes to form a company. Once this stage is reached the solicitor will:

(a) Discuss with the client the effect of incorporation and the legal requirements of running a company.

(b) Discuss with the client whether the company should be formed by the solicitor or whether an existing company should be bought 'off-the-peg' from a firm of law stationers.

(c) Prepare the documents leading to incorporation (after taking the client's instructions as to their contents). If an 'off-the-peg' company is decided on, this step will be unnecessary.

(d) Inform the client as to the steps to be taken after incorporation, as required by the Companies Act 1985 (as amended).

(e) Advise the client as to the problems which may arise if contracts are made in the name of, or on behalf of, the company before incorporation.

This chapter considers each of these matters (though not in chronological order). It should be borne in mind that, especially in relation to the proposed company's constitution, the circumstances of each case will be different. This Guide is particularly concerned with the problems likely to be faced by a two- or three-man business.

7.2   Steps Leading to Incorporation

For a company to be registered under the Companies Act, the 'promoters' (that is, the traders who wish to form the company) or their agents (for example, a solicitor or a law stationer) must deliver to the Registrar of Companies the following:

(a) a memorandum of association;

(b) articles of association (but see **7.2.2**, for adoption of Table A by reference in the memorandum);

(c) Form G10, setting out details of the registered office, the directors and secretary of the company;

(d) Form G12 — a statutory declaration of compliance with the requirements of the Companies Act;

(e) the Registrar's fee (currently £50).

In this chapter we will consider the formation of private limited companies only. Of the documents that have to be submitted to the Registrar the most important are the company's memorandum and articles; great care must be taken to ensure that they are suitable for the particular circumstances.

7.2.1   MEMORANDUM OF ASSOCIATION

Section 1 CA 1985 provides that every company must have a memorandum, which is sometimes described as the company's 'charter'. Its principal function is to set out the *raison d'être* of the company and to regulate its dealings with outsiders. Five compulsory clauses *must* be included in the memorandum. These relate to:

(a) the name of the company;
(b) the registered office;
(c) the objects of the company;
(d) the liability of the members;
(e) the authorised capital of the company.

Further clauses may be included, covering anything which could be contained in the company's articles, however, this is rarely done in practice.

The memorandum must also contain the 'association' and 'subscription' clauses. The former states that the persons who subscribe (i.e., sign) the memorandum wish to be formed into a company and that they each agree to take a specified number of shares in the new company. The latter sets out the names, addresses and descriptions of the subscribers and the number of shares each agrees to take. The memorandum must be signed by a minimum of two subscribers, who sign in the presence of at least one witness, and each subscriber must agree to take at least one share.

We will now consider each of the clauses which must be included, in turn.

7.2.1.1   The name

Choice of name   Generally, the promoters have freedom of choice as far as the company's name is concerned. The purpose of a company's name is to differentiate the company from all other registered companies. Sections 25-26 CA 1985, therefore, prohibit the Registrar from registering a company with a name which:

(a) does not end with the word 'limited' (or its Welsh equivalent 'cyfyngedig' if appropriate — see below) if the company is a private limited company. (However, s. 30 provides that a company limited by guarantee may apply for dispensation from using the word 'limited'. The objects of a company applying for this exemption must be the promotion of commerce, art, science, education, religion, charity or a profession and its memorandum or articles must prohibit the members from taking any profits out of the company.)

(b) is the same as that of an existing registered company; or

(c) in the opinion of the Secretary of State constitutes a criminal offence, or is offensive;

(d) includes the words limited, unlimited or public limited company (or the Welsh equivalents or abbreviations of these words) other than at the end of the name;

(e) includes words suggesting a connection with the Government or a local authority or particular words specified in regulations (made under s. 29 CA 1985). In such cases, however, the Registrar may give approval for registration of the name. In the case of words specified in the regulations, consultation with government departments or institutions specified in the regulations is sometimes required before the Registrar gives his approval.

If a name is rejected by the Registrar a certain amount of expense and delay is bound to occur, as the promoter will have to submit a further set of documents applying for formation with a new name. The new memorandum will have to be printed (although 'printing' in this context includes most types of photocopying) and so will the new articles (unless Table A is adopted by reference in the memorandum). To minimise the risk of a name being rejected the promoters should consult the index of company names kept by the Registrar of Companies shortly before the application for registration. If the name is already in use a new name should be chosen. If the name is not in use then the application should progress quickly as there is no procedure for reserving a name.

Passing-off   Registration of a company with a particular name does not give the company any protection against a passing-off action if an existing business trades under a similar name and its business is likely to be affected by the similarity. This potential problem can be partly avoided if the promoters inspect the trade marks register before applying for registration with any particular name.

Change of name   Section 28 CA 1985 provides that, after a company is formed, it is free to change its name by passing a special resolution subject to the same restrictions as apply to choice of name by a new company. Furthermore, the Registrar has the power to direct a company to change its registered name if it gives so misleading an indication of the nature of its activities as to be likely to cause harm to the public (s. 32 CA 1985).

7.2.1.2   Registered office

The second compulsory clause in the memorandum sets out the *situation* of the company's registered office. It does not state the address of the company's registered office (this appears in Form G10 — see **7.2.3**), but only that the office is situated in England (which includes Wales for this purpose) or Wales (to the exclusion of England) or Scotland as appropriate. The function of this clause is to determine the company's domicile, and it can only be altered by Act of Parliament.

If the office is to be in Wales (to the exclusion of England), the company's name may end in the word 'cyfyngedig' rather than 'limited'. The memorandum and articles may, in such cases, be printed in Welsh but a certified translation into English is required.

7.2.1.3   The objects and the ultra vires doctrine

The third compulsory clause specifies the company's objects, or purposes, and the powers it is to have.

Common law doctrine of ultra vires   Any contracts made, or acts done, by the company not within the objects clause or reasonably incidental thereto, used to be void as a result of the doctrine of 'ultra vires'. Because of this rule objects clauses have traditionally been drafted very widely. In particular it is usual to find many sub-clauses which seek to list all the businesses and activities which the company could conceivably wish to undertake in the future. These will be followed by a statement that each sub-clause should be construed as independent of each other. In *Cotman* v *Brougham* [1918] AC 514 it was held that this did in fact make each sub-clause an independent object. Without such a statement the later sub-clauses would be construed as being dependent on the 'main objects' stated in the first few sub-clauses.

In *Bell Houses Ltd* v *City Wall Properties Ltd* [1966] 2 QB 656 it was held that an objects clause saying that the company could carry on any business which the directors believed could be 'advantageously carried on by the company in connection with or ancillary to the company's other businesses' was valid.

Decisions such as these greatly reduced the significance of the ultra vires rule for companies.

Effect of the 1989 Act   The Companies Act 1989 has now all but abolished the rule in relation to transactions between a company and an outsider (however, the directors may be liable to the company if it loses as a result of a breach of the objects clause — see **Chapter 8**). Despite this, most companies still submit a long form of objects clause when they register. An alternative is now available under s. 3A CA 1985 (which was interpolated by the Companies Act 1989), and this provides:

Where the company's memorandum states that the object of the company is to carry on business as a general commercial company —

(a)   the object of the company is to carry on any trade or business whatsoever, and
(b)   the company has power to do all such things as are incidental or conducive to the carrying on of any trade or business by it.

Where a company adopts this simple form of objects clause the powers of the company will include power to carry on any trade or business.

How many companies will choose to be incorporated with an objects clause in the new simple form remains to be seen. It is likely that most companies will still choose the traditional form and companies formed before the 1989 Act came into force are unlikely to change their objects clauses. Some new companies are adopting a 'belt and braces' approach and have both the new form of clause and a traditional objects clause following it.

7.2.1.4   The liability clause

This merely states whether the members' liability for the debts of the company is limited or unlimited but it does not specify the manner in which the members' liability is limited. The clause is unalterable but if a company wishes to change the nature of liability it may re-register under ss. 49-52 CA 1985. The detailed provisions are complex, and beyond the scope of this book; the main requirements are that the unanimous consent of all the members is needed to convert from limited to unlimited but only a special resolution — that is, a 75% majority — is necessary to change from unlimited to limited.

7.2.1.5   The capital clause

The final compulsory clause in the memorandum states the amount of the company's 'authorised share capital' and how it is divided into shares of a specified nominal value (sometimes called the 'par value'). It is possible to divide the shares into different classes enjoying different rights (such as a preferential dividend entitlement) but this is normally done, if at all, under provisions in the articles.

The company's authorised share capital sets an upper limit on the number of shares which it can issue (although the shareholders can later resolve to increase this limit). Since the capital clause only deals with the nominal value of the share capital, it does not restrict the amount which can be invested in the company.

At this stage it may be useful to explain the different types of share capital:

(a)   *Authorised capital* limits the maximum number of shares which the company can issue.
(b)   *Issued capital* is the part of the authorised share capital which has been issued to the members. The issued capital is calculated by multiplying the number of shares issued by their nominal value.
(c)   *Paid-up capital* is the amount received from the members to date, whether in cash or in the form of assets. Since the company may, if it wishes, call for only part payment at the time when shares are issued, the paid-up capital may be less than the issued capital.

7.2.2   THE ARTICLES OF ASSOCIATION

The second document which must be drafted before the company is incorporated is the articles of association (s. 7 CA 1985). These regulate the company's internal affairs and contain the regulations dealing with such matters as directors' powers, proceedings at members' meetings and so on. The promoters decide what form the articles take.

7.2.2.1   Choice of form of articles

There are no compulsory clauses but the Companies (Tables A to F) Regulations 1985 contain a standard set of articles which set out regulations (called Table A) intended to be suitable for an 'average' company. The company may:

(a)   have prepared specially drafted Articles;
(b)   reprint Table A either with or without amendment; or
(c)   adopt Table A by special reference in its memorandum (in which case it need not submit a printed copy of its articles when applying for registration).

If this last procedure is followed the adopted Table A will be in the form laid down in the Regulations in force at the date of incorporation. While later Regulations and/or Acts may change Table A from time to time this will not affect companies already registered. Therefore, for the purpose of reference, copies of Table A in the appropriate form should be kept. It should be noted that the present Table A was introduced on 1 July 1985. It is substantially different from its predecessor (contained in the Companies Act 1948 and amended on a number of occasions) which will form the basis of the articles of most companies incorporated before July 1985 for many years to come.

Unless Table A is adopted by reference in the memorandum the articles submitted for registration must be 'printed' and must be signed by the subscribers to the memorandum in the presence of a witness. Photocopying is acceptable provided the print is permanent but typing is not, since this can be altered too easily.

When preparing to incorporate a company, one of the most important matters to discuss with the promoters is the contents of the articles and their effect. Because Table A is a standard form it may not be suitable for every company and should be altered to meet the circumstances. Other possible provisions are considered in **Chapter 26**.

7.2.2.2   Amendment of articles

Should the company be incorporated with unsuitable articles or should circumstances change, s. 9 CA 1985 allows amendments, provided a special resolution approving them is passed (see **Chapter 26**).

7.2.2.3   Table G

The Companies Act 1989 provides a further possibility as far as articles are concerned. This is the adoption of a new Table G which will contain articles for a 'partnership company'. Section 8A CA 1985 (interpolated by s. 128 CA 1989) defines a partnership company as 'a company limited by shares whose shares are intended to be held to a substantial extent by or on behalf of its employees'. At the time of writing, Table G has not been published.

7.2.3   FORM G10

This is a statutory form required by s. 10(2) and sch. 1 CA 1985 which is a statement of the first directors and secretary and intended situation of the company's registered office. The form is supplied with notes explaining its completion. The following points should be noted:

(a)   The *address* of the company's first registered office appears in this form, not in the memorandum; later it can be moved anywhere within the country specified in the 'office' clause in the memorandum. The registered office may be changed by giving notice to the Registrar. The change is effective in relation to service of documents when registered by the Registrar although service of documents at the old registered office remains valid for a further 14 days after registration. A company is required to keep certain registers and documents at its registered office and to make them available for public inspection (see **7.4.3**). A company is not liable for failing in this duty if it has to change its registered offices in circumstances where it is not practicable to notify the Registrar provided that it finds a new registered office as soon as practicable and informs the Registrar within 14 days (s. 287(6) CA 1985 as substituted by CA 1989).

(b) The company must have at least one director and if only one is appointed he must not also be the company secretary. This ensures that every company has at least two separate officers.

(c) The information required in relation to the directors includes details of other directorships.

(d) The persons named as directors and secretary, and who sign the form to signify their consent, automatically become the first directors and secretary of the company even if the articles provide otherwise.

7.2.4 FORM G12

This is a statutory declaration of compliance with the registration requirements of the Act. It must be completed by the solicitor engaged in forming the company or one of the company's directors or secretary named in Form G10.

7.2.5 THE FEE

The documents must be sent to the Registrar of Companies together with the fee of £50.

7.3 The Certificate of Incorporation

The Registrar will examine the documents and, provided they are in order and the chosen name is still available, he will sign a certificate of incorporation stating that the company was incorporated under the Companies Act 1985 and that the company is limited (if appropriate). The Registrar specifies the company's registered number on the certificate and this must be quoted on all official documents and business letters. Under s. 13(3), from the date of incorporation the company becomes a legal entity. At the same time as the Registrar issues the certificate, he must (under s. 711 CA 1985) 'officially notify' the fact of issue. This means he must place a notice to this effect in the Government's official newspaper (in England and Wales, the *London Gazette*).

7.4 Steps Necessary after Incorporation

Once the certificate of incorporation has been issued the company's existence begins. There are then certain procedural and statutory provisions to be complied with. In addition to matters such as the issue of shares and fixing the company's accounting reference date, which will be dealt with soon after incorporation, these steps relate to the following formal requirements:

(a) the company's seal (if there is to be one);
(b) the publication of the company's name;
(c) the keeping of certain statutory 'books'.

7.4.1 THE SEAL

After the enactment of the Companies Act 1989, there is no longer any need for a company to have a seal. If the company does have one, the company's name must be engraved on it. Whether or not the company has a seal, documents signed by a director and the secretary and expressed (in whatever form of words) to be executed by the company will have the same effect as if they were under the company's seal.

7.4.2   **PUBLICATION OF THE COMPANY'S NAME**

The Companies Act 1985 contains a number of provisions concerning publication of a company's name. A company is required to:

(a)   display its registered name outside every office or place of business in which its business is carried on, in a conspicuous position and in letters which are easily legible (s. 348 CA 1985);

(b)   ensure that its name appears on all business letters, notices, cheques, orders for money or goods, invoices, etc. (s. 349 CA 1985).

7.4.2.1   **Company name: liability of officers**

An officer of the company who uses an incorrectly engraved seal or issues a letter, invoice, etc. or signs a cheque, order for money, etc. on which the correct name does not appear is liable to a fine. However, where the document in question is a cheque, bill of exchange, promissory note, order for money or goods, there is additional, more serious, liability, in that the signer will be personally liable to the holder of the cheque, etc. This is a circumstance where the 'veil of incorporation' is lifted and is illustrated by the case of *Durham Fancy Goods Ltd* v *Michael Jackson (Fancy Goods) Ltd and Another* [1968] 2 QB 839. In this case the plaintiffs drew a bill of exchange on the defendants and wrote on it 'Accepted payable . . . for and on behalf of M. Jackson (Fancy Goods) Ltd'. On receiving the bill, a director of the defendant company signed his name and returned the bill. It was dishonoured by his company which then went into liquidation. The plaintiffs claimed against the director personally on the ground that he had contravened a provision of the Companies Act 1948 which was the same as s. 349 CA 1985. This was because the name included the word 'Michael' in full and not merely the initial 'M' as in the bill. It was held that this section had been contravened and that the director would have been personally liable but for the fact that it was the plaintiffs themselves who had written the incorrect name on the bill. It seems, however, that abbreviations may be used where they are in common usage as equivalents for the words for which they stand. Thus in *Banque de l'Indochine et de Suez SA* v *Euroseas Group Finance Co. Ltd* [1981] 3 All ER 198, an abbreviation of 'Company' to 'Co' was held not to be a breach of the section. Clearly these rules are important and should be drawn to the attention of the directors of a newly formed company.

7.4.2.2   **Company stationery**

A further practical point relating to the name and its publication is that the promoters will need to have stationery printed which complies with the statutory requirements. This cannot, however, be done until the certificate of incorporation has been issued, confirming that the chosen name was accepted and giving the company's number. Section 305 CA 1985 requires that if the name of *any* director appears on a business letter (other than in the text or as a signatory) on which the company's name appears, then the forenames (or initials) and surnames of *all* the directors who are individuals and the corporate names of all the corporate directors must appear in legible characters.

7.4.2.3   **Letters and order forms**

Section 351 CA 1985 requires the company's letters and order forms to specify:

(a)   the place (i.e., country) of registration of the company and its registered number;

(b)   the address of its registered office;

(c)   that it is a limited company if it has been granted a licence to dispense with 'limited' as the last word of the name.

Failure to comply makes the company and every officer authorising the issue of a letter, etc. liable to a fine.

7.4.3 THE STATUTORY BOOKS

7.4.3.1 The books

The Companies Act 1985 requires companies to keep certain 'books' (i.e., records — they need not be bound volumes). The company can prepare its own books or buy them from law stationers. As far as a private limited company is concerned the most important books it must keep at its registered office are:

(a) A register and index of members, containing each member's name, address, dates of entry on the register and cessation of membership together with details of the shares held.

(b) A register of directors and a register of secretaries setting out their names, addresses, and, for directors only, details of any other directorships. It is advisable to include details of the period of holding office since problems may arise in the future as to whether a board decision was validly passed and enquiries of the directors holding office at the time may be necessary; similarly for secretaries.

(c) A register of the interests of directors, their spouses and infant children in shares and debentures of the company, its holding and subsidiary companies as required by ss. 324-328 CA 1985. The purpose of this is to ensure that the extent of a director's direct or indirect control over the company is known.

(d) A register of charges which must be kept even if the company has not yet charged any of its assets. It sets out details of the property charged and the terms of the charge.

(e) Copies of the company's memorandum and articles.

7.4.3.2 Inspection of company books

All these books must be available for inspection by members, creditors and the general public for at least two hours daily during business hours. The Secretary of State has power, under CA 1989 to make regulations concerning the times when registers are to be available. Certain of the books may be kept at a place other than the registered office provided the Registrar is notified.

7.4.3.3 Other documents to be kept by a company

Other documents which should be kept at the registered office include:

(a) Copies of all instruments creating any charge over the company's property (whether or not registrable at the Companies Registry) and a register of brief particulars of the charges. The copies and register are available for inspection by members and creditors free of charge and by anyone else on payment of a fee to be prescribed by regulations.

(b) The directors' service contracts, which can only be inspected by members.

(c) The minute book of general meetings of the company, which can only be inspected by members.

7.5 Methods of Incorporation

The trader who wishes to trade using a limited company can have his company formed, following the procedure set out above, either by his professional advisers or by a firm of law stationers. Our aim is to make a comparison between a company which is 'tailor-made' to the trader's particular requirements in every way and one that is bought from the stock of 'shelf' or 'off-the-peg' companies maintained by law stationers.

7.5.1 THE 'TAILOR-MADE' COMPANY

If the company's documentation is tailored to the promoters' requirements the articles will include only those provisions appropriate to the particular circumstances of the case. Furthermore, the promoters may be the subscribers to the memorandum and articles and appear in Form G10, thus becoming the company's first members and officers.

The disadvantages are that there will be a delay between taking instructions and the company's incorporation and this method, at first sight, might appear more expensive.

7.5.2 THE 'OFF-THE-PEG' OR 'SHELF' COMPANY

If this type of company is bought from a law stationers the only part of the documentation which is likely to be entirely suitable to the trader's needs will be the objects clause of the memorandum, since stocks of companies carrying on most types of business are maintained. Companies will also be available, stating that their object is to 'carry on business as a general commercial company'. However, while the objects clause will almost certainly be satisfactory, the name probably will not be and the articles may not be.

7.5.2.1 Company name

On incorporation the 'shelf' company will have been given a name which will have no connection with the company's future powers. If the name of their company is unimportant to the promoters this will cause no problems but if they wish their company to trade under their own names or a chosen name, the name will have to be changed see **7.7**.

7.5.2.2 Use of business name

A cheaper alternative is to use a business name, provided the promoters comply with the requirements of the Business Names Act 1985. This Act requires that where a company does not carry on its business under its corporate name, the corporate name must appear on all business letters, orders for goods or services to be supplied to the business, invoices and receipts issued in the course of the business as well as on written demands for payment of debts arising in the course of the business. In addition, an address in Great Britain at which service of any document relating to the business will be effective must be set out. Furthermore, in any premises where the business is carried on and to which the customers of the business or suppliers of any goods or services to the business have access, the company must display prominently a notice setting out this name and address. The Act requires the company to supply this information in writing to anyone dealing in the course of business with the company who asks for it. Failure to comply with any of these requirements may lead to a fine.

7.5.2.3 Articles of association

As regards the articles, the law stationers will have incorporated the company by using either Table A alone or as amended by their standard 'special' or additional articles. Great care must be taken to ensure that the articles are suitable. If they are not, they will have to be amended in accordance with s. 9 CA 1985, which requires the members to pass a special resolution approving the change see **Chapter 26**. Having done so, a new print of all the articles will have to be delivered to the Registrar, which will take time and increase the expenses of formation.

7.5.2.4 Shelf company documentation

Employees of the law stationers will have signed the memorandum and the articles as well as being named in Form G10, with all the normal results this entails. Since they become the first members, their names should appear in the register of members and they would then have to transfer shares, incurring stamp duty payments. The law stationers have provided a solution to this problem by supplying a 'letter of renunciation' of rights as shareholders and company officers in favour of the company's shareholders. This means that the directors may allot the subscribers' shares to someone else.

7.5.2.5 Advantages and disadvantages

Arguably the greatest advantage of this method is speed, since the trader can have his company immediately but this must be set against the corresponding disadvantage that although such companies are cheap initially, the changes necessary to make them comply with the trader's requirements can increase the cost considerably.

7.6 Pre-incorporation Contracts

A difficulty can arise in relation to contracts made by the promoters on behalf of a proposed company. They may wish to make contracts to acquire premises, machinery, stationery and so on, without incurring personal liability but, for some reason, may be unable to wait until the company is incorporated. This creates a problem as the company cannot enter into contracts until it has been registered as it is not yet a legal person.

Provided the promoters are aware of the difficulty, it can be minimised either by entering into a draft contract which the company will finalise on incorporation, or entering into a binding contract under which the promoters are personally liable until incorporation, at which time the company assumes responsibility usually under the terms of a new contract with the agreement of the other party.

Should the promoters enter into a contract *on behalf of* the unformed company, s. 36(4) CA 1985 will apply. This provides that 'where a contract purports to be made by a company, or by a person as agent for a company, at a time when the company has not been formed, then *subject to any agreement to the contrary* the contract has effect as one entered into by the person purporting to act for the company or as agent for it, and he is *personally liable* on the contract accordingly'.

The safest course would be to enter into contracts only after incorporation, but if this is impossible care must be taken to avoid the problems indicated.

7.7 Change of Name

7.7.1 PROCEDURE

Section 28 CA 1985 gives companies power to change their names by special resolution (which requires 75% of the votes cast in order to be passed — see **Chapter 12**). A copy of the special resolution must be sent to the Registrar and within 15 days of the change a printed copy of the memorandum with the name changed should be delivered to the Registrar. The change becomes effective when the Registrar issues a certificate of incorporation 'altered to meet the circumstances' (that is, showing the new name of the company) under s. 28(6). Although a new certificate of incorporation is issued when the name is changed the company remains the same legal person so that its rights and obligations are not affected by the change (s. 28(7)). Once the name has been changed it must be used on the company's notepaper and other documents as required by ss. 348-9 CA 1985.

7.7.2 NOTIFICATION

The issue of a certificate of incorporation by the Registrar must be officially notified (that is, advertised by the Registrar in the *London Gazette*) under s. 711 CA 1985. The company is not entitled to rely on the change as against any person until it has been officially notified unless that person actually knew of the change, nor may it rely on the change for the first 15 days after official notification against a person who was unavoidably prevented from knowing about the change (s. 42 CA 1985). It is, therefore, in the company's interests to ensure that the change is officially notified.

7.7.3   CHOICE OF NAME

As on incorporation, a company has general freedom to choose whatever name it likes, but this is subject to restrictions contained in s. 26 CA 1985 preventing use of a name the same as that of an existing company, one which constitutes a criminal offence or is offensive. Approval of the use of certain words is required as on formation. The Secretary of State also has power to direct a change of name within 12 months if it is too like a name appearing in the index of names at the time of registration or the same as a name which should have been in that index. The Secretary of State may also direct a change of name within five years under s. 28(3) if misleading information was given at the time of registration (whether on first registration or on change of name). He may also so direct at any time under s. 32 CA 1985 if the name gives 'so misleading an indication of the nature of [the company's] activities as to be likely to cause harm to the public'.

7.8   Change of Objects

As we have already seen (**7.2.1.3**) most companies, especially those formed in recent decades, have objects clauses so widely drawn that the company can lawfully undertake almost any type of business without any danger of transactions being held to be ultra vires. However, it may occasionally be considered desirable for the company to widen its objects clause. There may also be occasions when a company wishes to alter its objects clause so that it is more obviously appropriate to present circumstances. For example, a company with a 'main object' giving it power to carry on business in manufacturing may now largely be in the wholesale business and may, therefore, wish to change its objects to reflect that fact.

Power to alter the objects clause is given by s. 4 CA 1985 as amended. A special resolution is required.

A company which takes advantage of s. 3A CA 1985 as substituted and has incorporated a statement to the effect that its objects are to carry on business as a general commercial company is unlikely to need to change its objects clause.

EIGHT

DIRECTORS

8.1 Division of Powers Within a Company

The power to take decisions on behalf of a company is divided between the directors and members. There are a number of powers which are exercisable only by the members under various provisions of the Companies Act — for example, the power to change the name, objects, articles and nominal capital and various powers in relation to the issue of shares and meetings. The members' power to remove directors from office is considered in **Chapter 9**. As far as the vast majority of powers are concerned, the company is free to choose its own procedures, which will be laid down in the articles. Usually these give very wide powers to the directors.

8.2 Appointment of Directors

8.2.1 INTRODUCTION

The first directors of a company are the people who have agreed to take office by filing Form G10 (see **7.2.3**); they automatically become directors as soon as the company is formed. From time to time it will be necessary to appoint further directors, either because one of the directors has ceased to hold office or because it is decided to increase the size of the board. Apart from a few statutory restrictions which will be dealt with shortly, the company is free to make whatever provision it wishes in its articles as to the appointment of directors. In particular, there is no general requirement that the directors should be shareholders, nor that they should be chosen by the shareholders. The provisions of Table A will be considered first and then some other possibilities.

8.2.2 APPOINTMENT OF DIRECTORS UNDER TABLE A

Article 64 provides that the minimum number of directors is two and that there is no maximum number. However, the members can by ordinary resolution fix a different minimum number (including one) and/or fix a maximum number. The minimum and maximum can then be changed by further ordinary resolutions.

The main power to appoint directors is given to the members by art. 78. This provides for appointment by ordinary resolution (that is, by a simple majority at a meeting of the company or by unanimous written consent of the members).

Appointments to fill vacancies on the board and appointments of additional directors (up to the maximum, if any, fixed by the members) may be made by the board itself. A person co-opted in this way holds office until the following annual general meeting (art. 79).

8.2.3 OTHER POSSIBILITIES

In most cases the provisions of Table A as to the appointment of directors will be entirely satisfactory. However, in some cases it may be considered appropriate to make permanent appointments to the board; this can be achieved by removing the retirement provisions discussed below. It is also possible for the articles to name the first directors and to make them permanent or life directors without affecting the method of appointment of other directors. However, such appointments are ineffective unless the directors are also named as the first directors in Form G10.

It should be noted that Table A does not require a director to be a shareholder. If the company wants to restrict membership to the board to shareholders an article to that effect must be adopted on formation or by later amendment.

8.3 Removal of Directors from Office

8.3.1 RETIREMENT BY ROTATION

If Table A or similar provisions apply, all the directors retire from office at the first annual general meeting and one third of them at each subsequent AGM (arts 73-74). The retiring directors are eligible for re-election and are automatically re-elected unless someone else is appointed, or the company resolves not to re-elect them, or the company resolves not to fill the vacancy (art. 75).

In the case of a private company provisions for retirement by rotation are unnecessarily cumbersome and are often removed so that, once appointed, directors hold office permanently until death, voluntary retirement, disqualification or removal from office under s. 303 CA 1985 (see **Chapter 9**).

8.3.2 DISQUALIFICATION

8.3.2.1 Company Director Disqualification Act 1986

Companies legislation contains a number of provisions under which directors are disqualified either automatically or by court order. The most important of these are now contained in the Company Directors Disqualification Act 1986. This Act provides for disqualification from acting as a director, liquidator, receiver or manager of a company and from being concerned with the management of a company for up to 15 years (five years if the order is made by a magistrates' court). Disqualification can be imposed following:

(a) conviction for an indictable offence in connection with the management of a company;

(b) a finding that an offence involving fraud has been committed in the course of winding up a company;

(c) persistent default in filing returns with the Registrar (persistent default is conclusively presumed following three convictions for failure to file returns within five years); the maximum period of disqualification in this case is five years even if the penalty is imposed by a court other than a magistrates' court;

(d) a finding that a person is 'unfit' to be concerned in the management of a company. The order may only be made against a person who is or has been a director of a company which has become insolvent while or after he was a director. For these purposes a company is insolvent if it goes into insolvent liquidation, an administration order is made against it or an administrative receiver is appointed. Where an order is made on the ground of unfitness, the disqualification period must be for a minimum of two years and a maximum of 15.

8.3.2.2 Disqualification under the articles

The articles of a company may, of course, make provision for disqualification or automatic retirement in circumstances other than those specified in the Act. Table A art. 81 states that the office of director is to be vacated:

(a) if a director becomes bankrupt;

(b) if a director is or may be suffering from mental disorder and is admitted to hospital under the Mental Health Act or a court order is made against him on matters concerning mental disorder;

(c) if a director is absent from directors' meetings (without the board's permission) for at least six months and the directors resolve that the office be vacated.

Article 81 also provides for the resignation of directors by giving written notice to the company. No particular period of notice is required. If the director has a service contract, as, for example, in the case of most full-time directors, there is an implied obligation to give reasonable notice but for the sake of certainty it is better to include a specific period in the contract.

8.4 Alternate Directors

Table A art. 65 gives a director power to appoint (subject to the approval of the board) an alternate director. Once appointed the alternate director has all the powers of the appointing director until he is removed by the appointing director or the appointing director ceases to be a director.

8.5 Shadow Directors

A 'shadow director' is defined by s. 741(2) CA 1985 as 'any person in accordance with whose directions or instructions the directors of a company are accustomed to act'. However, a person who simply gives professional advice to the directors is not to be taken to be a shadow director.

Shadow directors are deemed to be directors of the company under some provisions of the Companies Acts. Their names should be included in the register of directors under s. 288 CA 1985. Most significantly, shadow directors are deemed to be directors for the purpose of s. 214 Insolvency Act 1986 and so may be held liable for wrongful trading. They may also be disqualified from holding office or being concerned in the management of any company (under the Company Directors Disqualification Act 1986) as if they were directors.

8.6 Powers of Directors

8.6.1 DEFINING DIRECTORS' POWERS

The powers of the directors are laid down in the articles. Table A art. 70 gives the directors wide powers, including in particular power to manage the business of the company. Article 70 is in the following terms:

> Subject to the provisions of the Act, the memorandum and the articles and to any directions given by special resolution the business of the company shall be managed by the directors who may exercise all the powers of the company. No alteration of the memorandum or articles and no such direction shall invalidate any prior act of the directors which would have been valid if that alteration had not been made or that direction had not been given. The powers given by this regulation shall not be limited by any special power given to the directors by the articles and a meeting of directors at which a quorum is present may exercise all powers exercisable by the directors.

8.6.2 EXERCISE OF POWERS

It should be noted that under the general law and under art. 70, decisions of the directors must be taken either at a board meeting at which a quorum is present or by unanimous agreement. This is, however, subject to the directors' power to delegate (see **8.9**).

The powers of the directors must be exercised in accordance with the articles. Article 88, Table A allows the directors to decide how to regulate their own meetings and provides that any director may call a meeting or require the company secretary to do so at any time. No particular period of notice is required, so that a meeting will be validly held if reasonable notice is given. Notice need not be given to a director or alternate director who is absent from the UK.

8.6.2.1 Decisions at board meetings

Decisions at board meetings are taken by majority vote; if there is an equality of votes, art. 88 gives the chairman a casting vote. The chairman is chosen by the directors from among themselves (art. 91). The chairman's casting vote prevents deadlock (without it a resolution fails if there is an equality of votes), but it also means that the director who is the chairman has considerably more power than the others. In a company with only two directors he is, in effect, able to take decisions alone.

8.6.2.2 Prohibition on director voting on resolution in which he is interested

Article 94 prohibits a director from voting on any resolution concerning a matter in which he has an interest or duty which is material and conflicts or may conflict with the interests of the company. However, this prohibition does not apply to:

(a) a resolution concerning any guarantee, security or indemnity in respect of money lent to, or an obligation for the benefit of the company;

(b) an arrangement whereby the company gives a guarantee, security or indemnity to a third party in respect of an obligation of the company guaranteed or indemnified by the director;

(c) an interest arising from his buying any shares or other securities from the company; or

(d) a resolution relating to a retirement benefits scheme.

8.6.2.3 Decision by way of written resolution

Article 93 allows the directors to pass valid resolutions without holding a board meeting provided *all* the directors entitled to receive notice of meetings (including alternate directors) sign a written resolution.

8.7 Directors' Duties

8.7.1 FIDUCIARY DUTIES

Directors do not hold the property of their company on trust since the company is a separate legal entity and therefore is able to own property directly. However, directors do owe fiduciary duties to their company, that is, they are in the same position in respect of their powers as trustees or agents with respect to the company. Because of their fiduciary duties directors must not make any secret profit out of their position and they must exercise the powers given to them bona fide for the benefit of the company.

8.7.1.1 Secret profit

The concept of secret profit is a rather intangible one; it does not, of course, prevent directors from receiving remuneration for their services. A profit is a secret profit if it comes to the director because of his position as a director. Thus in *Cook* v *Deeks* [1916] 1 AC 554, two directors of a company negotiated a construction contract with the Canadian Pacific Railroad on behalf of their company. At a late stage in the negotiations they decided to take the contract in their own names. The Privy Council held that they were accountable to their company for the profit; it was only because they were directors of the company (which had previously contracted with the Canadian Pacific) that they were able to make the profit.

A secret profit must be paid over to the company even if the company itself could not have made the profit. This is well illustrated by *Boston Deep Sea Fishing Co.* v *Ansell* (1888) 39 ChD 339. The defendant was a director of the plaintiff company and negotiated a contract on its behalf for the supply of ice to a fleet of fishing smacks owned by the company. The defendant was a shareholder in the ice-making company which had a policy of paying 'bonuses' to any of its shareholders who introduced work to it. The court held that the defendant was liable to the company for the bonuses even though the company itself could not have obtained them since it was not a shareholder in the ice-making company.

Although the fiduciary duty is to hand over what are described as secret profits, it seems that secrecy in this context means failure to obtain permission rather than actual secrecy. This is illustrated by the rather hard case of *Regal (Hastings) Ltd* v *Gulliver* [1967] 2 AC 134 (note), in which the plaintiff company owned a cinema and wished to buy two others in the same town with a view to selling all three together. The company could not raise sufficient money to buy the other cinemas and so another company was set up partly owned by Regal (Hastings) Ltd and partly by some of the directors of Regal (Hastings) Ltd who had money of their own to invest. The new company then purchased the other two cinemas. The purchasers who wished to acquire all three cinemas then purchased all the shares in Regal (Hastings) Ltd and in the new company, thus acquiring control of the companies. The new board of directors then instituted proceedings on behalf of Regal (Hastings) Ltd against its former directors. It was held by the House of Lords that a secret profit had been made since the opportunity to invest in the new company only came to the defendants because they were directors of Regal (Hastings) Ltd. This profit was ordered to be paid to Regal (Hastings) Ltd even though that company had been unable to raise all the money needed for the purchase itself and even though, realistically, the consequences of the order was that the purchaser who had negotiated the purchase of the shares at a fair price got some of the purchase price repaid to their own company.

8.7.1.2 Exercise of powers bona fide in the interests of the company as a whole

The second requirement of directors' fiduciary duties is that the directors must exercise their powers bona fide in the interests of the company as a whole. This involves two separate restrictions on directors' powers: first, that powers are given to directors for a particular reason or group of reasons and so their decisions can be challenged if they exercise powers for some other reason; and second, directors must not exercise their powers for motives of personal gain (this second reason will often overlap with the rule against secret profits). Many of the cases on this type of breach of duty have been concerned with the issue of shares by directors (a power which is in any case now much restricted by legislation — see **Chapter 10**).

An illustration of the types of cases where directors exercise power for motives of personal gain is given by *Piercy* v *S. Mills & Co. Ltd* [1920] 1 Ch 77. In that case shares were issued, at a time when capital was not needed, purely for the purpose of strengthening and maintaining the directors' control of the company. The issue of shares was held to be invalid.

The fact that there is a breach of fiduciary duty where the directors exercise powers for reasons other than those for which they were granted even in the absence of personal gain, is illustrated by *Hogg* v *Cramphorn Ltd* [1967] Ch 254. In *Hogg* v *Cramphorn* directors issued shares to trustees for the benefit of the employees. The object of the directors in issuing the shares was to prevent the takeover of the company. It was held that the issue could be challenged even though the directors believed it to be in the interests of the company as a whole, since the power to issue shares is given to the directors so that they can raise capital.

8.7.1.3 Ratification of breach of fiduciary duty

A breach of fiduciary duty may be ratified by the members and the directors themselves may vote in favour of the resolution. However, ratification is not possible where there has been a 'fraud on the minority'. It is not easy to draw a distinction between cases where ratification is possible and those where it is not, but it seems that breach of fiduciary duty without personal gain to the directors is ratifiable, breach of fiduciary duty coupled with personal gain by the directors and actual loss to the company is not.

8.7.2 DUTIES OF CARE AND SKILL

Directors may be liable to their companies for their negligence as well as for breach of fiduciary duty. The courts are always reluctant to interfere with business decisions, however foolish they may seem with the benefit of hindsight. The duty of care and skill required from a director is, therefore, a low one. In particular, the test applied is a subjective one, that is, a director need not exhibit in the performance of his duties a greater degree of skill than may reasonably be expected from a person of his knowledge and experience. Directors may be liable for 'wrongful trading' if their company becomes insolvent: see **Chapter 24**.

8.7.3 STATUTORY DUTIES

8.7.3.1 Company records

The duty to make returns to the Registrar of Companies will normally be performed on behalf of a company by its secretary, but directors are in some circumstances also liable to a fine if returns are not made (s. 730(5) CA 1985) and persistent default can lead to disqualification. The directors are also under a duty to keep minutes of their own meetings and to deliver accounts.

8.7.3.2 Interests of employees

Section 309 CA 1985 provides that directors shall have regard to the interests of the company's employees in general as well as the interests of its members. However, this duty is only enforceable by the shareholders, not by the employees.

8.7.4 DIRECTORS' DUTIES TO THIRD PARTIES

A director does not generally owe any duty to a person dealing with his company. However, a director makes himself liable to such a person in a particular case if he claims an authority to bind his company which he does not have. The action resulting from such a liability is called an action for breach of warranty of authority: see further **8.11**.

8.8 Statutory Provisions concerning Directors

Because of the very high degree of control which directors are able to exercise over their companies a number of statutory provisions have been enacted for the protection of shareholders and the public generally.

8.8.1 DISCLOSURE OF INFORMATION

8.8.1.1 Register of directors

Section 288 CA 1985 requires every company to keep at its registered office a register of directors. In respect of each director (including any shadow director) the following information must be given:

(a) present Christian or other forename(s) and surname;
(b) any former names (there are limited exceptions, the most important being that married women need not state their maiden names or other names by which they were known before marriage);
(c) residential address;
(d) business occupation;

(e) other directorships held or which, during the last five years, have been held by the director other than directorships in dormant companies or in companies wholly owned by or wholly owning the company.
(It is also advisable to include dates of appointment and removal from office.)

The same information must also be sent to the Registrar of Companies. Form G10 is used for notification of particulars of the first directors and Form G288 must be sent to the Registrar within 14 days of any change in the particulars (whether because a director is appointed or ceases to hold office, or because of changes in the particulars of the continuing directors).

8.8.1.2 Register of directors' interests

A director is under an obligation to give to the company certain information about his interests in the company's shares and debentures (s. 324 CA 1985) and the company must keep a register of such interests. Any type of interest in shares or debentures must be reported, including, for example, outright ownership, options to purchase and charges — the register, therefore, includes information which cannot be obtained from the register of members which deals only with legal ownership. Notification and registration are also required of interests of the spouse and infant children (including step-children) of the director.

8.8.1.3 Service contracts

Copies of directors' service contracts must be available for inspection by the members (s. 318 CA 1985). If a director does not have a written service contract then a written memorandum of his terms of service must be kept instead.

8.8.1.4 Publicity as to names of directors

Section 305 CA 1985 prevents a company from giving publicity to the names of directors in business letters unless the names (including forenames or initials) of all the directors are given.

8.8.1.5 Disclosure of interests in contracts

Section 317 CA 1985 requires a director who is directly or indirectly interested in a contract or proposed contract with his company to declare the nature of his interest at a board meeting. Notice must be given at the first meeting at which the contract is discussed or at the first meeting after the director becomes interested in the contract. Where the director is a member of another company or firm he may give general notice stating that he is interested in any contract with the company, and then he need not disclose his interest each time such a contract is discussed.

8.8.2 RESTRICTIONS ON FREEDOM OF CONTRACT

8.8.2.1 Loans to directors

The latest of the successively more stringent provisions preventing loans to directors is contained in ss. 330-347 CA 1985. A private company may not make a loan or loans of more than £5,000 in aggregate to a director of the company or a director of its holding company nor may it guarantee or provide security in connection with a loan made by any person to such a director. However, a loan of any amount may be made if its purpose is 'to provide a director with funds to meet expenditure incurred or to be incurred by him for the purposes of the company or for the purpose of enabling him properly to perform his duties' provided that the members in general meeting give approval in advance or the loan is repayable within six months of the next annual general meeting (s. 337).

8.8.2.2 Directors' service contracts

The terms of directors' service contracts will usually be determined by the board although members are entitled to information about the terms of such contracts and a director may not usually vote on his own service contract (Table A art. 94). Section 319 requires the approval of the members in general meeting of a term in the service contract of a director under which he cannot be removed by notice for a period exceeding five years. Approval is also required where an existing contract is extended if the aggregate term exceeds five years. Although only the service contracts of directors require approval of the members in this way, it is not possible to circumvent the section by providing for employment in a capacity other than as a director (for example, as a consultant) after the directorship ceases.

8.8.2.3 Property transactions

A third restriction on the freedom of directors to contract with their companies is provided by s. 320 CA 1985. This requires the approval of the members in general meeting for the contracts to which it applies. Section 320 applies to any arrangement whereby a director or a person connected with a director is to acquire from the company one or more non-cash assets of the 'requisite value' or whereby the company is to acquire such assets from such a person.

The 'requisite value' depends on the net assets of the company as shown in the company's most recent balance sheet. A non-cash asset is of the requisite value 'if at the time the arrangement in question is entered into its value is not less than £2,000 but, subject to that, exceeds £100,000 or 10% of the amount of the company's relevant assets'. Thus if the company's net assets are £1,000,000 or more the requisite value is £100,000. If the net assets are less than £1,000,000 but more than £20,000 the requisite value is 10% of such assets. If the net assets are £10,000 or less the requisite value is £2,000.

If a contract is made in contravention of the section it is voidable by the company unless:

(a) restitution is no longer possible;
(b) third party rights (acquired for value without notice) would be affected by avoidance; or
(c) the contract has been affirmed by the members in general meeting.

Furthermore, the directors who authorised the arrangement (not just the one who is a party to the contract) are liable to indemnify the company against any loss. The director or connected person who is a party to the contract is liable to account for any profit made, although a connected person is excused from liability if he did not know the circumstances. For the purposes of s. 320 a connected person includes (among others) a director's spouse, child or step-child.

The main purpose of s. 320 is to prevent directors from making substantial profits in transactions with their companies and so reinforces the rules of equity concerning secret profits. One fairly common type of contract which is subject to its provisions is a contract under which a director receives shares in return for assets, so that if a director who owns business premises (of the requisite value) wishes to transfer them to the company in return for shares, the approval of the members in general meeting must first be obtained.

8.9 Managing Directors

8.9.1 APPOINTMENT

It is very common for one of the directors of a company to be appointed managing director. The functions actually performed by the managing director vary from company to company, but in practice he will usually be either the most senior director in the company's hierarchy or second in command to the chairman. A managing director cannot be appointed unless the articles (or, rarely, the memorandum) so provide. Table A, art. 84 does so provide and art. 72 provides that: '[the directors] may . . . delegate to any managing director . . . such of their powers as they consider desirable to be exercised by him'.

8.9.2 POWERS

The board are also given the power to specify what his powers are to be and to impose conditions. The powers granted may even be to the exclusion of the powers of the board but can be revoked or altered at any time by the board.

8.9.3 SERVICE CONTRACT

In practice, the managing director will usually have a service contract even if the other directors do not. The terms of the contract will be negotiated by the managing director and the board; the members' approval will be required if he is given security of tenure for longer than five years (s. 319 CA 1985 — see **8.8.2.2**). The managing director is both a director and an employee of the company; like other employees he has certain statutory rights against the company if he is unfairly dismissed or made redundant. Since he automatically ceases to be managing director if he ceases to be a director, the members can remove him from both offices by passing an ordinary resolution (s. 303 CA 1985) but this may result in heavy damages being payable by the company for breach of the service contract.

8.10 Removal of Directors (s. 303 CA 1985)

8.10.1 POWER TO REMOVE BY ORDINARY RESOLUTION

Shareholders appoint directors in most cases and, unless Table A has been altered, have an opportunity to get rid of them every three years when they retire by rotation. To give the shareholders a greater measure of control, s. 303 CA 1985 provides for removal of directors by ordinary resolution (i.e., by a majority vote of the shareholders in general meeting). The power given by the section overrides anything in the company's articles (even, for example, an article naming a life director) or in an agreement with the director. The importance of s. 303 can hardly be overstated; it is the most effective way in which majority shareholders who object to the way in which their company is being run can keep control of the company. Where the directors themselves are the majority shareholders, as they very frequently will be in the case of a private company, the other (minority) shareholders have limited rights to object to the way the board is running the company (see below).

8.10.2 PROCEDURE

A shareholder who wants to propose a resolution for the removal of a director under s. 303 must give 'special notice' of the resolution; this means that he must give notice to the company at least 28 days before the meeting at which the resolution is to be discussed (s. 379 CA 1985). However, this requirement is deemed to be complied with if a meeting is called *after* notice has been given for a date within the 28 days. It has been held (in *Pedley* v *Inland Waterways Association* [1977] 1 All ER 209) that the directors are not under an obligation to put the resolution for the removal of a director on the agenda of a meeting merely because they have received special notice. This detracts slightly from the effectiveness of s. 303 but any shareholders (or group of shareholders) with a 10% shareholding (5% in the case of an annual general meeting) can insist on the inclusion of a resolution on the agenda. Once the company has received the special notice a copy must be sent to the director whose removal is proposed (s. 304); he is also given a right to speak at the meeting even if not a member, and to require the company to circulate representations in writing of reasonable length to the members.

8.10.3 LIMITATIONS ON EFFECTIVENESS OF s. 303

8.10.3.1 Director's right to compensation

Although the right to remove a director is absolute, the director is not deprived of any right to compensation or damages which he may have (s. 303(5)). It may, therefore, be very expensive to remove a director, in which case the majority shareholders should consider other methods of control (e.g., by the appointment of additional directors).

8.10.3.2 Special voting rights

Secondly, the articles may validly give special voting rights to some of the shareholders either generally or in particular circumstances. In the case of *Bushell* v *Faith* [1970] AC 1099, the articles provided that 'in the event of a resolution being proposed at any general meeting of the company for the removal from office of any director, any shares held by that director shall on a poll in respect of such resolution carry the right to three votes per share . . .'. The director whose removal was proposed owned one third of the shares and so could not be removed. Nevertheless, the article was held to be valid, since all that s. 303 lays down is that an ordinary resolution may be used to remove a director and an ordinary resolution is one requiring a simple majority of votes. A clause of this type does not, therefore, prevent a resolution from being an ordinary resolution but effectively makes it impossible to remove the director without his consent.

The decision in *Bushell* v *Faith* has been criticised, but there are some circumstances where it may be appropriate to include in the articles a regulation which makes it impossible for the majority shareholders to get rid of a director who owns a minority of the shares. Such a regulation should be considered, for example, where a small number of people wish to run a company as a 'quasi-partnership' — that is, where they all intend to have a continuing right to take part in management. In other circumstances it may be appropriate to give the shareholders wider powers to remove directors than are given by s. 303 so that, for example, removal by ordinary resolution *without* special notice may be considered appropriate.

8.11 The Directors and Protection of Outsiders

8.11.1 INTRODUCTION

A company is not a natural person and so can only exercise its powers through agents. Usually contracts will be made on behalf of the company either by the directors or by more junior officials acting on the directors' authority. If a contract is made in accordance with the articles of the company it will be binding on the company, so that the 'outsider' with whom the company is dealing can sue the company if it fails to perform the contract. Where, however, a contract is made by the wrong people (e.g., the directors exercise a power which is vested in the shareholders, or an employee acts without the authority of the directors), or in the wrong way (e.g., a meeting is held but it has not been properly convened), the whole transaction is, prima facie, void. Contracts and other transactions decided upon without proper authority (or without a proper exercise of authority) are described as 'irregular'.

In dealing with irregular contracts the law is faced with a dilemma. If the contract is declared irregular and void the outsider will not be able to enforce it against the company even though he may be unaware of the irregularity. On the other hand, if the company is held to be bound by irregular contracts the directors will, in effect, be able to ignore the requirements of the company's articles to the possible detriment of the shareholders. The law deals with this dilemma by providing that irregular contracts, though prima facie void, are binding on the company in certain circumstances only. These circumstances result partly from statute, partly from decisions of the court concerned exclusively with company law rules, and partly from the general law of agency. The Companies Act 1989 has further extended the circumstances in which an irregular contract is valid.

8.11.2 STATUTORY PROTECTION

8.11.2.1 Sections 35A and 35B (as interpolated)

Statutory rules about the extent to which directors could bind their company despite irregularity were first included in the European Communities Act 1972. Similar provisions were included in s. 35 CA

1985. This section has now been significantly amended by CA 1989. The new provisions are contained in new sections 35A and 35B CA 1985. Section 35A(1) provides:

> In favour of a person dealing with a company in good faith, the power of the board of directors to bind the company, or to authorise others to do so, shall be deemed free of any limitation under the company's constitution.

The reference to the company's constitution (for this purpose) includes a resolution of the company and agreements between the company and its members as well as the memorandum and articles.

It should be noted that a person dealing with the company is entitled to assume that the directors have unlimited power to bind it. A similar assumption may also be made where the directors have purported to authorise 'others' to do so.

Shareholder's power to seek injunction If a shareholder believes that the directors are about to exceed their powers by entering into an irregular contract he can seek an injunction to restrain them. However, this right is lost once the company incurs any legal obligation to a third party (s. 35A(4)). If directors enter into an irregular contract they may be liable to the company for any loss. (Section 35 gives them no protection personally (s. 35A(5).)

Requirements of good faith The protection of s. 35A is given only to persons who act in good faith. However, good faith is presumed unless the contrary is proved (s. 35A(2)(c)) and knowledge that the directors are acting beyond their powers is not of itself sufficient proof of bad faith (s. 35A(2)(a)). Section 35B provides that a person dealing with a company is not under any obligation to enquire into the powers of its directors.

Transaction with connected party Section 322A CA 1985 (as interpolated by CA 1989) makes a limited exception to s. 35A. This applies where the board of a company exceed their powers in a transaction with a director or a person connected with a director. In such cases the transaction is voidable by the company. Whether or not it is avoided, the director or connected person and any director who authorised the transaction is liable to account to the company for any gain he makes and to indemnify the company against any loss. Where a transaction is irregular and is made between the company, a director and one or more third parties the court has a wide discretion which enables it to protect any innocent third party.

The company's right to avoid a contract under s. 322A is lost if restitution becomes impossible (i.e., if a third party who has acquired rights bona fide for value would be affected), if the transaction is ratified or if the company has been fully compensated by indemnity from the director.

8.11.2.2 Section 285 CA 1985

Section 285 provides that, 'the acts of a director or manager are valid notwithstanding any defect that may afterwards be discovered in his appointment or qualification'. This section protects the company, the outsider dealing with it, and the director, if there is some sort of procedural defect in the appointment (e.g., proper notice was not given of the meeting at which the appointment was made).

8.11.3 THE RULE IN *ROYAL BRITISH BANK* v *TURQUAND*

A number of common law decisions gave protection to outsiders where contracts were made without authority. In view of the enactment of ss. 35A and 35B the significance of these decisions is likely to be very slight in future.

These decisions held that a person dealing with a company was entitled to assume the correct procedures had been followed (*Royal British Bank* v *Turquand* (1856) E and B 327, 119 ER 886), that persons appearing to be directors had been properly appointed (*Mahony* v *East Holyford Mining Co.* (1875) LR 7 HL 869) and that a board meeting had been lawfully held (*Browne* v *La Trinidad* (1887) 37 Ch D 1).

8.11.4 AGENCY

8.11.4.1 General position

A company can only act through agents; the authority of agents to act for a company depends on the general law of agency. The actions of an agent are binding on a principal if the agent has actual authority or authority arising from estoppel. The agent may also be personally liable to the third party (i.e., to the outsider) if the principal (i.e., the company) is not liable.

8.11.4.2 Actual authority

The scope of the actual authority of a company's agents depends upon the memorandum and articles of the company. The board of directors, acting collectively, usually has very wide powers to act on behalf of the company. The articles will usually permit delegation to committees of directors and to a managing director (or to a number of joint managing directors).

8.11.4.3 Agency by estoppel

A company may be bound by the acts of a person acting on its behalf when it is estopped from denying that person's authority. Agency by estoppel may result either from 'holding out' (that is, an actual representation that the agent has authority) or from a representation that the agent is a member of a particular class of agent which is recognised to have certain powers to bind its principals. The estoppel may prevent the company from denying that the alleged agent is its agent or that he has power to bind the company in a particular way.

'Holding out' If a company is to be liable because an agent has been held out as having authority, the holding out must be done by the person or persons with actual authority to bind the company.

Usual or apparent authority It is a well established rule of the law of agency that a principal is estopped from denying that an agent of certain recognised classes has the authority normally associated with that class (unless, of course, he tells the third party that there is a restriction on the power of the agent). In relation to companies, this rule has been applied to managing directors. If a company describes one of the directors as a managing director, it is estopped from denying that he is a managing director (even if he has not been appointed) and that he has the authority of a managing director (even if his appointment includes terms restricting his authority). This type of authority is sometimes called 'usual authority' or 'apparent authority'.

Directors other than managing directors do not generally have authority to act alone, so a company is not bound by the action of a single director who is not a managing director unless either he has actual authority or the board have held him out as having authority in the particular transaction.

The company secretary has been held to have usual authority to bind the company to contracts concerning administration.

8.11.4.4 Liability of the agent to the third party

A person purporting to act as agent for a company will be personally liable for breach of warranty of authority if it turns out that he had no authority to bind the company.

8.11.4.5 Ratification

If a contract is made by an agent without authority so that the company is not bound by the contract, the company can ratify, and thus retrospectively validate, the contract. Ratification may be effected by the people with actual authority to bind the company (i.e., normally the board, but in some cases the members in general meeting). Ratification will usually be implied where the company has accepted performance of the contract.

8.12   The Company Secretary

Section 283 CA 1985 requires every company to have a secretary. The secretary may also be a director but, to ensure there are always two officers of the company, a *sole* director cannot also be secretary. The first secretary of a newly formed company is the person named in Form G10; subsequently the secretary is appointed and removed by the board who also decide on the terms of appointment (Table A art. 99). The secretary is responsible for keeping the various records of the company, such as minutes of board and general meetings and the various records which must be kept at the registered office. He is also an officer of the company and so is liable to a fine if the company is in breach of the provisions of the Companies Act which require information to be filed with the Registrar of Companies.

Many company secretaries are given powers far in excess of those contemplated by the Companies Act. Often the secretary is responsible for the administration of the company and performs the functions of an office manager as well as of a record-keeper. The courts have, therefore, recognised that an outsider is entitled to rely on a decision taken by the secretary which relates to administration even if it turns out that the decision was not authorised by the board (i.e., the secretary has ostensible authority to make such contracts). Thus in *Panorama (Developments) Guildford Ltd* v *Fidelis Furnishing Fabrics Ltd* [1971] 2 QB 711, the Court of Appeal held that a company was bound to pay for the use of cars hired by the secretary purportedly on behalf of the company but in fact for his own use.

Every company must keep a register of directors and secretaries and notify the Registrar of Companies within 14 days of any change (s. 288 CA 1985). In the case of a secretary the particulars to be given are the present and past names of the secretary (subject to the same exceptions as apply in the case of a director) and his usual residential address.

NINE

SHAREHOLDERS

9.1 Introduction

This chapter will deal with the position of shareholders in relation to a company. We will look at the following issues:

(a) registration of membership;
(b) the powers of shareholders in relation to their company;
(c) the legal protection given to shareholders by the rules of equity and by the Companies Act;
(d) the payment of dividends to shareholders.

You will find references to shareholders throughout this Guide so that this chapter is intended to deal with their position in the company in general terms. Bear this in mind as you progress through your studies — it is always dangerous to pigeonhole things too much. You cannot understand the position of shareholders fully until you understand the position of directors (and vice versa).

You already know (see **Chapters 6** and **7**) that all companies must have at least one 'member'. The vast majority of companies are incorporated with a 'share capital', that is with the right and expectation that one day they will issue shares to people who are in effect the owners of the company. Section 22(2) CA 1985 provides that: 'Every person who agrees to become a member of a company, and whose name is entered in its register of members, is a member of the company.' This means that membership begins when the member's name is entered in the register of members. The *right* to become a member may result from a contract between the company and the purchaser of new shares (this is called an allotment or issue of shares; see **Chapter 10**). The right may also arise because an existing shareholder transfers shares to someone else by sale or gift. It may also arise when a member dies or becomes bankrupt. At that time the shares are automatically transmitted to the personal representative or trustee in bankruptcy. From this we can see that it is the ownership of shares which makes someone a member of a company. Hence the terms 'member' and 'shareholder' mean almost the same thing.

When someone becomes a shareholder and is registered as a member he acquires some say in the way that the company is run.

In most companies (including those which have Table A as their articles), it is the directors who actually run the company (see **Chapter 8**). It is because there may be a conflict between the interests of the directors and the shareholders that the law steps in to provide a measure of protection to the shareholders. In giving advice on these matters it is vital to distinguish between shareholders in various categories. As we have already seen (see **8.10**) a shareholder with a majority of the votes has the power to remove the directors from office. When this power is available to a shareholder it is likely to be the most effective way in which he can control the company. Bear in mind also that with very many small companies the directors and shareholders are likely to be the same people so that they will have rights in both capacities. (These matters are dealt with more fully in **9.3** below.)

9.2 Registration of Membership

9.2.1 CONTENTS OF THE REGISTER

Every company must keep a register of its members and their shareholdings. The following information must be recorded (s. 352 CA 1985):

(a) the names and addresses of the members;
(b) the number of shares held and, where the company has more than one class of issued shares, the number of each class held by each member;
(c) the amount paid or agreed to be considered as paid on the shares of each member;
(d) the date at which each member was entered in the register;
(e) the date at which each member ceased to be a member.

No particular form of register is required (since 1967 it may be kept by a computer), but under s. 354 CA 1985 an index is required if the register is not kept in the form of an index and there are more than 50 members (this provision is of little relevance to private companies since very few of them have more than 50 members). The register must normally be kept at the registered office of the company and if kept elsewhere the Registrar of Companies must be notified (s. 353 CA 1985). The register of members itself is not sent to the Registrar but the annual return made by the company after each AGM contains details of the membership.

The register of members must be open to inspection (by members free of charge and by the public) during business hours for at least two hours during every business day.

9.2.2 TRUSTS

Section 360 CA 1985 provides that 'no notice of any trust . . . shall be entered on the register . . .'. This means that the company must treat the registered holder of shares as beneficially entitled to those shares even if it knows that they are held on trust. The company must, therefore, pay dividends to the trustee and allow the trustee to exercise any voting powers attached to the shares.

The effect of this rule is well illustrated by the case of *Simpson v Molson's Bank* [1895] AC 270. A shareholder died and the shares were registered in the name of his executors, one of whom was a director of the company. The executors transferred the shares in breach of the provisions of the will. A copy of the will had been sent to the company to prove the identity of the executors. The company was held not to be liable to the true beneficiary of the will since it was not entitled to take notice of any trusts over the shares. Once satisfied that the executors were entitled to be registered and once it had registered them the company was bound to allow them to transfer the shares.

Section 360 does not, of course, affect the position as between the registered owner and his beneficiary. The registered owner must, therefore, hand over to the beneficiary any dividend he receives and vote in accordance with the beneficiary's wishes.

9.2.3 RECTIFICATION OF THE REGISTER

Section 359 CA 1985 gives the court power to order rectification of the register of members if:

(a) the name of any person is, without sufficient cause, entered in or omitted from [the register]; . . . or
(b) default is made or unnecessary delay takes place in entering on the register the fact of any person having ceased to be a member.

One of the circumstances in which rectification may be applied for is when the company *wrongly* refuses to register a transfer. However, a person to whom shares are transferred does not always have a right to be registered (see **Chapter 11**).

In addition to its powers under s. 359 the court may order rectification of the register in other circumstances where it is just and equitable. Thus in *Burns* v *Siemens Brothers Dynamo Works Ltd* [1919] 1 Ch 225, shares were registered in the name of two joint holders. The articles of the company provided that where there were joint holders only the first named could vote (cf. Table A art. 55, which in such a case allows the second joint holder to vote only if the first does not). The person whose name appeared second sought rectification and the court ordered that half the shares should be registered with his name appearing first in the register.

9.3 Powers and Duties of Shareholders

9.3.1 SOURCES OF SHAREHOLDERS' POWERS

The powers of the shareholders are not easy to define succinctly. As we saw in **Chapter 8**, most of the decisions of a company are taken by the board of directors (unless the articles are very unusual), but certain powers are specifically given to the members by the Companies Act and these cannot be taken away by the memorandum or articles. In addition to these powers which are guaranteed by law, certain powers are also given to members by the articles. Thus, if Table A applies, the members have power to elect new directors and to declare dividends. It should be noted that the powers given to members are given collectively; therefore, a shareholder (or group of shareholders) who controls the majority of the votes at a company meeting is obviously in a far stronger position than a 'minority' shareholder.

9.3.2 POWERS OF CONTROL

In practical terms, a majority shareholder has extensive powers of control, exercisable ultimately by removing or threatening to remove the directors from office. A minority shareholder often has no real power (unless he is a director and/or can persuade the majority to agree with him), but his position is protected by a number of rights, mostly statutory, some of the most important of which are discussed later in this chapter. It should also be noted that both the powers and rights given to members depend in many cases on the holding of a particular proportion of the company's shares (or votes). For example, a number of types of decision require a special resolution (75% majority) — a shareholder who controls 75% of the votes is, therefore, able to exercise powers which a shareholder with a simple majority could not exercise alone. Conversely, a shareholder with more than 25% of the votes can block a special resolution even though he may not have enough votes to be in control of the company (this is sometimes called negative control).

9.3.3 DUTIES OF SHAREHOLDERS

Just as the powers and rights of members largely depend on the proportion of votes that they control, so the duties of members differ depending on whether or not they are in control of the company. The basic rule is that members (whether or not in control) can exercise their right to vote as they wish, so that they can take account of their own interests to the exclusion of conflicting interest of other shareholders. This does not mean that shareholders are *entirely* free to vote as they please; thus certain breaches of duty by directors cannot be ratified by the members (see for example, *Cook* v *Deeks*, **8.7.1**) while other breaches can be ratified (*Regal (Hastings) Ltd* v *Gulliver*, **8.7.1**). Shareholders may not commit a 'fraud on the minority', so that an alteration to the articles is invalid if it discriminates against some of the shareholders. Both these exceptions to the basic rule are well established, but the case of *Clemens* v *Clemens Brothers Ltd* [1976] 2 All ER 268, suggests that the duty of controlling shareholders may be much more extensive than was previously thought. The facts were as follows. The plaintiff owned 45% of the shares in the company and her aunt all the remainder. The directors were not shareholders. Under the articles a shareholder had a right of pre-emption if another shareholder wished to transfer shares so that one day the plaintiff hoped to obtain control of the company. The aunt passed a resolution for the issue of shares to the directors and to a trust for the employees of the company. The object of the resolution was apparently to deprive the plaintiff of her power to block special resolutions. The court set aside the resolution and declared it invalid because the aunt was held not to be: 'entitled as of right to exercise her votes as an ordinary shareholder in any way she pleases

. . . that right is subject to equitable considerations which will make it unjust to exercise it [in the way she has]'. This decision has not been relied upon in later cases but the provisions of ss. 459-461 CA 1985 strengthen the position of minorities considerably in this sort of case (see **9.8** below).

The powers of shareholders to control their companies are normally exercised by passing a resolution by the required majority at a meeting called by the appropriate notice at which a quorum is present. Alternatively, a written resolution may be used. Members who are absent do not, of course, count in the voting unless they have validly appointed a proxy to represent them. Company meetings and resolutions are dealt with in **Chapter 12**.

9.4 Internal Disputes — Introduction

The courts are very reluctant to get involved in disputes within a company. In particular they are not willing to do anything which might amount to interference with business decisions. Internal disputes must therefore usually be resolved under the terms of the company's articles. For example, if there are disputes about business policy the view of the majority of the board will prevail. In the case of an equal division on the board the dispute will be resolved by the chairman's casting vote if the articles so provide (as they usually will).

The power of the shareholders is rather limited. In this section we will look at four procedures which are, however, available to shareholders for their protection. The first of these (s. 14 CA 1985) provides any shareholder with a procedure for enforcing his personal rights in the company. The other three procedures are designed chiefly for the protection of minority shareholders when a dispute arises. In addition we dealt with removal of directors in **Chapter 8**. This gives a majority shareholder ultimate control of the company.

9.5 Section 14 Companies Act 1985

9.5.1 CONTRACT BETWEEN MEMBERS AND COMPANY

This important section creates a contract between a company and each of its members (without such a provision only the original owner of shares would have a contract with the company). Section 14 says

. . . the memorandum and articles . . . bind the company and its members to the same extent as if they respectively had been signed and sealed by each member, and contained covenants on the part of each member to observe all the provisions of the memorandum and of the articles.

Read literally only the members are bound by this contract since only they are deemed to have sealed the memorandum and articles and to have entered into covenants. However, the company has been held to be bound by the contract as well (*Re Compañía de Electricidad de la Provincia de Buenos Aires Ltd* [1978] 3 All ER 668).

9.5.2 CONTRACT BETWEEN MEMBERS

The contracts laid down in s. 14 have been held to bind the members contractually to each other. Thus in *Rayfield* v *Hands* [1960] Ch 1, the articles of the company required the directors to purchase the shares of any member who wished to sell his shares. This obligation was held to be enforceable against the directors since they were shareholders in the company and were, therefore, parties to a contract with each of its members. As we shall see shortly, s. 14 has often been held to apply only to obligations owed by or to members in their capacity as members, but the court was able to say (without giving any very persuasive reasons for doing so) that the obligation to buy shares was imposed on the directors in their capacity as members.

9.5.3 MEMBERSHIP RIGHTS

An obligation imposed by the memorandum or articles on a member or on the company for the benefit of a member is only enforceable under s. 14 if it relates to membership rights. The most obvious examples of membership rights which have been enforced as a result of actions based on the section include:

(a) the right to a dividend once lawfully declared (*Wood* v *Odessa Waterworks Co.* (1889) 42 ChD 636);

(b) the right to share in surplus capital on a winding-up (*Griffith* v *Paget* (1877) 5 ChD 894); and

(c) the right to vote at meetings (*Pender* v *Lushington* (1877) 6 ChD 70).

The most obvious obligation of a member which may be enforced by s. 14 is the obligation to pay for shares issued by the company.

9.5.4 OTHER RIGHTS

Obligations imposed by the memorandum or articles which do not relate to membership rights are not enforceable under s. 14. A member may, therefore, be left without any remedy even though the company has failed to observe an article which would have benefited him. This is illustrated by the case of *Eley* v *Positive Government Security Life Assurance Co.* (1876) 1 ExD 88. When the company was formed a provision was included in the articles naming the plaintiff as solicitor of the company. He was never, in fact, appointed to the office but did become a member of the company. It was held that he could not sue the company under the provisions of earlier legislation corresponding with s. 14.

It may seem harsh that a member cannot sue in such a case to enforce an article of the company, but the justification for the rule is that it would be wrong to allow someone to sue just because he was a member, and furthermore it would lead to great inconveniences if members could sue every time there was a breach of the articles.

Just as a member cannot enforce rights against the company which do not relate to his rights as a member, neither can the company enforce obligations imposed by the articles other than in connection with membership. For example, in *Beattie* v *E. and F. Beattie Ltd* [1938] Ch 708, a dispute arose between a company and one of its directors concerning the latter's right to inspect documents. The company wished to refer the matter to arbitration in accordance with an article requiring arbitration of disputes with members, but was held not entitled to insist on arbitration since the dispute was between the company and the plaintiff in his capacity as director not in his capacity as shareholder.

9.5.5 IMPLIED CONTRACTS AND SHAREHOLDERS' AGREEMENTS

The terms laid down in the memorandum or articles may be impliedly incorporated into a contract made with the company. This is most likely to occur in relation to directors' service contracts. Thus, in *Read* v *Astoria Garage (Streatham) Ltd* [1952] Ch 637, a managing director whose service contract did not specify how long he was to remain in office was held to have an implied contract allowing for his dismissal in accordance with certain provisions in the articles.

If the members of a company wish to be able to enforce all the terms of the articles against the company and/or each other they are free to enter into a separate contract to that effect. Such a contract is generally referred to as a 'shareholders' agreement' (see **Chapter 28**).

9.6 *Foss* v *Harbottle*

9.6.1 MAJORITY RULE

A shareholder is not usually permitted to sue where a wrong is done to a company of which he is a member. This rule is known as the rule in *Foss* v *Harbottle* (1843) 2 Hare 461, and there are two justifications for it. Firstly, since a company is a separate legal person distinct from its members the company is the proper plaintiff in an action where a wrong has been done to the company. Secondly, the decision whether or not to sue can be taken either by the directors or by the members in general meeting, and the court is unwilling to interfere with this decision by imposing its own views on the company. At the same time, the courts have recognised that in some circumstances it is appropriate to allow a shareholder to sue on behalf of the company since otherwise justice cannot be done. There are, therefore, a number of exceptions to the rule in *Foss* v *Harbottle*, under which a shareholder can bring an action if the company will not.

These exceptional cases should be contrasted with cases where the personal rights of a shareholder are affected. In such cases, as we saw in the last paragraph, the shareholder need not rely upon an exception to *Foss* v *Harbottle* at all, but may sue because of the contractual rights which he has under s. 14. It is not always easy to decide which actions are permitted by the exceptions to *Foss* v *Harbottle* and which by s. 14. Minority shareholders are also given a number of statutory rights which may be directly enforced against the company (for example, to have the register to members rectified under s. 359 CA 1985), and are given a right to sue where they are 'unfairly prejudiced' by the way in which the company's affairs are being conducted (s. 459 CA 1985) (see **9.8** below).

9.6.2 EXCEPTIONS TO *FOSS* v *HARBOTTLE*

The following are the circumstances in which a member can sue to remedy a wrong done to the company.

9.6.2.1 Where the majority exercise their votes so as to 'defraud' the minority shareholders

'Fraud' in this context is quite a wide concept, covering forms of conduct which do not amount to the commission of a tort. Thus in *Clemens* v *Clemens Brothers Ltd* [1976] 2 All ER 268, a resolution was declared invalid, the effect of which was to increase the degree of control which the majority shareholder and her associates could exercise.

9.6.2.2 Where directors who are in control of a company have been guilty of a breach of fiduciary duty

This exception will often overlap with the first exception, since a breach of fiduciary duty will often involve a fraud on the minority. The reason for this exception is that if the directors are in control of the company they will use their voting power so as to prevent action being brought against themselves. Therefore, unless a shareholder can sue on behalf of the company, there is no real chance of a remedy for the breach of fiduciary duty. Where a breach of fiduciary duty can be ratified by the members in general meeting (see, for example, *Hogg* v *Cramphorn*), an action by a shareholder may be stayed pending the holding of a meeting, but the court will not permit ratification in every case (see, for example, *Cook* v *Deeks*).

Where the directors are not in control of a company, an action cannot be brought by a shareholder based on breach of fiduciary duty, since the company in general meeting is then in a position to decide to sue. However, *Clemens* v *Clemens* shows that in such cases the way in which the majority shareholders vote may be subject to control by the court.

9.6.2.3 Where the company (usually as a result of a decision of the board) is proposing to act ultra vires or illegally

In such cases the action may result in an injunction against the directors or an order for compensation against the directors.

9.6.2.4 Where the company has purported to pass an ordinary resolution in circumstances where a special resolution or extraordinary resolution is required

Similarly, an action may be brought to restrain a threatened breach of the articles (which can only validly be altered by special resolution), although the exact scope of this exception is far from clear.

9.6.2.5 **Where the company proposes to act on the authority of a resolution which is defective because inadequate notice was given**

The notice may be inadequate either because the time between service and the holding of the meeting is too short or because the details given in the notice are insufficient to enable a member to decide whether to attend. For example, in *Baillie* v *Oriental Telephone Co. Ltd* [1915] 1 Ch 503, the notice referred to the fact that a resolution was to be proposed authorising certain payments of commission by a subsidiary company to the directors. It did not say that the payments effectively amounted to all the subsidiary's profits. This was held to be inadequate notice and, therefore, the resolution was set aside in an action brought by a shareholder.

9.6.2.6 **Where the court decides that an action by a shareholder is in the interests of justice**

There is some authority for saying that the list of exceptions to *Foss* v *Harbottle* is not closed and that the courts may allow actions in any circumstances where it is in the interests of justice. This was suggested in *Heyting* v *Dupont* [1964] 2 All ER 273 (although on the facts of that case the minority shareholder was refused a remedy). However, this view was doubted in *Estmanco (Kilner House) Ltd* v *GLC* [1982] 1 All ER 437, and in *Prudential Assurance Co. Ltd* v *Newman Industries Ltd (No. 2)* [1982] 1 All ER 354, the court observed that this was 'not a practical test'.

9.7 Actions by Shareholders — Procedure

When a member is able to bring an action under one of the exceptions to *Foss* v *Harbottle*, he is really doing so on behalf of the company. The plaintiff's interests are, therefore, the same as those of the other shareholders (other than any wrongdoers, usually the directors, who are defendants in the action). When a member sues to enforce the memorandum or articles under s. 14 he may be seeking a remedy for himself or for himself and a large number of other members whose rights have also been infringed. Order 15 r. 12(1) of the Rules of the Supreme Court makes provision for a representative action where 'numerous persons have the same interest in any proceedings'. This type of action may be brought where the cause of action arises under one of the exceptions to *Foss* v *Harbottle* or under s. 14. The plaintiff shareholder then represents the interests of all the shareholders (except the wrongdoers) and the judgment is normally binding on, and enforceable by, them.

If action is brought under one of the exceptions to *Foss* v *Harbottle*, the company will be made a nominal defendant. This type of action is sometimes described as a 'derivative action' because the right of the member to sue is not personal to him but derives from the right to sue which the company has failed to exercise. It should be noted that if this type of action is successful, the judgment will give a remedy to the company (which has been wronged) rather than to the plaintiff.

If action is brought under s. 14 it may or may not be representative but it will certainly not be 'derivative'. The right to sue is the plaintiff's own cause of action and in appropriate cases damages, specific performance or other directly beneficial orders will be made in his favour.

9.8 Section 459 Companies Act 1985

9.8.1 **UNFAIR PREJUDICE**

Section 459(1) provides that:

> A member of a company may apply to the court by petition for an order . . . on the ground that the company's affairs are being or have been conducted in a manner which is unfairly prejudicial to the interests of some part of the members (including at least himself) or that any actual or proposed act or omission of the company (including an act or omission on its behalf) is or would be so prejudicial.

9.8.1.1 Grounds

A shareholder may petition under s. 459 if he can show that he has suffered unfair prejudice. The prejudice must have arisen from the way in which the affairs of the company were being conducted or from an actual or proposed act or omission by the company. The prejudice must have affected the interests of at least some of the members of the company. If these things can be shown then the court will have to consider what remedy would be appropriate.

9.8.1.2 Test for unfair prejudice

The test as to what amounts to unfair prejudice is objective. It is not, therefore, necessary for the petitioning shareholders to show that anyone acted in bad faith or with the intention of causing prejudice. In *Re R. A. Noble (Clothing) Ltd* [1983] BCLC 273 the judge suggested that the unfairness of the behaviour could be tested by the 'reasonable bystander test'; that is, prejudice will be regarded as unfair if a hypothetical reasonable bystander would believe it to be unfair.

9.8.1.3 Rights *as shareholder* must have been prejudiced

If the petitioner is to succeed he must show that his rights as a shareholder have been prejudiced. In *Re Postgate and Denby* [1987] BCLC 8 it was held that such rights include all rights given under the company's memorandum and articles, statutory rights and also rights arising out of agreements and understandings between members. An important example of the last category is an understanding between members (often falling short of a contract) that the company will be run as if it were a partnership. In such cases of 'quasi-partnership' a member who is excluded from management of the company may claim unfair prejudice (*Re Cumana* [1986] BCLC 430). However, the mere fact that a member has been excluded from his share of management of a quasi-partnership does not guarantee that he will succeed in a claim for unfair prejudice. Thus, in *Re A Company (No. 004377 of 1986)* [1987] 1 WLR 102 the petition failed as the articles of the company laid down exactly what was to happen if the quasi-partnership ended for any reason. This included a right for a majority shareholder to buy the shares of the minority. The minority shareholder might indeed be prejudiced by such a provision but he could not claim that the prejudice was unfair as he had (by joining the company) agreed to this in advance.

9.8.2 POWERS OF COURT

9.8.2.1 Orders

If a petition under s. 459 is successful the court 'may make such order as it thinks fit for giving relief in respect of the matters complained of' (s. 461(1)). Subsection 461(2) lists particular types of order which may be made but is expressly stated to be without prejudice to the general power given by s. 461(1). The powers listed in s. 461(2) are:

(a) to regulate the conduct of the company's affairs in the future;
(b) to require the company to refrain from doing or continuing an act complained of by the petitioner or to do an act which the petitioner has complained it has omitted to do;
(c) to authorise civil proceedings to be brought in the name and on behalf of the company by such person or persons and on such terms as the court may direct;
(d) to provide for the purchase of the shares of any members of the company by other members or by the company itself and, in the case of a purchase by the company itself, the reduction of the company's capital accordingly.

9.8.2.2 Power to authorise civil proceedings

The power to authorise civil proceedings subject to terms may prove particularly useful. A shareholder may be deterred from fighting a complicated action, based on an exception to *Foss* v *Harbottle*, by the prospect of heavy costs. It may, therefore, be attractive to petition under s. 459 in the hope of obtaining an order for the action to be pursued by the company. The court will ensure that such a petition can be dealt with (in suitable cases) without the substantive issue being tried in the s. 459 proceedings.

9.8.2.3 Purchase of petitioner's shares

In practice the most common remedy awarded to a successful petitioner is that his shares should be purchased by the wrongdoers who have caused the unfair prejudice. The question of valuation causes considerable problems in such cases. The courts have held that the shares should be valued as at whatever date is fair to the petitioner. This usually means that the shares are valued at the date when the prejudice to the petitioner began. If a different date is chosen the court will usually order that the valuer should value the shares as if the prejudice had not taken place.

9.8.2.4 Alteration of memorandum or articles

The order made by the court under s. 459 may require an alteration to the memorandum or articles. If this is done, an office copy of the court order must be delivered to the Registrar within (usually) 14 days.

9.9 Just and Equitable Winding Up

Companies may be wound up on a number of grounds. Winding up is the process by which a company's existence is brought to an end; it usually results from the insolvency of the company. However, one type of winding up is available as a remedy to shareholders of solvent companies — this is winding up under s. 122(1)(g) Insolvency Act 1986, which provides for winding up where 'the court is of the opinion that it is just and equitable that the company should be wound up'. Winding up is a rather drastic solution to problems arising within a company and is now much less important, as a remedy for shareholders is available for cases of unfair prejudice.

9.10 Shareholders and Profits

Basically there are four ways in which a company can deal with its profits:

    (a)   retain them in the business;
    (b)   pay them as dividends to the shareholders;
    (c)   use them to pay interest on debentures;
    (d)   pay directors' fees.

If profits are retained in the business the proprietors (i.e., shareholders) ought to benefit in the long run, since the capital value of the company (and thus of the shares in it) will increase. A payment of interest on debentures will often be a payment to an outsider, which reduces profits available to the proprietors of the business. However, a long-term loan to a company is really a method of investing in the company without buying shares, and so the payment of interest on such a loan may properly be regarded as a payment to an investor in the business. Directors' fees are expenses of the business which an accountant would regard as reducing the profit available to shareholders, but in the case of most small, private companies the directors and shareholders are the same people; thus a payment of directors' fees is in a commercial sense equivalent to a payment of profit to the proprietors.

A company is not entirely free to choose between the four different uses of profits for the following reasons:

    (a)   it will often be contractually bound to make payments of interest and directors' fees;
    (b)   there are company law rules which prevent the company from paying dividends except to the extent of 'profits available for the purpose'. (The reason for this is that the original investment made in

the company by shareholders may not be returned to them, except in limited circumstances, until the company is wound up.);

(c) it will often be commercially unwise for the company to pay out all its profits, since some will be required to provide for future contingencies or for the expansion of the business.

The tax consequences of each method of using profits will be considered and a comparison will be made between them in **Chapter 16**.

9.11 Procedure for Declaring and Paying a Dividend

A dividend is a payment to the shareholders of the company which provides them with a return on their investment. It is not a payment of interest on the money invested, since the shareholder does not have an automatic right to the dividend — as we shall see, it becomes payable only if 'declared' by the company (or otherwise authorised under the articles) and only if the Companies Act permits payment in the circumstances.

9.11.1 TABLE A

The provisions of Table A in respect of dividend payments provide for the following procedure:

(a) During the course of an accounting period (i.e., a twelve-month period in respect of which the company's accounts are prepared), the directors may decide to pay an interim dividend (art. 103). However, the directors may only pay an interim dividend if it appears to them to be 'justified by the profits of the company available for distribution'.

(b) After the accounts have been prepared the directors will consider what dividend, if any, ought to be declared, and will make a recommendation to the members in general meeting.

(c) A meeting of the company will be held at which the question of declaring a dividend will be considered. In practice, this will be done at the AGM, although Table A does not prevent consideration of dividends at an EGM. The members may reject the directors' recommendation or declare a dividend smaller than that recommended, but Table A art. 102 prevents them exceeding the amount recommended by the directors.

The reason why the members may not declare a dividend in excess of the directors' recommendation is that the directors are the managers of the company's business, and so are in a better position than the members to assess the economic ability of the company to pay dividends; it is therefore probably a sensible provision to include in the articles. If members with a majority of the votes object to the dividend policy of the directors they can exercise their right to remove the directors from office under s. 303 CA 1985.

(d) Once the dividend has been declared, the members will be paid the dividend by the company. The amount of dividend paid to each member depends on the nominal value of the shares held, no account being taken of any premium paid on the shares. If there are different classes of shares they may have different rights to dividends. Thus, if there are preference shares, the ordinary shareholders will usually not be entitled to any dividend until the preference shareholders have received their dividend (which will be expressed as a fixed amount per share or a fixed percentage).

For example, a company has 2,000 £1 shares of which 1,000 are ordinary shares and 1,000 are 10% preference shares; the company declares a dividend of £150. The preference shareholders are entitled to their 10% (i.e., £100) and the ordinary shareholders get the balance (i.e., £50 or 5p per share).

9.11.2 OTHER POSSIBLE ARRANGEMENTS

The articles of the company may validly provide that directors are to declare dividends without holding a general meeting. It is also possible (although undesirable), for the articles to require payment of all the company's profits as dividends (subject to the legal restriction referred to below). If an elective resolution has dispensed with the need to hold an AGM a dividend could also be declared by a written resolution if the company does not choose to hold an EGM.

9.11.3 LEGAL ENTITLEMENT TO DIVIDEND

Once declared by the members in general meeting, a dividend is a debt due to the members from the company. The member is, therefore, entitled to sue the company if the dividend is not paid. An interim dividend is not, however, a debt due from the company, so that the members have no right to it until it is actually paid.

9.12 Restrictions on Sources of Dividends

9.12.1 THE BASIC RULE

So as to ensure that money invested by shareholders is not returned to them before the company is wound up, there have always been rules based on judicial decisions preventing the payment of dividends other than out of profits. The Companies Act 1985 now lays down clear rules as to what funds are available for the payment of dividends. These rules, which were first introduced in 1980, are designed to implement the European Communities' Second Directive on Company Law and differ somewhat from the rules previously established by the courts — the new rules are generally more restrictive.

Section 263(1) CA 1985 provides that: 'A company shall not make a distribution except out of profits available for the purpose.' The term 'distribution' is defined by s. 263(2) and includes all distributions of assets to members except:

(a) the issue of bonus shares;
(b) the redemption or purchase of its own shares by the company;
(c) reduction of capital (which requires the approval of the court; see **10.15.4**); or
(d) a distribution on winding-up.

Most dividends are paid in cash and are included in the definition of 'distributions', since cash is just as much an asset as other types of property.

9.12.2 'PROFITS AVAILABLE'

9.12.2.1 Definition

'Profits available for the purpose' of paying dividends are defined by s. 263(3) as 'accumulated, realised profits, so far as not previously utilised by distribution . . . less . . . accumulated, realised losses . . .'. This means that each year it is necessary to calculate the company's trading profit and any capital profits that have been made on the disposal of fixed assets. These are the 'realised profits' from which must be deducted any realised losses, that is, any trading loss or loss made on the disposal of a fixed asset. However, a dividend is only payable if there are *accumulated* realised profits in excess of *accumulated* realised losses. This means that the balance of realised profits can be carried forward from year to year. It is not, therefore, necessary to make a profit every year in order to pay a dividend — all that is required is that there should be a balance of profits taking this year and previous years together.

For example:

	Realised Profit/(loss)	Dividend
Year 1	4,000	1,000
Year 2	2,000	1,000
Year 3	(3,000)	1,000

The dividend in year 3 is lawful because in year 1 the realised profits were £4,000 and the dividend only £1,000, so that £3,000 worth of profits could be carried forward. In year 2 the realised profits were £2,000 and the dividend £1,000, so that a further £1,000 could be carried forward. In year 3 there was a realised loss of £3,000 which had to be deducted from the accumulated profits of £4,000, thus leaving £1,000 for a dividend.

Just as realised profits not used to pay dividends may be carried forward to later years and used to pay dividends in those later years, so realised losses which are not balanced by realised profits accumulated from previous years must be carried forward to later years and set off against realised profits before a dividend can be paid. Thus (continuing the example above):

	Realised Profit/(loss)	Dividend
Year 4	(2,000)	nil
Year 5	1,000	nil
Year 6	2,000	1,000

In year 4 there was a loss, and since no accumulated profits were available from years 1-3, no dividend could be paid. In year 5 a profit of £1,000 was made but this could not be used to pay a dividend since the accumulated realised loss (£2,000 from year 4) was more than the realised profit. In year 6 the £1,000 dividend was the maximum which could be paid because £1,000 of the loss from year 4 had to be set off against the profit.

9.12.2.2 Calculation of profits and losses

Section 263 CA 1985 does not lay down particular rules as to how profits and losses are to be calculated; normal accountancy practice must be applied in deciding whether a profit or loss has been realised. However, a few situations are specifically dealt with:

(a) A profit which has been 'capitalised' (in this context a profit is capitalised only if it is used to pay up bonus shares or to replace capital repaid to members) cannot be treated as a realised profit.

(b) A loss which has been written off in a reduction of capital is not treated as a realised loss. This is because when the capital is reduced the shareholders' investment is wiped out, with the approval of the court, to the extent of the reduction and so does not have to be maintained.

(c) If a 'provision' is made in the accounts of the company it must usually be treated as a realised loss (s. 275 CA 1985). A provision is an item shown in the accounts as an expense in respect of expected future expenses (e.g., it is usual practice to provide for depreciation of wasting assets — that is, to record the fact that they are declining in value). If the provision were not treated as a realised loss the company could write down the value of an asset in its accounts and then sell it for its written-down value thus (apparently) making neither a profit nor a loss, whereas in fact there was a substantial loss in value during the period of ownership of the asset.

9.12.2.3 Restriction on payment of dividends by a company's articles

The articles of a company may restrict the company's right to pay dividends further than is done by the Companies Act, for example, by preventing payment of a dividend out of a realised capital profit. Table A does not contain any such provisions. In most circumstances a company would be very unwise to distribute all the 'profits available' as defined by s. 263, since to do so would often create cash flow problems (a company always needs sufficient cash to buy stock, pay wages, etc.), and make expansion of the business more difficult.

9.12.2.4 Unrealised losses

It should be noted that, although realised losses must be made good out of realised profits before a dividend can be paid, there is no requirement that *unrealised* losses must be made good. For example, if a company owns land which it knows to be declining in value, it can still go on paying dividends out of realised profits, since the loss on the land is only realised when the land is sold. Similarly an unrealised profit cannot be used to pay a dividend. A company which is making small realised losses cannot, therefore, pay a dividend even if it knows its land is increasing in value by more than the losses.

9.12.3 THE 'RELEVANT ACCOUNTS'

Whether a company has got any profits available for distribution can only be judged by reference to properly drawn up accounts. Section 270 CA 1985 lays down rules as to which accounts are to be used at any particular time for deciding whether there are profits available. Usually the company must rely on the last set of accounts prepared in accordance with s. 226 CA 1985 (substituted by s. 4 CA 1989 — as we shall see in **Chapter 29**, these are the accounts which must be audited, laid before the members in general meeting and sent to the Companies Registry where they are available for public inspection). However, if the company wants to pay a dividend which is not justified by those accounts it can prepare 'interim' accounts specially for the purpose of showing that profits are available for distribution. This might be done, for example, if the company had made a loss and so could not pay a dividend but has now started to make profits again and does not want to wait until the next full set of accounts are produced. Similarly, if a company wishes to pay a dividend before it has prepared *any* accounts under s. 226 CA 1985 (i.e., broadly speaking, during its first year after incorporation) it can prepare 'initial' accounts to justify the dividend payment.

Interim and initial accounts must be prepared and audited in much the same way as the normal final accounts of the company. Because of the expense involved in preparing such accounts it will usually be better to wait until accounts are produced in the normal way before paying the dividend.

9.12.4 CONSEQUENCES OF UNLAWFUL DISTRIBUTIONS

Section 277 CA 1985 requires any member to repay a distribution which he 'knows or has reasonable grounds for believing' to be illegal. If a dividend is paid illegally the directors will normally be personally liable to the company, since they will have recommended and paid (or permitted payment of) the dividend in breach of their duty.

TEN

COMPANY FINANCE

10.1   Introduction

Once a company is formed it will need to spend money to get its business going. It may need to buy stock, buy or rent premises, pay wages, advertise and pay the general expenses involved in running a business. The money that the company needs to start its business is often called capital. Technically, however, 'capital' is the liability of the company to the people who have provided it with money on a long-term basis.

A company can raise money either in the form of an investment by shareholders or in the form of loans. Once the business is established profits may be retained in the business thus producing a third source of finance.

10.2   Issue of Shares

10.2.1   LEGAL NATURE OF SHARES

A share in a company is a chose in action. Its value to the shareholder depends on the particular contractual rights which he obtains from owning the share. These contractual rights are obtained when the shares are issued to him by the company if he is the original owner, or when they are transferred or transmitted to him. This section is concerned with the issue of shares by a company; transfer and transmission are dealt with in **Chapter 11**.

10.2.2   RIGHTS ATTACHING TO SHARES

The rights attached to shares vary from company to company and a company may issue different classes of shares with different rights attached to them. It is, therefore, difficult to generalise about the exact nature of a share but the following general points may be of assistance:

  (a) Nearly all shares give the shareholder a right to a dividend (i.e., a share in profits), but a dividend is only payable if the company has made profits and it is decided to declare a dividend (see **Chapter 9**).
  (b) Most, but not all, shares give the shareholder a right to vote at general meetings of the company.
  (c) If the company is wound up the shareholder will have a right to repayment of his investment (in the comparatively unlikely event that the company is then solvent) and in most cases a right to participate in any undistributed profit.
  (d) The Stock Transfer Act 1982 lays down a procedure for the transfer of shares but does not guarantee the shareholder a right to transfer.

(e) Shareholders are given certain rights as a matter of law by the Companies Act. Many of these rights are, however, only given to shareholders who have a right to vote at company meetings (e.g. the rights to remove directors and to appoint and remove auditors referred to in **Chapter 8**).

In the case of a private company the voting rights will often be as important as the financial rights. This is especially so in the case of a shareholding which gives voting control, since it effectively carries with it the right to control many major decisions of the company.

10.2.3 THE VALUE OF SHARES

The capital value of shares clearly depends to some extent on the rights attached to them but it also depends on other factors — particularly the profitability of the company and its asset worth.

All shares must have a 'nominal value' (also called 'par value') which is set out in the capital clause of the memorandum. This figure says little about the true value of the shares since, as we shall see shortly, shares can be issued for more (but not less) than nominal value and once issued their value will fluctuate either upwards or downwards as the company is more or less successful. The nominal value is really just a way of measuring one shareholder's interest against the interests of other shareholders.

10.2.4 THE POWER TO ISSUE SHARES

When new shares are created by a company they are said to be 'issued' or 'allotted' by the company to the people who have contracted to buy them. The articles of the company may give the directors the power to issue shares. Any power granted to the directors to issue shares is subject to the following restrictions:

(a) The powers of the directors to issue shares is restricted by s. 80 CA 1985. This requires the directors to be authorised to issue shares either by the company in general meeting or by the articles. The authorisation may be given either for a particular exercise of the directors' power or generally and may be unconditional or subject to conditions. Whether the authorisation is given by ordinary resolution of the members in general meeting or by the articles, it must state the maximum amount of shares which the directors may issue and the date when the authority will expire. The authority cannot be given for more than five years from formation of the company or the passing of the resolution (as the case may be) and can be revoked or varied by the company in general meeting at any time. Once given, the authority can be extended by up to five years by the further resolution of the company. Resolutions under s. 80 may be passed as ordinary resolutions (so that a simple majority is sufficient), even though they alter the articles. The resolution must, however, be registered with the Registrar of Companies as if it were a special resolution. If the directors issue shares without authority they commit an offence and presumably would be liable to the company for breach of duty but the issue of shares remains valid (s. 80(10)). At first sight this section gives very considerable protection to the shareholders but in most private companies the directors and majority shareholders are the same people, so that all that will be required is an extra procedural step (the calling of a meeting of the company) at some time within five years before the issue. The section is, therefore, of most importance to the comparatively few private companies where the directors are not the controlling shareholders, and to public companies. Following the enactment of the Companies Act 1989, in the case of privte companies, it is possible to dispense with this five-year limitation if the authority is given by an elective resolution in accordance with the provisions of s. 80A CA 1985.

(b) Shares may only be issued to the extent of the nominal capital of the company. If the articles give power to do so, the nominal capital may be increased under s. 121 CA 1985, but this requires the approval of the members by ordinary resolution in general meeting (see **10.14**).

(c) The directors may not issue shares in breach of their fiduciary duty, so that the approval of the members is required if the motive behind the issue is anything other than the raising of further investment in the company.

(d) The articles themselves may impose restrictions. For example, the power may extend only to issuing ordinary shares, the sanction of the members in general meeting being required for the issue of shares with special rights.

(e) Under s. 89 CA 1985 if it is proposed to issue shares to any person, they must first be offered to the existing shareholders, in proportion to their existing holdings, on terms at least as favourable as those proposed for the issue to that person. The members must be given 21 days to make up their minds. This right of pre-emption does not apply if the shares are to be issued for a non-cash consideration and can, in the case of a private company, be varied or removed by contrary provision in the articles. A special resolution can be passed, without altering the articles, to allow the directors to issue shares on a particular occasion as if s. 89 did not apply.

Section 89 gives shareholders a useful degree of protection in cases where the effect of issuing shares would be to water down their control of the company. A higher degree of protection will be given if the articles provide for pre-emption rights on *any* issue of shares, so that the company will not be able to offer shares for a non-cash consideration unless the members are willing to give up their rights. It should be noted that s. 89 is only concerned with the *issue* of shares. It is fairly common for articles to provide for pre-emption rights where an existing shareholder wants to *transfer* his shares (see **Chapter 11**).

10.2.5 PAYMENT FOR SHARES

10.2.5.1 Consideration

A contract for the issue of shares may provide for payment in cash or for some other consideration. If the agreement is for the payment of cash the full amount may be payable immediately or part of it may be left outstanding until the company makes a 'call' for the unpaid amount if the company goes into liquidation. Payment in full on issue of the shares is now usually required, so that partly paid shares are rather uncommon.

10.2.5.2 Premium

Shares are quite commonly issued at a premium, that is, for more than their nominal value. The premium is treated as 'capital' of the company (for the consequences of this, see **10.3.2**).

10.2.6 'RETURN AS TO ALLOTMENTS'

Section 88 CA 1985 requires a return of allotment to be made to the Registrar of Companies within one month of the issue of shares (this is known as 'Form G88(2)'). The form requires details as to the number and nominal amount of the shares, the names, addresses and descriptions of the shareholders, and the amount paid up on each share including any premium. Where there is a non-cash consideration, a written contract for the sale of the shares must also be sent to the Registrar or, if the contract was oral, particulars of the contract should be set out on Form G88(3) and also returned to the Registrar.

10.2.7 ISSUE OF SHARES TO THE PUBLIC

Section 81 CA 1985 makes it an offence for a private company to offer shares (or debentures) to the public or to issue them with a view to an offer for sale to the public.

10.3 Share Capital

10.3.1 MAINTENANCE OF CAPITAL

Once shares have been issued they are said to form part of the 'capital' of the company.

'Share capital' is really a liability of a company to its shareholders, since the company will one day be liable to repay the shareholders' investment (usually, in fact, only when the company is wound up). For the protection of people dealing with the company, share capital has to be 'maintained' by the company. This does not mean that the money invested has to be deposited or set aside as a fund to guarantee the company's creditors; it only means that it must not, normally, be returned to the members in any way while the company is a going concern.

Two major consequences of this rule are:

(a) That dividends may only be paid out of profits (see **9.12**).
(b) That capital invested cannot be returned to the members except:

(i) with the approval of the court (s. 135 CA 1985 deals with the cases where capital can be returned or the liability to members cancelled with the approval of the court); or
(ii) where the company redeems or purchases its own shares (see below and **Chapter 11**).

10.3.2 SHARE PREMIUM ACCOUNT

As has already been explained, it is common for shares to be issued for more than their nominal value. The excess is not strictly speaking share capital but is required by s. 130 CA 1985 to be credited to a 'share premium account' (i.e., an account showing the company to be liable to the members for the amount of the premium). The share premium account has to be maintained in the same way as share capital; thus assets representing it cannot be returned to members.

10.3.3 COMPANY AS MEMBER OF ITSELF AND PURCHASE OF OWN SHARES

10.3.3.1 The company as its own shareholder

A company may not be registered as its own shareholder. However, shares can be transferred to a trustee or nominee for the company.

10.3.3.2 Original prohibition on buy-back of shares

The traditional position was that it was illegal for a company to buy its own shares (*Trevor* v *Whitworth* (1887) 12 App Cas 409). This is because use of its money by a company to purchase its own shares is in effect a return to the shareholder of his investment and so is a reduction of capital.

10.3.3.3 Redeemable shares

Section 159 CA 1985 gives companies (if authorised by their articles) power to issue redeemable shares, that is shares which can be bought back by the company at the option of the company or the shareholder. Table A art. 3 gives the company power to issue redeemable shares.

10.3.3.4 Buy-back of shares

It was thought to be desirable for companies, particularly small family companies, to have the power to purchase their own shares as this would provide an additional market for the shares. Section 162 CA 1985, therefore, gives companies power to purchase their own shares if authorised to do so by their articles (Table A art. 35 gives such authorisation). Examples of cases where the power is useful include buying out dissident shareholders and the provision of funds to the estate of a deceased shareholder to assist in the payment of inheritance tax.

The contract for purchase must be approved by special resolution before the company enters into it. The members whose shares are to be purchased must not use the votes given to them by the shares which are to be purchased on that resolution. The resolution will be invalid unless a copy of the contract (or a memorandum of its terms) is made available for inspection by the members at the company's registered office for a period of at least 15 days ending with the date of the meeting and also at the meeting itself. Once the shares have been purchased by the company they are treated as cancelled.

Within 28 days after the shares have been purchased a return must be made to the Registrar of Companies stating the number and nominal value of the shares purchased and the date of purchase.

10.3.3.5 Financing buy-back or redemption

When shares are redeemed or purchased by the company the money used to pay for them must generally come out of profits or the proceeds of a fresh issue of shares. Where the shares are purchased or redeemed with assets representing profits the legislation requires the capital of the company to be maintained. Thus, s. 170 CA 1985 requires the company to open a 'capital redemption reserve' equal to the reduction in the share capital. This reserve is treated in the same way as share capital or the share premium account, that is, it is shown in the balance sheet as a liability due to shareholders which has to be maintained until the company goes into liquidation.

In the case of a *private* company payment out of assets representing capital is permitted. The use of assets representing capital to redeem or purchase its own shares means that a private company can reduce its capital without seeking the sanction of the court. In order to protect the interests of members and creditors detailed procedural requirements must be satisfied. The articles must contain an express power to use capital assets for this purpose. The general power to purchase its own shares is not sufficient. (Article 35 of Table A does contain such a power.) The directors must certify that the company will remain solvent and will, in their view, be able to carry on business as a going concern for at least a year. The directors' certificate must be supported by an auditors' report in which the auditors certify that they are not aware of anything which would indicate that the directors' view of the situation is unreasonable. Not later than one week after the date of the certificate a general meeting of the company must be held at which a special resolution approving the payment is passed. The members whose shares are to be purchased may not use the votes on those shares on this resolution. The payment for the shares must be made by the company not less than five nor more than seven weeks after the date on which the resolution is passed. This period is laid down so that members or creditors who object to the purchase have time to challenge the purchase in court.

10.4 Financial Assistance by Company for Purchase of Shares

Section 151 CA 1985 makes it illegal for a company to give financial assistance directly or indirectly to assist someone to purchase shares in the company but there are important exceptions to this rule which will be considered in **Chapter 11**.

10.5 Classes of Shares

In most companies, all the shares issued have the same rights attached to them. It is possible, however, for a company to issue shares with different rights. The shares are then said to belong to different classes. For example, a company may issue preference shares, that is, shares which have a better right to receive a dividend than ordinary shares. It is also possible to give some shareholders a greater measure of control over the affairs of the company either by creating voting and non-voting shares or by providing that all shares are to carry a right to vote but that some will have more votes than others.

10.6 The Power to Borrow

10.6.1 EXPRESS AND IMPLIED POWER

A trading company has an implied power to borrow for the purpose of its trade. This is because the trade will be authorised by its objects and the borrowing will be reasonably incidental to the power to carry on the trade.

A company with power to borrow also has an implied power to give security for the loan. It is preferable to include express powers if a full objects clause is adopted rather than to rely on implied ones. In practice, banks (and other professional lenders) would probably continue to check the company's express powers despite the abolition of the consequences of the ultra vires rule referred to in **10.6.2**.

10.6.2 ULTRA VIRES BORROWING

A lender to a company was formerly well advised to check the company's memorandum so as to ensure that the loan was within the powers of the company. However, the new s. 35 CA 1985 (as substituted by CA 1989) removes the need to do so by providing that 'the validity of an act done by a company shall not be called into question on the ground of lack of capacity by reason of anything in the company's memorandum'.

10.6.3 EXERCISE OF BORROWING POWERS

The power to borrow must be exercised in accordance with the company's articles of association. If the company has adopted Table A the directors will have power to borrow at least where the loan is to be used for the purposes of the business (art. 70).

The Table A in force before 1 July 1985 limited the powers of the directors to borrow on behalf of the company. Many companies formed before that date will therefore only be able to borrow substantial sums following approval of the loan by the members in general meeting. Restrictions on the power of the directors to borrow can, in the case of newly formed companies, be imposed by the adoption of a special article to that effect.

10.7 Secured Loans

10.7.1 TYPES OF SECURITY

A prudent lender will usually require security for a loan which he makes to a company. Any assets of the company may be charged by way of security.

Companies may give security for a loan in the form of a 'debenture'. Unfortunately, this is rather an ambiguous term. The legal definition seems to require only that there is:

(a) a document, which
(b) creates or acknowledges indebtedness by a company, and
(c) the indebtedness arises from a loan.

It should be noted that a debenture does not necessarily require that any security be given in the form of a mortgage or other charge over assets. The term 'debenture' is often used in practice to mean a long-term loan to a company for the purpose of its business (for details of this type of debenture see **Chapter 27**). Usually security will be required for such a loan in the form of a fixed charge, a floating charge or both.

In addition to a charge over the assets of the company a lender may frequently require personal guarantees from the directors. Where a personal guarantee is given, the benefit of limited liability is effectively lost to the extent of the guarantee.

10.7.2 FIXED CHARGES

A fixed charge is a mortgage of a particular asset. The mortgage may be either legal or equitable and the company, having created the charge, is not free to dispose of the asset without the consent of the mortgagee. When a bank lends money to a company, it will frequently require a fixed charge over any land owned by the company. Other assets owned by the company, such as plant and machinery and book debts, may also be available as security for a fixed charge.

10.7.3 FLOATING CHARGES

A floating charge is an equitable charge over assets of a particular description owned by the company from time to time. A floating charge can be given over assets which are repeatedly dealt with by the company. Perhaps stock-in-trade is the clearest example. A company cannot give a fixed charge over its stock since to do so would prevent it from selling that stock. However, if it gives a floating charge over the stock, the charge will 'float' over whatever stock the company owns from time to time — it can therefore sell the stock free from the charge and buy new stock to which the charge will automatically attach.

The nature of a floating charge was defined in *Re Yorkshire Woolcombers' Association Ltd* [1903] 2 Ch 284, in the following way:

> . . . if a charge has the three characteristics I am about to mention it is a floating charge.
> (a)   if it is a charge on a class of assets of a company present and future;
> (b)   if that class is one which, in the ordinary course of business of the company, would be changing from time to time; and
> (c)   if you find that by the charge it is contemplated that, until some future step is taken by or on behalf of those interested in the charge, the company may carry on its business in the ordinary way as far as concerns the particular class of asset I am dealing with.

At first sight a floating charge would seem to give no security at all to the lender since the company can continue to deal with the assets which are charged. However, a floating charge becomes a fixed charge on the charged assets owned by the company at the time when the charge 'crystallises'. A floating charge crystallises when:

(a)   The winding-up of the company commences (in the case of a winding-up by the court this is usually when the winding-up petition is presented (s. 524 CA 1985); in the case of voluntary winding-up it is when the winding-up resolution is passed (s. 574 CA 1985)).
(b)   A receiver is appointed by the court.
(c)   A receiver is appointed by the lender under a power given by the debenture.
(d)   Any other event occurs which the debenture specifies will cause crystallisation.

It should be noted that companies are the only type of business association which can create a floating charge.

10.7.4 ADVANTAGES AND DISADVANTAGES OF FLOATING CHARGES

As far as the borrowing company is concerned a floating charge has one great advantage over a fixed charge; that is, until crystallisation, it can deal freely with the charged assets without the permission of the lender.

From the lender's point of view a floating charge suffers from a number of disadvantages when compared with a fixed charge. In particular:

(a)   Its value as a security is uncertain until crystallisation.
(b)   It is postponed to execution and distress for rent completed before crystallisation.
(c)   It is postponed to preferred creditors on a liquidation of the borrowing company.
(d)   It is postponed to later fixed charges in certain cases (see **10.9.1** below).
(e)   It may be invalid as a security if the company goes into liquidation within a year (see **10.9.3** below).

10.8 Registration of Charges

10.8.1 SECTIONS 395 ff CA 1985

The Companies Act 1989 introduced a new system of registration of charges. References to CA 1985 in this paragraph are references to the sections substituted by CA 1989.

Section 396 CA 1985 lists the types of charge particulars of which a company must register. The list is quite extensive so that nearly all charges must be registered. In particular, registration is required of charges over land, goods (except where the chargee is entitled to possession of the goods or documents of title to them), goodwill, intellectual property and book debts owed to the company. Registration is also required where the charge is or includes a floating charge.

10.8.2 THE REGISTRATION PROCESS (s. 398 CA 1985)

Where a company creates a charge or acquires property which is already subject to a charge it must deliver (to the Registrar of Companies) 'prescribed particulars' within 21 days. At the time of writing, regulations prescribing the particulars which are to be registered have not been made. Although it is the duty of the company to register, any person with an interest in the charge has a power to register. Failure to register may lead to the charge being invalid (as to which see below) so that it is in the interests of the chargee to ensure registration. Once the charge has been registered the Registrar sends a copy of the registered particulars to the company and the chargee.

10.8.3 CONSEQUENCES OF FAILURE TO COMPLY WITH REGISTRATION REQUIREMENTS

10.8.3.1 Fine (s. 398(3))

If particulars of a charge are not registered within 21 days the company and every officer in default is liable to a fine.

10.8.3.2 No particulars delivered (s. 399)

If the particulars are not delivered within 21 days the charge is void against an administrator or liquidator of the company who is appointed after the creation of the charge. The appointment of an administrator or liquidator is a step in relation to the insolvency of a company (as to which see **Chapter 23**). It follows, therefore, that if a charge is not registered the charge is void in the insolvency of the company. The chargee will rank as an ordinary creditor without security.

Similarly, if particulars are not delivered within 21 days the charge is void against any person who, after the creation of the charge and for value, acquires an interest in or right over property subject to the charge. The unregistered charge would therefore be void against a subsequent chargee or a purchaser.

It should be noticed that in both these circumstances a charge is only void if it is not registered within 21 days of its creation.

10.8.3.3 Effect of late registration (s. 400)

Particulars may be registered outside the 21 day period. Where particulars are delivered late the charge is void against a liquidator or administrator appointed before delivery and against a person acquiring an interest in or right over the property before that time (see above). The charge is not, however, void against a liquidator or administrator appointed after the delivery unless the company is insolvent when the particulars are delivered (or becomes insolvent as a result of the charge) and insolvency proceedings begin within the 'relevant period'. The relevant period is six months from delivery of particulars (12 months in the case of a floating charge, two years in the case of a floating charge granted to a director or other connected person).

10.8.3.4 Examples of ss. 398-400

(a) Charge created 1 March.

Particulars registered 15 March.

The charge will be valid (unless there are other grounds for declaring it void e.g. as a preference — see **Chapter 23**).

(b) Charge created 1 March.

Liquidator appointed 10 March.

Particulars delivered 15 March.

The charge will be valid. (Where particulars are delivered within 21 days the charge is valid.)

(c) Charge created 1 March.

Liquidator appointed 10 March.

Particulars never delivered.

The charge is void against the liquidator.

(d) Charge created 1 March.

Particulars delivered 25 March.

Property sold 27 March.

The charge is not void against the purchaser. (Although particulars were delivered late they were delivered before the sale to the purchaser.)

(e) Charge created 1 March.

Property sold 25 March.

Particulars delivered 27 March.

The charge is void against the purchaser (opposite of last example).

(f) Fixed charge created 1 March.

Particulars delivered 25 March.

Liquidator appointed 27 March.

Prima facie this is like (d) above. However, the charge will be void against the liquidator if the company was insolvent on 25 March (as it almost certainly was since the liquidator was appointed two days later).

(g) Fixed charge created 1 March.

Particulars delivered 25 March.

Liquidator appointed 27 October.

The charge is not void. (Even if the company was insolvent on 25 March, the liquidator was not appointed within six months of the delivery of particulars.)

10.8.3.5 Errors and omissions (s. 402)

Provision is made for cases where particulars are delivered but the particulars are not complete and accurate. In such cases, the charge is void only in respect of rights not disclosed in the particulars and only to the extent that a person has been prejudiced by the error or omission.

10.8.3.6 Priorities between unregistered charges (s. 404)

Where a company creates two charges and particulars of neither are delivered the first is not void against the second under s. 399.

10.8.4 CRYSTALLISATION OF FLOATING CHARGES (s. 410)

The Secretary of State is empowered to make regulations requiring registration of crystallisation of floating charges. This means that notice will have to be given to the Registrar when the floating charge becomes a fixed charge (see **10.7.3** above). The regulations have not been made at the time of writing.

10.8.5 DISCHARGE OF CHARGES (s. 403)

When a charge ceases to affect the company's property, the company may deliver a memorandum of discharge to the Registrar. This is normally done on Form 403. This will be added to the company's file at the Companies Registry and so will be seen by anyone who searches the file.

10.8.6 COMPANY'S REGISTER OF CHARGES (ss. 406-408 CA 1985)

Under s. 408 CA 1985, as substituted, the company is required to keep a register of its charges (which must be available for public inspection). It must keep copies of all charges whether or not the charges need to be registered under s. 398, as substituted. Furthermore, any person is able to require the company to send him within ten days of request (and on payment of the appropriate fee) a copy of any charge kept by the company or any entry in the company's register of charges. If the company refuses to allow inspection or fails to send a copy which has been requested the company and every officer who is in default are liable to a fine and the court may compel the company to comply with its duties.

10.8.7 OTHER TYPES OF REGISTRATION: CHARGES OVER LAND

In addition to registration under the Companies Act, mortgages of land by a company may have to be registered at HM Land Registry or at the Land Charges Department (depending on whether the land is registered or unregistered respectively).

10.8.7.1 Fixed charges

A fixed charge on registered land must be registered at the Land Registry or else it is void against a subsequent purchaser for value of a legal estate (including a later legal mortgagee). A fixed charge over unregistered land must be registered at the Land Charges Department if the mortgagee does not have the title deeds. However, registration at the Land Charges Department is not required if the mortgage was created before 1970 (when the Law of Property Act 1969 came into force). In such cases registration at the Companies' Registry is sufficient.

10.8.7.2 Floating charges

Floating charges over land are unusual but not impossible. A floating charge over registered land must be registered at the Land Registry against each piece of land from time to time subject to the charge. The mortgagee will not be in a position to know what land the company owns from time to time and so the instrument creating the floating charge should place the company under an obligation to notify the mortgagee of acquisitions and should provide for crystallisation on failure of the company to notify. (When the charge crystallises the fact that it is now a fixed charge must be registered.)

A floating charge over unregistered land apparently need not be registered at the Land Charges Department even if created after 1969, although the position is not entirely free from doubt.

10.9 Priority of Charges

10.9.1 FIXED CHARGES

A company which creates a floating charge retains the right to deal with its assets. As we have already seen, this means that the value of the security may be reduced by the sale of the assets over which the charge floats. Furthermore, the company is free to deal with the assets by charging them. A floating charge, even though properly registered, is, therefore, normally postponed to a later fixed legal charge. This is because 'where the equities are equal the law prevails'. If the later fixed charge is equitable rather than legal the position is more complicated but the fixed charge will usually prevail since the fixed chargee will normally have a stronger claim to the security than the floating chargee.

The reason for the priority of later fixed charges is that the company is left free to deal with its property as it wishes. The floating charge will, therefore, have priority over later fixed charges if:

(a)   the instrument creating the charge prohibits the creation of later fixed charges ranking in priority to or *pari passu* (i.e., equal) with the floating charge; *and*

(b)   the later fixed chargee has *notice of this prohibition* at the time when he takes his charge.

Following the enactment of the Companies Act 1989, once a charge has been registered, s. 397(5) CA 1985 as substituted provides that any person acquiring a charge subsequently will be taken to have notice of matters disclosed on the register. Provided that a notice of prohibition is one of the prescribed particulars to be delivered to the Registrar, it should be included on the register and therefore any later chargee will have constructive notice of the prohibition. (The regulations have not, however, been made at the time of writing.)

10.9.2   FLOATING CHARGES

As between several floating charges, the first in time will have priority provided that it is properly registered. However, a floating charge over some particular type of asset will probably take priority over an earlier floating charge over the whole of a company's property (*English and Scottish Mercantile Investment Co.* v *Brunton* [1892] 2 QB 700).

10.9.3   AVOIDANCE OF CHARGES

In certain circumstances charges may be avoided, other than for non-registration, if made within a short period before the commencement of insolvency proceedings. This topic is dealt with in **Chapter 24.**

10.10   Remedies of Debenture-holders

10.10.1   EXPRESS AND IMPLIED POWERS

If the company fails to pay interest or principal money (i.e., the debt itself) the debenture-holder may sue as a creditor or petition for winding-up. In addition, the debenture may contain an express power of sale and a power to appoint a receiver (see below). The debenture will state the circumstances in which these powers are to arise. It may, for example, give such powers to the lender when his interest is in arrears for a specified period, when the company breaks any term of the debenture, when any other creditor of the company appoints a receiver and when the company suffers execution by a judgment creditor.

Section 101 of the Law of Property Act 1925 gives the lender implied power to sell and to appoint a receiver if the debenture is made under seal and interest is two months in arrears or principal money has not been paid three months after it becomes due. In drafting a debenture, express powers should be given since they can be made wider than the implied powers; if the debenture is not under seal, express powers are essential.

10.10.2   APPLICATION TO THE COURT

In the absence of express powers an application may be made to the court for sale or appointment of a receiver or manager if:

(a)   liquidation of the company has commenced; or

(b)   the company is in arrears with payment of principal or interest; or

(c)   the lender's security is in jeopardy.

If the court orders sale the chargee will be paid principal money and interest and any balance will be paid to the company. The assets will be treated as disposed of by the company so that a chargeable gain or allowable loss may result — thus affecting the company's corporation tax position (see **Chapter 15**).

10.11 Receivers

A receiver is appointed to realise the security of a debenture-holder. His position is, therefore, different from that of a liquidator, whose function is to wind up the company entirely. Once the receiver has paid the debenture-holder he will return any surplus to the company, which may then continue to trade. In fact, very often the appointment of a receiver by a debenture-holder will lead to the liquidation of the company, for example, because, after his appointment, the receiver finds that he can only obtain payment by winding up the company or because other creditors petition for winding-up.

For the effect of an appointment of an administrative receiver see **Chapter 23**.

10.12 Position of Debenture-holders

Many debentures are short-term loans to a company (typically by a bank) on which interest will be paid by the company at a fixed or variable rate in accordance with the loan agreement. The lender who takes such a debenture will consider the interest part of his general profits rather than as a source of investment income — he may take an interest in the running of the business as a financial adviser but will not consider that he is an investor in the business.

Some types of debenture are issued to people who have lent money to the company on a long-term basis and who may, therefore, be regarded as investors in the business. The nature of their investment is quite different from the investment made by shareholders. As we shall see in **Chapter 16**, the tax treatment of debenture interest is usually different from the treatment of dividends paid to shareholders. There are a number of other important differences between the two types of investment, which may be summarised as follows:

(a) Debenture-holders are not members and so do not have the right usually given to the members of voting at meetings.

(b) Debenture interest is payable out of capital if the company fails to make profits, so that a debenture is a safer investment (although if the company makes large profits the debenture-holders will not usually benefit).

(c) Debenture-holders are creditors on a winding-up and will usually have a charge over some or all of the company's assets, whereas shareholders are repaid their investment only if the company is solvent.

(d) Debenture-holders, unlike shareholders, may be repaid while the company is a going concern (usually at a fixed date or at the option of the company). Shareholders may only be repaid where capital is reduced or where the company redeems or purchases its own shares.

10.13 Steps to be Taken by a Lender to a Company

A person who wishes to lend money to a company should take the following steps either personally or through his advisers. Some of them are dictated by common sense, others by legal requirements:

(a) Investigate the financial standing and management of the company.

(b) Search at the Companies' Registry to see the company's last few sets of accounts and of what charge particulars have been registered.

(c) Search at the company's registered office — inspect copies of charges and obtain evidence of discharge of any registered charges.

(d) Search at the Land Registry or Land Charges Department (as appropriate) if a charge is to be taken over land.

(e) If there are any floating charges, make sure that they have not crystallised (until regulations requiring registration of crystallisation are made there is no machinery for ensuring this, but the directors of the company should be asked to certify that no events leading to crystallisation have occurred and, if possible, confirmation should be obtained from the chargees).

(f) Include in the debenture power to appoint a receiver and a power of sale. If the charge is a floating charge, provide for its crystallisation.

(g) Ensure that the charge is registered within 21 days.

10.14 Alteration to the Capital Clause

10.14.1 THE CAPITAL CLAUSE

As stated earlier, the capital clause merely states the company's authorised capital and how it is divided into shares of particular nominal value. In **10.2** we saw how shares are issued. The capital clause may be altered in a number of ways, the most important of which is by increasing the authorised capital. It should be noted that an issue of shares even long after incorporation does not always require an alteration to the capital clause. For example, the capital clause may say: 'The share capital of the company is £5,000 divided into 5,000 shares of £1 each.' Shortly after incorporation 1,000 of these shares may have been issued but this still leaves 4,000 unissued shares, so that an increase of capital will only be required if it is decided to issue more than 4,000 shares. If a further issue of shares is being considered, it is necessary to find out what the authorised capital is (by looking at the capital clause) and how much of it has been issued (by looking at the last annual return and any allotments since then).

10.14.2 THE POWER TO ALTER CAPITAL

10.14.2.1 Increase

Section 121 CA 1985 gives a limited company power to alter its capital in a number of ways provided that the articles authorise the alteration. The most important alteration permitted by s. 121 is the power for a company to 'increase its share capital by new shares of such amount as it thinks expedient'. If Table A applies, then the authorisation for an increase is given by art. 32, which says: 'The company may by ordinary resolution increase its share capital by new shares of such amount as the resolution prescribes'. Section 121(4) requires that the decision to alter capital must be taken by the company in general meeting.

10.14.2.2 Other alterations

Most alterations of capital under s. 121 will be increases of nominal capital but it is also possible under that section to consolidate or subdivide shares. Shares are consolidated if shares of a smaller amount are consolidated into a smaller number of shares of a larger amount (e.g., 1,000 £1 shares become 100 £10 shares); subdivision is the opposite (1,000 £1 shares become 10,000 10p shares). If Table A applies the company has power to consolidate or subdivide under art. 32. However, since the change is really only a nominal one, there will seldom be any advantage in making it unless the value of each share is either extremely large or extremely small, in which case subdivision or consolidation may be of some cosmetic value.

10.14.3 STEPS TO BE TAKEN ON INCREASE OF CAPITAL

The directors will normally propose the increase and so will summon a general meeting to consider an increase. The ordinary resolution will then be considered at the meeting. In the extremely unlikely event that the articles do not give the company power to increase capital, the articles will have to be changed first. In *MacConnell* v *E. Prill and Co. Ltd* [1916] 2 Ch 57, it was held that the same special resolution could be used both to alter the articles and to exercise the power to increase capital.

After the meeting, if the alteration has been approved by the members, s. 123 CA 1985 requires that notice must be given to the Registrar of the increase, together (on Form G123) with a copy of the resolution and (within 15 days of the change) a printed copy of the amended memorandum. (This is one of the comparatively few circumstances in which an ordinary resolution requires registration.) Following the increase of capital steps will, of course, usually be taken to issue further shares (usually an increase will only be considered when such an issue is intended).

10.14.4   REDUCTION OF CAPITAL

A reduction of capital is not generally permitted since capital must be maintained. However, a reduction of capital is permitted in limited circumstances following an application to the court.

ELEVEN

DISPOSAL OF SHARES

11.1 Introduction

In this chapter we will consider the various ways in which a shareholder in a company may dispose of his interest in the company either during his lifetime or on death.

On disposal of shares tax will often become payable, although there are a number of reliefs available; this topic is dealt with in **Chapter 18**.

A disposal of shares by a substantial shareholder will alter the control of the company, so that the disposal may affect the rights of the remaining shareholders in the company. The interests of the incoming shareholder and the remaining shareholders have to be balanced against each other, and arrangements for achieving a balance between those interests have to be anticipated and made in advance (usually by drafting suitable articles when the company is formed). It is, therefore, essential that potential problems should be foreseen and suitable arrangements made for the particular circumstances of each company.

11.2 Transfer of Shares

11.2.1 PROCEDURE ON TRANSFER

A transfer of shares may be made by means of a sale or a gift *inter vivos*. The death or bankruptcy of a shareholder gives rise to an automatic transmission of shares (which will be followed by a transfer) and the special rules for transmission are dealt with later in the chapter.

11.2.2 CONTRACT FOR SALE

A shareholder who wishes to sell his shares may make a contract in any form that he wishes. The contract for sale is sufficient to give the purchaser an equitable interest in the shares. As between vendor and purchaser, the vendor will be liable to account to the purchaser for any dividends received and to vote as directed by the purchaser. However, membership of the company does not begin until the purchaser is registered as a member in the register of members which the company is required to keep. An entry cannot be made in the register of members until the company has received an 'instrument of transfer'.

11.2.3 STOCK TRANSFER FORM

Section 1 of the Stock Transfer Act 1963 provides that a transfer of fully paid shares may be made on a stock transfer form signed by the transferor and specifying (in addition to the particulars of the consideration, of the description of the number or amount of the shares, and of the person by whom the transfer is made) the full name and address of the transferee.

Once the sale of the shares has been agreed the vendor should execute a stock transfer form and send it together with the share certificate to the purchaser, who pays the stamp duty (1% without any exemption for transfers under £60,000). The purchaser then applies to the company for registration by sending the stamped transfer and share certificate to the company. The transfer must be registered within two months of the application unless the directors have power to refuse registration, and the company must send the purchaser a share certificate within the same period (s. 185 CA 1985). The procedure explained above applies on a gift of shares as well as on a sale (save that no *ad valorem* stamp duty is payable).

11.2.4   RESTRICTIONS ON RIGHT TO TRANSFER

Unless the articles provide to the contrary every shareholder has a *right* to transfer his shares (which in effect means that the transferee has a right to be registered). However, the articles of the company can impose a restriction on the right to transfer shares. In the case of private companies a restriction is extremely common. A restriction is often thought to be desirable since it enables the company (usually through the directors) to refuse to allow unsuitable outsiders to join the company. Article 24 of Table A provides as follows:

> The directors may refuse to register the transfer of a share which is not fully paid to a person of whom they do not approve and they may refuse to register the transfer of a share on which the company has a lien. They may also refuse to register a transfer unless:
> (a)   it is lodged at the registered office or at such other place as the directors may appoint and is accompanied by the certificate for the shares to which it relates and such other evidence as the directors may reasonably require to show the right of the transferor to make the transfer;
> (b)   it is in respect of only one class of shares; and
> (c)   it is in favour of not more than four transferees.

Thus, the directors can refuse to register the transfer of partly paid shares or fully paid shares over which the company has a lien (however, where Table A applies unamended, there is only a lien for calls on partly paid shares) and fully paid shares (whether or not the company has a lien over the shares) unless the requirements set out in (a), (b) and (c) above are complied with.

The person responsible for drafting the articles of a company should consult his clients to see what restrictions, if any, they require.

Where there are restrictions on the right to transfer shares, the company must decide within two months of application for registration, whether or not to permit the transfer. If within that time the company has not given notice of refusal of registration to the transferee, the company and its officers who are in default are liable to a fine (s. 183(5) and (6) CA 1985) and the transferee becomes *entitled* to be registered.

It is not possible to consider all the possible types of restriction on the right to register but some of the more common restrictions will now be considered.

11.2.4.1   'The directors may, in their absolute discretion and without assigning any reason therefor, decline to register any transfer of any share, whether or not it is a fully paid share'

At one time a company could not be a private company unless there was a restriction, in its articles, on the right to transfer shares. (This requirement was removed by CA 1980, now consolidated in CA 1985.) The inclusion of this particular restriction in Table A before the enactment of the Companies Act 1980 means that it is very common. As with most restrictions on transfer it is the directors who have power to refuse registration. The power is a negative one, that is, the directors have power to *refuse* registration — their positive approval is not required. This may seem an unimportant distinction but it means that a resolution of the directors is required to refuse registration, and since a resolution requires a majority in favour, an equality of votes will not be sufficient (unless, of course, the chairman has a casting vote and is against registration). This should be borne in mind in the case of 'two-man' companies, since either director will be able to ensure a transfer of his own shares merely by voting against the resolution to refuse registration. The directors' power to refuse registration must be exercised in good faith but it is very difficult to prove bad faith. The directors do not need to give reasons for refusal even if the article does not specifically excuse them from doing so.

It should be noted that this restriction is a restriction on the right to transfer shares, it is not a restriction on the right to sell them. If shares are sold but the purchaser is not registered, the vendor will hold the shares on trust for the purchaser. The purchaser will not be able to sue the vendor for damages (or his money back) unless the vendor guaranteed that registration would take place.

11.2.4.2 'The directors may decline to register a transfer of any share in favour of a person of whom they disapprove or of a share over which the company has a lien'

This restriction gives the directors two grounds for refusing registration. If required to do so, the directors must say on which ground they rely but need not give reasons justifying their decision. However, if they specified refusal on the grounds of a lien and there was no lien over the shares, the transferee would be able to insist on registration. If, however, the directors specified disapproval of the transferee the latter would find it impossible in most cases to establish that they did not disapprove of him. If the directors choose to give reasons justifying their decision the court will enquire into them to see if they are cogent reasons for refusal.

11.2.4.3 'The directors may decline to register a transfer of any share except a transfer to [a member of the company or to a member of the family of the transferor]'

This type of restriction may be appropriate to restrict a shareholder in his right to bring in outsiders against the wishes of other members of the company; it leaves him free to transfer to insiders or his own family. The words in square brackets could be adapted to include various other groups of permitted transferees, e.g., named persons or employees of the company. The term 'family' must, of course, be defined by the articles.

11.2.5 PRE-EMPTION RIGHTS

The object of restrictions on the right to transfer shares is to keep a private company private. However, the restrictions referred to above are not entirely sufficient for that purpose since they are merely restrictions on *transfer* and do not prevent sale or gift of the equitable title to the shares. If it is decided that the company should be kept completely private, the articles should, therefore, include pre-emption rights. The usual provision is that a member who wishes to transfer shares must first offer them to the existing members of the company. In drafting an article providing for pre-emption rights the following points should be considered:

(a) Should the transferring member be free to transfer to any existing member of the company or should he be obliged to offer his shares to the existing members in proportion to their present holdings?

(b) Should the transferring member be obliged to transfer part of his holding to the existing members if they do not wish to take all the shares which he proposes to transfer?

(c) Should any exceptions be made to the pre-emption rights? For example, the articles may provide that the pre-emption rights do not apply on a transfer to a member's family as defined by the article.

(d) How is the price payable to be fixed? It is quite common for the price to be fixed by agreement or by the auditors if no price can be agreed between vendor and purchaser.

(e) How long are the other members to be given to make up their minds? A period should be specified for the avoidance of doubt.

(f)   How is the transferring member to give notice of his intention to sell? It is quite common for the article to require notice to be given to the company. The secretary will then inform the other members of the offer.

A pre-emption right is a right given to the other members of the company. It is also possible for the articles to provide that a member who wishes to transfer shares shall have a right to *require* the other members to buy his shares.

11.3   Transmission by Operation of Law

When a member of a company dies his shares vest automatically in his personal representative, who is entitled to any dividend paid by the company but may not vote at general meetings. The personal representative does not, however, automatically become a member of the company since membership begins only with an entry in the register of members. A personal representative will have to prove his title to the shares, by production of the grant of representation. Having done so, the personal representative has two courses of action open to him. Firstly, he can apply, by means of a letter of request, for registration by the company as a member (the entry in the register of members will not refer to his representative capacity). If the personal representative is registered as a member, a subsequent transfer to a beneficiary will require a stock transfer form to be completed. Secondly, and alternatively, if the personal representative wishes to sell the shares so as to raise cash for the purposes of the deceased's estate or when he wishes to vest the shares in the deceased's beneficiary, he can do so without himself being registered, by means of a stock transfer form. The articles of the company will usually contain a provision (such as Table A art. 30) permitting the personal representative to be registered as a member.

A restriction on the right to transfer shares does not apply to a transmission on death unless the articles specifically so provide.

11.4   Financial Involvement by the Company

11.4.1   BUY-BACK AND REDEMPTION

As we have already seen, a company can issue redeemable shares or buy its own shares in certain circumstances. If the company buys its own shares it must normally do so out of profits, although purchase out of capital is permitted provided: a special resolution is passed; the directors can certify that the company will be solvent after the purchase and will be able to continue in business for a year; and the creditors do not successfully apply to the court for cancellation.

11.4.2   FINANCIAL ASSISTANCE

Sections 151-158 of CA 1985 contain provisions whereby a company can give financial assistance *in specified circumstances* for the purchase of its own shares without itself buying those shares. The object of this legislation is to facilitate 'management buy-outs', that is, to enable the persons who run the company's business to buy out substantial shareholders (particularly controlling shareholders) who want to dispose of their interests. This is thought to be desirable because in the past, as a result of the fact that financial assistance from the company was not then lawful, companies often had to be put into liquidation when a controlling shareholder wanted to get out of the business and no one concerned with the company had the money to buy him out. The legislation is not limited to cases of management buy-out.

11.4.3   GENERAL PROHIBITION

Section 151(1) of CA 1985 makes financial assistance, direct or indirect, by a company for the acquisition of its own shares prima facie unlawful. Section 151(2) makes it prima facie unlawful for the company to give financial assistance, direct or indirect, for the purpose of reducing or discharging a liability incurred by any person in acquiring the company's shares. Both subsections apply to 'indirect' as well as direct assistance. It is, therefore, prima facie unlawful for a company to guarantee a loan made by a third party (e.g., a bank) to enable someone to buy shares in the company or to guarantee such a loan after the shares have been purchased. A gift is also treated as financial assistance for these purposes and so is any other transaction whereby the assets of the company are reduced (s. 152(1)(a)).

11.4.4 GENERAL EXCEPTION FOR ALL COMPANIES

Section 153(1) contains the first exception to the prohibitions referred to above. It applies to all companies, public and private, and says that a company is not prohibited from giving assistance 'for the purpose of an acquisition of shares in it . . .' if:

    (a) the company's principal purpose in giving the assistance is not to give it for the purpose of any such acquisition, or the giving of the assistance for that purpose is but an incidental part of some larger purpose of the company; and
    (b) the assistance is given in good faith in the interests of the company.

11.4.5 SPECIFIC EXCEPTION FOR PRIVATE COMPANIES

Section 155 CA 1985 contains the second exception to the prohibitions and gives private companies wide powers to give financial assistance for the purchase of their own shares (or for the reduction or discharge of liabilities incurred on purchase). The main requirement of the section is that the assistance must not reduce the net assets of the company or, if it does reduce them, must be provided out of profits available for dividend (s. 155(2)). Financial assistance by way of a loan would not normally reduce net assets since the reduction in assets (cash) caused by the lending would be balanced by the debt owed to the company by the borrower. Financial assistance by way of gift would, of course, reduce net assets.

Before financial assistance can be given under s. 155:

    (a) a special resolution must be passed approving the assistance (s. 155(4)); and
    (b) the directors must make a statutory declaration setting out the nature of the assistance and stating the directors' opinion that the company is solvent and will remain so for at least twelve months. The directors' opinion must be confirmed by the auditors in a report annexed to the statutory declaration.

Under s. 157 CA 1985 the special resolution must be passed within a week of the statutory declaration and 10% of the shareholders may apply to the court for cancellation of the resolution within 28 days.

The company must send copies of the special resolution, statutory declaration and auditors' report to the Registrar of Companies.

The financial assistance approved by the special resolution must not be given until four weeks after the resolution (or until the court approves it if an application for cancellation is made), and must not be given more than eight weeks after the directors make the statutory declaration.

TWELVE

COMPANY MEETINGS AND RESOLUTIONS

In this chapter we will look at meetings of shareholders and the resolutions which are passed at such meetings. In **Chapter 9** we saw that there are certain powers which can only be exercised within a company by the shareholders. In this chapter we are concerned with how those powers are exercised. The rules about these matters are sometimes quite technical but their importance cannot be overestimated. Unless correct procedures are followed the rights of shareholders may often be lost to them. A solicitor advising a company or shareholder may often be called upon to see that the correct procedures are adopted.

We are not concerned in this chapter with directors' meetings (which were dealt with in **Chapter 8**), we are only concerned with meetings of shareholders. Shareholders' meetings are also called 'company meetings' or 'general meetings'.

12.1 Types of General Meeting

The meetings of a private company are of two types: annual general meetings and extraordinary general meetings. The meetings are called 'general' meetings to distinguish them from board meetings (that is, meetings of the directors).

12.1.1 ANNUAL GENERAL MEETINGS

An annual general meeting (AGM) must normally be held once in every calendar year and must be within 15 months of the last AGM. However, a company need not hold an AGM during the (calendar) year of incorporation or during the next calendar year provided the first AGM is held within 18 months of incorporation.

Private companies are able to dispense with the need to hold an annual general meeting. In order to do so they must first pass an elective resolution (see **12.2** below).

12.1.2 EXTRAORDINARY GENERAL MEETINGS

Any meeting which is not an AGM is an extraordinary general meeting (EGM). An EGM is held as and when necessary. The procedure for calling such a meeting will be considered shortly, but first it is necessary to consider the types of resolution needed to transact business at general meetings.

12.2 Resolutions

A company in general meeting can only transact business by passing the appropriate type of resolution. There are four types of resolution: ordinary, extraordinary, special and elective.

12.2.1 ORDINARY RESOLUTIONS

An ordinary resolution is one which requires a simple majority of votes in favour if it is to be passed (a simple majority means more votes in favour than against — an equality of votes is not sufficient). Where there is an equality an ordinary resolution may, however, be passed on the chairman's casting vote if the articles so provide. Table A art. 50 gives the chairman a casting vote. In the case of a small company the decision as to whether to allow an article giving a casting vote may be crucial. The presence of a casting vote resolves the problem of deadlock but may in some cases be considered to give the chairman too much power. An ordinary resolution is suffcient to transact any business at a general meeting save in those cases where the Companies Acts require special, extraordinary or elective resolutions or where the articles require special or extraordinary resolutions.

12.2.2 EXTRAORDINARY AND SPECIAL RESOLUTIONS

An extraordinary resolution and a special resolution both require a three-quarters majority — that is, at least three votes must be cast in favour of the resolution for every one cast against it. The difference between an extraordinary resolution and a special resolution is that an extraordinary resolution (like an ordinary resolution) requires the same length of notice as the meeting at which it is to be considered (14 days at an EGM, 21 at an AGM), whereas a special resolution requires 21 days' notice even if it is to be considered at an EGM. An elective resolution depends on the unanimous approval of all the shareholders or their proxies (unanimous agreement by all who attend and vote is not sufficient) and 21 days' notice is required.

The Companies Act lays down many circumstances in which a special resolution is required. Among the most important from the point of view of the shareholder are resolutions to alter the articles or objects, and resolutions to exclude pre-emption rights on the issue of shares. Any generalisation as to when a special resolution is required is perhaps a dangerous simplification, but if there is a factor common to all the circumstances it is probably that they are all circumstances where minority shareholders need protection. It is a common mistake to suppose that all alterations to the memorandum require a special resolution. This is not so since, for example, capital can be increased by ordinary resolution if the articles so provide. A special resolution may be required by the articles of the company in any other circumstances where the Act does not require some other kind of resolution (an ordinary resolution is required by s. 303 for the removal of a director from office and an extraordinary resolution in the circumstances referred to below). It is, in fact, very uncommon for the articles to require a special resolution where the Act does not do so. If the company wishes to give the minority shareholders the greater protection of a three-quarters majority, the articles will usually provide for an extraordinary resolution.

An extraordinary resolution is provided for by the Companies Act in a small number of circumstances where it is considered that minority shareholders require protection but the matter is urgent. The most important of these circumstances is where a resolution is passed to commence a voluntary winding-up because of the company's liabilities (s. 572(1)(c) CA 1985). As with a special resolution, the articles can require an extraordinary resolution in any circumstances where the Act does not require some other sort of resolution.

12.2.3 ELECTIVE RESOLUTIONS

The Companies Act 1985, s. 379A (interpolated by CA 1989) allows a private company to simplify its own internal management by passing elective resolutions. Such resolutions may:

    (a)   authorise the directors to allot shares for an indefinite period (see **Chapter 10**);
    (b)   dispense with the need to hold a shareholders meeting for the consideration of accounts;
    (c)   dispense with the holding of an AGM (see **12.1** above);
    (d)   permit the holding of a meeting with short notice with the approval of 90% of the members (see **12.4** below); and
    (e)   dispense with the need to make annual appointment of auditors.

Once passed, an elective resolution may be revoked by an ordinary resolution.

12.3 Calling a General Meeting

As we saw in **Chapter 8**, directors' meetings can be called quite informally at the request of any one of the directors. The position in relation to general meetings is much more complicated. As with so many aspects of company law, the rules are partly statutory and partly depend on the provisions of the company's own articles. Most of the statutory rules are designed to protect the shareholders whose voting rights would be worthless if they were not backed up by rights to call meetings. The statutory rules will be considered first and then the provisions of Table A.

12.3.1 STATUTORY RULES

Section 367 CA 1985 provides that if default is made in holding an annual general meeting when required, the Department of Trade can call a meeting on the application of any member and can order that one person shall constitute a quorum at the meeting.

Section 368 is the most important statutory provision dealing with meetings as far as the shareholder is concerned. This section allows shareholders who are registered as owners of 'not less than one tenth of such of the paid-up capital of the company as . . . carries the right of voting at general meetings' to requisition a meeting. The requisition must be in writing and signed and must be deposited at the registered office. Once this has been done the directors *must* call a meeting for a date within 28 days of the issue of the notice. If within 21 days of the requisition, the directors have not taken the necessary steps to call the meeting, the requisitionists may call the meeting themselves at the company's expense. Section 368 does not say that the requisitionists have a right to specify what resolutions are to be discussed at the meeting but s. 368(3) clearly implies that they have such a right. Most private companies have only a very small number of members, so that wherever there is any real chance of success (i.e., of passing a resolution) there should be no difficulty in requisitioning a meeting. In fact, it should not be necessary in many cases to use s. 368, since the directors will usually be willing to call a meeting when required (for the directors' power to call general meetings, see below).

Section 370 provides a separate power for 'two or more members holding not less than one tenth of the issued share capital' to call a meeting. In the majority of circumstances this adds little to s. 368, but it should be noted that under s. 370 the shares need not represent one tenth of the *paid-up* capital but only of the *issued* capital, nor need the shares carry the right to vote. Section 370 has one substantial advantage over s. 368 — that is, the members can themselves call the meeting (although they must, of course, give proper notice), so that there will be less delay before the meeting is held than in the case of s. 368. Unlike s. 368, s. 370 only has effect 'in so far as the articles of the company do not make other provision in that behalf': that is, it can be excluded or varied by the articles. Table A does not exclude s. 370.

Section 371 gives the court power to order meetings 'if for any reason it is impracticable to call a meeting of a company in any manner in which meetings of that company may be called'.

12.3.2 TABLE A

Table A art. 37 gives the directors power to decide when to call the AGM and to call an EGM at any time. The vast majority of EGMs will be called in this way. Article 37 also provides that if there are not sufficient directors present in the UK to constitute a quorum at a board meeting, a single director or any member may convene a meeting.

12.4 Notice of Meetings

12.4.1 SERVICE OF NOTICE

Business at a meeting cannot be properly transacted or relied upon unless proper notice has been given of the meeting. Section 370(2) provides that 'notice of the meeting of a company shall be served on every member of it in the manner in which notices are required to be served by Table A (as for the time being, in force)'. The articles in Table A dealing with notices are numbers 38-39 and 111-116.

Article 38 requires notice of general meetings (of both types) to be given to all the members, persons entitled to a share in consequence of the death or bankruptcy of a member, the directors and auditors. Article 112 relieves the company from the duty to give notice to members who have no registered address in the UK, and art. 116 provides that notice need only be given to personal representatives and trustees in bankruptcy if they have supplied the company with an address to which notices are to be sent; if they have not done so, service on the dead or bankrupt member is deemed effective if sent to his registered address as if the death or bankruptcy had not occurred.

Article 112 provides for personal service or service by post. Where service is by post, it is presumed to have been served 48 hours after posting.

Article 39 provides that accidental omission to give notice to someone entitled to it, does not invalidate the meeting. Accidental omission would include clerical errors but not a failure to give notice resulting from a failure to apply the articles properly (*Young* v *Ladies Imperial Club Ltd* [1920] 2 KB 523).

12.4.2 LENGTH OF NOTICE

The length of notice required depends on the nature of the meeting and of the resolutions to be proposed at it. For an AGM, 21 days' notice is required. For an EGM, 14 days' notice is required, unless a special resolution (or, where Table A applies, a resolution appointing someone to be a director) or elective resolution is to be proposed, when the period is 21 days. Table A art. 38 provides that notice periods are to be 14 and 21 'clear days', that is, exclusive of the date of service and the date of the meeting. Thus, for example, if the directors wish to hold an EGM at which a special resolution is to be proposed and post the notices on Monday 1 March the meeting cannot be held before Thursday 25 March. (Notice deemed served on 3 March (art. 112), 4-24 March inclusive is the 21 clear days, so the meeting can be held on the next day.)

Section 369(3) and art. 38 provide that shorter notice than that normally required is valid if all the members attend the meeting and agree to short notice, in the case of an AGM, or a majority in number owning 95% (or such lesser percentage — but not less than 90% — as specified in an elective resolution) of the voting shares in the case of an EGM. For many private companies (especially family companies or companies where the members are all directors) this allows a meeting to be held at very short notice; it is not a practical alternative to the giving of proper notice for companies with large numbers of members.

12.4.3 CONTENTS OF NOTICE

The notice of a meeting must state the date, time, and place of meeting. It must also describe the business which is to be transacted sufficiently for members to be able to decide whether they wish to attend. It is a question of judgment in each case how much detail of the business needs to be stated, so that decided cases do not give much guidance to those drawing up the notice. One point that is clear, is that any personal interest of directors in the business of the meeting must be disclosed. In drawing up a notice it is better to err on the side of inclusion rather than exclusion.

If a special, elective or extraordinary resolution or a resolution which requires special notice (for example, a resolution to remove a director under s. 303 CA 1985) is to be proposed, it must be set out verbatim in the notice. Section 372 CA 1985 requires that the notice should tell the members that each of them is entitled to send a proxy (who need not be a member) to attend and vote on his behalf.

12.5 Proceedings at Meetings

12.5.1 QUORUM

A meeting cannot consider business unless a quorum is present at the time when the meeting proceeds to business. Unless the articles otherwise provide, two members personally present are the quorum (s. 370(4)).

12.5.2 AGENDA

Discussion of resolutions is limited by requirements as to the notice of meetings, that is, sufficient notice and description of the business should be given to enable members to decide whether to attend. Amendments may be moved but only within the scope of the notice; therefore, no amendment of substance is permitted to a special, elective or extraordinary resolution and amendments to ordinary resolutions are limited. Proxies as well as members may speak at a meeting of a private company.

12.5.3 VOTING

A vote on a resolution may be decided on a show of hands. On such a vote each member personally present has one vote (regardless of the number of shares owned), and a proxy cannot vote unless the articles provide to the contrary (Table A does not give a proxy a right to vote on a show of hands). Section 373 gives a right to demand a poll to: any five voting members; or any member or members with 10% of the voting rights; or any member or members with 10% of the paid-up capital with a right to vote. Table A art. 46 extends this by allowing any two members (instead of five) or the chairman to call for a poll. Proxies have the same right to call for a poll as the member or members they represent. When a poll is called, the votes are counted according to the voting rights of the members rather than according to the number of members. If necessary the meeting can be adjourned while the votes are counted but this is unlikely in the case of a private company.

12.6 Dispensing with Meetings

A private company may, as an alternative to holding a meeting, pass resolutions in writing under CA 1985 s. 381A. For such a resolution to be valid it must be agreed and signed by or on behalf of all the members who would have been entitled to attend and vote if a meeting had been held. A written resolution is passed when the last member signs. By way of exception, a written resolution may not be used to remove a director from office under s. 303 nor to remove an auditor under s. 391. In certain cases, the Companies Acts require documents to be produced to members at a meeting before a resolution is passed. In such cases the documents must be sent to each member if a written resolution is to be passed. (For example, if a director's service contract is to exceed five years its terms must be sent to the members before the written resolution is passed.)

12.7 Minutes and Returns

Minutes must be kept of all decisions taken at general meetings and must be available for inspection by the members at the registered office. Copies of certain resolutions must be sent to the Registrar of Companies within 15 days of being passed (s. 380 CA 1985). Included in this requirement are all special, elective and extraordinary resolutions.

TAXATION

THIRTEEN

THE TAXATION OF THE INCOME PROFITS AND LOSSES OF SOLE TRADERS AND PARTNERSHIPS

13.1 Introduction

In this chapter we will look at the way the income profits and losses of sole traders and partnerships are determined and assessed. We will first look at the general rules as they apply to any unincorporated business and then look at the specific rules relevant to partnerships.

13.2 Income Profits

13.2.1 THE TAX SCHEDULES

Sole traders pay income tax on income. For a receipt to be income it must usually be recurrent or capable of recurrence (but 'one-off' receipts can be income in some circumstances), and must be included in the definition of income under one of the five schedules of the Income and Corporation Taxes Act 1988 (commonly called 'the Taxes Act'). It is beyond the scope of this book to deal with the various definitions of income in the schedules but the following table will give an idea of what is covered:

Schedule A	Rents
Schedule C	Government securities
Schedule D Case I	Profits of a trade
Schedule D Case II	Profits of a profession or vocation
Schedule D Case III	'Pure income' (interest, annuities and annual payments)
Schedule D Cases IV & V	Income from foreign securities or possessions
Schedule D Case VI	Miscellaneous income (casual profits and certain items specifically allocated to this case)
Schedule E	Income from offices, employments or pensions
Schedule F	Dividends

Each schedule lays down rules for the deductibility of expenses in calculating income and for the allocation of receipts to a particular year of assessment (each year of assessment starts on 6 April and ends on the following 5 April and is commonly called a tax year).

For a sole trader Schedule D Case I (trade) or II (profession or vocation) is usually the most important case. The rules for these two cases are almost identical, and are in many respects quite different from the other cases of Schedule D and from the other schedules, both in respect of the definition of income and the time when it is taxed. To determine the amount of profits it is necessary to calculate the amount of income generated from trading activities and deduct from that the amount of deductible expenditure.

Once the income has been calculated the taxpayer is liable to income tax on the whole amount less certain payments known as charges on income and certain sums known as personal reliefs. Charges on income are defined by s. 8(8) Taxes Management Act 1970 as 'amounts which fall to be deducted in computing total income'. This somewhat unhelpful definition is not explained further. Charges on income include annuities and other annual payments and certain interest payments. A personal relief is a sum deducted in computing the taxable part of income, the amount of which depends on the taxpayer's circumstances. The tax is progressive, that is, the rate increases as income increases.

13.2.2   DEFINITION OF INCOME

Income must be distinguished from capital receipts. In most cases there is no problem in deciding which an item is. Thus profits received from the sale of stock-in-trade are income: profits made from the sale of fixed assets are capital. For example, if the business is a grocer's shop, the food which is sold is stock but the shop itself, its shelves and counters are fixed assets. The evidence of accountants as to general accountancy practice is valuable but not conclusive in deciding whether an item is income or capital.

Almost all businesses produce final accounts on an annual basis. These show the amount of profit made according to normal accountancy practice and how it is allocated to the proprietor(s). These accounts are not, however, necessarily suitable for tax purposes, as often there are special tax rules which define what is taxable as income and what is deductible as an expense.

13.2.3   DEDUCTIBLE EXPENDITURE

Deductible expenditure is not fully defined in the Taxes Act. Expenditure is deductible if it is of a revenue rather than a capital nature. This distinction is similar to the distinction between income and capital receipts, so that, again, evidence of accountancy practice is valuable. Section 74 ICTA 1988 prevents the deduction of expenses in 15 circumstances.

The first paragraph of s. 74 provides that, 'in computing the amount of the profits or gains to be charged under Case I or II of Schedule D, no sum shall be deducted in respect of any disbursements or expenses, not being money *wholly and exclusively* laid out or expended for the purposes of the trade, profession or vocation'. Expenditure, if it is to be deducted, must, therefore, be 'wholly' incurred for the purposes of the trade, so that if a sum of money represents partly a business expense but is excessively large so that it also partly represents a gift it is not deductible. Expenditure must also be 'exclusively' incurred for the purposes of the trade, so that if money is spent and the motive is partly connected with the trade and partly not so connected (e.g., there is an element of personal enjoyment), then the payment is not deductible.

Certain types of expenditure are not deductible because of the provisions of paras. (b)-(q) of s. 74. Many of these paragraphs refer to types of expenditure which would be non-deductible anyway because they are not revenue expenditure or not wholly and exclusively incurred for the purposes of the trade. The section, among other things, prohibits the deduction of provisions for bad debts (but not of actual bad debts); and most business entertainment expenses are non-deductible under the provisions of s. 577 ICTA 1988.

13.2.4   ACCOUNTING BASES

When calculating profit, it is important for any business, whether run by a sole trader, by a partnership or through a limited company, to apply a consistent method to determine whether receipts and expenses relate to one accounting period or to a later period. If it fails to do so its accounts are useless to the business for the purposes of comparison; what is more, the business could manipulate its receipts and expenses so as to avoid tax.

For tax purposes accounts have to be agreed with the Inland Revenue and must be prepared on one of three bases: the earnings, the cash, or the bills delivered bases.

(a) *The earnings basis* Accounts are prepared on the basis of income earned (even if not received) and expenses incurred (even if not paid) during the relevant accounting period.

The value of stock unsold at the end of an accounting period and/or the value of work-in-hand at the end of the accounting period must be included when calculating profit (see paragraph 1.5 below).

(b) *The cash basis* Accounts are prepared on the basis of sums actually received and paid. No account is taken of amounts owed or owing or of the value of unsold stock or work-in-hand. This basis may give a misleading picture of the true profit where credit is given and/or received.

(c) *The bills delivered basis* Accounts are prepared on the basis of bills delivered to customers and received from suppliers irrespective of whether the bills have been paid. No account is taken of amounts owed or owing but not billed or of the value of unsold stock and work-in-hand. The fact that work-in-hand need not be valued makes this basis particularly popular with professional partnerships.

Trading partnerships are assessed on the earnings basis. Professionals, such as solicitors and accountants, are usually assessed on this basis for the first three tax years during which the profession is carried on but in the fourth and subsequent years (provided an undertaking is given to deliver bills promptly), the Revenue will usually agree to the bills delivered basis. The Revenue is normally reluctant to allow the cash basis except in special cases.

13.2.5   THE NEED TO VALUE STOCK AND WORK-IN-HAND

As explained above, when a business is taxed on the earnings basis, it is necessary to value stock and work-in-hand at the end of an accounting period, otherwise the accounts are misleading. If a trading business which makes a profit by buying and selling goods or other property simply compared its receipts and expenses, the accounts would give no real idea of the amount of profit. For example, £1,000 worth of goods are bought during a particular period and half of them are sold for £1,200 — clearly the profit is more than £200 since half the goods remain. Ignoring other expenses (wages, rates, electricity bills, etc.) the profit could be said to be £700 since goods purchased for £500 have been sold for £1,200.

Clearly it would be impractical to record the sale price of each item and deduct from it the original purchase price. To calculate a trading profit, stock must be valued at the end of the period. If the closing stock figure (i.e., the value at the end of the year) is deducted from the total of the opening stock figure and the amount spent on stock during the year (which accountants call 'purchases') the cost of goods sold has been calculated. This figure can then be deducted from the receipts from the sale of stock (called 'sales') to calculate the gross profit.

Example

	£	£
Sales		50,000
Opening stock	10,000	
Add: Purchases	35,000	
	45,000	
Less: Closing stock	(12,000)	
		33,000
Gross profit		17,000

(Other deductible expenses such as wages are then deducted from the gross profit to arrive at the net profit which enters into the tax calculation.)

113

Clearly the amount of profit depends on the value placed on stock — the lower the closing stock figure the smaller is the profit (and, therefore, the tax on it). Stock is valued according to normal accountancy principles, which allow each item of stock to be valued at the lower of cost or market value. Thus where stock has risen in value an upward valuation is not required, but where it has fallen in value immediate relief is given by the revaluation. Once a closing stock figure has been arrived at for a period it becomes the opening stock figure for the next period.

A business which supplies services will not have trading stock left at the end of an accounting period. It will, however, have work-in-hand at that date (that is, work commenced but not yet billed). The same principles are applied as with trading stock. Thus, where the earnings basis applies, the work-in-hand at the end of the year will increase profits, whereas work-in-hand at the start of the year will reduce them.

13.3 The Basis of Assesssment for Income Tax

Almost all traders find that a suitable accounting period is twelve months. The period chosen need not correspond with the year of assessment (tax year). A trader pays tax on the income of the year of assessment according to the rates fixed for that year by the annual Finance Act (taking into account his tax-free personal reliefs for the year). Because the accounting period and year of assessment do not usually correspond, rules are needed for allocating the profits of accounting periods to years of assessment.

13.3.1 PRECEDING YEAR BASIS

In most circumstances the 'preceding year basis' applies to business profits (whether of a trade, profession or vocation). The profits taxable in each year of assessment are deemed to equal the profits of the accounting period ending in the preceding year of assessment. For example, a trader makes up his accounts to 31 December each year. His profits for the tax year 1993-94 will therefore be the profits of the accounting period which ended in the year of assessment 1992-93, i.e., the profits earned between 1 January 1992 and 31 December 1992.

Since the tax on trading profits is payable in two instalments — on 1 January during the year of assessment and on 1 July after its end — this effectively means that there is a considerable time-lag between an increase in profits and an increase in tax; the extent of this time-lag will depend on the date chosen for the end of the accounting period. (For example, if the accounting period ends on 5 April, the first instalment of tax for that period will be payable nine months later; if on 7 April, 21 months later.)

13.3.2 EARLY YEARS OF TRADE

The preceding year basis cannot apply in the early years of trade because there is no preceding year with profits. The rules for the opening years of assesment are as follows:

Year of commencement   Profits from date of commencement to following 5 April
Second year   Profits of first 12 months of trade
Third and subsequent years   Preceding year basis

In the second and third years only, the *taxpayer* has a choice and can elect to be taxed on the actual profits of both those years (but not on only one of them) if he wishes. Such an election is advisable if profits are falling.

Where necessary, profits taxed on the actual basis are calculated by apportioning the profits of one or more accounting periods on a time basis. the following examples should make the rules clearer:

(a)   A trader starts business on 1 January 1990. Accounts are made up to 31 December each year and profits are as follows:

1990	£5,000
1991	£6,000
1992	£7,000

The income for tax purposes is:

*Year of
assessment*

1989-90	£1,250 approx.	(actual basis, i.e., £5,000 apportioned to the period of 3 months)
1990-91	£5,000	(first 12 months)
1991-92	£5,000	(preceding year basis)
1992-93	£6,000	(preceding year basis)
1993-94	£7,000	(preceding year basis)

An election for the actual basis for 1990-91 and 1991-92 would produce incomes of £5,250 and £6,250:

	£	£
1990-91:		
6 April 1990 to 31 December 1990	$9/_{12} \times 5,000 =$	3,750
1 January 1991 to 5 April 1991	$3/_{12} \times 6,000 =$	1,500
		5,250

	£	£
1991-92:		
6 April 1991 to 31 December 1991	$9/_{12} \times 6,000 =$	4,500
1 January 1992 to 5 April 1992	$3/_{12} \times 7,000 =$	1,750
		6,250

Note: In doing this calculation we have worked in whole months for the sake of simplicity. In practice the calculation would be done on a daily basis.

The election for the actual basis should not be made.

(b)   A trader starts business on 1 January 1990. Accounts are made up to 31 December each year and profits are as follows:

1990	£8,000
1991	£6,000
1992	£4,000

Income for tax years:

	£	£
1989-90	£2,000 approx	(actual basis, i.e., £8,000 apportioned to the period of 3 months)
1990-91:		
6 April 1990 to 31 December 1990	$9/_{12} \times 8,000 =$	6,000
1 January 1991 to 5 April 1991	$3/_{12} \times 6,000 =$	1,500
		7,500

	£	£
1991-92:		
6 April 1991 to 31 December 1991	$9/_{12} \times 6,000 =$	4,500
1 January 1992 to 5 April 1992	$3/_{12} \times 4,000 =$	1,000
		5,500

1992-93	6,000 (preceding year basis)
1993-94	4,000 (preceding year basis)

An election for the actual basis of assessment for the second and third years would be made. If it was not made the profits assessed to tax for 1990-91 would be the profits of the first 12 months, £8,000 and those for 1991-92 on the preceding year basis would be £8,000.

13.3.3   CLOSING YEARS OF TRADE

Special rules also apply to the closing years of a trade (contained in s. 63 ICTA 1988), since if the preceding year basis continued to apply a trade could be artificially closed down and a new trade started after a particularly good accounting period without the profits of that period ever being used as the basis of a tax assessment.

The closing year rules are:

Last year	Actual profits from 6 April to discontinuance
Penultimate year	Preceding year basis
Pre-penultimate year	Preceding year basis
Earlier years	Preceding year basis

In the penultimate and pre-penultimate years the Revenue can elect to tax the profits on the actual basis if this produces a larger amount of profit taking both years together (they will do so if profits are rising).

Where necessary, profits taxed on the actual basis are calculated by apportioning the profits of one or more accounting period on a time basis.

The following examples should make the closing year rules clearer:

(a)   A trader ends his business on 31 December 1994. His accounts are made up to 31 December each year and the profits are as follows:

1994	£10,000
1993	£12,000
1992	£14,000
1991	£16,000
1990	£20,000

The income for the tax years is as follows:

1994-95	£7,500 approx	(actual profits 6 April 1994 to 31 December 1994, i.e., £10,000 apportioned)
1993-94	£14,000	(preceding year basis)
1992-93	£16,000	(preceding year basis)
1991-92	£20,000	(preceding year basis)

The Revenue would not elect to make the assessment on the actual basis for 1993-94 and 1992-93 since the profits would then be £11,500 and £13,500 respectively:

1993-94:	£	£
6 April 1993 to 31 December 1993	$^9/_{12} \times 12,000 =$	9,000
1 January 1994 to 5 April 1994	$^3/_{12} \times 10,000 =$	2,500
		11,500

1992-93:	£	£
6 April 1992 to 31 December 1992	$^9/_{12} \times 14,000 =$	10,500
1 January 1993 to 5 April 1993	$^3/_{12} \times 12,000 =$	3,000
		13,500

(b) A trader ends his business on 31 December 1994. His accounts are made up to 31 December each year and the profits are as follows:

1994	£16,000
1993	£12,000
1992	£ 8,000
1991	£ 6,000
1990	£ 4,000

The income for the years is as follows:

1994-95:
6 April 1994 to 31 December 1994 $\qquad \frac{9}{12} \times 16,000 = \underline{12,000}$

1993-94:
6 April 1993 to 31 December 1993 $\qquad \frac{9}{12} \times 12,000 = 9,000$
1 January 1994 to 5 April 1994 $\qquad \frac{3}{12} \times 16,000 = \underline{4,000}$
$\qquad\qquad\qquad\qquad\qquad\qquad\qquad \underline{13,000}$

1992-93:
6 April 1992 to 31 December 1992 $\qquad \frac{9}{12} \times 8,000 = 6,000$
1 January 1993 to 5 April 1993 $\qquad \frac{3}{12} \times 12,000 = \underline{3,000}$
$\qquad\qquad\qquad\qquad\qquad\qquad\qquad \underline{9,000}$

1991-92 (preceding year basis) 4,000

The Revenue would make the assessment on the actual basis for 1993-94 and 1992-93 since the profits on the preceding year basis would be £8,000 and £6,000 respectively — in fact, assessments will already have been made on those figures because it is not known until the end of 1994 that they are penultimate and pre-penultimate years. The assessments will, therefore, have to be retrospectively adjusted.

13.3.4   ASSESSMENT — CONCLUSIONS

The basis of assessment under Cases I and II is highly artificial. In practical terms some profits in the early years are taxed more than once and some near the end of the trade not at all. As long as the profits near the end of the trade are higher than those soon after the beginning the taxpayer may ultimately benefit, but even with inflation there is no guarantee that profits will be higher near the end of the trade.

If a trade is short lived, the opening years and closing years may overlap, in which case the closing year rules take priority.

It should be noted that the amount of tax paid by a trader does not depend on what he does with his profits. Subject to the deduction of charges on income, they are fully taxed whether withdrawn or retained in the business (unless a capital allowance can be claimed).

Following the publication of two consultative documents in 1991 and 1992, the Chancellor announced in the March 1993 Budget a proposal to introduce a major reform of the system for assessing personal tax. The reform is designed to make the process of making tax returns and payments simpler and fairer. The new system will apply from the 1996-1997 tax year. The detailed legislation will be introduced in the 1994 Finance Bill and, among other changes, will abolish the 'preceding year' basis of income tax for the self-employed.

13.4 Losses Under the Income Tax System

If a trader makes a trading loss (i.e., deductible expenses exceed income profits) during an accounting period, there will be a 'nil' assessment in the following tax year if the preceding year basis applies (as it will unless the trade is just beginning or is coming to an end). This does not give any relief for the loss, its effect being to reduce the income to nothing rather than to the negative figure which the loss represents. Loss relief is, however, given in a number of ways.

(a)   Under s. 380(1) ICTA 1988 the amount of the loss may, if the taxpayer so elects, be deducted from any income of the taxpayer taxable in the year of assessment during which the loss is made. Where, as is usual, the loss-making period is partly in one tax year and partly in another the Revenue will, in practice, allow the whole of the loss to be set off against the income of the tax year during which that period ends.

If a loss is not fully relieved under s. 380(1) either because the income of the year of the loss was insufficient or because the taxpayer did not elect to take the relief, a similar election may be made for the next year of assessment, provided that the trade is still being carried on by the taxpayer on a commercial basis (s. 380(2)).

It should be noted that under both subsections the loss may be set off against *any* of the taxpayer's income from whatever source: because of the preceding year basis this may (in the case of subsection (1)) include a profit from the same trade made in an earlier accounting period. A claim under s. 380 must be made in writing within two years of the end of the relevant tax year.

Special rules apply to prevent relief under s. 380 being given where the trade is not being carried on with a view to profit.

Trading losses can, in limited circumstances, be set against the taxpayer's capital gains in the tax year when the loss arises and in one following tax year under s. 72 Finance Act 1991. The relief under s. 72 only applies to such losses as have not been used up following a claim under s. 380.

(b)   Under s. 385 ICTA 1988 a loss may be set against income from the same trade (but not from any other source) in future years to the extent that it has not been completely relieved under s. 380, either because no relief was claimed or because the income was insufficient. Relief is given by means of a deduction from the income of the next tax year in which there are profits and then the year after that and so on until the loss is completely relieved.

The following example should make the operation of ss. 380 and 385 clear. The profits and loss of a trade made during accounting periods ending on 31 December each year are as follows:

1990	£ 5,000	profit
1991	£20,000	loss
1992	£ 6,000	profit
1993	£ 7,000	profit

In addition to his trade the taxpayer has a part-time employment producing an income of £2,000 per annum throughout the period. If claims for relief under ss. 380 and 385 are made the income tax position is as follows:

	1991-92	1992-93	1993-94	1994-95
DI income	5,000	nil	6,000	7,000
Schedule E income	2,000	2,000	2,000	2,000
	7,000	2,000	8,000	9,000
Loss relief	7,000*	2,000**	6,000***	5,000***
Final income	nil	nil	2,000	4,000

*s. 380(1)   **s. 380(2)   ***s. 385

Note:

    (i)   On these figures full relief is not given until 1994-95 even though the loss was made in 1991.

    (ii) It would probably be better not to claim relief for 1992-93 since much of the income for that year would have been covered by personal reliefs which are tax-free anyway. The loss relief is therefore wasted.

    (iii) The deduction in 1993-94 is only £6,000 because in that year no relief is given against income from other sources. After the deduction of £5,000 in 1994-95 full relief has been given for the loss.

  (c) Under ss. 388 and 389 ICTA 1988 a loss made during the last year of a trade may be deducted from income from the same trade in the three years of assessment before the discontinuance (relief under s. 380 will be available for the year of discontinuance), taking later years before earlier years. This section is really s. 385 in reverse since it allows the loss to be carried back rather than forwards. It should be noted that the relief only applies where the loss is made in the last year of a trade. If a business makes losses for a number of years before discontinuance there will be no loss relief unless the trader has other sources of income — s. 385 cannot help since there will be no future profits, nor can ss. 388 and 389, since the loss can only be carried back three years and those years will have had nil assessments because of the earlier losses.

  (d) Under s. 381 ICTA 1988 losses made during the first four years of a trade may be set off against income of the three tax years before the loss, taking earlier years before later years. The loss can be deducted from all the income of those years from whatever source and the rules of s. 380 dealing with the order in which relief is given where there is more than one source of income apply to s. 381. The principal effect of s. 381 is to allow a sole trader who starts a trade to set the loss off against income received before the business started.

As would be expected, all the sections giving relief prevent double relief being claimed in respect of the same sum (for example, if relief is claimed under s. 381 only the unrelieved balance, if any, may be carried forward under s. 385). In many cases relief is given by setting a loss off against income which has already been taxed; where this happens the relief is given by means of repayment of tax.

It should be noted that loss relief is not intended as a subsidy for unsuccessful business; there is no guarantee that just because a loss is made relief will one day be given. Where relief is given the saving is, of course, the amount of the tax on the amount of the relief, so that for the basic rate taxpayer a loss of £100 saves £20 in tax.

13.5   Income Tax Liability of Partnerships

A partnership is not a separate legal person. It is a group of individuals each of whom is taxed on his own share of the partnership profits or losses in the light of his own personal reliefs, charges on income and other sources of income. However, for the purposes of *assessment* and *collection* of tax the Revenue does recognise the partnership as an entity (see below).

The income on which the partnership is assessed to tax in a particular tax year is calculated according to the preceding year basis, the opening year rules (subject to the provisions of ss. 61 and 62 ICTA 1988 — see **14.3.2.1**) or the closing year rules as appropriate.

A trading partnership will be charged to tax under Schedule D Case I. It is normally assessed on the earnings basis. A professional partnership will be charged to tax under Schedule D Case II. It is also assessed on the earnings basis initially, although the Inland Revenue will normally agree to the bills delivered basis in the fourth and subsequent accounting periods, provided an undertaking to bill promptly is given (for a fuller discussion of the three bases see paragraph 1.4 above).

The taxable profit is calculated by applying normal income tax principles to ascertain taxable receipts and deductible expenses. However, in the case of a partnership, it is necessary to examine any payment made by the business to a partner to determine whether it is a deductible expense or merely an allocation of the taxable profit amongst the partners. A payment which falls into the latter category cannot reduce the taxable profit of the partnership.

The following items merit special attention:

(a) *Salary* The tax treatment of a 'salary' payable to a 'partner' depends on whether the Revenue regard the recipient as a true partner sharing in the profits in a particular, agreed way (the decision to allocate profits in this way is normally taken to ensure that one partner is entitled to an agreed portion of profit in priority to the other partners) or whether the recipient is merely an employee in receipt of a salary who is described as a 'partner'. In making their decision, the Revenue will consider all the facts and the terms of the partnership agreement entered into by the parties. The terms of the agreement are not conclusive (*Stekel* v *Ellice* [1973] 1 WLR 191). Where salary is treated as an allocation of profit, it is not deductible from the firm's taxable profits. Where it is a true salary, it is deductible and will be assessed under Schedule E with tax deducted at source under the PAYE procedure.

(b) *Interest* 'Interest' payable to a partner will not be a deductible expense if it is payable on a partner's contribution of capital to the firm. Such a payment is regarded as part of the agreed method of allocating profits. However, if a partner makes a loan to the partnership, interest payable on the loan will normally be a deductible expense.

(c) *Rent* Where a partnership pays rent to a partner for the use of assets owned by the partner the amount of the rent will be a deductible expense (unless it is excessive).

Once the taxable profit on which the partnership is to be assessed to tax in a particular year has been calculated, the 'precedent partner' must make a return of the partnership income to the Revenue. (The precedent partner is normally the partner whose name appears first in the partnership agreement.)

In addition, each partner submits a personal tax return to the Inland Revenue showing his share of the partnership profit (including any 'salary' and/or 'interest' on capital which falls to be treated as an allocation of profit, where appropriate), together with full details of other sources of income (if any) and his entitlement to personal reliefs and charges on income, if any. The Inland Revenue calculates how much tax is due from each partner on his partnership income and then, having added together all such amounts, issues a joint assessment in the partnership name for the total amount due (s. 111 ICTA 1988).

The Revenue provides the precedent partner with information as to how the bill was calculated so that the total tax bill can be apportioned amongst the partners. The tax is due in two equal instalments, on 1 January in the current tax year and 1 July in the following tax year.

The individual partners can remit their own share of the amount due to the Inland Revenue direct or the firm can pay the whole payment and charge the individual partners for their share.

Example A and B are in partnership sharing profits equally. A is a married man; he has charges on income of £2,000. B is an unmarried woman; she has charges on income of £5,000. The taxable profits of the partnership to be assessed in 1993-94 are £30,000.

	A £	B £
Share of partnership profit	15,000	15,000
Income from other sources	—	—
Personal reliefs: Single person's	(3,445)	(3,445)
Married couple's:	(1,720)	—
Charge on income	(2,000)	(5,000)
	7,835	6,555
Tax at 20% on first £2,500	500	500
Tax at 25% on balance	1,333.75	1,013.75

The partnership's tax liability is £3,347.50. A and B are jointly liable for the whole amount.

If there is a change in the profit-sharing ratio, the income is allocated to each partner for tax purposes according to the ratio in the year of assessment rather than that used in the accounting period to which the income relates.

For example, A and B are in partnership; they share profits equally until 6 April 1993 when A's share goes up to 75% and B's down to 25%. The profits for accounting periods ending on 31 December are:

1991	£10,000
1992	£10,000
1993	£20,000

The income for tax purposes will be:

	Partnership	*A*	*B*
1992-93	£10,000	£ 5,000	£5,000
1993-94	£10,000	£ 7,500	£2,500
1994-95	£20,000	£15,000	£5,000

Thus A pays tax on £27,500 during the three years of assessment even though during the corresponding three accounting periods his receipts from the partnership were:

1991	£ 5,000	
1992	£ 5,000	
1993	£13,750 approx	(½ share of profits 1 Jan-5 Apr i.e., 5,000 ÷ 2 = 2,500
		¾ share of profits 6 Apr-31 Dec i.e., 15,000 ÷ ¾ = 11,250)
	£23,750	

The rules applicable if a partner dies or retires or joins the firm are considered in **Chapter 14**.

When a partnership makes a loss, each partner can choose what type of relief to claim in respect of his share of the loss. For example, some of the partners may prefer to claim relief under s. 380 ICTA 1988 and s. 72 FA 1991 immediately; others may prefer to wait and claim relief under s. 385 ICTA 1988. The discontinuance caused by death, retirement or the admission of a new partner does not give the whole partnership a right to claim relief under ss. 388 and 389 ICTA 1988 (terminal loss relief) or under s. 381 ICTA 1988 (relief for losses of new trades): only the leaving or joining partners, respectively, may claim such reliefs.

Partners, being self-employed, are liable to make national insurance contributions at a rate lower than the rate applicable to employees (but the benefits are correspondingly lower), and they are entitled to deduct one half of their contributions when calculating their income tax liability.

FOURTEEN

THE TAX CONSEQUENCES OF LEAVING AND JOINING A PARTNERSHIP

14.1 Introduction

In **Chapter 5** we saw that it was possible for an individual to cease to be a partner on the happening of one of the following events:

(a) the dissolution of the partnership;
(b) his retirement; or
(c) expulsion from the partnership.

In **Chapter 5** we explained that if the partnership is dissolved the partnership will come to an end, whereas on retirement or on expulsion the remaining partners or partner can carry on the business, albeit through the medium of a newly constituted partnership or as a sole proprietorship.

Having considered the legal consequences of the occurrence of these events in **Chapter 5**, we will concentrate in this chapter on the tax consequences (particularly the circumstances in which tax charges can arise). We will only consider the tax exemptions and reliefs where they are of special relevance.

We will also consider the position of a new partner joining the firm, whether or not as a replacement for a deceased, retired or expelled partner.

In this chapter we will not repeat the legal consequences so the reader is recommended to review **Chapter 5** for this information.

14.2 The Tax Consequences of the Dissolution of a Partnership

14.2.1 INTRODUCTION

If a partnership is dissolved by one of the methods explained in **Chapter 5**, the partnership relationship ceases and the assets of the business must be realised. From this will flow various tax consequences.

14.2.2 INCOME TAX

The profits of the partnership are normally assessed to tax on the preceding year basis (see **13.3.1**) but if there is a permanent cessation (on a closure of the business) the closing year rules set out in s. 63 ICTA 1988 will be applied (see **13.3.3**).

Where there is a change in the persons engaged in carrying on any trade, profession or vocation under Case I or II of Schedule D, s. 113(1) ICTA 1988 provides that the closing year rules will apply to this deemed cessation. However, it is possible for an election to be made under s. 113(2) that the business be treated as continuing for tax purposes provided at least one 'partner' continues in the business before and after the change and all the partners involved in the business before and after the change make the election. (It should be noted that dissolution of the partnership will mean that there will be no *continuing* partnership. Therefore the special opening year rules set out in ss. 61 and 62 ICTA 1988 (see **14.3.2** below) will not apply.)

Where a partnership is dissolved, the business may sometimes be continued for a period pending the final realisation of assets. If, at the time of the dissolution, there is a change in the persons engaged in the partnership (for example, where one partner dies and the surviving partners continue the business pending realisation), the closing year rules will be applied at the time of the dissolution unless the election to have the business treated as continuing is made.

If the partnership has been claiming capital allowances on, for example, the plant and machinery used in the business, balancing charges may be levied if the assets are disposed of for more than their written-down value on cessation. Balancing allowances may be claimed if the market value of the assets is less than their written-down value.

Finally, if the partnership has made losses, loss relief under ss. 380 and 382 ICTA 1988 in respect of the final tax year of the trade may be claimed. Terminal loss relief under ss. 388 and 389 ICTA 1988 will permit the partners to carry back losses made in the final 12 months of the trade against the profits of the same trade during the immediately preceding three tax years.

14.2.3   CAPITAL GAINS TAX

If the partnership property is sold to outsiders following dissolution any gains realised by each partner on the disposal of his fractional share of the assets will be taxable in accordance with general principles. The general principles will also apply when a partner disposes of assets he owns personally but which have been used by the partnership.

The position is more complicated where the assets are disposed of to some of the former partners. In these circumstances para. 3 of the Revenue's Statement of Practice D/12 will be relevant. This provides that where a partnership distributes an asset in kind to one or more of the partners, a partner who receives the asset will not be regarded as disposing of his fractional share in it (although the other partners *will* be disposing of their shares in the asset). The Statement of Practice requires that a computation be done of the gains which would be chargeable on the individual partners if the asset had been disposed of at its current market value. Where this results in a gain being attributed to a partner not receiving the asset, the gain will be charged at the time of the distribution of the asset. Where, however, the gain is allocated to a partner receiving the asset concerned there will be no charge on distribution. Instead, his capital gains tax acquisition cost which is to be carried forward will be the market value of the asset at the date of distribution as reduced by the amount of his gain. (The same principles will be applied where the computation results in a loss.)

Example   A, B and C decide to dissolve their partnership and agree that, in satisfaction of his right to share in the asset surpluses, A should receive one particular partnership asset which the partnership acquired for £60,000 in 1983 and which is now worth £90,000. (The partners shared profits and asset surpluses equally.) The changes in their respective interests in the asset are as follows:

	Before £	Current market value £	After £
A	20,000 (⅓)	30,000 (⅓)	90,000
B	20,000 (⅓)	30,000 (⅓)	—
C	20,000 (⅓)	30,000 (⅓)	—

Taking into account para. 3 of the Revenue's Statement, the gain realised on a notional disposal at current market value is calculated. This means that B and C will each be charged to CGT on £10,000 (subject to indexation). A is not charged on a gain of £10,000 (subject to indexation), his acquisition costs for the purposes of calculating his future CGT liability will be the market value of the asset less his share of the notional gain, i.e., £90,000 − £10,000 = £80,000. Thus para. 3 effectively gives rise to an automatic hold-over of A's gain.

14.2.4 INHERITANCE TAX

If the assets of the partnership are disposed of at full market value on dissolution, there will be no reduction in the value of the transferor's estate and, therefore, no transfer of value. If there is no transfer of value there cannot be any IHT liability. However, a charge to tax can arise on dissolution caused by death although (provided the necessary conditions are satisfied) business property relief will be available and this is considered in paragraph **14.4.4** below.

14.3 The Tax Consequences of the Retirement of a Partner

14.3.1 INTRODUCTION

As we explained in **Chapter 5**, while 'retirement' implies a person retiring from full-time work having reached normal retirement age, in the partnership context 'retirement' simply means leaving the partnership voluntarily so that the age of the 'retiring' partner is irrelevant. In this section we have examined the tax charges which can arise when there is such a change in the partnership.

14.3.2 INCOME TAX

14.3.2.1 Deemed cessation under s. 113 ICTA 1988

On retirement, whenever there is a change in the persons engaged in carrying on any trade, profession or vocation under Case I or Case II of Schedule D, this will result in a deemed discontinuance of the partnership under s. 113(1) ICTA 1988. This deemed discontinuance applies when a new partner joins the partnership (whether or not he replaces a retired partner) and when a partnership is dissolved.

The deemed discontinuance will result in the closing years rules set out in s. 63 ICTA 1988 applying to the partnership as originally constituted and the opening years rules in ss. 60-62 ICTA 1988 applying to the changed partnership. (The opening and closing years rules are considered in **Chapter 13**.)

However, the deemed discontinuance imposed by s. 113(1) only applies to the profits of the partnership, not to any losses realised. Therefore, terminal loss relief under ss. 388 and 389 ICTA 1988 will only be available to a retiring partner, not to a continuing partner. Similarly, relief under s. 381 ICTA 1988 (for losses realised by new, unincorporated businesses) will only be available to new partners.

It is possible, under s. 113(2), to elect that the business be treated as continuing. In cases where the opening and closing year rules would be disadvantageous for the business, such an election should be made. Broadly speaking, the deemed discontinuance can be disadvantageous where the profits of the partnership increase regularly from year to year. This is because the preceding year basis (as to which see **13.3.1**) ensures that the partners' taxable income, in any tax year, will be less than their actual share of profits received in that year. (The interrelation between the opening and closing years rules is such that a cessation occurring at the end of the fifth year of the life of a firm used to give rise to part of the profit for that five-year period escaping tax. This benefit has been restricted by ss. 61 and 62 ICTA 1988, which is considered below.)

If the profits of the firm remain steady, or actually decline, the deemed discontinuance may be advantageous because the partners will be assessed on the actual profits realised in the relevant tax years, which may be less than the profits on which they would have been assessed under the preceding year basis.

The election must be made within two years of the change. It must be made, in writing, by all partners, both old and new. If a deceased partner is being treated, under the terms of the partnership agreement, as a retiring partner so that the partnership can continue, his personal representatives must join in an election.

Because of the need for all the partners, both old and new, to concur in the s. 113(2) election, the partnership agreement should provide that new partners must agree to the election before joining the firm. Furthermore, there should be a provision to the effect that retiring partners (and the personal representatives of a deceased partner, if appropriate) can be required to concur with the election if the continuing partners so request.

If the election is made, the newly constituted partnership will be assessed on the preceding year basis. In the year of the change, this will mean that the partners in the new firm will be assessed on the profits earned by the partners in the old firm. While this can result in the partners in the newly constituted firm paying tax on profits they never received, this will only be a disadvantage if they pay *more* tax than they would have done had the opening year rules applied.

In order to give protection should any of the partners in the new firm be prejudiced, it is customary for the retiring partners (or the personal representatives of a deceased partner if appropriate) to give an indemnity against any *additional* tax which becomes payable by the partners in the new firm. However, the former partner does not necessarily have to make a payment under the indemnity provision.

It used to be possible to take advantage of the relationship between the opening and closing years rules to gain a tax advantage. Some successful firms made a practice of making a change in the membership of the partnership every five years but not electing for continuance. In order to prevent the opening and closing years rules being abused, ss. 61 and 62 ICTA 1988 were enacted. They provide that (save where the new partnership genuinely carries on a business which is different from that carried on by the old partnership, when ss. 61 and 62 apply) following a change in the persons engaged in the partnership business within s. 113(1), when no s. 113(2) election is made, the opening years of the new partnership will be assessed as follows:

Year of change and the three subsequent years	Actual profits of each tax year
Fifth and subsequent years	Preceding year basis

The partnership will have the option to elect for the actual basis to be applied in assessing the profits of the fifth and sixth tax years.

14.3.2.2 Provision of income for retired partners

The methods by which former partners can provide themselves with an income during their retirement are considered in **Chapter 19**. The income tax consequences of retirement annuities (whether paid under approved annuity contracts or by the former partners) and consultancy arrangements are not considered further here.

14.3.3 CAPITAL GAINS TAX

Disposals by a firm are subject to the normal CGT principles in determining whether a gain has arisen. However, the lack of a comprehensive body of legislation dealing with the taxation of capital gains realised by partners led to difficulties. The Revenue's Statements of Practice D/12, SP 1/79 and SP 1/89 set out the Revenue's view of the way in which general capital gains tax principles apply in a partnership context. The underlying principle on which the Statement of Practice D/12 is based is that each partner is to be treated as owning a fractional share of each of the chargeable assets of the partnership (including goodwill). This concept forms the basis of the rules which follow.

In this section we will consider the capital gains tax consequences which arise, according to the Statements of Practice, when there is a change in the personnel of the partnership (principally on the retirement of a partner or when a new partner is admitted). In addition, the effect of changing the asset surplus sharing ratio will also be considered.

Where one partner retires from the business he will normally relinquish his interest in the partnership assets in consideration of a capital sum and/or the provision of an income. The retiring partner's present interest in the business is shown on his capital account. He will be treated as making a disposal of that interest to the continuing partners (and to any new partners who are being admitted on his retirement). The continuing (and new) partners will acquire his interest and will thereafter have a greater interest in the business.

Example A, B, C and D share profits (and asset surplus) equally. The assets of the firm were acquired for £60,000. A is retiring and once he has retired, all the profits will be divided equally between B, C and D. The asset-sharing ratio will change as follows:

	Before £	*After* £
A	15,000 (¼)	(—)
B	15,000 (¼)	20,000 (⅓)
C	15,000 (¼)	20,000 (⅓)
D	15,000 (¼)	20,000 (⅓)

A has disposed of his ¼ interest to the continuing partners and is left with nothing. Each of the continuing partners receives ⅓ of A's ¼ share (i.e., $^1/_{12}$th share in the partnership property).

It can be clearly seen from the above example that the retiring partner has made a disposal to the continuing partners. The question then arises of whether or not the disposal has realised a gain (or a loss). Where the assets have not been revalued in the accounts and the retiring partner receives an amount equivalent to the balance on his capital account, he is simply receiving the return of his original capital contribution. There will be no gain and no loss (D/12 para. 4). For example, in the above illustration, if A was paid £15,000 he would realise neither a gain nor a loss.

However, there will be a gain on disposal where assets have been revalued in the accounts (D/12 para. 5). Where assets have increased in value since the date of acquisition the partners may wish to record this increase in the accounts; the process is referred to as a 'revaluation'. The values of the various assets are increased in the accounts and the balances on the partners' capital accounts are increased by a corresponding amount in order to reflect the increase in the worth of the business. A revaluation of itself gives rise to no charge to CGT since there has been no disposal. However, if after a revaluation there is a change in the asset surplus sharing ratio, for example on retirement, the disponer partner will receive more than his original capital contribution and (subject to indexation and other reliefs) there will be a charge to capital gains tax.

Example The facts are as in the previous example but the partnership decides that prior to A's retirement the assets should be revalued from £60,000 to £90,000. A's ¼ share will be worth £22,500. Therefore A will be treated as disposing of assets for £22,500 which were acquired for £15,000, and will have a capital gain of £7,500.

	Before £	On revaluation £	After £
A	15,000 (¼)	22,500 (¼)	—
B	15,000 (¼)	22,500 (¼)	30,000 (⅓)
C	15,000 (¼)	22,500 (¼)	30,000 (⅓)
D	15,000 (¼)	22,500 (¼)	30,000 (⅓)
	60,000	90,000	90,000

B, C and D will each be treated as acquiring ⅓ of A's share in the assets and therefore their respective base costs will increase from £22,500 to £30,000. They are, therefore holding assets which have increased in value to them from £15,000 to £30,000. When they realise the assets, there will be a CGT liability (subject to indexation).

An apparent way for a retiring partner to avoid a CGT liability where assets have increased in value would be for the partnership to refrain from revaluing the assets in the accounts and simply to return to the retiring partner the balance on his capital account. After that the continuing partners would make a cash payment to the retiring partner outside the accounts. However, the Revenue's Statement of Practice (D/12) states that when, on a change of partnership sharing ratios, payments are made directly between two or more partners outside the framework of the accounts, the payments represent *an additional consideration* for the retiring partner's share in the assets. Thus, such payments increase the value received by the retiring partner on the disposal.

Example The facts are as in the first example. Instead of revaluing the assets in the accounts, the partners agree that they will pay A the £15,000 due to him on his capital account *and* will pay him an additional £7,500 outside the accounts as a separate matter. As a result of the Statement of Practice, A is to be treated as receiving £15,000 + £7,500 and will, therefore, have a capital gain (subject to indexation) of £7,500.

The members of the partnership, in order to minimise the burden of finding large capital sums, may agree not to revalue assets as and when partners retire. It could be argued that this is a gift by each retiring partner of his share in the increased value of the asset. In the case of a gift (or sale at an under-value), the Revenue can treat the disposal as made for market value unless it was a bargain made at arm's length. In the case of connected persons, transfers are always treated as otherwise than by way of bargains made at arm's length. Partners are normally connected but will not be when transferring property to each other provided the disposal *was pursuant to a bona fide commercial arrangement*. Thus, provided there is some bona fide commercial reason for not revaluing, the Revenue will not seek to substitute market value.

Even where the partners are connected other than by partnership (for example, father and son) the Revenue have stated that they will only seek to substitute market value where the transaction would not have been entered into by persons who were not at arm's length.

14.3.3.1 Entitlement to reliefs

If a charge to tax arises on the disposal by a partner of his interest in partnership property, the disponer will be entitled to claim the benefit of the CGT exemptions and reliefs in the normal way. One relief which may be of special relevance is the retirement relief given by ss. 163 and 164 of and sch. 6 to the Taxation of Chargeable Gains Act 1992.

An individual aged 55 or an individual who has retired under that age on the grounds of ill-health, is entitled to claim a full exemption from charge for gains up to a maximum of £150,000 and an exemption for 50% of gains between £150,000 and £600,000 for gains realised on the disposal of its assets. A former partner who satisfies the age or ill-health condition must have owned the interest in the partnership for at least one year before he qualifies for any relief. Once he has owned the interest for exactly one year he is entitled to a proportion of the full available relief; the limits of £150,000 and £600,000 are scaled down. Thus if a partner has owned an interest for one year he is entitled to a full exemption for gains up to a maximum of one-tenth of £150,000 (i.e., £15,000) and an exemption for 50% of gains from £15,000 to one-tenth of £600,000 (i.e., £60,000).

14.3.3.2 Changes in the asset surplus sharing ratios

The principles dealt with above, applicable where one partner is retiring from the firm and giving up his entire interest in the firm, apply equally where a partner gives up part of his interest in a firm. This may be done because new partners are admitted or it may be done in order to give existing partners a greater share in the assets of the partnership.

The partners who are reducing their interest in the assets are treated as making a disposal of part of their interest.

Example A and B share profits and assets surplus equally. The assets were acquired for £60,000. A and B agree that A will make a disposal to B of one half of A's interest so that, in future, the ratio will be ³⁄₄ : ¹⁄₄.

A is giving up half of his existing entitlement and is, therefore, disposing of assets acquired for £15,000.

	Before	*After*
	£	£
A	30,000 (½)	15,000 (¼)
B	30,000 (½)	45,000 (¾)

A is making a disposal. As in the case of retirement the question arises of whether there has been a gain (or loss). The same principles apply. Thus, if there has been no revaluation, there is no gain on the disposal. If there has been a revaluation in the accounts there will be a gain on the disposal (subject to indexation). If there is no revaluation but a payment is made outside the accounts the payment is treated as an additional part of any consideration received by the disposing partner.

A partner may decide to dispose of part of his interest in the partnership assets to existing (or new) partners without requiring full consideration. The question will arise of whether or not the Revenue can treat the disposer as disposing of the asset at market value. As stated above, no such substitution will occur as between partners who are not otherwise connected, provided the disposal is made pursuant to a bona fide commercial arrangement.

If there is no bona fide commercial arrangement (or if the partners are connected otherwise than by partnership and the transaction is not such as would have been entered into by persons at arm's length), the Revenue can substitute market value. The partners can elect for hold-over relief of the gain attributable to the gift element.

14.3.3.3 Goodwill

Goodwill presents particular problems. In recent years partners (particularly in professional firms) who paid for a share in the goodwill of the firm when they were admitted to partnership have agreed not to charge incoming partners for a share (the burden of finding a large capital sum being regarded as too great). The effect of this is that the old partners write off goodwill. It is clear that when an old partner retires and receives no payment for the goodwill he makes a loss on that asset. Many partnerships have argued that the old partners are entitled to make a claim for CGT loss relief when the value of goodwill is written off. (Section 24(2) Taxation of Chargeable Gains Act 1992 provides that where an inspector is satisfied that the value of an asset has become negligible he may allow an immediate loss.) The Revenue resist such claims, taking the view that the goodwill still has a value and does not become negligible simply because the partners choose not to charge for it. However, claims for immediate loss relief have been successful in front of the General and the Special Commissioners. The position is unsettled and the practice varies between inspectors, some being prepared to allow such claims and some not.

14.3.3.4 Payment of annuities

A partnership may agree to pay a retiring partner an annuity. The annuity will be subject to income tax in the hands of the recipient partner. If it is more than can be regarded as reasonable recognition of the past contribution of work and effort by the partner to the partnership, the Revenue will treat the capitalised value of the annuity as consideration for the disposal of the retiring partner's share in the assets. An annuity will be regarded as reasonable for this purpose if:

(a) the former partner had been in the partnership for at least 10 years;
(b) the annuity is no more than ⅔ of his average share of profits in the best three of the last seven years in which he was required to devote substantially the whole of his time to acting as a partner.

For periods of less than 10 years, fractions other than ⅔ will be used.

14.3.3.5 Disposal of assets owned by partners personally

Where a partner disposes of an asset which he owns personally but which is used by the partnership, the Statements of Practice are not relevant. On such disposals the normal CGT principles are applied to ascertain whether a gain or loss has arisen. Similarly, the disposing partner will be able to claim any relevant exemptions or reliefs, save that retirement relief will only be available to relieve the gain realised on the disposal of such an asset if the disposal is associated with the partner's disposal of his share in the partnership on reaching 55 or on retirement under that age on ill-health grounds.

14.3.4 INHERITANCE TAX

Normal principles of IHT apply in the partnership context. Thus, where a partner sells an interest in the partnership for full consideration there is no transfer of value and therefore no charge to IHT arises. If a partner sells an interest for less than full consideration or transfers it for no consideration at all, prima facie a charge to IHT will arise. However, s. 10 IHTA 1984 provides that a disposition is *not* a transfer of value if it was not intended to confer gratuitous benefit and was either made at arm's length between unconnected persons or, if between connected persons, was such as might be expected to be made between unconnected persons. Partners are not connected persons in respect of transfers between partners of partnership assets pursuant to bona fide commercial arrangements. Thus many transfers which might appear to be chargeable may escape IHT on the ground that there was no intention to confer a gratuitous benefit.

It is common for partners to agree that on their retirement (or death) their share of goodwill is to accrue automatically to the other partners without payment. This has the benefit of relieving the partnership of the need to pay for portions of goodwill as and when partners retire. Section 163(1) of IHTA 1984 provides that where a person enters into a contract which excludes or restricts the right to dispose of any property the exclusion or restriction will be ignored in valuing the asset when it is next transferred except to the extent that consideration for the exclusion or restriction was given. The effect of s. 163 is that, unless consideration is given for the accruer clause, the clause will be ignored when the goodwill is valued on the next transfer and the full value of the retiring (or deceased) partner's share in the goodwill will be charged to tax. (There is also a possibility of an immediate charge to tax on the entry into the clause; in that case, however, credit is given on the later transfer for the value brought into charge on entering into the agreement (s. 163 IHTA 1984).) However, it seems likely that the Revenue will follow the approach in *Att.-Gen.* v *Boden* [1912] 1 KB 539, and look at the covenants entered into by all the partners (which may include an agreement to pay an annuity to the former partner) to assess whether what is given up is a fair equivalent of what is received.

In the event that an inter vivos transaction is regarded as the transfer of value it will be potentially exempt. If the transferor dies within seven years the transfer will be treated as if it had always been chargeable. An interest in the partnership is relevant business property qualifying for business property relief at 100% provided:

   (a)   the transferor had owned the property for at least two years at the time of the transfer;

   (b)   the transferee still owns the property (or replacement property) and it still qualifies as relevant business property.

Where there is a gift of land, buildings, plant or machinery owned by a partner personally but used wholly or mainly for the purpose of the partnership of which he is a member, a reduction of only 50% is available.

The transferor's annual exemption may be available for the tax year of transfer and the preceding tax year, in which case it will reduce the value transferred.

When ascertaining the rate of tax chargeable on the inter vivos transfer it will be necessary to cumulate any chargeable transfers made in the seven years before the transfer in question. Tapering relief will be available if the transferor survives three years from the date of the transfer. The burden of the inheritance tax will fall on the transferee (unless the transferor provides otherwise in his will). In cases where the potential liability is large the transferee may wish to consider insuring the transferor's life. The option to pay inheritance tax by instalments will be available. The first will be due six months after the end of the month of the transferor's death. Interest will not be payable unless an instalment is late.

14.4   The Tax Consequences of Death

14.4.1   INTRODUCTION

As we saw in **Chapter 5**, death causes the automatic dissolution of a partnership, although it is common to provide in partnership agreements that the deceased partner is to be treated as if he had retired (thus avoiding the automatic dissolution of the partnership). In this section, we look at the tax consequences of the death of a partner.

14.4.2   INCOME TAX

Whether the death is treated in the same manner as a retirement (because of the provisions of the partnership agreement) or as causing a dissolution of the partnership (because the partnership agreement is silent on the point), the death will result in a change in the persons engaged in carrying on the partnership's trade, profession or vocation. There will, therefore, be a deemed cessation of the business under s. 113(1) ICTA 1988 and the closing years rules will apply unless an election under s. 113(2) ICTA 1988 is made to have the partnership's trade assessed on a continuing basis (see **14.3.2** above). The personal representatives of a deceased partner will have to join in the election if the partnership is not being dissolved and it is, therefore, desirable that the partnership agreement should include a term requiring them to do so.

14.4.3   CAPITAL GAINS TAX

The deceased partner's interest in the partnership assets is *acquired* by his personal representatives at market value on the date of death. Since a disposal is a prerequisite for liability to CGT, this means that no CGT is payable on death and that unrealised gains arising during the deceased's lifetime escape the charge to tax.

The continuing partners may incur a capital gains tax liability if, in order to pay the amount due to the deceased partner's estate (and/or dependants) they have to sell partnership assets which have increased in value since acquisition.

14.4.4   INHERITANCE TAX

The estate of a deceased partner will include his interest in the partnership assets. Under s. 4(1) IHTA 1984, the partner is deemed to make a transfer of value on his death and the value transferred is the value of the assets in his estate immediately before his death. Accordingly, subject to exemptions, reliefs and the deceased partner's cumulative total at the date of death, IHT will be payable in respect of the market value of his share in the partnership.

Changes in the value of assets resulting from death are taken into account for IHT purposes. If all or part of the value of the goodwill of the business was personal to the deceased partner the value of the goodwill, and therefore of the business, will fall as a result of the death. The reduced value of the deceased partner's share in the business will then be included in his estate for IHT purposes.

The value of the deceased's share may be reduced as a result of an option to purchase held by the other partners. Thus, if the partnership agreement provides that on the death of a partner, his fellow partners will have an option to buy the deceased partner's share in the partnership assets for a fixed sum, the value of the assets for the purposes of IHT will be the agreed fixed sum, provided the option was granted for consideration in money or money's worth (s. 163 IHTA 1984) which was considered in more detail in **14.3.4** above concerning automatic accruer clauses in relation to the goodwill of the business. The points made in connection with such clauses applying on retirement apply equally on death. Therefore, provided full consideration was given for the clause, no IHT liability will arise on the death of one of the partners (*Att.-Gen.* v *Boden* [1912] 1 KB 539).

Where an IHT liability does arise on death it may be reduced by virtue of the relief for business property given by ss. 103-114 IHTA 1984 (and considered above in **14.3.4**).

However, there is no entitlement to claim the relief if the assets are the subject of a binding contract for sale at the time of death. A clause in the partnership agreement to the effect that the surviving partners are *obliged* to buy and the personal representatives of the deceased partner are *obliged* to sell the deceased partner's share may have been included in the agreement for sound commercial reasons but it will result in the loss of business property relief. This is because the Revenue regard such clauses as amounting to binding contracts (see Statement of Practice 12/80 dated 13 October 1980). If there is no *obligation* to buy and sell, the relief is available and so this difficulty can be avoided by the use of an option arrangement or an automatic accruer clause.

IHT attributable to an interest in partnership property can be paid in 10 yearly instalments under ss. 227 and 228 IHTA 1984. The first instalment is due six months after the end of the month of death and no interest is due unless an instalment is late. If the interest in partnership property is sold all outstanding IHT must be paid off. Where the continuing partners purchase the interest of a deceased partner the instalment option will not thereafter be available to the deceased partner's estate.

14.5   The Tax Consequences of Expulsion from a Partnership

In **Chapter 5** we saw that s. 25 of the Partnership Act 1890 provides that the majority of the partners can expel any partner unless a power to do so has been conferred by express agreement between the partners. If the partnership agreement does contain such a power and it is exercised, the tax consequences of expulsion are the same as for retirement.

14.6   The Tax Consequences of Admission of a New Partner

14.6.1   INTRODUCTION

Although this chapter is primarily concerned with leaving a partnership, the admission of new partners is a topic so closely connected that it seems appropriate to deal with it here. The tax consequences of a new partner joining the firm have largely been dealt with in connection with retirement but for the sake of completeness a brief summary will be given here.

14.6.2 INCOME TAX

When a new partner joins a partnership, there will be a change in the persons engaged in carrying on the partnership's trade, profession or vocation. This will result in a deemed cessation of the business under s. 113(1) ICTA 1988 and the application of the closing years rules (see **14.3.2** above) unless an election under s. 113(2) is made by all the partners both old (or their personal representatives, if appropriate) and new. Since the s. 113(2) election will result in the partnership's profits being assessed on the preceding year basis, the new partner will be assessed on profits he never received. To avoid him being prejudiced by this, the partnership agreement should contain a clause under which the partners in the old firm will indemnify him against this additional tax liability.

If the new partner has to borrow money to raise the funds to buy into the partnership, the borrower will be able to deduct the interest as a charge on his income. The same relief is available if the borrower uses the funds to contribute additional capital to the partnership or to make a loan to the partnership, if it is used exclusively for the partnership's business purposes.

14.6.3 CAPITAL GAINS TAX

A newly admitted partner will acquire an interest in the partnership assets either by purchase or by gift. Thus, if the old partners give the incoming partner a one-third share in profits and asset surpluses, he will acquire one third of the value of the partnership assets at that date. That value will be his acquisition value.

Example A and B, who share profits and assets equally, decide to admit C and to share profits and assets equally thereafter. The partnership assets are shown in the accounts as worth £120,000 at the date of C's admission.

	Before	*After*
	£	£
A	60,000 (½)	40,000 (⅓)
B	60,000 (½)	40,000 (⅓)
C	—	40,000 (⅓)

C's acquisition value is, therefore, £40,000. A and B have disposed of a part of their share in the assets surplus. As discussed above there will be no charge to CGT on such a disposal provided there has been no upward revaluation of the assets in the accounts and provided no payment is made. The old partners are treated as making a disposal for a consideration equal to their capital gains tax cost so that there will be neither a chargeable gain nor an allowable loss at that point. They will carry forward a smaller proportion of cost to set against a subsequent disposal of their assets. The Inland Revenue will not seek to substitute market value in such a case since the transaction is likely to be a bona fide commercial transaction where the continuing partners dispose of a share in the asset surpluses but in consideration of the incoming partner covenanting to devote himself to the partnership. If there has been an upward revaluation in the accounts there will be a potential charge to CGT.

If the incoming partner makes a payment of cash the effect of such a payment depends upon whether it is a contribution of capital which is to be credited to his capital account or whether it is a payment to the old partners. In the former case no cash has been paid to the old partners and so there is no assessment to CGT; in the latter case there can be an assessment to CGT irrespective of whether the payment is made through the accounts (in which case the amount paid will be credited to the capital accounts of the old partners) or whether it is made outside the accounts to each partner individually.

14.6.4   INHERITANCE TAX

Inheritance tax is unlikely to be an immediate problem for a newly admitted partner. However, he might be the recipient of a potentially exempt transfer of value. If so, it is possible that the transfer will become chargeable if one or more of the transferor partners dies within seven years. The donee of an inter vivos transfer of partnership property may exercise the right to pay by way of 10 equal yearly instalments, the first due six months after the end of the month of transfer. Interest is not charged unless an instalment is late.

FIFTEEN

THE CORPORATION TAX SYSTEM

15.1 Introduction

In this chapter, we will look at how the corporation tax system works and the chapter will concentrate on the tax liability of companies. The tax liabilities of the recipients of income from companies (whether the income be in the form of dividends, debenture interest or directors' fees) will be considered in **Chapter 16**. The inheritance tax and capital gains tax liabilities of shareholders in respect of shares will be considered in **Chapter 18**.

15.2 Calculation of Profits — Corporation Tax

15.2.1 INCOME

Companies pay corporation tax on their profits. For the purposes of the tax, unincorporated associations (such as members' clubs), other than partnerships, local authorities and local authority associations, are taxed as companies (s. 832(1) ICTA 1988). 'Profits' means income and capital gains (s. 6(4)(a) ICTA 1988).

Income profits are calculated according to income tax principles (see **Chapter 13**), so that the various schedules of income are as relevant for corporation tax as for income tax. Similarly, the rules for deduction of expenses which apply for income tax purposes also apply to corporation tax (s. 9 ICTA 1988). There are some exceptions to these rules, particularly in relation to dividends, losses, charges on income and capital allowances. Companies, unlike individuals, have no right to claim any personal allowances.

15.2.2 CHARGES ON INCOME

A charge on income is defined for corporation tax purposes as any yearly interest, annuity or other annual payment and any other interest (i.e., interest on a loan for a period which cannot exceed a year) paid to a bank. Sums which are deductible as business expenses are not within the definition. A charge on income payable out of profits may be deducted from profits liable to corporation tax. Deduction is not, however, permitted unless the charge was incurred for valuable and sufficient consideration. Individuals may also deduct certain items as charges on income in computing tax liability (see **13.2**), but the definition of charges on income is in some respects wider (for example, mortgage interest relief is available) and in others narrower (some covenanted payments are not deductible) than for corporation tax purposes. Charges should be distinguished from business expenses (which are deductible from receipts in calculating profits rather than from profits once calculated). A charge on income is deducted when paid, whereas a business expense is deducted when it accrues due.

15.2.3   CAPITAL ALLOWANCES

Companies are entitled to claim the allowances at the same rates as individuals (see **Chapter 17**). Capital allowances of companies are treated as trading expenses of the accounting period in respect of which they are claimed, and balancing charges are treated as trading receipts of that period. For income tax purposes, capital allowances and balancing charges are technically not trading expenses and receipts, but the practical differences between the two systems are slight.

15.2.4   CAPITAL GAINS

Capital gains of companies are calculated according to capital gains tax principles (s. 345(2) ICTA 1988).

Since companies are not individuals they are not entitled to annual exemptions. A company can, however, claim the relief for gains realised when replacing business assets set out in CGTA 1979, ss. 115-121 (see **Chapter 18**).

Retaining appreciating assets in a company can lead to an element of double taxation since, on realisation of the asset, the company pays tax (subject to the relief for replacement assets). The company's gain after tax may be reflected in an increase in the value of the company's assets. This will cause the value of the shares in the company to increase which will result in a greater gain being realised (subject to exemptions and reliefs) on a subsequent disposal of shares by the shareholder.

15.3   Assessment — Corporation Tax

15.3.1   BASIS OF ASSESSMENT

Although income tax and capital gains tax rules are used to calculate the amount of profit, the basis of assessment for corporation tax is quite different from either of those taxes. For income tax different bases apply for the various cases and schedules (for Schedule D Cases I and II see **Chapter 13**), and capital gains tax is payable on the gains made in each tax year. For corporation tax purposes, tax is calculated by reference to each accounting period of the company (s. 12 ICTA 1988). An accounting period is normally twelve months ending with the company's accounting date, that is, the date to which its accounts are made up. If the accounts are made up for a period of less than twelve months, then the accounting period is also less than twelve months; if for a longer period, special rules apply and the profits are divided on a time basis between two or more accounting periods, none of which may be longer than twelve months. Corporation tax is payable nine months after the end of the accounting period or, if later, one month after assessment (s. 10(1) ICTA 1988), so that the date chosen does not affect the length of time between the end of the period and the date of payment. Companies are generally liable to pay tax on trading profits considerably earlier than sole traders and partners, since the preceding year basis does not apply.

(With effect from 30 September 1993, unless the Revenue opts to delay its implementation, the new pay and file system under which companies will make their own assessments of their liability to corporation tax will come into effect. The new system will not affect the due date for payment of corporation tax, rather it will introduce a more efficient system for assessing and collecting corporation tax. Under the new system, companies will be required to complete a corporation tax return in which the company itself calculates its own corporation tax liability. The return must be delivered to the Revenue within 12 months of the end of the period to which it relates.)

15.3.2   RATES OF TAX

Although companies pay tax on the profits of their own accounting periods, the rate of tax is fixed for financial years, that is, periods starting on 1 April and ending on the following 31 March. For the financial year 1993 (i.e., the period 1 April 1993 to 31 March 1994) the rate is 33%.

Unless the company happens to make up its accounts to 31 March the profits will have to be apportioned (on a time basis) between two financial years if the rate changes. For example, a company makes up its accounts to 31 December. Its profits for the accounting period ending on 31 December 1994 are £1,460,000 — the rate of corporation tax for the financial year 1993 (1 April 1993—31 March 1994) is 33%, for the financial year 1994 (1 April 1994—31 March 1995) the rate is yet to be fixed. Assuming the rate for 1994 were 40%, corporation tax for the accounting period would be:

$$\begin{array}{ll} & \text{£} \\ \dfrac{90}{365} \times 1,460,000 \times 33\% = & 118,800 \\[2mm] \dfrac{275}{365} \times 1,460,000 \times 40\% = & 440,000 \\ & \overline{558,800} \end{array}$$

The normal rate of corporation tax for the financial year 1993 is 33%. However, s. 13 ICTA 1988 makes provision for a reduced rate in the case of a company with small profits. For this purpose 'profits' include income profits, capital gains and 'franked investment income' (i.e., dividends from another company except a company in the same group of companies). Loan interest may be deducted in calculating this figure. The reduced rate for the financial year 1993 is 25% and applies where the profits do not exceed £250,000 (the 'lower relevant maximum amount'). Where profits exceed the 'higher relevant maximum amount' (£1,250,000 for the financial year 1993) all profits, not just the excess over that figure are taxed at 33%. Where the amount of the profits falls between the two maximum amounts the effective rate of tax is between the lower and higher rates of tax. In such a case the rate can be calculated for 1993 by treating the first £250,000 as taxable at 25% and the excess at 37.5%. If the profits include franked investment income the calculation is more complicated since only the income profits get the benefit of the lower rate. The Act provides that the tax is first calculated at the full rate and then reduced by an amount expressed by the formula $(M - P) \times (I/P) \times$ (the statutory fraction) where M is the higher relevant maximum amount (£1,250,000), I is the profits other than franked investment income and P the total profits — the statutory fractions for the financial year 1993 is one-fiftieth.

15.4 Loss Relief under the Corporation Tax System

Trading losses of companies are relieved in a number of ways; the scheme of the legislation is very similar to the one which applies for income tax (see **Chapter 13**). When assessing the company's income liable to tax, losses are deducted from the profits of the relevant accounting period before charges on income are deducted.

Under s. 393 ICTA 1988, the company can carry forward a trading loss and use it to reduce the profits derived from the same trade in future accounting periods. The claim for relief under this section must be made within six years of the end of the accounting period in which the loss was made. This relief is similar to s. 385 for sole traders or partners. Section 393 can give relief for a charge on income which cannot be fully set off against trading profits provided the charge is made 'wholly and exclusively for the purposes of the trade'.

To illustrate the application of s. 393, the company has an accounting period corresponding with calendar years and its profits and losses are as follows:

	Trade I £	Trade II £	Capital Gains £
1990	75,000	25,000	Nil
1991	100,000	50,000	Nil
1992	100,000	50,000	20,000
1993	(300,000) loss	50,000	30,000
1994	100,000	50,000	Nil
1995	200,000	50,000	Nil

Under s. 393 the £300,000 loss incurred in Trade I in 1993 can only be carried forward against future profits of that same trade. Therefore, the profits made by Trade I in 1994 and 1995 will be wiped out but the profits from Trade II and the capital gains realised in the years 1993, 1994 and 1995 will all remain taxable.

In addition to or instead of the relief given by s. 393, a company may set a loss made during an accounting period off against any profits of the same accounting period if a claim for relief is made within two years of the end of the accounting period in which the loss was made. 'Profits' for corporation tax include both income and capital gains so that the company may set an income loss (from a trade) against a chargeable capital gain. If the loss is not entirely relieved by setting it off against profits of the same accounting period in which the loss was made, the company may also make a claim requiring the unrelieved part of the loss to be set against profits (including capital gains) for the previous three accounting periods (s. 393A ICTA 1988). A loss cannot be carried back under this provision to a period when the company was not carrying on the business and there are no corporation tax provisions corresponding with s. 381 ICTA 1988 (income tax loss relief for the early years of a new trade). Where relief is being claimed in respect of a loss which has been carried back under this provision, the carried back loss will be taken into account before charges on income incurred in the earlier accounting period are deducted but any loss made in the earlier year is taken before the carried back loss.

To illustrate the application of s. 393A and using the figures set out above, the £300,000 loss made in Trade I in 1993 can be used to wipe out the Trade II profits and capital gains for that year, reducing the loss to be carried back to £220,000.

Under s. 393A, any loss which is carried back must be set off against the profits of later periods first. The as yet unrelieved loss will, therefore, be set against the profits of 1992, leaving only £50,000 of the loss to be set against the profits of 1991. (This section replaces the relief for terminal losses which used to be available under s. 394 ICTA 1988.)

In deciding which method of relief to use, the company will wish to ensure, so far as possible, that the maximum tax saving is achieved (but setting the loss against those profits which are subject to tax at 33% rather than 25%). However, the cashflow problem of having to meet a tax bill at a time when the cash reserves may be low often means that it is preferable not to carry forward the relief but to claim the relief as soon as possible.

The possibility of carrying forward losses is lost in certain cases where there are substantial changes in both the ownership of the company and in the nature of its trade. This is an anti-avoidance provision designed to prevent the purchase of a company simply to take advantage of its tax losses.

If a company makes a capital loss (calculated in the same way as a capital gain), it may be set off against capital gains of the same accounting period and, if unrelieved, may be carried forward and set off against capital gains of later accounting periods. Although trading losses may be set off against capital gains there are no provisions allowing capital losses to be set off against income profits.

Section 402 ICTA 1988 makes provision for group relief. In outline, where a company is a member of a group it may surrender its loss to another company in the same group. The latter then deducts the loss from its profits as if it were its own loss. Companies are in the same group, broadly speaking, if one is the 75% subsidiary of the other or both are 75% subsidiaries of a third company. It should be noted that a taxpayer who runs a business liable to income tax and who also owns a company cannot set off a loss made in the trade against income of the company unless it is paid to him as income (e.g., as director's fees or dividends), in which case relief under s. 380 ICTA 1988 would be available. If the company makes a loss the proprietor cannot set it off against his income at all.

15.5 Close Companies

A close company is a company controlled by five or fewer participators or participators who are directors (s. 414 ICTA 1988). 'Participators' are shareholders, loan creditors and certain others entitled to participate in the distributed income of the company. 'Control' includes, inter alia, ownership of a majority of the share capital or a majority of the votes or a right to a majority of the dividends. In assessing control, the rights of 'associates' must be added to the rights of a participator — associates include, among others, the participator's spouse, parents, remoter forebears, children, remoter issue, brothers and sisters. The above definition is only a very brief summary but it is sufficient to show that nearly all private companies are close companies (for example, if a company has nine or fewer shareholders, it must be under the control of some five of them even if none of them is related to each other — it will therefore be a close company unless it falls into one of the small number of cases excluded from the definition).

Close companies are subject to certain special tax rules. These are designed to prevent the use of the company as a vehicle for tax avoidance.

If a loan is made to a participator or his associate, then under s. 419 ICTA 1988 the company must pay a levy equal to the rate of advance corporation tax on the loan. This currently means that for every £3 lent an additional £1 must be paid to the Revenue. When the loan is repaid so is the levy, but if the loan is written off or released, the levy becomes irrecoverable. Furthermore, the borrower is liable to income tax on the amount written off or released as if it were a payment of income to him net of basic rate tax. It will be remembered that loans to directors are generally prohibited by the Companies Act 1985, s. 330 (see **8.8.2.1**).

If close companies provide living accommodation or other 'benefits in kind' for a participator or his associates the company will be treated as making distribution. This charge will *not* apply if the recipient of the benefit is subject to the normal benefit in kind rules under Schedule E. It is, therefore, designed to ensure that the provision of such benefits to shareholders who are neither directors nor higher paid employees of the company is assessed to tax. If a charge is applicable, the cost of providing these benefits is treated like any other 'distribution' (see **Chapter 16**).

If the close company is a 'close investment holding company', the small companies rate of corporation tax of (25%) will not be available. The company will instead pay corporation tax on its profits, whatever the amount, at the full rate of 33%. To fall within this category of close companies, the company must not be a trading company nor a member of a trading group. Companies which deal in land, shares or securities and companies carrying on property investment on a commercial basis are all treated as trading companies and so outside the scope of this anti-avoidance provision.

Companies are not normally liable to inheritance tax if they make gifts. However, if a close company makes a gift (or other transfer of value) this is deemed to be a gift made by all the shareholders in the company (except those with very small interests) in proportion to their shareholdings. If the shareholders fail to pay inheritance tax on this deemed gift, the company becomes liable (ss. 94-102 and 202 IHTA 1984).

SIXTEEN

TAXATION OF DIVIDENDS, DEBENTURE INTEREST AND DIRECTORS' FEES

16.1 Introduction

In **Chapter 15** we looked at the corporation tax system for charging companies tax on their profits (or allowing them relief on their losses). Assuming that the company makes profits, the company has, put simply, a choice of one of four ways of dealing with those profits:

(a) retaining them in the business;
(b) paying them as dividends to the shareholders;
(c) using them to pay interest on the debentures; or
(d) paying directors' fees.

If profits are retained in the business the proprietors ought to benefit in the long run so that the capital value of the company (and thus the value of the shares in it) will increase. The payment of interest on debentures will often be a payment of interest to an outsider, which reduces profits payable to the proprietors of the business. However, a long term loan to a company is really a method of investing in the company without buying shares and so the payment on such a loan would probably be regarded as a payment to invest in the business. Directors' fees are expenses of the business which an accountant would regard as reducing the profit available to shareholders but in the case of most small, private companies the directors and shareholders are the same people. Thus a payment of directors' fees is really a payment of profit to the proprietors.

A company is not entirely free to choose between the four different uses of profits. Firstly, the people are often contractually bound to make payments of interest and directors' fees. Secondly, there are company rules which prevent the company from paying dividends except to the extent of gross profits available for the purpose. (The reason for this is that the original investment made in the company by shareholders may not be returned to them, except in limited circumstances, until the company is wound up.) Thirdly, it will often be commercially unwise for a company to pay out all of its profits since some will be required to provide for future contingencies or for the expansion of the business.

In this chapter, we will consider the tax consequences of each method of using profits. The company rules dealing with the distribution of profits are set out at **9.10** and those relating to the company's power to borrow are set out at **10.6**. We will not repeat those rules in this chapter.

16.2 Taxation of Distributions

16.2.1 DEFINITION OF DISTRIBUTION

A shareholder is liable to income tax under Schedule F on any 'distribution' which he receives in respect of shares. The definition of distribution for this purpose is extremely complicated but the following types of receipt are the most important of those included in the definition:

    (a) any dividend paid by the company including a capital dividend (s. 209(2)(a) ICTA 1988);

    (b) any other distribution out of assets of the company . . . in respect of shares . . . (s. 209(2)(b));

    (c) any interest on securities (i.e., debentures) where the interest varies with the profits of the company (s. 209(d)(iii));

    (d) in some circumstances, the issue of bonus shares following a reduction of capital or the repayment of share capital after a bonus issue.

The issue of bonus redeemable shares (i.e., shares which do not have to be paid for and which will one day be repaid by the company) is also a distribution, but is described as a 'non-qualifying distribution' and is taxed in a special way. (In general terms, the shareholder receiving the shares pays tax on the value of the shares received but the income is treated as having borne tax at the rate of 20% and the company does not have to pay ACT (see below) on the distribution.)

It should be noted that an issue of bonus shares (that is, shares treated as paid up out of the profits of the company) is not a distribution for tax purposes unless share capital has previously been reduced. However, if the shareholders are given a *choice* between receiving a cash dividend (which is, of course, a distribution) or bonus shares, those who choose to take the bonus shares are taxed on the amount of cash dividend forgone in almost the same way as if it were a distribution (s. 249 ICTA 1988).

When a company redeems or purchases its own shares there is usually no income tax liability on the members (this topic will be dealt with in **Chapter 18**). It is possible to obtain clearance in advance ensuring no income tax liability in respect of such a scheme.

16.2.2 TAX CONSEQUENCES ON THE COMPANY OF DISTRIBUTIONS

16.2.2.1 Advance corporation tax

The payment of a dividend (or other distribution) is neither an expense of a company's business nor a charge on its income. The amount of the dividend cannot, therefore, be deducted in computing the company's liability to corporation tax.

When a company makes a qualifying distribution it must pay advance corporation tax (always referred to as ACT) to the Revenue (s. 14 ICTA 1988). All the types of distribution referred to in **16.2.1** above are qualifying distributions except the issue of bonus redeemable shares or securities. ACT is payable on a quarterly basis so that a company must usually report the payment of the distribution within, at the most, three months of the payment and must pay the ACT within 14 days of assessment. The ACT serves a dual purpose — it is a prepayment of part of the company's corporation tax liability and also a payment of at least part of the shareholders' income tax (see **16.2.3** below).

The rate of ACT is calculated by the formula:

$$\frac{I}{(100-I)}$$

where I is 22.5% for the tax year 1993/94 and is 20% for the tax year 1994/95. This means that for 1993/94, ACT is $22.5/(100 - 22.5) = \,^9/_{31}$. For 1994/95 ACT will be $20/(100 - 20) = \,^1/_4$. Thus for 1993/94 in which the distribution of £7,750 is paid, ACT will be £2,250. The amount of ACT is, therefore, equal to 22.5% on the *gross* amount of the distribution (i.e., it is equal to 22.5% on the amount of the distribution plus the ACT on it). For tax years prior to 1993/94, the rate of ACT was geared to the basic rate of income tax. However, in the Budget of 1993, the Chancellor announced that in future he wanted to ensure that dividends attracted tax at the lower rate of 20% (and the rate of 22.5% is transitional provision which will apply to the paying company only in 1993/94).

16.2.2.2 Set-off of ACT

A company is normally liable to pay corporation tax nine months after the end of its accounting period. The amount of ACT paid may be deducted from the corporation tax then due. For example, a company makes trading profits of £3 million during the transitional year of 1993/94 and pays a dividend of £310,000 during the accounting period. Its corporation tax liability will be £990,000 (33%) but from this the company can deduct the £90,000 (£310,000 × $^9/_{31}$) paid as ACT. The balance of £900,000 is called mainstream corporation tax (MCT). Had the profits been made and dividend been paid in 1994/95 or subsequent years, the amount of ACT would have been one quarter of the dividend payment.

From the company's point of view a payment of ACT, therefore, adversely affects its cash flow (since ACT has to be paid before the normal date for payment of corporation tax), but does not affect the total amount of tax paid. However, the maximum amount of ACT which may be set off against mainstream corporation tax liability for an accounting period is '. . . the amount of advance corporation tax . . . in respect of a distribution . . . of an amount which, together with the advance corporation tax so payable in respect of it, is equal to the company's income charged to corporation tax for that period' (s. 239(2) ICTA 1988). This apparently complicated rule really only means that a company cannot set ACT against MCT if the distribution is paid out of *capital* profits or out of income profits accumulated from an earlier accounting period. The maximum amount of ACT set-off is, therefore, in effect, 22.5% of the current year's income profits (for 1993/94). It will be 20% for 1994/95 and subsequent years.

For example, a company has income profits of £2 million in the accounting period ending 31 March 1994 and pays a dividend of £1,860,000. ACT will be £540,000 but the maximum ACT set-off is £450,000, i.e., 22.5% of £2 million (this is because ACT on £1,550,000 is £450,000 — add those together and you have income profits of £2 million), so that the company will pay £540,000 ACT and £120,000 MCT. (The corporation tax liability at 33% on £2 million is £660,000 from which is deducted £450,000 to produce the MCT figure of £120,000.)

In this type of case the company has 'overpaid' corporation tax (in this example, to the extent of £120,000). The amount of overpayment is called surplus advance corporation tax (SACT). SACT may be carried back to the company's six previous accounting periods and may be reclaimed to the extent that *gross* distributions in those years were less than income profits. If the SACT cannot be reclaimed it may be carried forward and used to pay ACT in future accounting periods (subject to the same limit to the amount that may be set-off). The effect of these rules is that a company which pays gross distributions in excess of its income profits will suffer a cash flow disadvantage, but the overall amount of corporation tax is not increased in the long run, except in the unlikely event that the distributions for all years taken together exceed the income profit for all years taken together.

16.2.3 TAXATION OF THE RECIPIENT

A shareholder who receives a qualifying distribution from a company is liable to income tax under Schedule F on the amount of the 'franked payment'. The franked payment is the amount of the distribution plus the tax credit (i.e., ACT) on it.

With effect from 5 April 1993, shareholders will be liable to tax on franked payments at the lower rate of 20%. This means that a shareholder who receives a dividend of £80 is liable to tax on £100 but with a tax credit for £20. (It should be noted that for the tax year 1993/94 there is a transitional rate of 22.5% which applies only to the *company* paying the dividend. The recipient shareholder will not be able to claim the corresponding extra tax credit of 2.5%.) The effect of fixing the rate of income tax on dividends at 20% will mean that shareholders who are exempt from tax, will be entitled to a rebate equal to 20% of the dividend received grossed up at 20%. If a dividend is paid to an individual shareholder whose income falls within the lower rate band of income tax charged at 20%, the 20% tax credit in respect of the dividend will discharge the shareholder's tax liability. For shareholders who are liable to tax at the basic rate of income tax of 25%, they will only be subject to tax on the dividend grossed up at 20% with the result that the tax credit they receive will discharge their liability in full. Individual shareholders who are liable at the higher rate of income tax of 40% will be liable to pay tax at the rate of 40% on the dividend received grossed up at 20%. They will, however, have the benefit of the tax credit. In each case, dividends received will be treated as the top slice of the taxpayer's income. The shareholder with income other than dividends will have the full amount of the lower rate band of 20% available to set against the other income. The shareholder liable to the higher rate will pay an additional 20% tax on dividends to the extent that those dividends fall above the threshold for the higher rate.

These rules may seem somewhat complicated and, therefore, by way of illustration:

(a)   An individual with taxable income (after allowances and reliefs) of £4,000 of which £500 is dividend income (including the tax credit), will be liable to tax:

— at 20% on the first £2,500;
— at 25% on the next £1,000; and
— at 20% on the 'top slice' of £500 of dividends.

(b)   An individual with taxable income of £25,000, of which £5,000 is dividend income (including the tax credit), will be liable to tax:

— at 20% on the first £2,500;
— at 25% on the next £17,500 of non-dividend income; and
— in relation to dividend income, at 20% to the extent that it falls below the basic rate limit of £23,700 (so £3,700 will be taxed at 20%) and at 40% on the remaining £1,300.

(c)   An individual with taxable income of £35,000 of which £5,000 is dividend income (including the tax credit) will be liable to tax:

— at 20% on the first £2,500;
— at 25% on the next £21,200; and
— at 40% on the balance (including the dividend income) of £11,300.

16.2.4   FRANKED INVESTMENT INCOME

When a company makes a distribution to another company it must pay ACT in the normal way (unless the companies are both members of the same group of companies — i.e., one company owns more than half the shares in the other — when the distribution can be made without payment of ACT). The recipient company does not have to pay corporation tax on the distribution (which, in its hands, is called 'franked investment income'), and when it makes a distribution to its own shareholders out of the franked investment income it does not have to pay ACT. The reason for this is that it would be unfair to tax the same profits over and over again merely because they pass from company to company before reaching an individual shareholder.

16.3   Interest on Debentures

16.3.1   TAX CONSEQUENCES ON THE PAYING COMPANY

Interest is a 'payment by time for the use of money' (per Rowlatt J in *Bennett* v *Ogston* (1930) 15 TC 374). The payment of a distribution to shareholders is not, however, treated as interest even in the case of a fixed dividend paid to preference shareholders. A payment of interest by a company will usually result in a tax saving to the company, either because the interest will be a business expense deductible in computing trading profits or because it is a charge on income deductible from profits before tax is computed on them. This distinction can be important in some cases, since a business expense is deducted when it accrues due, a charge on income when it is paid. There are also small differences in the way that relief is given if a loss results from the payment. Yearly interest is treated as a charge on income and so is short interest paid to a bank in the UK (s. 338(3) ICTA 1988). Short interest paid other than to a bank is deductible as a business expense provided it is 'wholly and exclusively incurred for the purposes of the trade' (s. 74 ICTA 1988; see **13.2.3**). 'Short interest' means interest for a period which *cannot* exceed a year and 'yearly interest' means interest for a period which can exceed a year.

16.3.2 DEDUCTION OF TAX

The company must deduct basic rate income tax (currently 25%) from interest which it pays (s. 349 ICTA 1988). Deduction is not, however, made where the interest is short interest or where it is yearly interest paid to a bank in the UK. When the company deducts tax it must account to the Revenue for the tax deducted. For example, a company borrows £1,000 at 10% interest from an individual. Each year (assuming tax rates remain the same) it will pay £75 to the lender and £25 to the Revenue.

The deduction of tax by the company is required to assist the Revenue with the collection of tax and does not affect the company's liability to corporation tax. It does not matter to the company whether it pays interest gross to the lender — e.g., £100 is paid to the lender, or net — £75 to the lender and £25 to the Revenue. Deduction is required where the recipient is another company even though companies do not pay income tax (the recipient company will be able to treat the tax deducted as a part payment of its corporation tax).

16.3.3 TAXATION OF THE RECIPIENT

The gross amount of interest received by a debenture-holder is taxed under Schedule D Case III. As we have just seen, the company usually deducts basic rate tax from the payment so that the amount received is a net amount. To calculate the amount of tax payable it is, therefore, first necessary to calculate the gross amount of interest. This is done by multiplying the net amount by 100/75 (e.g., £75 × 100/75 = £100). If the basic rate changes so will the fraction — the '75' really represents 100 minus the basic rate of tax.

The gross amount of interest is investment income in the hands of the recipient and is liable to higher rate tax if the recipient's income is large enough. If the recipient has unused personal reliefs the basic rate tax can be reclaimed to the extent that the reliefs are not set against other income. This means that, from the recipient's point of view, the receipt of dividends (or other distributions) and interest are exactly the same. The saving in tax from paying interest rather than distributing profits is made by the company — interest is usually a charge on the company's income whereas a distribution is not.

16.4 Directors' Fees

16.4.1 THE EMPLOYING COMPANY'S PERSPECTIVE

16.4.1.1 General

If a trade or profession is carried on through the medium of a company, the company will want to ensure that any payment of salary, pension or compensation for loss of office or any provision of a benefit in kind entitles it to claim a pre-tax deduction so as to reduce its profits taxable under Schedule D Cases I or II. It will be remembered from **Chapter 13** that to be deductible, any expense must satisfy two conditions, namely that the payments must be:

(a) of an income nature as opposed to a capital outlay; and

(b) incurred wholly and exclusively for the purpose of the trade or profession and must not fall within any of the disallowed deductions listed in the ICTA 1988.

In this section of the chapter, we will look at the tax rules as they apply to the payments to directors of companies but the rules can apply to other employees (including employees of sole proprietors or partnerships).

16.4.1.2 Limitation on deductibility

The payments that *are* deductible include the payment of salaries, wages, pensions and even lump sum payments in compensation for loss of the employee's office. However, this is subject to certain qualifications.

(a) *'Wholly'*

In respect of all such payments, the word 'wholly' in s. 74 relates to quantum, so that excessive payments cannot be deducted. In *Copeman* v *William J. Flood and Sons Ltd* [1941] 1 KB 202, it was decided that where such a payment is held to be excessive, such proportion of the payment as is reasonable in the light of the employee's work can be deducted.

With regard to pensions, the pension paid to an ex-employee is deductible even if it is paid voluntarily by the employer. In practice most employers who provide pensions do so by setting up a fund managed by an insurance company. Contributions paid into the fund by the employer are deductible as business expenses provided that the scheme is a retirement benefit scheme as defined by s. 590 ICTA 1988.

(b) *Compensation for loss of office*

Lump sum payments for loss of office are deductible provided they satisfy the conditions set out above, even though they may be one-off payments. Thus, in *Mitchell* v *B. W. Noble Ltd* [1927] KB 719, compensation payments made to directors who were liable to dismissal because of their misconduct but who resigned to avoid bad publicity, were held to be deductible on the basis that the retirement was in the interests of the business. Conversely, payments made to former employees to persuade them to enter into restrictive covenants have been held not to be deductible, since the payments were intended to buy off potential competitors and so amounted to a capital payment (*Associated Portland Cement* v *Kerr* (1945) 27 TC 108 (CA)). Such a receipt is taxable in the employee's hands under the provision of s. 313 ICTA 1988. If the employee is redundant and receives a redundancy payment, s. 579 ICTA 1988 provides that such payments are deductible under Schedule D Cases I and II and are treated as having been paid on the last day on which the business was carried on if made after the discontinuance of the trade, profession or vocation. Although s. 579 only deals with statutory redundancy payments, s. 90 ICTA 1988 allows additional payments to redundant employees (subject to a limit of three times the statutory redundancy payment) to be deductible. This includes payments over and above the employees' statutory entitlement made on the cessation of business in accordance with the power to make payments to employees in these circumstances given by s. 719 CA 1985.

(c) *The provision of benefits*

Many employers provide their employees with benefits over and above their salary, such as company cars, free meals and so on. The cost of providing such benefits will be deductible if the payments are made wholly and exclusively for the purposes of the trade. Thus if cars are provided for salesmen, the outlay will be deductible, but if they are for private use they will only be deductible if they can be regarded as reasonable remuneration.

16.4.1.3 Social security contributions

Although it is beyond the scope of this book to consider the social security legislation in detail, it should be noted that the employer is obliged to make social security contributions in respect of each employee (as well as deducting the contributions of the employee before paying over the net wages). The employer's contributions are deductible in computing the tax liability of the employer.

16.4.2 THE EMPLOYEE'S PERSPECTIVE

16.4.2.1 The Schedule E charge

Under s. 19 ICTA 1988 as amended, tax under Schedule E is charged in respect of emoluments from an office or employment as well as pensions and income (such as compensation payments) specifically charged to tax under the schedule. Tax is collected on a receipts year basis. That is to say, the employee pays tax on the emoluments received during the tax year whether or not they are for that year or for some other year. The tax is usually collected by deduction at source under the PAYE scheme.

(a) *Office*

The word 'office' is not defined in the statutes but Rowlatt J in *Great Western Railway Co* v *Bater* [1920] 3 KB 266, said it meant 'a subsisting, permanent, substantive position which had an existence independent of the person who filled it, which went on and was filled in succession by successive holders', although Lord Wilberforce and Lord Lowry, in *Edwards* v *Clinch* [1981] 3 All ER 543, felt the definition should be refined. Lord Wilberforce accepted 'that a rigid requirement of permanence is no longer appropriate . . . and continuity need not be regarded as an absolute qualification. But still, if any meaning is to be given to "office" in this legislation . . . the word must involve a degree of continuance (not necessarily continuity) and of independent existence: it must connote a post to which a person can be appointed, which he can vacate and to which a successor can be appointed'. Over the years office holders have been held to include directors of UK companies, NHS consultants, bishops, judges and personal representatives.

(b) *Employment*

'Employment' is equally difficult to define, but Pennycuick V-C said in *Fall* v *Hitchen* [1973] 1 All ER 368, that, 'unless some special limitation is to be put upon the word "employment" in any given context, the expression "contract of service" appears to be coterminous with the expression "employment" '. The case involved a ballet dancer who entered into a contract having the attributes of a contract of service, in that he was paid weekly regardless of whether a performance was given or a rehearsal attended, the 'employer' paid national insurance contributions on the dancer's behalf as if he were an employee and the dancer worked only for the employer. This contract was therefore assessable under Schedule E, even though it had been entered into in the normal course of carrying on his profession of dancer. Conversely, if it can be shown that the taxpayer's method of earning a livelihood does not consist of obtaining a post and remaining in it (as was the case in *Fall* v *Hitchen*), but consists of engagements and moving from one engagement to another, he is assessed under Schedule D and not Schedule E, provided the engagements are entered into as part of his profession (*Davies* v *Braithwaite* [1931] 2 KB 628).

(c) *Emolument*

Section 131 of ICTA 1988 defines emoluments as including 'all salaries, fees, wages, perquisites and profits whatsoever'. To be assessable the emoluments must arise out of the office or employment and be in money or convertible into money (although there are special statutory rules dealing with benefits in kind which are dealt with below).

16.4.2.2 Taxable receipts by employees

(a) *What is taxable?*

A director or other employee who receives salary or wages from his employer is obviously assessable under Schedule E. Gifts, bonuses or tips, will be taxable if the taxpayer holds an office or employment and the receipt derives from the employment even if paid by third parties. A pension paid to a former director or employee (or his dependants) is taxable under Schedule E even if it is voluntary or can be discontinued.

(b) *Payments made on employee's behalf*

Such payments will be assessable if the employer discharges a debt owed by the director or employee (*Nicholl* v *Austin* (1935) 19 TC 531).

16.4.2.3 Benefits in kind

(a) *The general rule*

The emoluments on which an employee is assessed to tax may include 'perquisites' as well as salary or wages. (The term 'perquisites' in this context includes assets or benefits provided by the employer.) For such receipts to be assessable emoluments, according to normal tax principles, they must be in the form of money or convertible into money (although it is not necessary that the asset or non-cash benefit *is* actually converted into money). Thus, free meals in a staff canteen fail this convertibility test (and so are tax-free) since the employee cannot sell the meal; the mere fact that it saves the employee money is not enough. However, a cash allowance in lieu of such a benefit attracts a tax charge (*Sanderson* v *Durbridge* (1955) 36 TC 239), as does a benefit which is provided in return for a deduction from the salary of the employee (*Machon* v *McLaughlin* (1926) 11 TC 83 (CA)) even if the deduction is voluntary in the sense that the employee is free to restore his income to its original level in exchange for giving up his right to receive the benefit (*Heaton* v *Bell* [1970] AC 728).

If the benefit is convertible into money, the employee is taxed on the monetary value of the benefit to him at the time it was received. This was held, in *Wilkins* v *Rogerson* [1961] Ch 7 (where suits were provided for employees) to mean that the employee should be assessed on the second-hand value of the benefit. If the emolument is a benefit in the form of money (such as a cash allowance), the cash value of the benefit will be the taxable emolument.

These rules make the provision of benefits in kind (this is to say, benefits in the form of assets or services) very attractive since the employees who receive them will either not be taxed at all on them (because their nature is such that they cannot be converted into cash) or be taxed on the second-hand value of the asset (which in the case of clothes, cars and similar items will be considerably less than the 'new value' of the asset). Therefore, to prevent abuse, various statutory provisions have been introduced (these are considered below). While, strictly speaking, the convertibility test applies to all employees, effectively the test is superseded when the special rules apply (see paragraphs (b) and (c) immediately below).

(b) *Statutory rules applicable to all employees*

(i) *Living accommodation* Under s. 145 ICTA 1988, an employee who occupies premises by reason of his employment is taxed on the greater of the rent paid by his employer or the 'annual value' of the accommodation less the rent actually paid by the employee. 'Annual value' means the market rent that could be obtained for the premises on the assumption that the landlord will bear the costs of repair and insurance (s. 837 ICTA 1988). This tax charge can be avoided if the 'representative occupier' exceptions laid down in s. 145 apply. There is, therefore, no charge if the accommodation is supplied:

— where it is necessary for the proper performance of the employee's duties (such as in the case of resident caretakers or lighthouse keepers);

— for the better performance of the employee's duties and his is one of the kinds of employment in which it is customary for employers to provide their employees with living accommodation (such as in the case of the police or fire officers);

— where there is a threat to the employee's security and he resides in the accommodation as part of the security arrangements (such as in the case of the Prime Minister).

Under s. 146 ICTA 1988, employees who receive the benefit of taxable living accommodation which costs more than £75,000 to provide will be treated as receiving an emolument equal to the official rate of interest (which will be kept in line with typical mortgage rates) on the excess over the £75,000 limit (less any rent paid in excess of the annual value of the accommodation calculated as above).

(ii) *Vouchers* Where vouchers, stamps or similar documents are provided, which can be converted into money or goods, the employee is taxed on the cost of providing the voucher, etc., incurred by the employer (s. 141 ICTA 1988). However, by virtue of an Inland Revenue concession, luncheon vouchers are exempt up to 15p per day provided they are not transferable.

(c) *The statutory rules applicable to directors and higher-paid employees*

   (i) *The persons subject to the rules*   Where the recipient of a benefit is a 'director or higher-paid employee', certain provisions of ICTA 1988 as amended by FA 1989 apply. Under s. 167 the special rules apply if the taxpayer receiving the benefit is an employee earning £8,500 per annum or more or a director. The term 'director' includes any person in accordance with whose directions or instructions the directors of the company are accustomed to act, and a member, if the company's affairs are managed by the members. However, the rules do not apply to:

— a director without a material interest in the company (i.e., his total shareholding together with that of his family, partners, and trustees of a settlement created by him or a relative, does not exceed 5% of the company's ordinary share capital) who works full-time for the company but earns less than £8,500 per annum; or

— a director of a charity or non-profit making body and again earns less than £8,500 per annum.

   (ii) *The special rules*

— Expense accounts. Under s. 153 ICTA 1988 if an expense account is provided, the director or employee is taxed on its full amount less any expenses incurred wholly, exclusively and necessarily in the course of his employment. Thus, if, for example, the employee has an expense allowance of £1,000 and he uses only £750 'wholly, exclusively and necessarily in the course of his employment' and the rest for his personal benefit, he adds £250 to his taxable emoluments.

— Benefits given to employees and directors. In the case of other benefits in kind which are given outright to the employee, he is treated as receiving emoluments equal to the 'cash equivalent' of the asset, which means the cost to the employer of providing them less any sums paid by the employee. In *Rendell* v *Went* (1964) 41 TC 641 (HL), the employee was assessed on an amount equal to the legal fees paid by his employer arising out of a criminal case. If the employee is given an asset which has depreciated in value, the cash equivalent is its market value at the time of transfer.

— Benefits lent to employees and directors. If the asset is lent to the director or employee, its cash equivalent is the 'annual value' of the use of the asset, plus any expenses incurred by the employer in providing it, less sums paid by the director or employee, or the rent paid by the employer whichever is greater. The annual value depends on the nature of the asset lent.

In the case of land the 'annual value' is the market rent on the assumption that the landlord will repair and insure.

For cars the 'cash equivalent' that is to be added to the employee's emoluments where a car is made available for use by the director or higher-paid employee or their families is determined by Sch. 6 ICTA 1988 which sets out the cash equivalents by reference to the car's age, its original market value and the cylinder capacity. The cash equivalent is increased by one-half if either the car is used only for private purposes or the business use does not exceed 2,500 miles in each tax year. Cars taken from a pool do not attract the tax charge. The provision of car fuel attracts a charge to tax subject to certain limitations.

— Beneficial loan arrangements. Generally, beneficial loans would not be benefits in kind, since they are not convertible into money. However, s. 160 ICTA 1988 provides that if an employer makes an interest-free or cheap loan, the recipient director or employee is taxed on its cash equivalent unless this does not exceed £300 or the loan would qualify for interest relief. The 'cash equivalent' is the difference between the official rate of interest fixed by statutory instrument and the rate paid by the employee. The tax charge arises if the loan is made to the director's or employee's relatives unless he personally derives no benefit from the loan.

If any loan is written off in whole or in part, the amount released is treated as a taxable emolument. Where the release is made on the termination of the employment, there is a tax charge unless the release is caused by the director's or employee's death. If a director or employee (or his family) acquires undervalued shares, the amount of the undervalue is treated as an interest-free loan. Payments made by the director or higher-paid employee reduce the 'notional loan', but it remains outstanding until either: the full value of the shares is paid; or the debt is released; or the shares are disposed of; or the employee or director dies. If the second or third situation arises, the employee or director is taxed as if the amount equal to the outstanding 'loan' had been released or written off.

For the purpose of deciding whether an employee or director is earning over £8,500, it is assumed that the special rules apply, (i.e., that the cost of providing the benefit incurred by the employer is added to the employee's salary). Thus if an employee earning £8,400 is given a suit that cost the employer £250 to buy, the cost to the employer is added to his salary to make his emoluments £8,650 and therefore sufficient to make him a 'higher-paid employee' for all purposes. This will be the case even if the second-hand value of the suit was only £50. Furthermore, although the special rules only apply to benefits provided for the director or employee by reason of his employment, s. 168 ICTA 1988 prevents the tax charge being avoided by giving the benefit to the director's or employee's family.

16.4.2.4 Terminal payments

(a) *General principles*

The mere fact that the payment is made on the termination of the contract (or the alteration of its terms) does not preclude its taxation under the rules of Schedule E, if it is 'something in the nature of a reward for services, past, present or future' (per Upjohn J in *Hochstrasser* v *Mayes* [1959] Ch 22). As a result of this, sums paid in accordance with the terms of the employment contract will be taxable since they will represent deferred or advance remuneration (*Dale* v *De Soissons* [1950] 2 All ER 460). Thus if an employee is to be paid £10,000 a year for 10 years but under the contract is to receive a lump sum of £50,000 on either the commencement or termination of the term, the sum is fully taxable under Schedule E (see *Williams* v *Simmonds* [1981] STC 715). Similarly, sums paid to an employee to induce him to withhold his resignation or to work for a lesser salary are assessable, since they represent a reward for future services. However, to fall in this category the payment must represent a reward for services, so that if its purpose is to induce the employee to accept a reduced pension, it is not taxable (*Tilley* v *Wales* [1943] AC 386).

(b) *'Golden handshakes'*

A lump sum payment made to compensate the employee for an early termination of the contract by the employer (sometimes called a 'golden handshake') is not assessable under the general principles. However, it may be taxable under s. 148 ICTA 1988. This taxes a payment on retirement or removal from office or employment that is not otherwise chargeable to tax (under the general principles), 'which is made, whether in pursuance of any legal obligation or not, either directly or indirectly in consideration or in consequence of, or otherwise in connection with, the termination of the holding of the office or employment or any change in its functions or emoluments, including any payment in commutation of annual or periodical payments [such as pensions] (whether chargeable to tax or not) which would otherwise have been made'. The assessment can be made on the personal representatives of a dead taxpayer and payments to a member of the taxpayer's family are also assessable under this section.

Section 148 does not apply if:

(i) the terminal payment is paid on the death, injury or disability of the holder of the office or employment (s. 188(1)(a));
(ii) the sum falls to be taxed under s. 313 (see **16.4.2.5** below) (s. 188(1)(b));
(iii) the payment does not exceed £30,000 (s. 188(4)). However, any excess over this figure is taxable and the subsection prevents the tax charge being avoided by paying the terminal payments in instalments.

If a terminal payment exceeds the £30,000 limit, the excess is taxable in the year of receipt as earned income.

16.4.2.5 Restrictive covenant payments

If an employee receives a payment in consideration of entering into a restrictive covenant, this is regarded as being a capital outlay by the employer. As such, it should be a capital receipt in the hands of the employee and so not taxable as part of the employee's income. However, s. 313 ICTA 1988 levies tax on such payments. They are fully taxed in the recipient's hands and the paying employer can deduct them when calculating profits.

16.4.2.6 Expenses

(a) *The test of deductibility (s. 198 ICTA 1988)*   If an employee incurs expenses, they will only be deductible if they are incurred wholly, exclusively and necessarily in the actual performance of his duties. This is narrower than the expenses rule for Schedule D Case I or II taxpayers. Two separate requirements can be extracted. These rules are of limited practical importance since an employee is usually indemnified by his employer for any such expenses which he incurs.

(i) *Incurred in the performance of duties*   Firstly, the expense must be incurred in the performance of the duties of the office or employment and an expense incurred merely to enable the employee to perform his duties more efficiently will not satisfy this requirement (even where the employee's contract requires him to incur the expense). In *Brown* v *Bullock* (1961) 40 TC 1, Donovan LJ summarised the position by saying: 'The test is not whether the employer imposes the expense but whether the duties do, in the sense that, irrespective of what the employer may prescribe, the duties cannot be performed without incurring the particular outlay.'

(ii) *The expense must be 'necessary'*   The second requirement which must be satisfied is that the expense has to be necessary, in so far as the nature of the job itself must be such that it cannot be done without the outlay. If the employee can show the expense is 'necessary' it does not give him a right to claim an unlimited deduction, since not only must the expense be necessary but also the amount of the expense must be no more than is necessary to perform the duties (any excess would not be deductible).

(b) *Travelling expenses*   Section 198 provides that the expenses of travelling in the performance of the duties of the office or employment are deductible from the emoluments, provided the employee is necessarily obliged to pay those expenses from his emoluments. The effect of this is that while expenses incurred when travelling on business are deductible (such as travelling from the employer's head office to a sub-office), the expense of travelling from home to the place where the employee is employed is not.

(c) *Subscriptions and business entertainment*   While subscriptions to professional societies are not generally deductible, s. 201 ICTA 1988 permits subscriptions to certain professional bodies, including those of architects, dentists, solicitors, and veterinary surgeons, to be deductible even though they are not 'necessary'.

16.4.2.7 Social security contributions

The contributions deducted by the employer from the employee's salary (see **16.4.1.3** above) are not deductible when calculating the employee's tax liability. Employees' contributions are greater than those levied on the self-employed but, in compensation, the benefits available to employees are greater than those available to the self-employed. (The details of the benefits are beyond the scope of this book.)

16.5   Retained Profits

16.5.1   CORPORATION TAX

Profits retained by the company are liable to corporation tax at the rates explained in **Chapter 15**. It does not generally matter why the profits are retained, although sums used for certain types of capital expenditure are eligible for relief under the capital allowance system (see **Chapter 17**).

16.5.2   FUTURE TAXATION OF RETAINED PROFITS

The only tax liability on retained profits *at the time they are made* is corporation tax. However, such profits will usually be subject to tax at some time in the future. Thus, if those profits are distributed in a later year Schedule F tax will be payable by the recipient shareholders. If the profits are retained for many years they will be reflected in the value of the shares in the company so that CGT and IHT liability on disposal of the shares will be increased (capital tax liability on disposal of shares is considered in **Chapter 18**).

Furthermore, under s. 703 ICTA 1988 the Revenue has wide powers to charge tax so as to counter tax advantages gained on a transaction involving (among other things) the sale of shares at a profit. The profits accumulated in the company and reflected in the value of shares may be taxed in this way when the shares come to be sold. (Section 707 ICTA 1988 provides a procedure for obtaining 'clearance in advance', i.e., the Revenue will state before the transaction is completed whether they will seek to assess tax under s. 703.)

16.6   Raising the Funds to Invest in the Company

An individual who wishes to put money into a company can, as we have seen in this chapter, use the money either to buy shares in the company or to make a loan to the company. The individual may have the funds to make this investment from his own resources but in many cases the investor will have to borrow money to raise the necessary funds.

Such an individual can deduct the interest on the loan as a charge on income if the loan is used to acquire ordinary share capital in a close trading company, or if the funds raised on the loan are in turn lent on to such a company, provided the money lent is used wholly and exclusively for the business of the company. The investor (whether buying shares or lending money to the company) has to show that either he is a shareholder in the company and works for the greater part of his time in the management or conduct of the company, or that he controls more than 5% of the ordinary share capital of the company. The investor will be able to aggregate the shareholdings of his 'associates' (which include his relatives, partners, the trustees of a settlement which he created and the trustees of a settlement holding shares for the benefit of the investor) when deciding whether he controlled more than the required 5% of the ordinary share capital in the company.

16.7   Conclusion

It is impossible to come to any very general conclusion as to which type of use of profits is most beneficial because the circumstances of each case are so different. However, the tax efficiency of the various possibilities dealt with above can be illustrated by the following example.

An individual decides to set up a company with £1,500,000 on 6 April 1993 and expects the company to make income profits during the first year of £500,000. He wishes to receive £100,000 p.a. from the company before tax. He is single (so his personal relief is £3,445), he has no other source of income and he has no charges on income. When he forms the company he has a choice of investing the money as share capital or of lending it to the company. If the money is lent to the company 10% interest will be paid. If it is invested as share capital the profits may be retained, paid out as directors' fees or used to pay dividends. (For completeness, the effect of retaining *all* the profits will also be considered.) For the purposes of these illustrations, National Insurance contributions have been ignored.

16.7.1   PART OF PROFITS OF £500,000 USED TO PAY DIRECTOR'S FEES OF £100,000

(a)   Corporation tax on £400,000 (since the fees can be deducted as a trading expense)

	£
On first £250,000 @ 25%	62,500
On balance of £150,000 @ 37.5%	56,250
Company's total tax	118,750

(b)   The proprietor's tax under Schedule E on £100,000

		£	
On first £3,445		nil	(personal relief)
On next £2,500 @ 20%		500	(lower rate)
On next £21,200 @ 25%		5,300	(basic rate)
On remaining £72,855 @ 40%		29,142	(higher rate)
Proprietor's tax under Schedule E		34,942	(deducted at source under PAYE system)

16.7.2   PART OF PROFITS OF £500,000 USED TO PAY 10% INTEREST ON £1,500,000 (i.e., £150,000)

(a)   Since the interest payment is a charge on income, the corporation tax position is the same as when director's fees are paid.

(b)   The proprietor's/lender's position is basically the same as when director's fees are paid. (The interest is investment income and so, for example, cannot be used as the basis for calculating pension contributions. The basis on which the tax is assessed will be the Schedule D basis not PAYE, so that basic rate tax will be deducted at source and higher rate tax will be paid on the preceding year basis except in the year of the loan.)

16.7.3   PART OF PROFITS OF £500,000 USED TO PAY DIVIDEND OF £80,000 net

(a)   Corporation tax on £500,000

	£
On first £250,000 @ 25%	62,500
On balance of £250,000 @ 37.5%	93,750
Company's total tax	156,250

Note: dividends are neither a business expense nor a charge on income.

The company now has £343,750 from which it can pay a dividend of £80,000. It will have to pay 9/31 of that sum as ACT (in 1993/94). Therefore, ACT is £23,225 (payable within three months of the dividend). This sum is deductible from the MCT liability, so that the MCT will be £156,250 − £23,225 = £133,025 (payable nine months after the end of the accounting period).

(b)   The proprietor's/shareholder's income after Schedule F is £80,000 + £20,000 = £100,000. Tax under Schedule F on £100,000 is £34,942 (since the rates of tax are the same as those applying under Schedule E to the director's fees).

16.7.4   WHOLE OF PROFITS OF £500,000 RETAINED IN FULL

(a)   Corporation tax on £500,000 = £156,250.

(b)   The proprietor's tax is nil since he has received no income.

16.7.5   SUMMARY

The position can be summarised as follows:

(1)   *Director's fees*

	£
(a) The company is left with £500,000 − (100,000 + 118,750)	281,250
(b) The proprietor is left with £100,000 − £34,942	65,058
	346,308

(2) *Interest*

		£
(a) The company is left with £500,000		
− (100,000 + 118,750)		281,250
(b) The proprietor is left with £100,000		
− £34,942		65,058
		346,308

(3) *Dividends*

		£
(a) The company is left with £500,000		
− (180,000 + 156,250)		163,750
(b) The proprietor is left with		65,058
		228,808

(4) *Retained profits*

		£
(a) The company is left with £500,000		
− £156,250		343,750
(b) The proprietor is left with		nil
		343,750

It can be seen that the most tax-effective ways of distributing profits appear to be the payment of director's fees or interest. We will now examine the reasons for this.

Whether profit is distributed to the proprietor by way of director's fees or interest, the tax effect is the same for the company. Both payments are deductible; the fees are deductible expenses; the interest is a charge on income.

So far as the proprietor is concerned the only tax distinction between fees and interest is that one is earned income and the other is investment income. This distinction is normally of no significance. (Investment income, unlike earned income, can never be taken into account when assessing pensionable income.)

Distributing profit by way of dividend is less tax-effective for the company than either of the other two methods. Dividends are not deductible expenses nor are they charges on income. So far as the proprietor is concerned, distributions by way of dividend may be less tax-effective than the two previous methods. Where profit is distributed by way of dividend by a company which pays tax at a rate of 33%, the company can only pass on to the shareholder a 20% tax credit (see **16.2.3** above). In such a case the full benefit of the profit distributed by way of dividend is not received by the shareholder.

A company which retains all its profit will have no deductible director's fees nor interest payments to reduce its taxable profits. The proprietor will have received no income from the company and will therefore have no income tax liability relating to it. There may be commercial reasons for retaining some or all of the profit (e.g., to fund expansion of the business), but a proprietor may not be able to do without substantial receipts from the company. If the proprietor cannot do without such receipts, distributions of cash will *have* to be made. If the proprietor can do without such receipts, the company must decide whether it is tax-effective to retain all of its profit or to distribute some.

In cases where the company's average rate of tax is lower than the taxpayer's, it is preferable to retain profits. In cases where the company's average rate of tax is higher than the taxpayer's it is preferable to distribute, *provided* this can be done by way of director's fees or interest. (As explained above, these payments reduce a company's taxable profit.)

Where profit can only be distributed by way of dividend, an overall tax saving cannot be achieved because the taxpayer will get only a 20% tax credit and will have to pay higher rate tax from his own resources, getting no benefit from the company's payment of higher rates of tax.

From a tax viewpoint, it can be seen that distributions by way of fees and/or interest are likely to be the most effective.

However, tax considerations alone cannot decide the matter. Other relevant factors to be considered are:

(a) There may be shareholders who are not directors and who therefore cannot receive directors' fees.

(b) A company may *have* to borrow money on loan for commercial reasons. Thereafter, it will be obliged to pay interest.

SEVENTEEN

CAPITAL ALLOWANCES

17.1   Introduction

Most businesses will need to acquire fixed assets for use in the business. The depreciation in the value of those assets due to wear and tear arising from their use in the business is not an allowable deduction from the business's profits for income tax purposes, even though their acquisition is essential to the future profitability of the business. However, certain limited types of fixed assets do attract relief in the form of capital allowances which can be deducted when calculating taxable profits.

Relief is only available if the capital expenditure has been incurred in respect of the items of expenditure prescribed by the governing statute, the Capital Allowances Act 1990. Under this Act, the principal allowances relate to expenditure incurred on 'plant and machinery' and 'industrial buildings' (although expenditure on other items if deductible under the terms of the Act).

The allowances can be claimed by companies, partnerships or individuals. Capital allowances of companies are treated as trading expenses of the accounting period in respect of which they are claimed and 'balancing charges' (see below) are treated as trading receipts for that period. For income tax purposes, capital allowances and 'balancing charges' are technically not trading expenses and receipts but the practical differences between the two systems are slight. The effect of claiming the allowances may be to create an allowable loss for which the taxpayer can claim loss relief (see **Chapter 13** for income tax relief and **Chapter 15** for corporation tax relief).

In this chapter we will look at the capital allowance system in outline, concentrating on the allowances available for 'plant and machinery' and 'industrial buildings'.

17.2   Plant and Machinery

17.2.1   DEFINITION

The Capital Allowances Act 1990 does not define either 'plant' or 'machinery' and therefore whether the expenditure will attract the allowances will depend on the facts in each case. In *Yarmouth* v *France* (1887) 19 QBD 647, Lindley LJ said that the term 'plant':

> . . . includes whatever apparatus is used by a businessman for carrying on his business, not his stock-in-trade which he buys or makes for sale; but all goods and chattels, fixed or movable, live or dead, which he keeps for permanent employment in his business.

On the basis of this guidance (which has been followed in subsequent cases), the term 'plant' will not apply to (and so allowances will not be available in respect of) an item which is not used for carrying on the business, the stock in trade of the business or the premises or place in which the business is carried on. However, if a building or structure can be properly described as 'apparatus for carrying on the business or employed in the business', such as a dry dock, then it could be 'plant'.

A fuller description of the definition of the term is beyond the scope of this book. The reader is referred to one of the standard tax textbooks for further detail.

17.2.2 THE WRITING DOWN ALLOWANCES

If the expenditure is incurred on an item of 'plant or machinery', it will qualify for a 'writing down allowance' of up to 25% of the 'qualifying expenditure' in the first and subsequent years. The term 'qualifying expenditure' means the original cost of the asset less any allowances already given. The allowance must be claimed by sole traders or partners, whereas a company will be given the allowance automatically unless it disclaims all or part of the allowance. (This distinction will be removed once the pay and file scheme is introduced — see **15.3.1**.)

For example, machinery is purchased for £50,000 on 1 January 1990 and the full writing down allowance of 25% is claimed. This would mean that an allowance of £12,500 will be available. If the owner of the machinery decides to claim the full 25% allowance in subsequent years, the allowance available will be as follows:

	Written Down Value	*Allowance*
Second year	£50,000 − £12,500 = £37,500	£9,375
Third year	£50,000 − £21,875 = £28,125	£7,031
Fourth year	£50,000 − £28,906 = £21,094	£5,273

When the asset is sold there is a balancing charge on the difference between the sale price and the written down value. In the above example, the written down value after the fourth year was £15,821, so if the machinery was sold for £17,821 there would be a charge to tax (under Schedule D Case VI) of £2,000. This charge is known as the 'balancing charge'. This means that, taking all the years together, the amount on which relief is finally given is equal to the amount of the depreciation. (Should the item be sold for *less* than the current written down value, a 'balancing allowance' will be available as a way of granting relief.) The balancing charge can never be on more than the amount of allowance given — any actual profit made on the sale of the assets being liable to capital gains tax, if taxable at all.

The illustration set out above shows that the allowances are of up to 25% of the *unrelieved expenditure* (that is to say, the purchase price less the allowances already taken). Thus, the annual allowance is a percentage of an ever-reducing balance so that it can take many years for the entire expenditure to be set against profits, subject to a balancing charge becoming payable.

So far, we have looked at the rules as they apply to the acquisition and subsequent disposal of a single item of plant or machinery. If several items of plant and machinery are owned by the business (as is more likely to be the case) the allowances are given by reference to a 'pool' of expenditure. This will mean that all of the assets in the pool are treated as if they were one asset. The amount of the writing down allowance on the 'pool' of expenditure will be up to 25% of the total of expenditure on machinery and plant less all allowances so far claimed. Where one item included in the pool is disposed of, the sale price of that item is deducted from the written down value of the pool (this deduction being known as a 'balancing adjustment'), so that smaller allowances will be available in later years. A 'balancing charge' will only apply where pooled items are sold for more than the written down value of the whole pool.

Motor cars which are used only for business purposes qualify for full writing down allowances. However, motor cars which are used for private as well as business purposes qualify for a 25% writing down allowance subject to a maximum allowance calculated on the basis that the original cost was £12,000. Motor cars which are not used solely for business purposes do not enter into the pool.

If an asset acquired after 31 March 1986 is expected to be disposed of at less than the purchase price less capital allowances within a period of five years from its acquisition, an election can be made (within two years of the year of acquisition) for the asset to be dealt with outside the pool of plant and machinery. Allowances for such assets which have been removed from the pool continue to be on the 25% reducing balance basis. Provided that the asset is either disposed of or scrapped within the five year period, the balancing allowance or charge will be calculated by reference to its own capital allowance history. If the asset is not, in fact, sold or scrapped within the five year period, its written down value will be added to the pool of plant and machinery and thereafter treated as if it had never been de-pooled.

17.2.3 USING THE ALLOWANCES

When expenditure, attracting the writing down allowance, is initially incurred to buy an item of plant and machinery the allowance will be deductible from the profits of the accounting period in which the expenditure was incurred.

The allowances will reduce the taxable profits and if the allowance for the relevant year exceeds those profits, the unused allowance can be carried forward and set against future profits. Alternatively, they can be used as a loss and the relief described for losses incurred by sole traders or partnerships (see **Chapter 13**) or companies (see **Chapter 15**) will be available.

17.2.4 SPECIAL RULES ON PLANT AND MACHINERY

The Capital Allowances Act 1990 contains special rules on the availability of capital allowances to the lessor when plant and machinery is bought in order to be leased (see Part II, Chapter V, Capital Allowances Act 1990). It also contains special rules which apply to expenditure on plant or machinery which are regarded as 'tenant's fixtures' under a lease (see s. 61 Capital Allowances Act 1990). Detail of these rules is beyond the scope of this manual and the reader is referred to one of the standard tax textbooks.

17.3 Industrial Buildings

17.3.1 DEFINITION

The Capital Allowances Act 1990 allows for allowances to be claimed in respect of the construction and purchase of industrial buildings and structures (such as factories, but not offices) for manufacturing (but not distributive) trades. The Act defines the term 'industrial building' at some length and it can include a mill, a factory and a warehouse. The allowances are not available in respect of the expenditure laid out to acquire the land. Expenditure incurred subsequently when the industrial building is improved can attract the allowances. If part of a building which satisfies the definition of an 'industrial building' is used for non-industrial purposes, the allowance can still be claimed provided expenditure on the non-industrial purpose does not exceed 25% of the expenditure incurred in respect of the whole building.

17.3.2 THE ALLOWANCE

A writing down allowance of 4% of the original cost of construction (or purchase) of an industrial building can be claimed for every year when the building is in use. Since the writing down allowance is a percentage of the *original* cost price, full relief for the expenditure will have been obtained once 25 years have elapsed. If an industrial building has declined in value and is sold, a balancing charge will be levied if the decline in the building's value is less than the allowances which have been given to date. A balancing allowance will be available if the decline is greater than the allowances given to date. These adjustments will not, however, be made once the 4% annual writing down allowance has been claimed for 25 years. This is because the value of the building will be regarded as having been written down to nil by then.

Where the vendor who has been claiming this allowance sells the building, the purchaser can claim a writing down allowance. In this case, the allowance is calculated by spreading the 'residue of expenditure' over the balance of the period of 25 years commencing when the building was originally built or purchased by the first claimant of the allowances. The 'residue of expenditure' is the written down value of the building at the date of the sale plus any balancing charge or less any balancing allowance. For example, a taxpayer buys a factory for £200,000 and claims the 4% writing down allowance for each of the first five years of his ownership (giving a total of allowances claimed of £40,000). After five years, the original owner sells the building for £170,000, which represents £15,000 above the written down value of the building for the purposes of the allowance. The vendor will suffer a balancing charge on the sum of £15,000. The purchaser will be able to claim the writing down allowance in respect of the sum of £175,000. The purchaser will be able to spread the 'residue of expenditure' of £175,000 over the balance of the original period of 25 years, that is to say, over the next 20 years. It should be noted that the writing down allowance which the purchaser in these circumstances can claim is not limited to the 4% figure.

17.4   Other Expenditure which Attracts Capital Allowances

The Capital Allowances Act 1990 provides that capital allowances can be available in respect of:

(a) agricultural forestry buildings;
(b) assured tenancies;
(c) scientific research;
(d) patents and 'know-how'; and
(e) mines, oil wells, mineral rights, cemeteries, crematoria and dredging.

EIGHTEEN

CAPITAL GAINS TAX AND INHERITANCE TAX ON BUSINESS ASSETS

18.1 Introduction

One of the principal motivations for people going into business, whether alone, in partnership or through the medium of a company, is to earn a living from the income they derive from the enterprise. For many people an equally important motivation is to create a capital asset which they can either sell or give away (whether during their lifetime or on death). The tax charges which can arise if any of these events occur will, therefore, be of importance to most business people and in this chapter we will examine the capital gains tax and inheritance tax charges which can arise. For both of those taxes, we will firstly explain how the tax liabilities can arise in outline and then look at the specific rules as they can apply to partnerships and companies.

18.2 Capital Gains Tax

18.2.1 GENERAL

Capital gains tax is payable, under the provisions contained in the Taxation of Chargeable Gains Act 1992 (TCGA 1992), when a taxable person makes a disposal of chargeable assets giving rise to a chargeable gain unless an exemption or relief applies. Capital gains tax is charged by reference to gains made during a tax year (as with income tax).

A taxable person for CGT purposes is anyone who is resident or ordinarily resident in the UK (including the personal representatives of a deceased person). For the charge to tax to arise, the taxable person must make a 'disposal', a term which is not exhaustively defined in the Act but which covers a sale, gift or part disposal. The definition of 'assets' for capital gains tax purposes is contained in s. 21(1) TCGA 1992 which widely defines it as including 'all forms of property . . .'. Only *chargeable* assets can give rise to a liability to the tax but virtually all 'assets' are chargeable assets subject to a few exceptions (such as motor cars and sterling).

For the tax to become payable, the disposal of chargeable assets has to give rise to a gain, which will occur if the 'consideration for disposal' exceeds the 'allowable deductions' permitted by the Act. The 'consideration for disposal' equals the sale price of the asset unless there is a gift or a gift element in which case the market value of the asset is substituted. The 'allowable deductions' are:

(a) the initial expenditure (that is, the original purchase price or market value if the asset was acquired by way of gift) plus incidental costs incurred in acquiring the asset;

(b) subsequent expenditure (such as money spent on enhancing the value of the asset); and

(c) incidental costs of disposal.

Special rules apply in relation to the allowable deductions if there was a partial disposal of the asset. The effect of these rules is to permit the taxpayer to deduct only a proportion of the 'allowable deductions'. This proportion is equal to the proportion which the part of the asset disposed of bears to the whole asset. For example, if the total 'allowable deductions' in respect of a piece of land owned by a sole trader are £100,000 and he sells one half of the land for £75,000, he is only allowed to deduct one half of the total 'allowable deductions' (namely, £50,000) when calculating his liability to capital gains tax on the subsequent partial disposal.

When capital gains tax was originally introduced, no allowance was given for inflation. The result was that, in times of raging inflation, taxpayers had to pay tax on 'gains' arising as a result of inflation, rather than as a result of a real increase in the asset's value. This unfairness has been addressed by the introduction of an 'indexation allowance' which permits taxpayers to increase the 'allowable deductions' available in respect of the initial and subsequent expenditure. This allowance is only available for disposals which took place on or after 6 April 1982. The allowance is calculated by multiplying the initial and subsequent expenditure by a decimal fraction (rounded to three decimal places) produced by the following formula:

$$\frac{RD - RI}{RI}$$

where RD is the retail prices index for the month of disposal and RI is the retail prices index for March 1992 or, if later, the month in which the expenditure was incurred. Inflation before March 1982 is not taken into account. There are special rules for assets held on 6 April 1965 (the date when capital gains tax first came into force) and on 31 March 1982 (when the indexation allowance was first permitted). Tax has never been levied on gains arising before 6 April 1965 and in March 1988 it was announced that the base date for capital gains tax would be changed. For all disposals made on or after 6 April 1988, no capital gains tax will be levied on gains arising prior to 31 March 1982. The effect of this is that taxpayers are treated as having disposed of assets on 31 March 1982 and as having reacquired them at their market value at that date.

It may be that the 'allowable deductions' in respect of a particular asset exceed the sale price or market value. In those circumstances, the loss arising can be set off against other gains made during the current tax year. The gains in the current year must be reduced to nil (even though the taxpayer is entitled to an annual exemption of, currenlty, £5,800). Only the balance of the loss once all other gains have been completely wiped out can be carried forward. Such losses can be carried forward indefinitely until gains arise in future years (although a carried forward loss must be set off against future gains as they arise). In contrast to the position for the year in which the loss initially arises, carried forward losses need only be set against the gains of future years to the extent necessary to bring that year's gains down to the amount of the then current annual exemption.

Assuming that a gain has arisen after the 'allowable deductions' have been deducted from the 'consideration for disposal', whether a *chargeable* gain will arise will depend on the availability of the exemptions and reliefs. The TCGA 1992 contains a variety of exemptions, the details of most of which are beyond the scope of this book. They include exemption for the taxpayer's only or main residence (s. 222 TCGA 1992), items of tangible movable property having a predictable useful life not exceeding 50 years (s. 45 TCGA 1992) and chattels where the consideration for disposal does not exceed £6,000 (s. 262 TCGA 1992).

If an exemption is not available in respect of a particular disposal, the following reliefs from tax may help produce (or wipe out) the liability to tax:

(a) the first £5,800 of gains arising on the disposals later in the current tax year (the 'annual exemption') (s. 3 TCGA 1992); and

(b) gains on disposal of business assets by a taxpayer aged 55 (or older), or a taxpayer who has retired on ill health grounds below that age (the 'retirement relief') (ss. 163-164, Sch. 4 TCGA 1992). In outline, this relief means that gains up to £150,000 are exempt and 50% of any gains realised between £150,000 and £600,000 are relieved. However, the maximum relief is available only if the taxpayer has owned the business assets for 10 years or more and no relief is available for business assets owned for less than one year. (Where shares in a company are disposed of, certain special conditions must be satisfied if the relief is to be available — see **18.2.3** below.)

In addition to the exemptions and reliefs outlined above it is possible, in certain circumstances, to postpone or defer the payment of tax. If the disposal is by way of a gift, or there is a sale with a gift element, the donor and donee can elect to 'hold over' any gain arising. This will result in the donee being treated as acquiring the asset at the donor's acquisition value. In certain circumstances, where the owner of certain types of assets sells them (even at full value), he can elect to 'roll over' the gain arising in to replacement assets. The effect will be to reduce the acquisition cost of the new assets by the amount of the 'rolled over' gain. If the 'hold over' or 'roll over' election is made, the whole of the gain arising must be held or rolled over, even if this means the taxpayer will lose the benefit of the annual exemption.

There are a number of hold over and roll over reliefs which will be looked at separately. Hold over relief is available in circumstances including:

(a) transfers between spouses (s. 58 TCGA 1992);

(b) gifts or sales at undervalue of business assets (s. 165 TCGA 1992), in which case a joint election can be made by the transferor and transferee but any gain arising will be held over (for these purposes, business assets are those used for the purposes of a trade, profession or vocation carried on by the transferor or his personal company and also include shares in an unquoted company or in the transferor's personal company; 'personal company' means that the donor holds at least 5% of the voting rights); and

(c) transfers chargeable to inheritance tax in which case a joint election can be made by the transferor and transferee that any gain arising can be held over but the relief is only available to disposals which are initially chargeable to inheritance tax, not those which are initially *potentially exempt* but which subsequently become chargeable because of the transferor's death within seven years.

The circumstances in which the roll over relief is available include:

(a) the replacement of business assets (including land, buildings, plant and machinery) provided the replacement asset is purchased in the period 12 months before or three years after the disposal of the old asset (ss. 152-160 TCGA 1992); and

(b) on the incorporation of a business provided the business is transferred as a going concern to a company in exchange for shares (s. 162 TCGA 1992). In those circumstances, the gain realised by the disposal of the assets to the company can be rolled over into the shares the company issues (which will mean that the shares, in effect, are acquired for the same value as were the assets which have been transferred).

If after taking into account all available exemptions, reliefs and deferments, a chargeable gain still remains, capital gains tax is payable calculated as if the gain was the top slice of the taxpayer's income (so that tax at the appropriate rates of 20%, 25% or 40% will be payable).

Finally, there is no capital gains tax payable when a person dies. The beneficiaries of the estate under the will or intestacy are deemed to acquire the asset at market value at the time of death. The absence of a deemed *disposal* avoids the liability to tax.

18.2.2   PARTNERSHIPS

When a firm disposes of one of their assets, normal CGT principles apply in determining what gain, if any, the firm has made. There are difficulties involved in applying the normal CGT principles to a partnership context. The problems are most clearly seen in connection with changes in the membership of the partnership. In **Chapter 14**, we looked at the Statements of Practice published by the Revenue which set out the way in which they regard the principles as applying in this context. As we explained in **Chapter 14**, the premise on which the Revenue statements are based is that each partner is to be treated as owning a fractional share of each of the chargeable assets of the partnership (including goodwill) and not, for this purpose, as owning an interest in the business as a whole. When the firm disposes of an asset to an outsider, each partner is treated as making a disposal of his fractional share in the asset.

The assessment and collection of CGT is treated differently from the assessment and collection of income tax. The president partner delivers a return to the Inland Revenue giving full details of disposals. The assessment is made on the individual partners. Each partner's share in the gain is calculated in accordance with his share in the asset disposed of.

In order to calculate the CGT liability of the individual partners in relation to the disposal of assets it is, therefore, necessary to know the proportions in which assets are owned. This is often referred to as the partners' 'assets surplus share'.

The partnership deed may specify the proportions in which asset surpluses are to be shared. If it does, it is conclusive. If there is no express provision in the partnership deed the asset surplus sharing ratio is deemed to be the ratio in which profits are shared. It is common for a partnership deed to provide an asset surplus sharing ratio which is different from the profit sharing ratio. For example, the agreement may provide for an individual partner's right to share in an asset surplus to be greater than his right to share in income profits, to reflect the fact that he has made a substantial capital contribution to the firm while contributing comparatively little to earning income profits.

When an asset is acquired by a partnership, each partner's share in the acquisition value is determined by his share in the asset surplus *at that time*. Similarly, in a disposal, each partner's share in the proceeds of disposal is determined by his share in the asset surpluses *at that time*.

For example, A and B are in partnership. They share profits equally and have made no special agreement as to sharing asset surpluses. They acquire an asset for £20,000. The acquisition value for each partner is:

A	½	£10,000
B	½	£10,000

They sell the assets for £36,000. The share in the proceeds of the disposal of each partner is:

A	½	£18,000
B	½	£18,000

The chargeable gain of each partner is (ignoring indexation):

A	£18,000 − £10,000 = £8,000
B	£18,000 − £10,000 = £8,000

Each partner is personally liable for his own chargeable gain and will be assessed for tax at the rates appropriate to his level of income.

Particular difficulties are involved in the application of the CGT rules to partnerships where the asset share ratio has changed (whether or not there is also a change in the personnel of the partnership). The effects of such a change are considered in **14.3.3.2**.

If there is a gain realised on the disposal, the exemptions and reliefs referred to in **18.2.1** above may be available. To the extent that there is a gift element in a disposal, hold over relief is available to postpone the payment of tax. This relief can be claimed not only in respect of partnership assets but also in respect of assets owned by an individual partner which are used by the firm. (However, in this case, there may be a potential inheritance tax liability to take into account as well.)

A disposal of partnership property in circumstances where the partners intend to reinvest the sale proceeds can attract roll over relief (under ss. 152-160 TCGA 1992). This option to postpone payment of tax is also available to a partner who owns an asset which is used by the partnership (irrespective of the terms on which the asset is used by the firm).

Where the disposal occurs when a partner is aged 55 (or earlier if the retirement is due to ill health), the partner disposing of his share can claim retirement relief provided he has owned his interest in the partnership for a least one year. (He will qualify for the full 100% relief if his ownership covers at least 10 years.) Relief can be claimed irrespective of the size of the partner's share in the partnership. If the partner owns assets which are not partnership property, relief is available if the disposal is associated with the disposal of the partner's share. If the partnership has been providing consideration for the use of the asset by paying a full market rent, the 'retiring' partner will not be able to claim a relief, save for a fraction of it which is in proportion to his share of the rent. A larger proportion of the relief will be available if the rent charged is less than the full market rent.

18.2.3   COMPANIES

A capital profit on the sale of shares may be liable to income tax under s. 703 ICTA 1988 (see **Chapter 31**), or when the sale is to the company in which the shares are held (see below). In other cases, the tax liability, if any, will be a liability to capital gains tax and the general principles set out in **18.2.1** above will apply.

It is not our intention to repeat those general principles but there are certain points in relation to the availability of reliefs on the disposal of shares in a company which merit particular attention.

18.2.3.1   Retirement relief

The conditions to be satisfied on the disposal of shares are that they are shares in a personal trading company or a personal holding company and the individual must be a full-time working officer or employee of the personal trading or personal holding companies or of another company in the group. (We explained in **18.2.1** that a personal company is one in which the transferor owns 5% of the voting rights.) To be entitled to relief at all, the individual must be able to show that these conditions have been satisfied throughout a period of at least one year prior to the disposal. Normally, this period of one year must end with the date of disposal. However, in certain cases, the relief is still available provided the conditions are satisfied by reference to a period ending on an earlier date. Thus, for example, a full-time officer or employee who decides to devote less of his time to the company can still claim the relief on a subsequent disposal of his shares if all the conditions were satisfied at the time he ceased to work full-time. However, having gone part-time, he can only preserve his rights to relief if he remains a director of the company and devotes at least 10 hours per week to the service of the company in a technical or managerial capacity throughout the period, starting with the date he ceases to work full-time and ending with the date of the disposal. There is no limit on the length of time the officer or employee can work part-time.

The relief is only given in relation to 'chargeable business assets'. In the case of a disposal of shares it is, therefore, necessary to calculate how much of the gain reflects chargeable business assets of the company (or of the whole trading group where shares in a holding company are being disposed of) and how much reflects other assets (such as stock in trade, which is not chargeable at all, and investments, which are not business assets). The relief is then restricted to the part of the gain resulting from chargeable business assets.

Where before disposal the business was owned personally by the transferor for part of the ten year period and by the company in which he owns the shares for part of that period, the period of personal ownership can be counted in calculating the proportion of the maximum relief which is available. Relief is also available where the asset disposed of is something owned personally by the transferor but used by his company.

Retirement relief is available on gifts as well as sale, subject to the same conditions. In those circumstances, to the extent that the chargeable gain exceeds the maximum amount of retirement relief which the donor can claim, the balance of the relief can be held over under s. 165 TCGA 1992.

18.2.3.2 Roll over relief on re-investment

Many business people have claimed that the existing capital gains tax reliefs have left them with a large tax liability when they sell their business. They have claimed that this often prevents them from starting new businesses, or from investing their capital and their own experience in other businesses. In the 1993 Budget, the Chancellor introduced a new relief (which will become s. 164A TCGA 1992) to remove this disincentive.

To get the relief, claimants must reinvest some or all of the gains from the said shares in their businesses in qualifying unquoted trading companies. The claimants must:

(a) sell shares in an unquoted trading company;

(b) have been the full time director or employee engaged in a managerial or technical capacity with that company;

(c) have, for at least one year owned more than 5% of the shares in that company; and

(d) reinvest in the qualifying unquoted trading company by acquiring or adding to a holding of at least 5% within a period beginning one year before and ending three years after the sale of the original shares. (A 'qualifying unquoted trading company' will include retail and manufacturing companies but not those with more than 50% of their assets in land or carrying on financial, leasing or land dealing activities.)

Any gains are to remain deferred while shares in a qualifying investment are held. It is possible for a person to sell one holding of qualifying shares and acquire another. However, the deferred gain will become taxable if the claimant emigrates, or sells the shares without replacing them with other qualifying shares or if, within three years of the reinvestment being made, the company involved ceases to be a qualifying company for the purposes of the relief.

18.2.3.3 The purchase by a company of its own shares

Where a company redeems, repays or buys its own shares under the provisions of ss. 159-181 Companies Act 1985 (see **Chapter 10**), tax will usually become payable. The amount received from the company is in some cases treated as a dividend (and so is subject to income tax) to the extent that it exceeds the original investment in the company. However, s. 219 ICTA 1988 contains provisions excluding such a payment from the definition of a distribution in certain circumstances. Where the payment is so excluded, capital gains tax will be payable on any increase in the value of the shares during the period of ownership (the redemption or repayment is treated as a disposal for CGT purposes as if it were a sale).

A redemption, repayment or purchase by the company is excluded from the definition of a distribution if the company is a trading company and the transaction is made 'wholly or mainly for the purposes of benefiting a trade carried on by the company'. Presumably, the transaction will be made for such a purpose if the object of it was to enable a shareholder of the company who disagreed with the policy of the directors to retire from the business if the company had more capital than it required. A transaction designed to enable the proprietors to take an income tax-free profit would not be covered, and this is reinforced by the further requirement that the main purpose or one of the main purposes of the scheme must not be 'to enable the owner of the shares to participate in the profits of the company without receiving a dividend or the avoidance of tax'. A redemption, repayment or purchase is also excluded from the definition of a distribution and the proceeds are intended to be used (and are used within two years) for the payment of IHT. The IHT must have arisen on a death and the shareholder must show that undue hardship would have arisen if the shares had not been purchased by the company.

In addition to the basic requirements of s. 219, income tax is only avoided if the following conditions are satisfied:

(a)   that the owner of the shares is resident and ordinarily resident in the UK at the time of the purchase;

(b)   that he has owned the shares for five years;

(c)   that the sale is of a substantial part of his shareholding taking into account any holding of his associates (which terms includes close relatives, partners and trustees of certain settlements); and

(d)   certain special conditions apply only in the case of groups of companies.

The object of these rules is to ensure that tax avoidance or tax advantages cannot be obtained by a purchase of its own shares by a company, but that 'genuine' transactions should give rise to CGT liability only. It is possible to apply for advance clearance when a scheme to buy back shares is proposed which, if granted, will ensure that putting the proposal into effect will not give rise to an income tax charge.

Payments to buy back members' shares are not deductible in calculating the company's profits for corporation tax purposes.

18.3   Inheritance Tax

18.3.1   GENERAL

Inheritance tax is payable under the provisions of the Inheritance Tax Act 1984 (IHTA 1984) where there is a *chargeable transfer*. The chargeable transfer is defined as 'any *transfer of value* which is made to an individual but is not . . . an exempt transfer'. A transfer of value is defined as 'a *disposition* made by a person . . . as a result of which the value of his estate immediately after the transfer is less than it would be but for the disposition . . .'. Inheritance tax is payable on the *value transferred* which is the amount by which the value of the transferor's estate is reduced as a result of the disposition.

Transfers of value can be made either *inter vivos* as a result of gifts or sales with a gift element or on death. In this section, we only give an outline of the principal aspect of the tax. The reader is referred to one of the standard tax text books for full details of all of the aspects of the tax.

There are three types of transfer which can give rise to inheritance tax (subject to the availability of any exemptions or reliefs). These are:

(a)   a transfer on death which will attract tax at the full rate;

(b)   a potentially exempt transfer which is an *inter vivos* transfer of value made by an individual as a result of which property becomes part of the estate of another individual or is transferred to certain types of trust. A potentially exempt transfer will become fully exempt if the transferor lives for seven years after the transfer. Death within those seven years will result in the transfer becoming chargeable at the rates of tax in force at the date of death; and

(c)   a chargeable transfer made before death which is immediately taxable but at only half the rates which apply on death. The death of the transferor within seven years will lead to the transferee becoming liable to tax at the full rates in force at the date of death.

There are now only two rates of inheritance tax. There is a nil rate band of £150,000 and any excess is taxed at the rate of 40% (subject to the points made below). Whether or not the nil rate band has been used up in relation to a particular chargeable transfer will depend on the total value of all previous chargeable transfers which the transferor has made within the immediately preceding seven years. This process of cumulation will mean that the tax on the present transfer will be calculated as if it were the top slice of a single transfer equal in value to all of the transfers (including the one with which we are concerned) made during the last seven years.

The full rate of 40% only applies where the transfer is made on death or within three years of death. Subject to that, if the chargeable transfer is made before death, inheritance tax is charged at the time of the transfer at half the full rate (currently 20%), assuming the nil rate band has been exhausted. If the transfer is a potentially exempt transfer or a chargeable transfer and the transferor dies within seven years, but not less than three years of the transfer, a sliding scale applies to determine the value of the transfer which will be subject to tax at the full rates in force at the time of death. Here a gift is made *inter vivos*, the transferor and the transferee can agree which of them will pay the inheritance tax. If the tax is paid by the donor, the loss to the donor will be the value of the gift plus any inheritance tax on it. This will mean that the inheritance tax calculation will be based on the gross loss to the donor. In those circumstances, it will be necessary to 'gross-up' the net gift before the calculation of the tax can be made.

It is not our intention to cover in this book any of the other detailed rules on the calculation of tax, such as the rules relating to gifts with a reservation or changes in values of gifts within seven years of death.

Clearly, the value of the property transferred plays an important part in the calculation of the liability to inheritance tax. For the purposes of inheritance tax, the value of particular items which have been given away will be the price which the property might reasonably be expected to fetch if it was to be sold in the open market at the time of the gift. However, there is no presumption that the value of the property will be reduced because it was all placed on the market at the same time. The latter reference will be of particular relevance when valuing a large holding of shares in a private company. In addition, there are certain special valuation rules which apply to shares. Quoted stocks and shares are usually valued by taking the lower of the two prices quoted in the Stock Exchange Daily Official List for the relevant day and adding to it one quarter of the difference between the lower and the higher quoted prices or, if it produces a lower figure, by taking a figure half way between the lowest and highest prices at which bargains were struck on the relevant day. The value of unquoted shares will be determined by the normal market value rule but it is sometimes extremely difficult to value such shares accurately. The facts that have to be taken into account include the company's profitability, its dividend record, the level of retained earnings and the value of the assets which the company owns. Should the shares be sold subject to pre-emption rights, the market value will be determined on the assumption that the pre-emption rights did not apply to the hypothetical sale. However, those rights will be assumed to apply to the hypothetical purchaser (which will mean that the value so determined would be the one which a purchaser was likely to pay in the full knowledge that the pre-emption rights will apply to their shares in the future).

Although not exclusively applicable to shares, a further rule which is of particular relevance when valuing shareholdings is the rule relating to 'related property'. This rule recognises the fact that some assets can be more valuable when combined with other assets of the same type than when they are owned individually. Shares which form part of a majority holding in a company will, for example, be more valuable than shares which form part of a minority shareholding. The IHTA 1984 defines a variety of items of property as being related property. This can include any item of property owned by the transferor's spouse at the time of the transfer. If the transfer is made of related property, the property actually transferred and the property to which it is related are valued as a single asset and tax is then calculated on the proportion of the total value which is transferred.

Finally, when valuing any property, transferred liabilities are taken into account to the extent that they were incurred for consideration in money or money's worth or imposed by law and provided there is no right to reimbursement.

At the start of this section, we stated that a chargeable transfer was any transfer of value which is not an *exempt* transfer. An exempt transfer will not attract tax and it will not be included in the transferor's cumulative total. The exemptions which can be claimed include the spouse exemption which is available both *inter vivos* and on death (and means that all gifts, irrespective of the value, between spouses are exempt from inheritance tax provided the recipient spouse is domiciled in the UK). An annual exemption of £3,000 per year is available on transfers made before death. If the annual redemption for any year is not used either wholly or partially, the unused part can be carried over for one year but no longer. Furthermore, outright *inter vivos* gifts worth up to about £2,500 per transferee are exempt.

In addition to the exemptions, the IHTA 1984 also makes various reliefs available which include quick succession relief, agricultural property relief and business property relief. The effect of a relief being available is to reduce the value of the relevant property with a resultant reduction in the amount of inheritance tax payable. In this section we will look only at business property relief which is available provided the property was 'relevant business property'. This term is defined as:

(a) property consisting of a business or an interest in a business (and so it includes the interest of a sole proprietor or a partner in a business);

(b) shareholdings in unquoted companies or companies quoted on the Unlisted Securities Market which alone, or with other shares owned by the transferor, or with related property gave the transferor control of the company;

(c) shareholdings in unquoted companies or companies quoted on the Unlisted Securities Market which alone or with related property carried more than 25% of the votes in the company;

(d) shareholdings in quoted companies which alone or with other shares owned by the transferor or with related property gave the transferor control immediately before the transfer;

(e) shareholdings in unquoted companies or the companies quoted on the Unlisted Securities Market which gave the transferor 25% or less of the votes; and

(f) land or buildings, or machinery or plant used immediately before the transfer wholly or mainly for the purposes of a company controlled by the transferor or of a partnership of which he was a member.

The relief on such a property is a reduction in the value transferred of 100% (in the case of property falling within (a)-(c) above) or 50% (in the case of property within (d)-(f) above).

For the purposes of this relief, 'business' includes a profession or a vocation but does not include a business carried on otherwise than for gain. Agriculture is a type of business and so business property relief may be available to the extent that agricultural relief is not. If the business consists of dealing in securities, stocks, shares, land or buildings or of holding investments, the relief is not available. The reduction in value is given on the net value of the business property (that is to say, after the liabilities have been deducted). Even if the property falls within the categories set out above, relief will not be available unless the transferor has owned the property throughout the two years before the transfer. If property replaces other relevant business property (other than in the case of minority shareholdings), relief is available provided the aggregate period of the ownership of the original and replacement property exceeds two years in the five years before the time of transfer. If the transferee of relevant business property himself makes a transfer of the same property before he has owned the property for two years, this will not prevent the relief being claimed provided the relief was available on the original transfer and one of the transfers was a transfer on death. If property is received on the death of a spouse, the surviving spouse can aggregate the deceased spouse's period of ownership with his own in order to satisfy the two year period of ownership requirement.

It is not our intention to deal with the complex rules for determining who is liable to account for inheritance tax to the Inland Revenue on death, nor to consider the rules on the burden or incidence of inheritance tax.

Tax on a chargeable transfer made before death must be paid six months after the end of the month in which the transfer is made or, if the transfer is made after 5 April and before 1 October, at the end of April in the next year. Tax in relation to a death is payable six months after the end of the month in which the death occurred. If tax is paid late, interest will be charged.

Inheritance tax on certain types of property can be paid by ten annual instalments. The instalment option is available in respect of:

(a)   land of any description;

(b)   shares or securities in a company giving the transferor control of the company immediately before death;

(c)   unquoted shares or securities which do not give the transferor control (provided paying the tax in one lump sum will not cause any hardship);

(d)   unquoted shares or securities are not giving the transferor control in the company, provided at least 20% of the tax paid by the person paying the tax on the shares is either tax on those shares or on those shares and other instalment options;

(e)   unquoted shares which did not give the transferor control and the value of which exceeds £20,000, provided they are at least 10% of all the shares of the company or are ordinary shares and at least 10% of the ordinary shares in the company; and

(f)   business or interest in a business including a profession or vocation.

Shares quoted on the Unlisted Securities Market are still 'unquoted' for these purposes. Control means voting control on all questions affecting the company. The relief is available whether the transfer is on death or *inter vivos* but, in the latter case, the relief is only available if the *transferee* pays the inheritance tax. The instalment option must be claimed by a written notice to the Revenue and the outstanding instalments must be paid off if the assets are sold within the ten year period.

If the instalment option is available, the first instalment is generally due six months after the end of the month in which the gift has been made. No interest is charged on the tax provided the instalments are paid on time. Although the instalment option does not reduce the amount of tax, the relief is nonetheless beneficial. The donor will often be able to pay the tax out of income derived from the business.

18.3.2   PARTNERSHIPS

The IHT legislation contains few provisions dealing specifically with partnerships. According to the general principle of IHT, any transfer of a partnership asset, or of an interest in a partnership, will be a transfer of value by the individual partners if the transfer is by way of gift or there is an element of gift in the disposition.

The transfer will be exempt if it is made between spouses. It will also be exempt if it was not intended to, and was not made in a transaction intended to, confer any gratuitous benefit and either it was an arm's length transaction between unconnected persons or was such as might be expected to be made between unconnected persons.

As a result of this provision, many *inter vivos* transfers which might appear to be transfers of value will escape inheritance tax. For example, when a new partner is admitted and is given a share in the assets without making a payment, there would be a transfer value were it not for this provision. This was considered in **Chapter 14.**

On death, a deceased partner's interest in the partnership will be part of his estate. The position was considered more fully in **Chapter 14** but business property relief (see **18.3.1**) will normally be available.

18.3.3   COMPANIES

The gift of shares may give rise to inheritance tax (and capital gains tax) since inheritance tax is chargeable on the 'loss to the donor's estate'. This normally means the market value of the asset given away, but in some cases the loss is considerably more than market value. For example, if a controlling shareholder gives away enough shares to lose control of the company, the loss to his estate will be very much more than the value of the shares given away.

The most important (but not only) 'reliefs' which will be relevant when shares in a company are given away are 'business property relief' and the instalment option (considered in **18.3.1** above). These reliefs exist because the Government recognises that too high a tax burden on the disposal of shares in a company could lead to the break-up of a company as being the only way of raising funds to pay the tax. Whether these two 'reliefs' will be available will depend on whether the conditions set out in **18.3.1** are satisfied. It should not be forgotten that the general exemptions (such as the spouse exemption and the annual exemption) will be available in respect of business property as well as the business property relief.

A shareholder, particularly a controlling shareholder, should consider the possible impact of tax on his family from a relatively young age. It should be clear from the rules described in this chapter that there is a very considerable fiscal advantage in disposing of shares *inter vivos* so as to take account of the fact that the IHT lifetime rates are lower than the death rates, and tax can be avoided altogether if the donor survives seven years after a potentially exempt transfer has been made. Since transfers of value are only cumulated for seven years after they are made (i.e., transfers made more than seven years ago are ignored in calculating the amount of tax), there is an advantage to be gained from making gifts of shares over a considerable period of time rather than all at once. However, it should be remembered that at some point one of the gifts will involve loss of the control of the company (and consequently a large transfer of value) and that once control is lost the future gifts will be eligible for 50% business relief rather than 100% relief. The burden of IHT can also be reduced in the long run by making use of the spouse exemption to ensure that both husband and wife lend enough to take maximum advantage of the nil rate band.

NINETEEN

RETIREMENT PROVISION

19.1 Introduction

Ensuring financial security during retirement is a matter which becomes of increasing concern to many individuals as they progress through their working lives. This chapter is concerned with the principal methods of providing for retirement which are available to directors, and employees, of companies and to partners. Different individuals will have different priorities and requirements so far as retirement provision is concerned. For some building up a capital fund during their working lives which can be invested to produce income and further capital growth will be of paramount importance; for others, the main aim will be to ensure they have a steady source of income.

For individuals who wish to enjoy the benefits of a capital fund on retirement, the sale of shares in their trading company or the sale of their interest in a sole proprietorship or partnership may be a convenient way of achieving their aim. The consequences of following this course of action were considered in **Chapter 18**. However, this option may not be available, or may be unattractive to the individual involved who may, therefore, need to ensure he receives a pension during his retirement.

This chapter is primarily concerned with the provision of income during retirement, whether from some form of pension fund or by means of payments from the former employer or former partners of the individual. A pension is taxable as earned income under Schedule E.

19.2 Retirement Provision for Directors and Employees

19.2.1 PRIVATE OCCUPATIONAL PENSION SCHEMES (ss. 590-612 ICTA 1988)

Many (though not all) employers provide private occupational pension schemes for their employees. The funds which provide the pensions are built up by contributions from the employer and the employee. These funds are usually managed by trustees who not only invest the contributions received but also administer the payment of pensions. Alternatively, under some schemes the contributions are paid, by way of premiums, to an insurance company which provides the pensions.

In theory a very wide range of schemes could be made available. However, one type of scheme (an 'exempt approved retirement benefits scheme') is eligible for very favourable tax treatment and so is very widely used. Such a scheme is one which is approved by the Occupational Pensions Board and accepted as exempt by the Inland Revenue Superannuation Funds Office. (The Revenue will grant exemption where the scheme is established under irrevocable trusts or where there are special circumstances justifying exemption.)

To be an approved scheme the following requirements must be complied with:

(a)   The scheme is bona fide established for the sole purpose of providing benefits in respect of the service of the recipient as an employee.

(b)   The scheme is established in connection with a trade or undertaking carried on in the UK by a UK resident.

(c)   The administrator of the scheme is a UK resident.

(d)   The scheme is recognised by both the employer and employees, and every employee has been given written details of its principal provisions.

(e)   The employer is a contributor to the scheme.

(f)   Contributions made by the employees under the scheme cannot be repaid.

(g)   The benefits are payable to the employee or his surviving spouse, children, dependants or personal representatives.

(h)   Any benefit for an employee is a pension on retirement which is first paid at an age not before 60 (for men) or 55 (for women) and not after 70, which does not exceed $^{1}/_{60}$th of the employee's average annual remuneration for the last three years of service for each year of service up to a maximum of 40 years.

(i)   Any benefit for the employee's spouse is a pension on the death or retirement of the employee which does not exceed $^{2}/_{3}$rds of the pension which would have been payable to the employee.

(j)   It must not be possible to surrender, commute or assign the pension in whole or in part, save that commutation in exchange for a lump sum is allowed provided the lump sum does not exceed $^{3}/_{80}$ths of the employee's final annual remuneration multiplied by the number of years of service up to a maximum of 40 (subject to an overall maximum of 1½ times the final remuneration).

(k)   No other benefits are payable under the scheme.

An earnings limit of £75,000 applies for the purpose of calculating certain benefits paid and contribution levels for approved schemes established on or after 14 March 1989 (this limit also applies to new entrants to existing schemes who join on or after 1 June 1989).

The Inland Revenue have a discretion to grant approval to schemes which do not satisfy certain of the requirements relating to the amount or type of benefit which can be received under the terms of the scheme. This discretion can be exercised to grant approval for schemes, providing, *inter alia*, higher pensions, death in service pensions for spouses, lump sum death in service benefits of up to four times the final remuneration or refunds of contributions.

If the scheme is a qualifying exempt approved scheme, the tax consequences are as follows:

(a)   Income derived from investments and deposits held for the purposes of the scheme are exempt from income tax.

(b)   The contributions to the scheme made by the employer can be deducted from profits when computing liability to tax under Schedule D Cases I and II.

(c)   The employee is allowed to deduct any ordinary annual contribution paid under the scheme when calculating his liability to Schedule E tax.

(d)   All pensions and annuities paid under the scheme are chargeable to tax as earned income under Schedule E. (The PAYE system applies for the purposes of collection of tax.)

19.2.2   RETIREMENT ANNUITY SCHEMES

An employee whose employer has not set up an occupational pension scheme is in the same position as a self-employed person. Accordingly, employees who are in non-pensionable employment often provide for their own retirement by means of a personal pension scheme (see **19.3.2** below).

19.2.3   FEES PAID TO NON-EXECUTIVE DIRECTORS

In cases where the employee wishing to ensure security of income during his retirement is a director of a company, it may be possible to secure an appointment as a non-executive director. Such an appointment is akin to an appointment as a consultant to a partnership. Provided the fees can properly be regarded as deductible expenses, the employer will be able to deduct the fees in calculating its taxable profits. The recipient will be receiving emoluments deriving from an office and will be assessed to tax under Schedule E. However, the company could remove the non-executive director from office and so this may not be a very secure method of providing for retirement.

19.2.4 THE STATE PENSION

In addition to the possible sources of pension benefits referred to above, a statutory state pension is available at present to every individual who has made National Insurance contributions.

The state pension scheme is funded by contributions made by both the employer and the employee. The terms of the state scheme provide for two types of pension, namely the flat-rate pension and the earnings-related pension (although the government is considering abolishing the earnings-related pension).

The flat-rate pension is payable at present at 65 (for men) and 60 (for women) to every individual who has contributed to the scheme for $^9/_{10}$ths of his or her working life, although the age limits are to be revised in line with European legislation.

In contrast the earnings-related scheme (under which an additional pension is provided, the amount of which is linked to the employee's earnings) is only available to employees whose employers have not 'contracted out' and there is a limit on the amount of earnings which are pensionable. (An employer can contract out if a private pension scheme is provided.)

The employee is not entitled to deduct any National Insurance contributions when calculating his tax liability.

19.3 Retirement Provision for Sole Proprietors and Partners

19.3.1 RETIREMENT ANNUITY CONTRACTS

On 1 July 1988 it ceased to be possible to take out new retirement annuity contracts since they were replaced by personal pensions (see **19.3.2** below). Since it is possible to continue to contribute to existing contracts, such contracts will continue to be of relevance for some years to come. Their key elements are explained below.

These schemes are available to the self-employed, employees whose employers do not run an occupational scheme and employees who opt out of their employer's scheme. The future pensioner gets income tax relief on contributions to the scheme up to a maximum of 17½% of net relevant earnings. Higher percentages apply where the premium is paid by a taxpayer aged 51 or older. On retirement, an annuity is purchased with the money in the accumulated fund. At that stage no capital gains tax is payable although the annuity when received is, of course, liable to income tax. A lump sum may be taken in cash on retirement provided that it does not exceed three times the value of the annuity payable (after the lump sum has been taken) subject to an overall maximum for the lump sum of £150,000.

19.3.2 PERSONAL PENSIONS

Such pensions (which replace retirement annuity contracts) can be taken out by the self-employed. They can also be taken out by employees in non-pensionable employment or those in pensionable employment who wish to 'top up' their occupational pensions or who have 'contracted out' of their occupational schemes.

The future pensioner will get income tax relief on his contributions up to a maximum of 17½% of net relevant earnings. However, if the taxpayer is aged 36 or over, the percentage for which relief is available increases on a sliding scale dependent on the payer's age.

As with occupational pensions, the tax relief is limited to contributions on earnings of up to £75,000 per annum. For personal pension plans entered into on or after 27 July 1989 the £150,000 ceiling applicable to the maximum tax free lump sum has been removed. Instead the maximum lump sum which can be taken at retirement is 25% of the total fund; the rules for determining the 'total fund' are beyond the scope of this book.

19.3.3 PARTNERSHIP ANNUITIES

While personal pensions may be the only method of providing a pension which is available to sole proprietors and employees in non-pensionable employment, it may be possible for a retiring partner (or his spouse and dependants) to receive an annuity from the continuing partners.

The terms of the payment of such an annuity are a matter to be agreed between the partners and that agreement should be reached well in advance of the retirement date.

This method of providing a pension has the attraction, so far as the retiring partner is concerned, of not requiring him to make payments prior to retirement (as is the case with a personal pension). However, the continuing partners may object since they will be supporting a person who is no longer contributing to the profits of the business.

The amount of the annuity will be a matter of negotiation. It can be linked to the profits of the partnership and so it may be possible to ensure that the income of the retired partner keeps pace with inflation.

Where an individual has ceased to be a member of a partnership on retirement, by reason of age or ill-health, or on death and an annuity is paid for his benefit or the benefit of his widow or dependants the annuity is treated as earned income, subject to a limit. The annuity must be paid under the partnership agreement, or an agreement replacing or supplementing the partnership agreement, or an agreement with an individual who has acquired all or part of the partnership business; it will be paid net of basic rate tax.

So far as the continuing partners are concerned, they will each bear the cost of the annuity in the same proportions as they share profits. The gross amount of the annuity payment is treated as a charge on their incomes and so will reduce their taxable share of profits. They will pay the annuity to the former partner net of basic rate income tax.

19.3.4 APPOINTMENT AS A CONSULTANT

The retiring partner may wish to retain some contact with the activities of the business by continuing to be involved as a consultant. Such an arrangement may give rise to the practical advantage that the partnership retains the benefit of the personal goodwill the retiring partner has built up over the years.

From a tax viewpoint, as the consultant is no longer a partner, the consultancy fees can be deducted in computing the partnership's profits provided they are wholly and exclusively incurred for business purposes.

The consultant will receive earned income taxable under Schedule E, although the nature of the consultancy arrangement may be such that he can show he is exercising a profession or vocation in which case he will be assessed under Schedule D Case II. This is more likely to be the case if the retiring partner has a number of consultancy arrangements.

19.3.5 THE STATE PENSION

Self-employed individuals, such as partners, pay Class 2 and Class 4 National Insurance contributions. Class 2 contributions are paid at a flat rate and, subject to satisfying certain requirements as to contribution history, entitle the individual at present to receive the flat-rate state retirement pension at

65 for men and 60 for women (but not the earnings related pension). Class 4 contributions are based on a percentage of taxable profits within certain limits. The payment of Class 4 contributions does not give rise to entitlement to any benefits; in effect, they operate as a form of additional income tax. Section 617 ICTA 1988 introduces provisions which allow tax relief to be given on 50% of the Class 4 contributions paid by a self-employed individual.

THE EUROPEAN COMMUNITY

TWENTY

THE EUROPEAN COMMUNITY: THE RIGHT OF ESTABLISHMENT AND THE RIGHT TO PROVIDE SERVICES

20.1 Introduction

In this chapter we will examine two closely related rights established by European Community law. These are the 'right of establishment' and the right to provide services. The right of establishment is the right of a national of one member State to set up business in another member State. The right to provide services is a right to do business in another member State in ways which fall short of setting up a business. Free movement of goods, persons and capital are provided for separately (in Article 60 of the Treaty of Rome) and so is freedom of transport (Article 61). Under Articles 58 and 66 the right of establishment and the right to provide services are extended to 'companies or firms formed in accordance with the law of a member State and having their registered office, administrative centre or principal place of business within the Community'.

20.2 Establishment and Services

Article 52 provides (in part):

> . . . restrictions of the freedom of establishment of nationals of a member State in the territory of another member State shall be abolished . . . such . . . abolition shall also apply to the setting up of agencies, branches or subsidiaries by nationals of any member State established in the territory of any member State.

> Freedom of establishment shall include the right to take up and manage undertakings in particular companies and firms . . . under the conditions laid down for its own nationals by the law of the country where such establishment is effected . . .

Article 59 provides (in part):

> . . . restrictions on freedom to provide services within the Community shall be . . . abolished . . . in respect of nationals of member States who are established in a State of the Community other than that of the person for whom the services are provided.

Services are defined as services 'normally provided for remuneration'.

These provisions effectively mean that nationals of all member States are to be treated as being on the same footing as far as doing business in any member State is concerned. A French national is, for example, free to set up business in the UK either on his own account, in partnership or through the medium of a company. Furthermore it would be illegal in terms of Community law for UK law to discriminate against him in respect of such a business.

However, companies formed in a member State are effectively excluded from this right unless their business is established in one of the member States. The reason for this is that such a company is not really an economic entity within the Community.

20.3   Limitations on the Rights of Establishment and Provision of Services

The basic principle of the provisions we have just examined is that nationals of any member State should be treated the same as nationals of the member State where they have set up their establishment where they are providing services. For example a Greek national who is undertaking a business in Germany should be treated in the same way, under German law, as a German conducting the same business.

At first sight this would seem to give complete protection to the Greek national. However, the Community has decided that further protection is needed in some cases. This is because national law might lay down requirements for its own nationals which they could easily achieve but which nationals of other states could not easily achieve. For example, a language requirement could be imposed simply for the purpose of giving a preference to nationals of the State concerned. The Community is therefore progressively abolishing such restrictions. However, it is recognised that such restrictions are reasonable in certain cases where the restriction relates to the education and training requirement of particular types of work or where it relates to rules of professional conduct in any member State.

The Community is, therefore, undertaking a process whereby Directives will be made under which professional and other qualifications will be recognised throughout the Community subject to safeguards in respect of reasonable requirements of the host State. To implement this process the basic requirement is that all States should recognise qualifications acquired in all other States. There are limited exceptions to this in the form of satisfying the host State's requirements in term of length of training. In certain cases an adaptation period may also be required during which the national of a member State may not practise on his own account in the host State. The period of additional training and the adaptation period together cannot exceed four years. The applicant to the profession (who is qualified in another member State) may take an aptitude test instead of undergoing the adaptation period.

A special exception is made for the legal profession and other professions which require knowledge of the law of the host State. In these cases the proper authority in the host State may require all applicants to take an aptitude test rather than undergoing a period of adaptation (they may not, however, require both).

TWENTY ONE

TREATY OF ROME ARTICLES 85 AND 86

21.1   Introduction

Articles 85 and 86 relate to the competition policy of the European Community. They are among the most important provisions of the Treaty. The object of the Treaty is to ensure that there is a free market which enables goods to move freely between the member States. Article 85 furthers this objective by outlawing certain agreeements which prevent, restrict or distort competition within the Community. Article 86 prohibits abuse of a dominant position in the common market or a significant part of it in so far as it may affect trade between member States.

In addition to the provisions of the Treaty itself regulations have been made by the Council of Ministers and by the Commission which supplement the provisions of the Treaty. The Court of Justice of the European Community and the Court of First Instance have also been called upon to develop a considerable body of case law relating to the competition policy of the Community.

The Council of Ministers has granted wide powers to the Commission in relation to competition law. In particular the Commission both makes policy decisions and enforces them (as to enforcement, see below). Parties aggrieved by a decision of the Commission are entitled to appeal, on points of law, to the Court of First Instance, and ultimately from there to the Court of Justice of the European Community itself.

21.2   Article 85

Article 85(1) prohibits 'all agreements between undertakings, decisions by associations of undertakings and concerted practices which may affect trade between member States and which have as their object or effect the prevention, restriction or distortion of competition within the common market'.

Agreements are defined as including informal agreements which may fall short of being contracts. The concept of a 'concerted practice' is even wider. This has been held to include any case where 'practical co-operation' between undertakings (i.e., businesses) have been set up in opposition to the concept of competition. An example of a concerted practice is where different undertakings keep their prices in line with each other. The fact that prices have risen at the same time is not, however, sufficient to prove a concerted practice. There must be evidence that the activities of the undertakings involved are such as to distort the market.

Decisions by associations of undertakings include such things as price fixing by trade associations. Decisions which have the effect of fixing prices are subject to Article 85 even if they are not binding on the members of the association, provided they are likely to be complied with at least to the extent that the free market will be affected.

The object of this provision is to ensure free movement of goods within the Community. However, it should be noted that what is prohibited is any agreement which may *affect trade between member States*. This does not, however, mean that an agreement which is made between undertakings in only one member State is automatically valid. An agreement between undertakings which only relates to activities within one country may indirectly prevent other companies from entering that market from a different member State.

21.2.1   VERTICAL AGREEMENTS

A vertical agreement is one between undertakings at different levels within the market. For example a manufacturer's agreement with a wholesaler or a wholesaler's agreement with a shop are vertical agreements. (An agreement between two manufacturers would be a horizontal agreement.) Examples of horizontal agreements include agency agreements and supply agreements. Vertical agreements are not usually considered to be as anti-competitive as horizontal agreements and so are less likely to fall foul of Article 85.

21.2.2   HORIZONTAL AGREEMENTS

Horizontal agreements are made between undertakings which are at the same level of the economic chain. These agreements are unlikely to be valid in view of the provisions of Article 85.

21.2.3   ARTICLE 85(3)

Article 85(3) provides an exemption from the basic rule contained in Article 85(1) where the operation of the rule would be inconsistent with the more general principles of competition law. Article 85(3) allows the Commission to consider agreements notified to it. The Commission can then issue a Decision to the parties which may exempt them from Article 85(1). The Commission will grant exemption to an agreement or decision of an association if it:

> contributes to the improvement of the production or distribution of goods or to promoting technical or economic progress, while allowing consumers a fair share of the resulting benefits, and which does not impose [unnecessary] restrictions on the undertakings or [allow] the undertakings to avoid competition.

21.2.4   IS IT POSSIBLE TO AVOID FALLING FOUL OF ARTICLE 85?

Article 85 is widely drawn so it is not possible to contract out of it. However, there are a number of effective exemptions.

21.2.4.1   Agreements of Minor Importance

The Commission has itself issued a notice on Agreements of Minor Importance which lays down guidelines allowing small scale agreements in circumstances where a similar agreement on a larger scale would be void (broadly speaking this applies where the parties control less than 5 per cent of the market in the Community).

21.2.4.2   Article 85(3)

We have already seen that Article 85(3) itself provides for exemption where the agreement is beneficial. An undertaking which believes that its agreement should be exempt under that provision can apply for an individual exemption which confirms the exempt status of this agreement.

21.2.4.3   Block exemptions

A system of block exemptions has been devised by the Commission. This provides that certain types of agreement are not to be regarded as infringing Article 85. In relation to each type of agreement the Commission will usually produce lists of terms which will be regarded as acceptable in such agreements ('the white list') and terms which will exclude the agreements from the block exemption ('the black list').

21.3   Article 86

Article 86 provides:

> Any abuse by one or more undertakings of a dominant position within the common market or in a substantial part of it shall be prohibited as incompatible with the common market in so far as it may affect trade between member states.

Notice that Article 86 (unlike Article 85) may be infringed by one undertaking acting alone. The key requirements here are that there must be a dominant position in the market and that that position must have been abused. The European Court of Justice has decided that a dominant position is one which 'enables the undertaking [or undertakings] to prevent effective competition . . . by giving it the power to behave to an appreciable extent independently of its competitors, customers and ultimately of its consumers' (*United Brands Co.* v *Commission* (Case 27/76) [1978] 1 CMLR 429). To be actionable the dominance must exist in a particular market. This is sometimes defined as the relevant product market which means the market for the goods in question together with any other goods which are effective substitutes for the goods in question.

Article 86 itself provides a list of activities which may be regarded as an abuse. This list is not intended to be exhaustive:

(a) imposition of unfair prices or trading conditions;
(b) limiting production markets or technical development to the prejudice of consumers;
(c) discriminating between different trading parties;
(d) by including terms in contracts which are collateral to the subject of the contract.

The abuse which is prohibited by Article 86 might also constitute a breach of Article 85. The two Articles are not designed to be mutually exclusive.

21.4   Enforcement of Competition Policy

21.4.1   DIRECT EFFECT

The provisions of Articles 85 and 86 have 'direct effect' in each of the States of the EC. This means that they are part of the law of each of the member States (in the UK as a result of the European Communities Act 1972). If there is any conflict between the provisions of EC law and the pre-existing UK law the EC law is to prevail. This means that UK courts must recognise and give effect to the competition law of the Community.

Agreements made in the UK which according to the principles of contract law may be valid, may be rendered void as a result of the competition law of the Community. In some cases, however, it may be possible for an English court to apply the principle of severance; that is, the court may be able to declare the clause in the agreement which offends competition law to be void, but uphold the rest of the contract. Whether the court can do this depends on the principles of English law. The traditional approach is that the court will not order severance if to do so would effectively require a re-writing of the agreement, either because the offending part cannot be separated within the agreement or because it is so fundamental to the agreement that to sever it would amount to imposing a new contract on the parties.

In addition to the possibility of action by another party to the contract it is also possible for third parties to sue under either Article if they have suffered loss. The position in English law is not entirely clear, but it would seem that the court can impose an injunction or award damages for breach of 'statutory' duty.

21.4.2   ENFORCEMENT BY THE COMMISSION

Many of the Commission's powers to investigate possible breach of Articles 85 and 86 are contained in Regulation 17/62. This enables the Commission to obtain information by (for example) inspecting premises, books and other records. The Commission has powers to impose fines of up to 1,000,000 ECU, or 10 per cent of the undertaking's turnover in the last accounting period, whichever is higher.

21.5   UK Competition Law

UK competition law is still relevant to UK cases to the extent that it does not conflict with EC law; if there is a conflict then the EC law will prevail. Among the principal rules of UK law in this area are:

(a)   The common law principles whereby certain agreements are void on grounds of public policy (e.g., restrictive covenants in employment contracts).
(b)   The Restrictive Trade Practices Act 1976 which requires registration of certain agreements which restrict competition.
(c)   The Resale Prices Act 1976 which prohibits (with limited exceptions) the right of manufacturers to fix what their customers may charge for goods.

INSOLVENCY

TWENTY TWO

BANKRUPTCY

22.1 Introduction

The risk of personal bankruptcy is a spectre which haunts many partners and sole traders. If a partner or sole trader finds that he is unable to pay his debts as they fall due, he may be made personally bankrupt. Thus, the partner or sole trader may be made bankrupt if his liabilities exceed his assets; he faces the same risk if he has insufficient liquid assets to pay his current liabilities even if the value of his total assets exceeds the value of his total liabilities.

It is to avoid this risk that many entrepreneurs choose to trade through a limited company. However, it should not be forgotten that the directors and members of a company may face personal bankruptcy where, for example, a director or shareholder has personally guaranteed a loan to the company or where a director is liable for 'wrongful' trading.

The members or partners may, of course, also find themselves facing bankruptcy as a result of a financial collapse entirely unconnected with the business of their own company or partnership.

The law of bankruptcy is now mostly contained in the Insolvency Act 1986 together with delegated legislation made under its provisions.

In this chapter we will summarise the law under the following headings:

(a) The procedure for making a person bankrupt.
(b) The appointment, function and removal of the trustee in bankruptcy.
(c) The effect of the bankruptcy order on the bankrupt personally.
(d) The provisions relating to the assets in the bankrupt's estate.
(e) The distribution of the bankrupt's assets.
(f) The duration of the bankruptcy and the discharge of the bankrupt.
(g) The rules governing voluntary arrangements contained in the Insolvency Act 1986.

A debtor who finds himself unable to meet all his debts in full may:

(a) be adjudicated bankrupt; or
(b) have his estate administered by a qualified insolvency practitioner under a voluntary arrangement (see **22.6** below).

189

22.2 The Bankruptcy Procedure

22.2.1 INTRODUCTION

Bankruptcy proceedings are commenced by the presentation of a petition for a bankruptcy order. The petitioners (who, broadly speaking, simply have to prove that the debtor is unable to pay his debts) are:

(a) a creditor (or creditors jointly) whether secured or unsecured; or
(b) the debtor personally; or
(c) a supervisor of, or a person bound by, a voluntary scheme; or
(d) the Director of Public Prosecutions.

22.2.2 PROCEDURE ON A CREDITOR'S PETITION

22.2.2.1 Prerequisites for presentation of a creditor's petition

The court will only entertain a petition presented by a creditor or creditors if certain conditions are satisfied:

(a) The debtor must normally be domiciled or personally present in England and Wales when the petition is presented.
(b) The debt (or debts) which are the basis of the petition must be for a liquidated sum.
(c) The debt (or debts) must amount to at least £750. (This sum can be changed from time to time by statutory instrument.)
(d) The debt must be unsecured. A secured creditor can present a petition but only if he relinquishes his security or petitions only for the unsecured part of the debt.

22.2.2.2 Grounds for presenting a creditor's petition

The petitioning creditor must allege that the debtor appears either:

(a) to be unable to pay, or
(b) to have no reasonable prospect of paying

the debt or debts specified in the petition and that there are no outstanding applications to have a 'statutory demand' set aside. (A 'statutory demand' is a demand in a form which complies with the Insolvency Rules 1986, r. 6.1.) The functions of the demand are described below.

22.2.2.3 Proving inability to pay debt

Before the court will make the order, the debtor's inability to pay his debt or debts may be proved in one of two ways:

(a) By showing that a 'statutory demand' served on the debtor requiring him to pay, secure or compound for the debt to the satisfaction of the petitioning creditor has not been complied with within three weeks.
(b) By showing that execution or other process issued in respect of the debt as a judgment or order of any court has been returned unsatisfied in whole or in part.

22.2.2.4 Grounds on which court may dismiss petition

Once a petition has been presented by a creditor the court may dismiss the petition if it is shown that the debtor can pay all his debts, including contingent and prospective debts; if the creditor has unreasonably refused any offer made by the debtor in response to a 'statutory demand'; or if it is appropriate to dismiss the petition for any reason, including a breach of the rules.

The court *must* dismiss a petition if a 'statutory demand' has been complied with.

22.2.3 PROCEDURE ON A DEBTOR'S OWN PETITION

The debtor himself may present a petition provided he has a connection with England and Wales. Accordingly the debtor must be able to show that he satisfies the requirements set out in **22.2.2.1 (a)** above.

The only ground on which the petition can be based is that the debtor is unable to pay his debts. When presenting the petition, the debtor must lodge a 'statement of affairs' giving full details of his assets, liabilities and creditors. Once presented, the petition can only be withdrawn with leave of the court.

In most cases the court will order an insolvency practitioner to inquire into the debtor's affairs and report on whether the debtor is willing to make a proposal for a composition with his creditors and/or whether the creditors should be summoned to a meeting at which they will consider such a proposal. Having considered the report of the insolvency practitioner the court can, if it considers it appropriate, make a bankruptcy order. Otherwise the voluntary composition will be pursued or the court can issue a certificate of summary administration.

22.2.4 PRESENTATION OF A PETITION BY A SUPERVISOR OF, OR A PERSON BOUND BY, A VOLUNTARY SCHEME

The supervisor of, or a person bound by, a voluntary scheme (the details of which are considered below in **22.8**) may base a petition on the following grounds:

    (a) that the debtor has failed to comply with his obligations under the scheme (or failure to comply with the supervisor's reasonable requests in connection with the scheme);

    (b) that the debtor has provided false or misleading information in connection with entry into the scheme.

22.2.5 PRESENTATION OF A PETITION BY THE DIRECTOR OF PUBLIC PROSECUTIONS

The DPP has power (under the Powers of Criminal Courts Act 1973) to apply to have a person made criminally bankrupt if the person has been convicted of an offence where loss in excess of a specified value has occurred.

22.2.6 CONSEQUENCES OF PRESENTING A PETITION

22.2.6.1 Restrictions on dispositions

A debtor who is the subject of a bankruptcy petition may be tempted to dispose of property before he is adjudicated bankrupt. The Insolvency Act 1986 makes void any disposition of property or payment of money made after the presentation of a petition if the debtor is subsequently adjudicated bankrupt unless the court approves the transaction either before or after it takes place.

22.2.6.2 Restrictions on proceedings

The court has power to stay any action, execution or legal process against the debtor or his assets while bankruptcy proceedings are pending.

22.2.7 MAKING THE BANKRUPTCY ORDER

Once the petition has been presented, the court may exercise its discretion to make a bankruptcy order (or, in the case of a petition presented by the debtor personally, to make an interim order so that a voluntary composition with the creditors can be arranged).

22.2.8 PROCEDURE FOLLOWING THE MAKING OF THE BANKRUPTCY ORDER

22.2.8.1 The official receiver becomes receiver and manager of the estate

Unless a trustee in bankruptcy is appointed at the time the bankruptcy order is made, the official receiver (who is an official of the court) will become the receiver and manager of the bankrupt's estate on the making of the order, pending the appointment of a trustee in bankruptcy.

22.2.8.2 Statement of affairs by the bankrupt

The bankrupt must, unless the official receiver dispenses with the requirement, prepare a statement of his affairs within 21 days (although this time-limit may be extended by the official receiver). Failure to do so is contempt of court.

When the debtor presents his own petition he must prepare a statement of affairs which is lodged with the petition.

22.2.8.3 Public examination of the bankrupt

At any time after the order is made and before the bankrupt is discharged, the official receiver can apply for an order that the bankrupt be required to attend a public examination of his affairs.

22.2.8.4 Appointment of a committee of creditors

Following the making of the bankruptcy order, a committee of creditors can be appointed by the creditors (unless the official receiver has been appointed as trustee in bankruptcy in which case the Secretary of State performs the function of the committee).

22.3 The Trustee in Bankruptcy

22.3.1 INTRODUCTION

The Insolvency Act 1986 provides that the administration of a bankrupt estate should be carried out by a trustee in bankruptcy.

22.3.2 APPOINTMENT

The procedure for appointing a trustee in bankruptcy and the date on which his appointment takes effect differ depending on who makes the appointment.

22.3.2.1 Appointment by creditors

If the official receiver is acting as receiver and manager of the bankrupt's estate, he has 12 weeks from the making of the order to decide whether to call a meeting of the creditors for the purpose of appointing a trustee. If he decides to call such a meeting he must notify the creditors within the 12-week period. He *must* call such a meeting if one-quarter (by value) of the creditors demand it and if he decides not to call a meeting, one-quarter (by value) of the creditors can override his decision. Provided the creditors do not object to no meeting being called, on notifying the court that no meeting will be held, the official receiver automatically becomes the trustee.

22.3.2.2 Appointment by the court

If the order is based on the debtor's own petition, the insolvency practitioner who is appointed to report on the debtor's affairs can be appointed as the trustee.

22.3.2.3 Appointment by the Secretary of State

The Secretary of State has power to appoint the trustee if the creditors fail to make an appointment at their meeting.

22.3.3 FUNCTIONS OF THE TRUSTEE

The function of the trustee is to get in, realise and distribute the bankrupt's estate in accordance with the provisions of the Act.

22.3.4 POWERS OF THE TRUSTEE

The Act gives the trustee wide powers which he may exercise in the course of administering the bankrupt's affairs. He may:

(a) Sell any part of the property for the time being comprised in the bankrupt's estate, including the goodwill and book debts of any business.
(b) Give receipts for any money received by him.
(c) Prove, rank, claim and draw a dividend in respect of such debts *due* to the bankrupt as are comprised in the bankrupt's estate.
(d) Exercise in relation to any property comprised in the bankrupt's estate any powers which the Act vests in him as trustee.
(e) Exercise all the powers of a receiver appointed by the High Court to enable him to collect or retain the bankrupt's estate.
(f) Exercise all the powers the bankrupt could exercise to transfer shares, stock or other property.
(g) Exercise extensive powers to require delivery, production or inspection of books, documents and records.
(h) Apply to the court for orders directing the bankrupt to do any act in connection with the administration of the estate.
(i) Hold property, make contracts, sue and be sued, employ agents, execute documents and do any act which may be necessary or expedient for the exercise of his powers.
(j) Disclaim onerous property (e.g., unprofitable contracts).

There are certain further powers which are only exercisable with the consent of the committee of creditors (if there is one) or of the court. These include:

(a) Power to carry on the bankrupt's business with a view to a beneficial winding up.
(b) Power to mortgage or pledge assets with a view to raising money for the estate.
(c) Power to make any compromise or arrangement as may be expedient with the creditors of the estate.
(d) Power to require the bankrupt to do any acts in the management or carrying on of the bankrupt's business.

22.3.5 RETIREMENT, REMOVAL AND RELEASE

22.3.5.1 Resignation

A trustee in bankruptcy may resign only if the resignation is accepted either by a creditors' meeting or by the court. Resignation must arise out of ill-health, retirement from practice, conflict of interest or other sufficient causes.

22.3.5.2 Removal

The appointees of creditors can be removed either by the court or by the creditors themselves at a general meeting summoned specially for the purpose.

22.4 Effect of the Bankruptcy Order on the Bankrupt Personally

If the court exercises its discretion to make a bankruptcy order against the debtor, he will become an undischarged bankrupt and will be deprived of the ownership of his property.

An undischarged bankrupt suffers certain disabilities, for example he cannot practise as a solicitor or barrister nor act as a director, nor be involved in the management, of a company. Furthermore, an undischarged bankrupt faces criminal liability if he commits one of the offences specified in the 1986 Act. These include making gifts of property, concealing property, and obtaining credit without disclosing the bankruptcy.

22.5 Assets in the Bankrupt's Estate

22.5.1 INTRODUCTION

The trustee in bankruptcy is under an obligation to collect the bankrupt's assets and distribute them among the bankrupt's creditors. In this section, we consider which assets can be claimed by the trustee towards payment of the bankrupt's debts.

22.5.2 AVOIDANCE OF DISPOSITIONS MADE AFTER THE PRESENTATION OF THE PETITION

Any disposition made by the bankrupt in the period between presentation of the petition and the date the estate of the bankrupt vests in the trustee in bankruptcy is void, unless the court gave prior consent (or subsequently ratifies) the disposition.

22.5.3 VESTING THE ASSETS IN THE TRUSTEE

Once the bankruptcy order is made, the undischarged bankrupt is deprived of the ownership of his property.

22.5.4 PROPERTY NOT AVAILABLE TO THE TRUSTEE

If the bankrupt enjoyed a purely personal right, such as the benefit of the Rent Act statutory tenancy, this is not available to the trustee. The following items are also not available for distribution:

(a) Property held by the bankrupt in trust for any other person.

(b) The tools of his trade, as well as such wearing apparel and bedding as is necessary to satisfy the basic needs of the bankrupt and his family.

(c) The personal earnings of the bankrupt to the extent that those earnings are not in excess of what is required to satisfy the reasonable domestic needs of the bankrupt and his family.

22.5.5 EXTENSION OF TRUSTEE'S TITLE TO BANKRUPT'S PROPERTY

The Act gives the trustee power to claim assets which are no longer in the possession or ownership of the bankrupt in the circumstances set out below.

22.5.5.1 Transactions defrauding creditors (sections 423 to 425)

Grounds Section 423 of the Insolvency Act 1986 can be used to give relief in respect of transactions defrauding creditors. To be within the scope of s. 423 a transaction must be:

(a) a transaction at an undervalue entered into between one person and another; and

(b) be accompanied by the requisite intent, namely that it is done for the purpose of putting assets beyond the reach of a person who is making, or may at some time make, a claim against the relevant person, or of otherwise prejudicing the interests of such a person in relation to the claim which he is making or may make.

Time limit   The transaction which is the subject of an action under s. 423 can have taken place at any time; there is no time-limit.

22.5.5.2   Undervalue transactions

If a person who is subsequently made bankrupt has transferred property to, for example, a member of his family or to trustees to hold for the benefit of his family with a view to putting assets beyond the reach of his creditors the transaction may be voidable under s. 339 of the Insolvency Act 1986.

Grounds on which transaction voidable   If the transaction is at an undervalue and is with a person who is not an associate of the transferor, it is voidable at the instance of the trustee in bankruptcy (or administrator where a voluntary arrangement has been made) if the transaction took place within the five years ending with the day on which the bankruptcy petition which ultimately led to the individual being adjudged bankrupt was presented (unless the debtor was solvent at the time of, and despite entering into, the transaction). However, if the individual entered into the transaction at an undervalue within two years of the presentation of the relevant bankruptcy petition, the transaction is voidable irrespective of whether the debtor was insolvent at the time of, or as a result of, the transaction.

Transfer to associate   In circumstances where the transferee is an 'associate' of the transferor, transactions entered into during the period of five years preceding the presentation of the petition are presumed, unless it can be *proved* to the contrary, to have taken place at a time when the transferor was insolvent. 'Associate' is defined as the bankrupt's spouse or former or reputed spouse, and, in relation to any of them or the bankrupt, a brother, sister, uncle, aunt, nephew, niece, lineal ancestor or lineal descendant (including relatives of the half-blood, stepchildren, adopted and illegitimate children. A company controlled by the bankrupt or any associate(s), as defined, is an associate.

22.5.5.3   Voidable preferences

A debtor who is in financial difficulties may not only make an undervalue transaction (as described in **22.5.5.2** above) but he may also be tempted to give a 'voidable preference' (Insolvency Act 1986, s.340).

Grounds   A 'voidable preference' consists of the debtor doing or suffering anything to be done at a time when he is insolvent which 'has the effect of putting [the person who benefits from the preference] into a position which, in the event of the [debtor's] bankruptcy, will be better than the position he would have been in if that thing had not been done'. Thus, a debtor discharging one of his unsecured, ordinary creditor's debts in full at a time when his assets are insufficient to discharge *all* his debts in full may have given a voidable preference.

If the trustee in bankruptcy considers that a voidable preference has been made, he may apply to the court to remedy the preference. However, an order can only be made where it can be proved that the debtor was 'influenced in deciding to give it by a desire' to improve the position of the creditor. Under these provisions the intention to prefer the particular creditor need not be the *dominant* intention.

Preference given to 'associate'   In cases where the preference is given by an individual to his 'associate' (see **22.5.5.2** above), there is a *presumption* that the debtor was influenced by the desire which would make the preference voidable, unless the contrary is proved.

Time limits   A preference is voidable if it takes place within the two years ending with the presentation of the bankruptcy petition, if the person preferred is an associate, but in other cases the preference is only actionable if it took place in the six months preceding the presentation of the petition.

22.5.5.4   Family homes

The Insolvency Act contains provisions designed to protect the family home of the bankrupt for the benefit of his family.

If the family home is owned in the sole name of the bankrupt the 1986 Act charges the right of occupation of the spouse of the bankrupt on the interest of the trustee in bankruptcy in the matrimonial home. If an application is made to realise the bankrupt's interest in the house the court will consider certain factors when deciding whether to grant an application for sale of the house. These factors include the creditors' interests, the needs and resources of the spouse, the needs of the children, whether the spouse's conduct contributed to the bankruptcy and all other relevant circumstances. (If the matrimonial home is owned in joint names by the bankrupt and his spouse, the discretionary factors listed above will be taken into account when the trustee applies under s.30 of the Law of Property Act 1925 to realise the bankrupt's interest.) If the application is made after one year has elapsed since the bankrupt's property vested in the trustee in bankruptcy, the interests of the creditors will be paramount.

If the bankrupt's minor children lived in the home at the time of presenting the petition and when the bankruptcy order was made, the bankrupt cannot be evicted without a court order. The court will consider the creditors' interests, the bankrupt's financial resources, the needs of the children and all the circumstances when deciding whether to make the eviction order. If the application is made after one year has elapsed since the bankrupt's estate vested in his trustee the interests of the creditors will outweigh all other considerations, unless the circumstances are exceptional.

22.6   Distribution of the Bankrupt's Assets

22.6.1   DISTRIBUTION PROCEDURE

Having realised as much of the bankrupt's assets as possible without needlessly protracting the administration of the estate, the trustee must notify the creditors that he intends to declare a final dividend (or that no dividend will be declared). The notice must also state a final date for the proving of claims (although the court has power, on application by any person, to postpone this date). Subject to any postponement, any creditor who fails to prove by the final date may be ignored in the final dividend.

22.6.2   ORDER OF PRIORITY FOR PAYMENT OF DEBTS

The distribution of the bankrupt's assets must be made strictly in accordance with the statutory order for payment of debts which is as follows:

(a)   Secured creditors, who take the mortgaged or charged property in priority to all other claims. However, if the security is insufficient to meet the debt, as far as the excess is concerned, the secured creditor claims as an ordinary creditor.

(b)   The administration costs of the bankruptcy paid to the official receiver, the trustee in bankruptcy and others, including professional advisers who have given assistance.

(c)   Certain sums paid to masters by their apprentices.

(d)   The preferential debts which are the same as those relevant on a company liquidation. These debts are calculated by reference to the 'relevant date', which, generally, is the date the bankruptcy order is made (unless an interim receiver is appointed following the presentation of the petition in which case the date is that on which the receiver is first appointed), and include:

(i)   Sums due from the debtor in respect of deductions of PAYE from his employees' wages in the 12 months prior to the relevant date.

(ii)   VAT claims up to six months before the relevant date.

(iii)   National insurance contributions for 12 months prior to the relevant date (for Class 1 or 2 social security contributions) or one year's assessment of Class 4 contributions before 5 April prior to the relevant date.

(iv)   Employees' arrears of wages or salary (including time or piece work and commission) for four months prior to the relevant date subject to an overall financial limit prescribed by delegated legislation (currently £800). These sums include sick pay, protective awards, and payments for time off work, such as on trade union work.

(v)   Accrued holiday remuneration.

(e)   The ordinary unsecured creditors.

(f)   Statutory interest which will be paid if a surplus remains after all previous claims have been paid. This interest is paid from the date of the order to the date of payment and the rate is the greater of the rate provided for in s.17 of the Judgments Act 1938 and the rate the bankrupt would have had to pay on the debt if he had not been made bankrupt.

(g)   The postponed creditors such as the spouse of the bankrupt who has a provable debt as a result of a loan to the bankrupt spouse.

(h)   The bankrupt receives any surplus.

Each class of creditor must be paid in full before the next class receives anything. If the assets are insufficient to meet the debts owed to the creditors of the class, they are paid rateably according to value.

22.7   Duration of the Bankruptcy and Discharge of the Bankrupt

22.7.1   DISCHARGE OF THE BANKRUPT

The Insolvency Act 1986, in relation to the majority of bankruptcies, provides for a bankrupt to be automatically discharged once the period of time specified by the Act has elapsed. In most circumstances this period is three years. The Act contains provisions which will prevent the 'automatic' discharge being available if the circumstances justify it.

22.7.2   EFFECT OF DISCHARGE

Once the bankrupt has been discharged, he is normally freed from the disqualifications suffered by undischarged bankrupts and from liability to meet his bankruptcy debts.

22.8   Voluntary Arrangements

22.8.1   INTRODUCTION

While formal bankruptcy may be the appropriate method of dealing with many debtors who find themselves in financial difficulties, there will be certain cases where the debtor involved may be able to come to terms with his creditors without involving the full rigour of the bankruptcy procedure. Although deeds of arrangement entered into under the Deeds of Arrangement Act 1914 were intended to satisfy this particular need, that procedure is not entirely satisfactory since only the creditors who agree to the deed of arrangement are bound by its terms. The procedure under the 1914 Act has been little used and is not considered further in this book. Therefore, the Insolvency Act 1986 has introduced a new alternative method by which debtors can come to binding arrangements with their creditors.

22.8.2 INTERIM ORDER

22.8.2.1 Application by debtor

If a debtor in financial difficulties wishes to propose a composition or scheme of arrangement to his creditors, he may apply to the court, even if a petition for his bankruptcy has already been presented, for an interim order to be made.

22.8.2.2 Effect of interim orders

Once the interim order is made, no bankruptcy petition can be presented against the debtor and no other proceedings, execution or legal process can, without the leave of the court, be commenced or prosecuted against the debtor or his assets.

22.8.2.3 Period of interim order

The interim order is relatively short-lived since it will cease to have effect at the end of the period of 14 days beginning with the day after the order was made, although the court has power to extend the period.

22.8.3 PROCEDURE FOLLOWING THE MAKING OF THE INTERIM ORDER

22.8.3.1 Debtors to provide statements to nominee

After the order has been made the debtor must provide the nominee (that is to say, the proposed 'trustee' of the arrangement) with a statement giving details of the proposed composition or scheme. He must also give a statement of his affairs, which will give details of his assets and liabilities. Failure to do so may result in the interim order being discharged.

22.8.3.2 Failure by nominee to deliver report to court

Should the nominee fail to deliver the report to the court before the interim order expires, the debtor can apply to the court to have the order renewed or extended and the debtor may also apply to have the nominee replaced.

22.8.3.3 Discharge of interim order

If the nominee decides that a meeting of creditors should not be called and the court agrees, the interim order may be discharged.

22.8.4 CONSIDERATION OF THE DEBTOR'S PROPOSALS

If the nominee has submitted a report to the court recommending that a creditor's meeting be called to consider the debtor's proposals, subject to any directions made by the court, the nominee gives notice of the meeting (at the date, time and place specified in his report to the court) to all creditors of whom he is aware.

At the meeting the proposals will be considered and the proposals may be approved as proposed or with any changes thought appropriate.

22.8.5 EFFECT OF ACCEPTING THE PROPOSAL

Once the proposal is approved, all persons who had notice of the meeting and who were entitled to vote at the meeting (irrespective of whether they did so vote) are bound by the composition or scheme as if they were parties to it.

Subject to any challenges within the 28-day period referred to in **21.8.6** below, once the proposal has been accepted, any interim order in force ceases to have effect and any bankruptcy petition which was stayed by the interim order is deemed to have been dismissed (subject to a court order to the contrary).

22.8.6 CHALLENGING THE DECISION OF THE CREDITORS' MEETING

22.8.6.1 Parties who may challenge

Once the creditors' meeting has reported its decision to the court, at any time during the 28 days commencing with the day the report is made to the court, that decision may be challenged by:

(a) the debtor;
(b) any person who was entitled to vote at the meeting;
(c) the nominee (or his replacement).

22.8.6.2 Grounds

The grounds of challenge are limited to the following:

(a) that the composition or scheme accepted by the meeting unfairly prejudices the interests of a creditor; and/or
(b) that there was a material irregularity at, or in relation to, the meeting.

22.8.6.3 Effect of challenge

If the court confirms the challenge, the approval of the meeting may be revoked or suspended. Alternatively, the court may order a further meeting to be held to consider any revised proposal or (if the challenge is based on 'material irregularity' in relation to the meeting) order that the meeting be held again to reconsider the proposal.

Having ordered a further meeting to be held, the court can extend or renew the interim order. However, if the court is satisfied that no revised proposal will be submitted by the debtor, the order to hold a further meeting will be revoked and the approval given at the original meeting will be revoked or suspended.

TWENTY THREE

COMPANY INSOLVENCY PROCEEDINGS

23.1 Introduction

All statute references in this chapter are to the Insolvency Act 1986 except where otherwise stated.

In this chapter we deal with the procedures which are available when a company is insolvent and with the procedures which are designed to prevent insolvency where a company is having financial problems.

The law relating to these matters is now largely contained in the Insolvency Act 1986. There are four principal procedures available where a company is insolvent or has financial problems:

23.1.1 ADMINISTRATION ORDER

This is a procedure which may be ordered by the court with a view to saving the business of the company (or part of it), or with a view to a more beneficial realisation of assets than could be achieved by winding up, or with a view to obtaining approval for a voluntary arrangement.

23.1.2 VOLUNTARY ARRANGEMENT UNDER THE INSOLVENCY ACT 1986

This procedure enables a variety of schemes to be implemented (with the agreement of the company and its creditors) either so as to avoid or to supplement other types of insolvency procedure.

23.1.3 ADMINISTRATIVE RECEIVERSHIP

An administrative receiver is appointed by a lender who holds a floating charge. The main responsibility of the receiver is to take control of the company so as to pay off the appointing creditor. However, the law recognises that this may have a considerable and permanent effect on the company and its other creditors and so various statutory powers are granted to the receiver and a number of obligations are imposed on him.

23.1.4 LIQUIDATION (OR WINDING UP)

There are three types of liquidation: liquidation by the court (or compulsory winding up), members' voluntary liquidation and creditors' voluntary liquidation. There are many procedural and other differences between these types of liquidation but each is designed to achieve the same thing, that is, the collection and distribution of all the company's assets. The effect of liquidation is that the company ceases to exist as a *commercial* entity. When the liquidation is over the company is 'dissolved', that is, it ceases to exist as a *legal* entity.

The administration procedure and liquidation by the court are initiated by petition, applications to the court are required at various stages of the procedures for these remedies and also in relation to voluntary schemes, administrative receivership and voluntary winding up. The High Court has jurisdiction to deal with any such petition or application where the company is registered in England and Wales. This type of business is assigned to the Chancery Division. In addition the county court of the district in which the company's registered office is situated has concurrent jurisdiction where the company's paid-up share capital does not exceed £120,000.

23.2 Administration Orders

Administration is intended as an alternative to winding up. It is used principally in circumstances where a company is in difficulties but where something can be saved.

23.2.1 APPLICATION AND GROUNDS

23.2.1.1 Who may present a petition

A petition for the making of an administration order may be presented by the company, or its directors, or by a creditor or creditors (including any contingent or prospective creditor or creditors) or by any or all of those people together.

23.2.1.2 Grounds

The petitioner must show that the company is unable to pay its debts or is likely to become unable to pay its debts. The petitioner must swear an affidavit setting out the grounds for the petition. This may be supported by a report from an independent insolvency practitioner which sets out the practitioner's reasons for believing that at least one of the objectives can be achieved. If no such report is annexed to the petition the petitioner must explain why none has been produced. In practice a petition not supported by a report is unlikely to succeed except perhaps in cases of great urgency.

The circumstances in which a company is treated as being unable to pay its debts are the same as for compulsory winding up (see **22.5.2.1**). In addition to proving inability to pay debts the petitioner must also satisfy the court that the making of the administration order would be likely to achieve one or more of the following objectives:

(a) the survival of the company, and the whole or any part of its undertaking as a going concern;
(b) the approval of a voluntary arrangement or a composition in satisfaction of the company's debts, or a compromise or arrangement between the company and some or all of its members under s. 425 CA 1985; or
(c) a more advantageous realisation of the company's assets than would be effected on a winding up.

As we will see shortly, the making of an administration order imposes a moratorium on the collection of debts by the company's creditors. A 'breathing space' is, therefore, created during which the administrator appointed by the court can seek to do one of these three things for the benefit of the creditors of the company generally.

23.2.1.3 Discretion of the court

The court has a discretion as to whether or not it will make an administration order. Very many companies are insolvent (unable to pay their debts) because of the 'balance sheet test' (that is, the value of the assets is less than the amount of the liabilities taking into account contingent and prospective liabilities). However, the court will exercise its discretion and refuse to make an administration order in cases where the company is viable even though technically insolvent.

23.2.2 CONSEQUENCES OF PETITION

23.2.2.1 Creates moratorium

The presentation of the petition for an administration order has an immediate and dramatic effect on the company. From the time when the petition is presented until the time when the court decides to make the order or to dismiss the petition a 'moratorium' is imposed on the company's debts. This means that creditors may not:

(a) take any steps to enforce any security over the company's property (this does not, however, prevent appointment of an *administrative* receiver — see **23.2.5**);

(b) repossess goods in the company's possession under a hire-purchase agreement, a conditional sale agreement, a chattel leasing agreement or an agreement under which the vendor has retained title;

(c) commence or continue proceedings, execution or other legal process against the company or its property;

(d) levy distress against the company's property.

However, any of these things can be done with leave of the court. The object of these rules is to preserve the assets of the company so that if an order is made the administrator will have a better chance of saving the business.

23.2.2.2 Stay on winding up

During the period between the petition and the making of the order or the dismissal of the petition the company cannot be wound up. (A petition for winding up may, however, be presented — it will be considered only if the court dismisses the petition for administration.)

23.2.3 CONSEQUENCES OF ADMINISTRATION ORDER

23.2.3.1 Administration manages company's affairs

The administration order directs that the affairs, business and property of the company are to be managed by an administrator appointed by the court. The administrator must be a qualified insolvency practitioner.

22.2.3.2 Continuation of moratorium

While the administration order is in force the moratorium preventing creditors from enforcing their rights continues. The restrictions are the same as those following the petition (see **23.2.2** above) save that the restrictions can be waived by the administrator as well as by the court. In addition, no appointment of an administrative receiver is possible while the order is in force.

22.2.3.3 Effect on other insolvency procedures

Once the order is made any petition for the winding up of the company is dismissed, any administrative receiver vacates office (see **23.4.2** for the definition of an administrative receiver and note that an administration order cannot normally be made where an administratve receiver is in office — see **23.2.5**). The administrator can also require any other receiver to vacate office.

23.2.4 THE ADMINISTRATION PROCESS

23.2.4.1 Powers and duties of the administrator

General   As we have already seen the administrator is appointed to run the company and its business with a view to saving the viable parts of the business or with a view to obtaining approval for a voluntary scheme or with a view to advantageous realisation of assets. The administrator is given very wide powers to achieve these things. He is given power to do 'all such things as may be necessary for the management of the affairs, business and property of the company' (s. 14(1)(a)) and also certain particular powers listed in sch. 1. These include power to bring and defend proceedings, sell assets, borrow money, insure and appoint agents. In cases of difficulty the administrator may apply to the court for directions.

Property subject to a floating charge   Section 15 gives the administrator power to deal with certain property of (or in the possession of) the company free from the claims of other persons. Section 15(1) allows the administrator to dispose of property which is subject to a floating charge as if the property were not subject to the floating charge. This provision applies also where the property is subject to a charge which was a floating charge when created even though it has since crystallised and thus turned into a fixed charge. Where property is disposed of by the administrator under s. 15(1), the holder of the floating charge (or former floating charge) is entitled to the same priority in respect of the property directly or indirectly representing the property disposed of as he would have had in respect of the property which was subject to the charge and which was disposed of by the administrator. Thus the position of the floating chargee is, in theory, as secure as it was before the administration order was made. However, the holder will have to wait for payment, possibly for a considerable time, and formidable problems may arise in trying to identify what property is to be regarded as 'directly or indirectly representing the property disposed of'.

Fixed charge and other property   Section 15(2) allows the administrator to dispose of property which is subject to a fixed charge and of property in the possession of the company under a hire-purchase agreement, a conditional sale agreement, a chattel leasing agreement or a retention of title agreement. However, in this case the administrator can only dispose of the property with the agreement of the court which must be satisfied that the disposal is likely to promote the purpose for which the administration order was made. The court order must direct that the proceeds of sale (and any sum required to make good any difference between the proceeds and market value of the assets) shall be used to discharge the company's liability to the secured creditor or owner of the goods which have been disposed of as the case may be.

23.2.4.2 Statement of affairs

The administrator must require a statement of affairs to be prepared (s. 22). This will usually be required from the directors but the secretary, former directors, certain employees and former employees and the directors and certain employees of certain associated companies may also be required to make the statement. The statement must usually be prepared within 21 days but the administrator or court can extend this period. The statement must set out details of the company's assets, debts and liabilities, creditors and securities.

23.2.4.3 Proposals

Preparation   Because of the moratorium created by an administration order the creditors of the company are forced to bear some of the risk inherent in the whole process of administration (that is the risk that, if the administration fails to save the business, the company will be in a weaker position when the administration ends than when it began). The creditors are, however, given a measure of control over the administration process. Section 23 requires the administrator to prepare proposals as to how he is going to achieve the purpose for which he was appointed. These proposals must be sent to the Registrar of Companies and to all creditors (so far as the administrator is aware of their addresses) within three months of the making of the order unless the court extends the period. Copies of the proposals must also either be sent to all the members or the members must be given an opportunity to ask for free copies.

Meeting of creditors   The administrator must hold a meeting of the creditors within three months of the order (unless the court extends the period) at which the proposals are considered. If the proposals are accepted by the creditors' meeting then the administrator must manage the company in accordance with the proposals. The creditors' meeting may propose modifications to the proposals but, as he is the person who will have to implement them, the administrator can reject such modifications.

If the creditors' meeting rejects the proposals the administrator must go back to the court. In such a case the court will usually discharge the administration order but it may also make any other order as it sees fit including a further administration order.

Revision of proposals   During the course of the administration the administrator may need to revise the proposals which have been accepted by the creditors. If he does so, and the revision appears to him to be substantial, then he must seek approval of the revision from a creditors' meeting (s. 25).

23.2.4.4   Discharge of administration order

The administrator may apply to the court for discharge of the order at any time. He *must* make such an application when it appears to him that the purpose for which the order was made has been achieved or has become incapable of achievement, or when required to do so by a creditors' meeting.

23.2.5   ADMINISTRATION AND OTHER REMEDIES

23.2.5.1   Winding up

Administration is an alternative to winding up. An administration order cannot, therefore, be made once the company has gone into liquidation. This means that the passing of a winding up resolution by the company (see **23.5.3.1**) or the making of a winding up order (see **23.5.2.2**) preclude the making of an administration order. Similarly the making of an administration order prevents winding up.

23.2.5.2   Administrative receivership

Administration and administrative receivership are also mutually exclusive. Thus when a petition for an administration order is presented notice must be given to any person who has appointed or is entitled to appoint an administrative receiver (see **23.4.2** — broadly speaking a floating charge holder can make such an appointment). An administration order cannot be made if, by the time of the hearing, an administrative receiver has been appointed unless either the creditor who made the appointment consents or it is shown that his charge would be liable to be set aside under ss. 238, 239 or 245 (see **Chapter 24**). Once an administration order has been made no appointment of an administrative receiver is possible. These rules give a creditor who can appoint an administrative receiver a right to veto administration but if he wishes to do so he must act quickly as the right to veto is lost if no appointment has been made by the time the petition for administration is heard.

23.3   Voluntary Arrangements (Sections 1 to 7)

23.3.1   PROPOSALS AND NOMINEE'S REPORT

The Insolvency Act 1986 seeks to promote agreement between a company in difficulties and its creditors. The directors or (where the company is being wound up) the liquidator or (where an administration order is in force) the administrator may make proposals to the company and its creditors. These proposals must, if they are to be put into effect under the Act, nominate a qualified insolvency practitioner to act in relation to the composition or scheme which is proposed. Where the nominee is not the liquidator or administrator, the person making the proposal (that is, the liquidator, administrator or directors) must submit details of the proposals and of the company's creditors, debts, liabilities and assets to the nominee. The nominee must then submit a report to the court stating whether or not he thinks that meetings of members and creditors should be called to consider the proposals.

23.3.2 MEETINGS OF MEMBERS AND CREDITORS

Where the nominee recommends that meetings should be held he may call the meetings unless the court orders otherwise. Notice must be given to every creditor of whose claim and address the person calling the meeting is aware.

The meetings of members and creditors then consider the scheme, which they may reject, approve or approve with modifications. A simple majority is required at the members' meeting (members having the voting rights attached to their shares by the articles). The position is more complicated at the creditors' meeting but basically the resolution is only validly passed if approved by at least three-quarters (by value) of the unsecured creditors *and* by a simple majority (by value) of the unsecured creditors together with such of the secured creditors as are not connected with the company.

The result of the meetings must be reported to the court. The court can reject the scheme on grounds of unfair prejudice or material irregularity.

23.3.3 IMPLEMENTATION OF APPROVED SCHEME BY SUPERVISOR

Where both meetings approve a scheme the scheme becomes binding on all persons who had notice of the shareholders' or creditors' meeting and were entitled to vote at that meeting. However, unless he agrees, the scheme cannot affect a secured creditor's right to enforce his security nor a preferred creditor's preference.

Once approved, the scheme is implemented by the supervisor (who is the same person as the nominee unless the court or meetings decide otherwise).

23.3.4 RELATIONSHIP BETWEEN VOLUNTARY SCHEMES AND ADMINISTRATION

The proposal that a voluntary scheme should be implemented does not create a moratorium so that, unless and until the scheme is approved, any creditor can seek payment of his own debt (by court action, petition for winding up, repossession or any other lawful means available to him). Even when the scheme is approved it does not prevent secured creditors enforcing their security. A voluntary arrangement is, therefore, more likely to succeed if an application for administration is made first thus giving rise to the moratorium. The administrator may then be able to put together a satisfactory voluntary scheme which he can supervise.

23.4 Receivership

23.4.1 NATURE OF RECEIVERSHIP

A receiver is a person who is appointed by or on behalf of a creditor to realise a security. His principal duty is to the appointing debenture holder. Receivers may be appointed by the debenture holder (provided that the debenture so provides) or by the court. In practice nearly all appointments are made by the debenture holder. The powers of the receiver are derived from the debenture although administrative receivers, as defined by the Insolvency Act 1986, have certain statutory powers.

23.4.2 ADMINISTRATIVE RECEIVERS — DEFINITION

Most receivers come within the definition of an 'administrative receiver' (s.29(2)). The Insolvency Act 1986 imposes certain duties on and grants certain powers to administrative receivers which do not apply in the case of other receivers. Only a qualified insolvency practitioner can be appointed as an administrative receiver. An administrative receiver is:

(a) a receiver or manager of the whole (or substantially the whole) of a company's property appointed by or on behalf of the holders of any debentures of the company secured by a charge which, as created, was a floating charge, or by such a charge and one or more other securities; or

(b) a person who would be such a receiver or manager but for the appointment of some other person as the receiver of part of the company's property.

In practice the person with a floating charge over the whole or substantially the whole of the company's property will usually be a bank. The bank is also likely to have fixed charges over land owned by the company and certain other assets (e.g., book debts) but these do not prevent it from appointing an administrative receiver.

23.4.3 ADMINISTRATIVE RECEIVERS — POWERS AND DUTIES

The administrative receiver, when appointed, effectively replaces the directors in the management of the company. His appointment is, therefore, a matter of great importance to the members, creditors and employees of the company. The law recognises this and so grants powers to and imposes obligations on an administrative receiver which make his position very similar to the position of an administrator. The administrative receiver is chosen by the debenture holder, not by the court, but can only be removed by the court.

23.4.3.1 General powers

An administrative receiver has all the powers conferred on him by the debenture under which he is appointed and also certain powers listed in the Insolvency Act 1986. The statutory powers include power to deal with the assets of the company, take or defend proceedings in its name and power to carry on the business of the company. These powers are the same as those granted to an administrator.

Disposal of property subject to prior charge Section 43 gives an administrative receiver power to go to court to obtain an order for the sale of assets free from any security with priority over the debenture under which he was appointed. The court may only authorise the administrative receiver to dispose of such property if it is likely to promote a more advantageous realisation of the company's assets. The court might, for example, authorise such a disposal so as to enable the receiver to sell the business of the company as a going concern. The proceeds of disposal (plus any difference between those proceeds and market value) must be paid to the person who was entitled to the security.

23.4.3.2 Legal position

The administrative receiver is deemed to be the agent of the company (s.44). Any contract which he makes is, therefore, binding on the company. The agency, however, ends when the company goes into liquidation. Section 44 also makes the administrative receiver personally liable on any contract which he himself makes and on any contract of employment which he 'adopts'. What amounts to an adoption of a contract is unclear. The administrative receiver is entitled to an indemnity against personal liability out of the assets of the company and, if the debenture so provides, will have an indemnity from his appointor.

23.4.3.3 Duty to pay preferential creditors

The primary duty of any receiver is to realise the security of the debenture holder who appointed him. A receiver appointed on behalf of a floating charge holder (whether or not he is an administrative receiver as defined) is, however, under a duty to pay preferential creditors (see 23.8) in priority to the debt secured by the floating charge.

23.4.3.4 Investigation and report into company's affairs

An administrative receiver is entitled to a statement of affairs from the directors (or in certain cases other officials) of the company. Within three months of his appointment (or longer if the court so directs) he must make a report which he must send to the court and to creditors.

The report must give details of the events leading to the appointment of the receiver, his dealings with the property of the company, his payments to the creditor who appointed him and to preferential creditors and an assessment of what will be available (if anything) to ordinary creditors.

23.4.4 CHOICE OF REMEDY

23.4.4.1 Position of floating chargeholder

A bank or other creditor with a floating charge will often be faced with a choice if its customer gets into difficulty. It may go to court to seek an administration order, or it may appoint its own administrative receiver, or it may seek winding up. As we have already seen (at **23.2.5**) the debenture holder loses the right to appoint an administrative receiver once an administrator has been appointed but, until that time, can effectively veto administration by appointing an administrative receiver.

23.4.4.2 Comparison of administration and administrative receivership

Administration and administrative receivership are in many ways very similar but are different from each other in the following principal respects:

(a)   The administrative receiver is chosen by the debenture holder, the administrator is appointed by the court.
(b)   The administration procedure leads to a moratorium, administrative receivership does not.
(c)   Administration blocks winding up petitions by other creditors.
(d)   In administration certain transactions may be set aside (see **23.8** below).
(e)   In administration owners of goods in the company's possession under hire-purchase and retention of title agreements cannot repossess without leave of the administrator or court.

23.5 Liquidation or Winding Up

23.5.1 TYPES OF WINDING UP

There are two types of winding up: compulsory liquidation and voluntary liquidation. Compulsory liquidation is initiated by petition to the court. Voluntary liquidation is initiated by a decision of the members of the company. Both types of winding up are designed to bring the existence of the company to an end and to distribute its assets to those entitled to them.

23.5.2 COMPULSORY WINDING UP

23.5.2.1 Grounds

Compulsory liquidation begins with a petition to the court (Chancery Division or, in some cases, county court — see **23.1** above). A petition can be presented on a number of grounds. By far the most common ground is that the company is unable to pay its debts. A company is treated as being unable to pay its debts if:

(a)   a demand for payment, in the prescribed form, for more than £750 (this figure may be changed from time to time by regulations) has been left at the company's registered office and the company has neglected to pay the debt, or to secure or compound for it (that is, agree to a reasonable compromise) to the reasonable satisfaction of the creditor for three weeks; or

(b) execution or other process issued on a judgment, decree or court order is returned unsatisfied; or

(c) it is proved that the company is actually unable to pay taking into account contingent and prospective liabilities; or

(d) it is proved that the value of the company's assets is less than the amount of its liabilities taking into account contingent and prospective liabilities.

Apart from inability to pay debts there are other grounds on which a company may be wound up. These are, however, seldom resorted to and are not considered in this book save that the 'just and equitable' ground is considered briefly in **Chapter 9**.

23.5.2.2 Locus standi

A petition for compulsory winding up may be presented by the company itself, any creditor or creditors (including contingent or prospective creditors), any contributory or contributories (the term 'contributory' includes the members of the company and certain former members) and, in very limited circumstances, by the Department of Trade and Industry. In practice the overwhelming majority of petitions are presented by creditors.

23.5.2.3 Court's discretion to refuse order

Even where a creditor has proved grounds for winding up, the court has a discretion to refuse to make an order winding up the company. An order will normally be refused where:

(a) The petitioning creditor (together with any supporting creditors) is owed £750 or less. This is by analogy with the rule whereby a statutory demand for more than £750 can be used as proof of inability to pay debts.

(b) The majority by value of the creditors oppose the winding up of the company.

23.5.3 VOLUNTARY WINDING UP

23.5.3.1 Commencement

By s.84 a company can be wound up voluntarily if:

(a) a special resolution to wind up is passed; or

(b) an extraordinary resolution is passed to the effect that the company should be wound up as it cannot continue in business because of its debts (that is, the company is, in effect, insolvent).

The winding up commences from the date of passing the appropriate resolution. A notice of the resolution must appear in the *London Gazette* within 14 days of its being passed.

23.5.3.2 Types of voluntary winding up

There are two types of voluntary liquidation; a members' voluntary winding up and a creditors' voluntary winding up.

Members' voluntary winding up The liquidation will be a members' voluntary winding up if, within the five weeks immediately preceding the date of the resolution (or on that date but before the resolution is actually passed) the directors (or the majority of them if more than two) make a statutory declaration, setting out the company's assets and liabilities, and stating that they have made a full enquiry into the company's affairs and are of the opinion that the company will be able to pay its debts in full within 12 months of the commencement of the winding up. The declaration must be delivered to the registrar within 15 days after the day the resolution was passed.

Creditors' voluntary winding up If no such 'declaration of solvency' is filed the winding up is a creditors' winding up. A meeting of the creditors must be called for a day not later than the 14th day after the day on which the meeting at which the members pass the winding-up resolution is held. Notice of the meeting must be posted to the creditors at least seven days before the creditors' meeting and the meeting must also be advertised in the *Gazette* and at least two newspapers.

Conversion from members' to creditors' voluntary winding up During the course of a members' voluntary winding up, it may become clear that the company will be unable to pay its debts within 12 months of commencement of the winding up. If this happens the liquidator must report the fact to the creditors, call a creditors' meeting and convert the liquidation into a creditors' voluntary winding up.

23.6 Liquidators

23.6.1 COMPULSORY LIQUIDATION

When a winding-up order is made the official receiver of the court becomes the liquidator of the company and continues in office until someone else is appointed (s. 136(2)). The official receiver may summon meetings of creditors and contributories with a view to the appointment of a liquidator. He must either do so or give notice that he intends not to do so within 12 weeks of the winding up order and may be required to call such meetings by one-quarter (by value) of the creditors.

Where meetings of creditors and contributories are held each meeting may nominate a liquidator. If the same person is nominated by each meeting, he becomes the liquidator. If different people are nominated the creditors' nominee takes office unless a creditor or contributory successfully applies to the court for the appointment of the contributories' nominee (either alone or jointly with the creditors' nominee) or of some other person.

Any liquidator must be a qualified insolvency practitioner.

23.6.2 CREDITORS' VOLUNTARY WINDING UP

As we have already seen, in a creditors' winding up a meeting of creditors must be held within 14 days of the meeting (of the members) at which the winding-up resolution was passed. The creditors may nominate a liquidator at their meeting. He will then become liquidator of the company but any director, member or creditor may apply to the court for the appointment of the members' nominee (either alone or jointly with the creditors' nominee) or of some other person.

The members will often have appointed a liquidator at the meeting at which the resolution for creditors' winding up was passed. Such a liquidator is entitled to act until the creditors' meeting is held but during that period his powers are restricted to collecting the company's property, disposing of perishable goods or other goods which may decline in value and taking other steps to protect the company's assets.

The liquidator must be a qualified insolvency practitioner.

23.6.3 MEMBERS' VOLUNTARY WINDING UP

The liquidator (who must be a qualified insolvency practitioner) is appointed by the members in general meeting.

23.6.4 FUNCTIONS OF LIQUIDATORS

The function of the liquidator of a company is to collect in the assets of the company and to pay their value to those creditors who are entitled according to the statutory order for payment (see **23.8**). If there is anything left after all creditors have been paid their debts and interest, the surplus goes to the members. If there are two or more classes of shares some members may have priority over others in claiming the surplus.

Sections 165 and 167 give liquidators extensive powers to assist them in performing their functions. These powers include:

(a) Power to pay any class of creditors in full.

(b) Power to enter into a compromise or arrangement with creditors (this can be made binding without the agreement of all the creditors in certain cases provided that the voluntary arrangements procedure (**23.3** above) is used).

(c) Power to compromise claims to which the company is entitled.

(The liquidator can only exercise the above powers with the sanction of an extraordinary resolution in the case of members' winding up, of the court, a committee of creditors or creditors' meeting in the case of creditors' winding up and of the court or committee in the case of compulsory winding up.)

(d) Power to bring or defend legal proceedings.

(e) Power to carry on the company's business for the purpose of beneficial winding up.

(Sanction is required in the case of compulsory winding up only.)

(f) Power to sell the company's property.

(g) Power to execute documents (including deeds).

(h) Power to borrow on the security of the company's assets.

(i) Power to act through agents.

(j) Power to do 'all such other things as may be necessary for winding up the company's affairs and distributing its assets'.

(No sanction is required for items (f) to (j) in any type of winding up.)

23.6.5 PROCEEDINGS AGAINST THE COMPANY

It would obviously be unfair if one creditor could start an action after the liquidation had begun and so obtain priority over the other creditors. Therefore, once an order for compulsory winding up has been made, no action can be started or proceeded with unless the leave of the court is obtained (s.130), and at any time between presentation of the petition and the making of the order, the company, or any creditor or contributory, can apply to have any action pending against the company stayed (s.126). Furthermore, any execution, attachment, sequestration or distress started after the commencement of a compulsory liquidation is void. However, if the attachment or execution was begun before presentation of the petition it can only be avoided by the liquidator if it was completed after commencement of the liquidation. This last provision also applies to voluntary liquidations, the operative date being the date the resolution to wind up the company was passed.

With regard to voluntary liquidations, the liquidator, any creditor or member, may apply to the court to have actions stayed. Such a stay is not granted automatically although, if the action is begun after the date of passing the resolution to wind up an insolvent company, it will normally be granted.

23.7 Collection and Distribution of Assets in Liquidation

23.7.1 PROPERTY OF THE COMPANY

23.7.1.1 Power to sell or charge

The liquidator has power to sell or mortgage the property and to satisfy the claims of the various people entitled in the company's liquidation (see **23.6.4** above).

23.7.1.2 Power to disclaim

An important power of the liquidator in relation to the company's property is the right of disclaimer given by s.178. The section gives the liquidator power to disclaim any of the company's property which consists of unprofitable contracts, or other property that is unsaleable or not readily saleable.

23.7.2 ASSETS IN THE HANDS OF THE COMPANY

23.7.2.1 Assets held on trust

The creditors of an insolvent company are entitled to payment from its assets. They are not entitled to any assets of which the company is the legal owner but which it holds on trust for a third party. This has been held to apply in certain cases where a company holds cash for its customers. In *Re Kayford Ltd* [1975] 1 All ER 604, the company put money received from mail order customers into a special trust account from which it only made withdrawals when goods were delivered to the customers. When the company went into liquidation it was held that the money in the account belonged to the customers whose orders had not been fulfilled and so was not available to the liquidator.

23.7.2.2 Assets subject to retention of title

Many suppliers of goods supply goods under contracts which contain retention of title clauses. These are clauses which state that the vendor retains title to the goods supplied until the purchaser pays for them. Such clauses have been considered in a number of reported cases (the leading case is *Aluminium Industrie Vaasen BV v Romalpa Aluminium* [1976] 2 All ER 552). Their effect varies depending on the exact wording which is used and on the circumstances of the case. A straightforward reservation of title clause is effective in ensuring that the vendor, not the liquidator, is entitled to the goods (or the proceeds of their further sale) if the company becomes insolvent. However, clauses which have tried to extend the unpaid vendor's rights (for example, by purportedly transferring them to newly manufactured goods only partly consisting of the goods which he originally supplied) have generally failed. (For the powers of an administrator to dispose of goods despite a retention of title clause see **23.2.4.1** above.)

23.8 Order of Entitlement to Assets

The principal duty of the liquidator of a company is to distribute the assets to those entitled. In a large majority of cases there will be insufficient funds available to pay all the creditors in full. There is, therefore, an order in which the assets must be paid to the creditors.

23.8.1 CREDITORS WITH FIXED CHARGES

Creditors with fixed charges are entitled to payment out of the assets which are charged to them before those assets are used for any other purpose. As between creditors with fixed charges over the same assets priority is governed by registration under s. 395 CA 1985 (but remember that a fixed charge gives priority over a floating charge, even though the latter is created and registered first, unless the floating charge prohibited the creation of later fixed charges ranking in priority to it and the fixed chargee had notice of this prohibition when he took the charge).

If the security of a fixed charge is inadequate (that is, the value of the charged assets is less than the amount of the debt), the chargee may claim the balance of the debt as an ordinary creditor. If the debt is oversecured (that is, the value of the charged assets is more than the amount of the debt), the chargee will be paid in full and the balance will be available for other creditors.

23.8.2   COSTS OF WINDING UP

Costs of winding up, including liquidators' fees and expenses, are paid in full before any other creditors (except those with fixed charges who are paid first to the extent of their security).

23.8.3   PREFERENTIAL CREDITORS

After payment of costs and expenses the next category of creditor is the preferred creditor. Preferred debts are:

(a)   Sums owed to the Inland Revenue for PAYE deducted from employees' wages in the 12 months before the relevant date.

(b)   VAT (and certain other sums due to Customs and Excise) referable to the six-month period before the relevant date.

(c)   Certain social security contributions and contributions to occupational pension schemes.

(d)   Wages owed to an employee in respect of the four months before the relevant date up to a maximum of £800 per employee (this figure may be varied from time to time by statutory instrument). Certain categories of holiday pay are also preferential.

(e)   Money lent to an employer so as to enable it to pay debts in category (iv) above and which was in fact used for that purpose. (Thus a bank is a preferential creditor if it allows an employer to overdraw a 'wages account' so as to keep on the workforce in the four months before the relevant date.)

The 'relevant date' is usually the date of the winding-up resolution, appointment of liquidator or date of appointment of a receiver.

Preferred creditors (to the extent of their preference) are entitled to payment in full before ordinary creditors or holders of floating charges receive any payment. If the assets are insufficient to pay the preferred creditors in full they rank equally *inter se* and so each is paid the same proportion of the preferred debt.

28.8.4   CREDITORS WITH FLOATING CHARGES

Floating chargees rank after preferred creditors but, to the extent of their security, before ordinary creditors. Priority is determined by date of registration where there are two or more floating charges over the same property.

28.8.5   ORDINARY CREDITORS

Ordinary creditors rank after all preferred creditors and secured creditors. They rank equally *inter se*.

28.8.6   INTEREST ON DEBTS

Once all creditors have been paid in full any surplus is first used to pay interest on debts from the date of liquidation. This interest is paid to all creditors equally regardless of whether their debts ranked equally for payment.

28.8.7   SHAREHOLDERS

Any surplus after payment of debts and interest goes to the members according to the rights attached to their shares.

23.9   Dissolution

Once winding up is complete the company may be dissolved. This is achieved in the following ways:

(a)   In compulsory liquidation the liquidator gives notice to the Registrar of Companies that he has completed the winding up. The company is then automatically dissolved three months later.

(b)   In voluntary winding up the liquidator holds a final meeting and files certain returns with the Registrar of Companies. The company is then automatically dissolved after three months.

(c)   The Registrar may dissolve a company by striking it off the register in certain circumstances where the company has ceased to trade.

TWENTY FOUR

LIABILITIES ARISING FROM INSOLVENCY

In this chapter we will look at a number of rules which enable insolvency practitioners to claim assets which are not held by the insolvent company itself.

24.1 Wrongful Trading (Section 214)

The directors of a company which is being wound up may be made liable, by the court, to contribute to the assets of the company if they are found to be guilty of wrongful trading.

24.1.1 GROUNDS

A person is guilty of wrongful trading where:

(a) the company goes into insolvent liquidation;

(b) that person knew or ought to have concluded (at some time before the commencement of winding up) that there was no reasonable prospect that the company would avoid going into insolvent liquidation; and

(c) that person was a director of the company at that time.

24.1.2 DEFENCE

A defence is available to a director who shows that he took every step with a view to minimising the potential loss to the company's creditors as he ought to have taken. However, in judging whether this defence is available the court must assume that the director knew what a reasonably diligent person having the general knowledge, skill and experience that it is reasonable to expect of a person carrying out his functions in relation to the company would have as well as taking into account the general knowledge, skill and experience which he actually had.

The steps which a director must take to avoid liability for wrongful trading will vary depending on the circumstances of the case. They might include, for example, proposing that the board should apply to the court for an administration order.

24.2 Transactions at an Undervalue and Preferences

Certain transactions which a company has entered into may be set aside on the ground that they are transactions at an undervalue or preferences. An application to the court by the liquidator is required for such transactions to be set aside. (The same rules apply where an administration order has been made save that the application is then made by the administrator.)

24.2.1   TRANSACTION AT AN UNDERVALUE

An undervalue is defined (by s.238) as a transaction where the company makes a gift to any person and where the company receives no consideration or where the consideration is worth significantly less than the consideration provided by the company. However, an undervalue cannot be set aside if it was entered into in good faith for the purpose of carrying on the company's business and at a time when there were reasonable grounds for believing that the transaction would benefit the company. For this reason a transaction cannot be set aside when the company sells stock or other assets at a reduced price so as to overcome cash flow problems.

24.2.2   PREFERENCE

A preference (s.239) is given if the company does anything or suffers anything to be done which puts a creditor, or a surety or guarantor of a debt of the company, into a better position on liquidation than he would have been in if that thing had not been done. Examples of preferences include payment of a debt to a particular creditor who would only have received partial payment on winding up or the giving of security to a creditor. However, a transaction cannot be set aside as a preference unless the company was influenced in deciding to give the preference to a person by a desire to put that person into a better position on liquidation than he would have been in if it had not been done. Such a desire is presumed where the preference was given to a connected person, which includes any director of the company. Where payment was made or security was given to a creditor because he was threatening proceedings or otherwise insisting on payment he will usually be able to show that this defence is available.

24.2.3   COURT CAN MAKE ORDER AS IT SEES FIT

Where it is shown that a transaction can be set aside as a transaction at an undervalue or preference the court can make such order as it sees fit for restoring the position to what it would have been if the transaction had not been entered into. This could include, for example, ordering the person who entered into the transaction or who received the preference to return property or its value to the company. The position of a bona fide purchaser for value is, however, protected.

24.2.4   'RELEVANT TIME' REQUIREMENT

Undervalue transactions and preferences can only be set aside if they were entered into at a 'relevant time', that is, a time when both of the following requirements are satisfied:

(a)   in the case of a transaction at an undervalue, the time is within two years before commencement of winding up or presentation of the petition for administration or, in the case of a preference, within six months before that date; and

(b)   in the case of either an undervalue or preference, the time is a time when the company is insolvent or a time when the company becomes insolvent as a result of the transaction.

24.2.5   TRANSACTION WITH 'CONNECTED PERSON'

Where a preference has been given to a connected person the six-month limit is extended to two years. Where an undervalue transaction has been entered into with a connected person insolvency is presumed unless it can be disproved.

24.3   Transactions Defrauding Creditors

Sections 423-425 contain another provision by which transactions at an undervalue can be set aside. This provision is not restricted to cases of winding up or administration orders and the undervalue transaction can be set aside whenever it was made. However, the person who applies to the court to have the transaction set aside under this provision must show that the company in entering into the transaction did so with the purpose of putting assets beyond the reach of that person.

24.4   Floating Charges (Section 245)

A floating charge is prima facie invalid if:

  (a)   it was made within 12 months before the presentation of a successful petition for winding up or for an administration order or before the passing of a winding-up resolution; and

  (b)   it was made at a time when the company was unable to pay its debts or became unable to do so as a result of the charge.

Where the company has created a floating charge in favour of a connected person the charge is prima facie invalid if it was made within *two* years before the petition or resolution. The charge is prima facie invalid in such a case even if the company was (and remained) solvent when the charge was created.

A floating charge created within the time-limits (and so prima facie invalid) is valid to the extent of:

  (a)   consideration for the charge consisting of money paid or goods and services supplied to the company at or after the creation of the charge; and

  (b)   consideration consisting of discharge or reduction of any debt of the company at or after the creation of the charge; and

  (c)   interest on (a) and (b) above.

Section 245 is designed to prevent a company benefiting a creditor by giving a charge for existing debt. The exceptions are designed to ensure that a company may still give security in order to obtain money or supplies even though in some difficulty. This should not in principle cause any harm to existing creditors.

SPECIAL TOPICS

TWENTY FIVE

THE PARTNERSHIP AGREEMENT

25.1 Introduction

In this chapter we will look at the provisions which should be considered for inclusion in a partnership agreement. Much of the contents of a partnership agreement will address issues raised by the provisions of the Partnership Act 1890 which we considered in **Chapters 1-5**, or which may be relevant to the tax provisions applicable to partnership which we considered in **Chapters 13, 14, 18 and 19**. Those detailed provisions should be borne in mind when reading this chapter.

Before we look at the possible contents of a partnership agreement, we will consider whether a formal, written agreement is necessary at all and at the end of the chapter we have included a section dealing with the points which a prospective new partner might wish to consider before putting his signature to a partnership agreement.

25.2 Is a Written Partnership Agreement Necessary?

A written agreement is not required for the formation of a partnership. This contrasts with the position of a company where the memorandum and articles, which have contractual effect under s. 14 CA 1985, must not only be in writing but must also be registered with the Registrar of Companies.

In practice, many partnerships decide that the agreement between the partners, as to how the business is to be regulated, should be in the form of a written agreement. Such an agreement is often called a partnership agreement, a partnership deed or articles of partnership.

The draftsman of a partnership agreement should bear in mind that many provisions of the Partnership Act 1890 apply to regulate the relationship of the partners except to the extent that there is contrary agreement. However well intentioned and however well drafted such legislation is, it is unlikely that it will entirely coincide with the wishes of a particular group of businessmen setting up a partnership.

The draftsman's task in drafting a partnership agreement is more onerous than his task in drafting articles of association for a company. In the case of a company a 'model' set of articles (Table A) is provided, which will suit the needs of most companies with comparatively minor alterations. The provisions of the Partnership Act are both more out of date and less comprehensive than those of Table A. The nature of a partnership agreement must, of course, depend upon the circumstances but we have set out in the next paragraph the most important matters which need to be considered.

25.3 The Clauses of the Partnership Agreement

25.3.1 THE PARTIES

The parties to the agreement will be the partners, old and new.

25.3.2 THE COMMENCEMENT DATE AND TERM OF THE PARTNERSHIP

While most partnerships will be partnerships 'at will' (and so can last indefinitely subject to notice to dissolve the partnership being given), it is possible to specify the length of the partnership's 'life'. Although the date the partnership agreement was entered into can determine the commencement of the partnership (which could be a newly constituted partnership following the retirement or admission of partners), partnership agreements often include a term stating the date on which the partnership commenced.

25.3.3 THE NATURE OF THE PARTNERSHIP'S BUSINESS

The ultra vires does not apply to a partnership. The business should, however, be specified so that a partner who objects to what is being done by way of new types of business can insist on the agreement being followed. Unless the partnership agreement provides to the contrary, the clause specifying what business is to be carried on can only be altered with the unanimous agreement of the partners (s. 24(8) PA 1890). This clause may also specify where the partnership is to carry on business.

25.3.4 THE PARTNERSHIP NAME

The business name and the partnership should be specified. The requirements as to approval for and publicity of business names were dealt with in 1.7.

25.3.5 THE INCOME OF THE PARTNERSHIP

If the partnership agreement is silent on the point, the partners will share the income (and liabilities) of the partnership equally. Even if this is in accord with the partners' wishes, it is best to state specifically the way in which the partnership's profits will be shared. However, in many partnerships, this simple position is not what the partners require. The share of profits between the partners may be unequal to reflect differing levels of contributions of capital, or differing levels of involvement in the partnership's business. Some partnerships may choose to build a mechanism into their partnership agreements for regular reviews of the profit sharing ratios to take into account the relative achievements of the partners. Other partnerships adopt a 'lock step' arrangement by which a partner's share of the profits may increase by a fixed amount annually over a period of years. If the partners have agreed among themselves that some or all of them should receive 'interest' on capital or 'salary' (see 13.5), these arrangements should be set out in the partnership agreement. However, care should be taken to ensure if a 'salary' is paid to the partner that the Revenue cannot argue that the recipient was, in reality, an employee rather than a full equity partner (if the latter is what the partners were trying to achieve).

25.3.6 THE CAPITAL OF THE PARTNERSHIP

A clause (or group of clauses) should be included dealing with the financial relationships between the partners. This should state what investment each partner is to make in the business, how each partner will satisfy his obligation to contribute capital (for example, whether in cash or assets) and over what period (if the capital contribution is not to be made in full on admission to the partnership). Although it may be difficult to specify the circumstances, it is worth giving thought to the circumstances in which further capital might have to be introduced. The reverse of these provisions is what should happen to the capital when the partnership is dissolved or a partner retires. What are the arrangements for a partner to withdraw capital and how is the goodwill of the business to be dealt with when a partner leaves?

25.3.7 THE PROPERTY OF THE PARTNERSHIP

The partnership agreement should include provisions specifying which property is to be regarded as partnership property and which is to remain the property of individual partners.

25.3.8 THE MANAGEMENT OF THE PARTNERSHIP

Small partnerships of two or three people will usually be run by the partners (perhaps in conjunction with a small number of employees) and each partner will have an equal say in management. In a large partnership (especially a professional partnership where there may be dozens of partners), a more complex management structure may be considered desirable and the structure should be specified. In the absence of contrary agreement all partners have an equal say in management. Among the more mundane, but very vital, matters which should be considered under this heading are questions such as where will the partnership maintain its bank account, who should be entitled to sign cheques for the partnership, who will allocate work to the employees, what authority is each partner to have in relation to buying stock, paying bills and so on. In most cases, the clause dealing with management of the partnership should be stated in general terms. It is better, for example, to say that junior partners are to have such functions as are assigned to them by the managing or senior partners than to list in minute detail what they are to be authorised to do.

25.3.9 THE EFFECT OF PROLONGED ABSENCE

It is now common to find included in partnership agreement clauses dealing with the consequences for a partner who is absent from the business for a prolonged period. This may be through illness, maternity leave or compassionate leave. The nature of the provisions will be determined by the necessity for the partners to balance the needs of the business with supporting their fellow partner. However, these provisions often mirror corresponding provisions found in employment contracts (so that a partner may be permitted to be away from the partnership's business for six months due to illness before he can be expelled, or the partnership agreement may provide maternity leave provisions similar to the statutory provisions which employees enjoy).

25.3.10 RESTRICTIONS

Terms may be included dealing with the partners' obligations to the firm. It is quite common, for example, to provide that the partners are to give their whole time to the business of the firm or to provide that they are only to take up other businesses with the approval of their partners. Consideration should also be given to the inclusion of a clause preventing competition with the firm during the lifetime of the partnership (even if the partners are not full time), although such competition would in any case normally be a breach of the partners' duty of good faith. Similarly, it is often desirable to include a restrictive covenant to prevent competition with the firm by a partner after he has left the firm. Such a term must be reasonable otherwise it may be declared void as being a term in unreasonable restraint of trade. The partners may also decide to place specific restrictions on the activities of particular partners in relation to the running of the business. For example, a partnership agreement could prevent an individual partner from charging or selling any of the partnership's assets.

25.3.11 PARTNERSHIP DISPUTES

It is sensible to anticipate that problems may arise within the partnership and so provide for how disputes should be resolved. Commonly, clauses dealing with disputes require the partners to refer the dispute (whatever subject matter of the dispute may be) to an independent arbitrator. This approach may lead to the resolution of the dispute and thus avoid the dissolution of the partnership.

25.3.12 DISSOLUTION, DEATH, RETIREMENT AND ADMISSION OF PARTNERS

It is sensible to set out the circumstances in which the partnership will be dissolved or in which a partner can be expelled from the partnership. If the partnership comes to an end, tax liabilities can arise (see **Chapter 14**) and the partnership agreement should include a provision as to whether the firm should set aside a proportion of each partner's profit share to provide a fund to discharge any tax liability which might arise on a 'cessation'. It will be remembered from **Chapter 14** that it is possible to make an election under s. 113 ICTA 1988 for the partnership to be taxed on a continuing basis despite a change in the make-up of the partnership (which would normally give rise to a 'cessation'). As a result, firstly, it is common to find in partnership agreements an obligation imposed on outgoing partners (or their personal representatives if appropriate) to enter into the s. 113 election if requested. Any outgoing partner, if he is retiring, will be concerned to secure an income during his retirement. While the partner can create a fund from which a pension can be paid during his years as a partner (see **Chapter 19**), many partnerships provide annuity or consultancy arrangements for former partners. The terms of such arrangements should be set out in the partnership agreement. Secondly, since the election for assessment on the continuing basis can mean that an incoming partner can be taxed on a share of profits in excess of the amount he actually receives, it is also common for the incoming partner to be indemnified by the existing partners for any extra tax he suffers as a result. The agreement should specify how new partners are to be admitted to the partnership. In the absence of agreement to the contrary, new partners may only be admitted with the unanimous consent of the existing partners (s. 24(7) PA 1890).

25.4   Issues for an Incoming Partner

We have seen the legal consequences of admission to a partnership in **Chapter 3** and the tax consequences of admission in **Chapter 14**. However, before accepting the offer of a partnership, a prospective partner needs to consider whether the partnership's business, management and finances are such as to justify the risk of taking on unlimited liability with his future fellow partners.

The partnership agreement will be a useful source of information about the way the partnership's affairs are handled but the agreement will be, by no means, the only document the prospective partner will want to examine. Other documents will include previous years' signed accounts, as well as previous years' budgets and management accounts (which will show whether the business has suffered an unexpected shortfall in income or cost overruns which will need to be explained). The prospective partner should try to anticipate any future financial problems the partnership may face by investigating whether there are any contingent liabilities, whether the firm's insurance cover is adequate, and what steps the firm is taking to make provision for bad debts. Perhaps the most significant protection against problems in the future would be if the firm has a carefully thought out, effective business strategy and the prospective partner will need to satisfy himself that he considers the strategy to be appropriate given the firm's position in its particular market place.

TWENTY SIX

THE ARTICLES OF A PRIVATE COMPANY

In this chapter we will look at the articles of a private company. We saw in **Chapter 7** that all companies are required to have articles of association and that these articles define the relationships within the company. We also saw that a company can either adopt Table A as its articles or have articles drafted for the company. Table A is a model set of articles contained in the Companies (Tables A to F) Regulations 1985 as amended.

In this chapter we will look at some of the major terms which it may be desirable to include in the articles of a private company. We will also look at the methods by which the articles of a company can be altered.

26.1 Table A

Most companies will find it advantageous to use Table A as the basis of their articles. The main advantage of doing so is that a great deal of work in drafting will be saved. Furthermore, although Table A has been amended over the years, much of it has been in use for many decades. As a result of this most of the problems in interpretation which might arise have been ironed out (often by decisions of the courts). However careful a draftsman is in preparing new articles which do not follow Table A as a precedent, there are bound to be difficulties of interpretation. Table A also has the advantage of providing a set of articles which have been used by very many companies. This means that any difficulties of application of the provisions have been resolved (ultimately by amendments to Table A).

As a result of the advantages mentioned above we would advocate that Table A should be used as a basis by companies unless there are very strong reasons to the contrary. We will, therefore, be concentrating in the first part of this chapter on possible amendments to Table A.

The first time when these amendments should be considered is when the company is formed. At that stage the draftsman of the articles should discuss the needs of this particular company with those who wish to have the company formed and should suggest possible amendments to Table A. Future problems should be anticipated as far as possible at this stage. For example, will the suggested articles be suitable if the company grows in the future?

The articles should also be kept under review as they may need to be changed from time to time. It may also be appropriate to consider amending the articles if a new Table A is introduced. If a company adopts Table A as its articles it will get the Table A which is in force at the time of its incorporation. Its articles will not be automatically amended when a new Table A is introduced.

26.2   Provisions Concerning Shares and Membership

26.2.1   SHARE CAPITAL

The first part of Table A deals with shares and membership of the company. It provides for the creation of different classes of shares (arts. 2 and 3). There are also provisions which deal with partly paid shares and the company's lien for amounts unpaid on shares (i.e., if shares are issued without being paid for in full the company has a lien (a charge) over the shares to secure payment for them). There are now relatively few cases where shares are issued by private companies without payment in full at the time of issue so that these provisions are unlikely to need amendment. You will sometimes see an extension to the lien so that it applies to any money that the shareholder owes to the company and to any shares whether fully paid or not.

26.2.2   ISSUE OF SHARES

Table A does not give the directors authority to issue shares. (Remember even if such a provision is included in the articles it can only last for five years from the date of incorporation of the company; see **10.2.2**.) It may be considered desirable to include such power in the articles of a newly formed company so that a meeting of members is not needed for the issue of shares when the company is newly formed.

If there are no provisions in the articles any issue of shares for cash has to be offered to the existing members pro rata (see **10.2.2**). Those drafting the articles should consider whether this is appropriate. A number of amendments is possible and the following, in particular might be considered.

(a)   A provision which disapplies these pre-emption rights so as to allow the shares to be issued to non-shareholders or other than pro rata (provided the directors are authorised to issue shares under s. 80).

(b)   Alternatively it may be decided that the power of the existing members to take shares issued for cash is insufficient. In this case the provisions of Table A could be amended to say that the shares are to be offered to the existing members in all cases whether or not the directors' primary intention is to issue the shares to outsiders for a non-cash consideration.

26.2.3   TRANSFER OF SHARES

Transfer of shares is dealt with in articles 23-28. A shareholder is free to transfer his shares to anyone in most cases. The directors have power to refuse only if the shares are not fully paid or the company has a lien on them (the company will only have a lien if the shares have not been fully paid for unless there have been other amendments to Table A).

In the case of many private companies it is considered appropriate that a shareholder should not be free to transfer his shares to anyone he chooses. The reason for this is that if an existing shareholder is free to transfer to anyone he is, in effect, in a position to decide who his fellow-shareholders' future associates should be. There is a considerable range of possibilities as far as restrictions are concerned. We will consider the most common and most important of them.

26.2.3.1   A simple restriction giving the directors power to refuse to register a transfer

This type of restriction is very common (indeed it was included in Table A at one time). It allows the directors to refuse to register any transfer of shares. Notice that with this type of provision a majority vote of the directors is needed to refuse to register the transfer. If the directors are equally divided and there is no casting vote (as to which see **8.1**) the transferee will become entitled to be registered. Notice also that if the directors have not refused registration within two months of the application for registration, the transferee again effectively becomes entitled to be registered (Companies Act 1985, s. 185).

If a restriction of this type is considered desirable, the article should say that the directors need not give any reason for their refusal to register the transfer.

Sometimes the article says that the directors may refuse to register if they disapprove of the transferee. This wording is undesirable as the directors may wish to refuse registration for other reasons.

The power of the directors to refuse to register a transfer does not prevent the existing shareholder from selling his shares or giving them away; it simply prevents the transferee from becoming the legal owner of the shares. If the registration is refused then the existing shareholder holds the shares on trust for the purchaser or donee who becomes the equitable owner of the shares.

26.2.3.2 A requirement that a member who wishes to sell should first offer the shares to the existing members pro rata

This type of right is usually called a pre-emption right. It should not be confused with the statutory pre-emption right which arises on the issue of new shares for a cash consideration (and which was referred to above). Neither the Companies Act 1985 nor Table A give any pre-emption rights where a shareholder wishes to transfer shares. In its simplest form a pre-emption right which applies on transfer will provide that if a shareholder wishes to transfer his shares he must first offer them to some or all of the existing shareholders, either in all circumstances or in some specified circumstances. The details of such clauses vary very considerably. An attempt is usually made to be fair to both the shareholder who wishes to transfer his shares and to those who may wish to buy. In drafting such a clause the following are among the matters which should be considered:

(a)   Are all the other shareholders to be entitled to buy some of the shares? (The right could be restricted for example, to the directors or to shareholders of the same class.)

(b)   Are the shares to be offered to those entitled according to the proportion of shares which they own? (This is by far the most likely arrangement.)

(c)   If a shareholder does not wish to buy, then what is to happen to the proportion of the shares which he could have bought? (In such a case the article could provide for a second round of offers to those shareholders who did take up the initial offer, or it could allow the selling shareholder to sell to whoever he chooses once the initial offer has been rejected.)

(d)   How is the price to be fixed? (It is important that there should be a mechanism otherwise the shareholder who wishes to sell to an outsider could circumvent the pre-emption procedure by offering to sell at an excessive price. The article may require an independent valuation by a specially appointed accountant, may provide for valuation by the company's own auditor or may fix the price in some arbitrary way.)

(e)   Are there to be time limits? (There should be, otherwise the procedure will be unfair to the shareholder who wishes to sell as the others will be able to cause him delay.)

(f)   Are there to be any safeguards in case the selling shareholder refuses to make the offer? (A common provision is to say that the directors are his agents and so can make the offer on his behalf.)

(g)   Are there to be any exceptions to the pre-emption rights? (It is quite common to provide that the shareholder is free to sell to his own family members (which must be defined) or to existing members or to both those categories without the pre-emption rights applying.)

26.2.3.3 A requirement that members must buy the shares of a member who wishes to sell

In a sense this sort of provision is the opposite of a pre-emption right. In this case once a member wants to leave the company he can require the other shareholders to buy him out. Many of the same problems as arise with pre-emption rights will arise here. In particular valuation and time limits will have to be provided for.

26.3 Provisions Concerning Meetings of Shareholders

Table A makes provision for company meetings which are likely to be satisfactory in most cases. However, it may be considered appropriate to remove the chairman's casting vote (art. 50). It may also be considered unnecessary to require 21 clear days' notice of a meeting at which a director is to be appointed (art. 38). However, if it is decided to remove this requirement, then the procedure for giving notice of the intention to propose the appointment of a director (which is contained in art. 76) should also be simplified.

26.4 Provisions Concerning Directors

Table A (arts. 73ff) makes elaborate provision for directors to retire by rotation (one third of the board retires each year in most circumstances). Such provisions are unnecessary in the case of a private company and it may be desirable to remove them (especially if it is contemplated that an elective resolution will be passed to dispense with the need to hold annual general meetings).

Table A also contains a provision (art. 94) which prevents directors from voting at board meetings on anything in which they have a personal interest. Although such a provision may have beneficial consequences as far as prevention of fraud is concerned, it is usual to remove this provision in the case of a small private company. If art. 94 is not amended or removed, then it may be difficult to transact business in certain cases as there may not be enough directors qualified to vote who can constitute a quorum at the meeting.

Table A art. 70 gives the directors very wide powers to run the company (see **8.6**). In some cases it may be considered appropriate to restrict the powers of the directors. However, in general the balance struck by Table A and the Companies Act is suitable for most companies.

The members of the company have power to remove a director from office by ordinary resolution (see Companies Act 1985 s. 303 and **9.3**). It may be considered appropriate to include in the articles a *Bushell* v *Faith* clause. This is a clause which says that if a director's removal from office is proposed he has weighted voting rights which effectively give him the power to defeat the resolution for his removal.

26.5 Alteration of Articles

26.5.1 POWER TO ALTER

Section 9 CA 1985 gives a company power to alter its articles by special resolution. The power of alteration is expressed to be 'subject to the provisions of this Act' — all this really means is that the altered articles may not conflict with other parts of the legislation (so that, for example, they cannot deprive the shareholders of a right to remove directors from office under s. 303 CA 1985). Anything which could have been included in the original articles may be included in the altered articles (s. 9(2)), so that the articles may not be made unalterable. However, an alteration requiring the members to buy more shares or otherwise invest more money is void as against persons who were members at the time of the alteration (s. 16 CA 1985).

The memorandum of association is regarded as being of greater authority than the articles, so that an article (whether included on incorporation or later) which contradicts the memorandum is invalid.

26.5.2 REGISTRATION

Once the special resolution altering the articles has been passed, the resolution and a printed copy of the amended articles must be sent to the Registrar within 15 days. The Registrar officially notifies his receipt of these documents and the company cannot rely on the changes until he has done so under the same rules as for change of name and alteration of objects. The company must ensure that copies of the altered articles are available, so that the directors and secretary may consult them and in case any member exercises his statutory right to a copy of the articles (s. 19 CA 1985).

26.5.3 ALTERATION TO BE FOR THE BENEFIT OF THE COMPANY

26.5.3.1 Shareholders may decide for themselves

There are no provisions in the Companies Act giving shareholders, or any particular proportion of the shareholders, power to challenge the validity of an alteration to the articles. However, the courts have held that an alteration is invalid if it is not 'bona fide in the interests of the company as a whole' (per Lord Lindley MR in *Allen* v *Gold Reefs of West Africa Ltd* [1900] 1 Ch 656). The test is very much easier to state than to apply to the facts of particular cases. As we have already seen in relation to the rule in *Foss* v *Harbottle* (see **9.6**), the court is very reluctant to interfere with business decisions merely because some of the shareholders object to what has been decided.

The court will normally regard an alteration as being in the interests of the company if the majority of the shareholders are in favour of the alteration (as they must be since a special resolution will have been passed before any question as to the validity of the alteration can arise). Thus in *Allen* v *Gold Reefs of West Africa Ltd* the articles contained a provision imposing a lien on partly paid shares. One shareholder owed money to the company and the articles were altered to impose a lien on fully paid shares as well as on partly paid shares. The court regarded the fact that one (and only one) shareholder was indebted to the company at the time of alteration as something exciting suspicion as to the bona fides of the company, but nevertheless came to the conclusion that the alteration was in the interests of the company as a whole. Clearly it is in the interests of a company that it should have security for money due to it and no discrimination against particular members was expressed in the altered articles.

Shuttleworth v *Cox Brothers and Co. (Maidenhead) Ltd* [1927] 2 KB 9, is perhaps a stronger illustration. The majority of the directors suspected that one of the board had been guilty of misconduct but they had insufficient proof of any grounds giving a right to dismiss him. They therefore altered the articles to say that any director would cease to hold office if requested to resign by the majority of the directors. The test applied by the court was whether any reasonable man could come to the conclusion that the alteration was in the interests of the company. If it was open to a reasonable man to come to that conclusion, the alteration would only be invalid on proof of actual bad faith. The court was satisfied that a reasonable man could come to the conclusion that the alteration was in the interests of the company and so, since the plaintiff could not prove actual bad faith, the alteration was held to be valid.

26.5.3.2 Discrimination

The courts have recognised that an alteration to the articles cannot be in the interests of the company as a whole if it discriminates against some members, however few. At first sight this seems strange in view of the two cases mentioned above, both of which appear to involve actual discrimination against a particular shareholder. However, on closer analysis neither of those cases involved any discrimination. In *Allen* v *Gold Reefs of West Africa* the lien applied, potentially, to all the fully paid shares whoever owned them, so that it might apply to any shareholder at some time. Similarly in *Shuttleworth* v *Cox* the new article potentially applied to any shareholder who became a director and who fell into disfavour with the rest of the board. A good illustration of the type of case where an alteration *is* discriminatory and so void is given by the Australian case, *Australian Fixed Trust Proprietary Ltd* v *Clyde Industries Ltd* (1959) SR (NSW) 33. In that case the articles were altered so as to require shareholders who were unit trust managers to obtain the approval of the majority of their unit-holders before exercising the voting rights attached to their shares. This clearly discriminated against shareholders who happened to be unit trust managers and so was void.

The narrowness of the distinction between cases which are, and cases which are not, discriminatory is well illustrated by the cases of *Sidebottom* v *Kershaw, Leese and Co. Ltd* [1920] 1 Ch 154, and *Brown* v *Abrasive Wheel Company* [1919] 1 Ch 290. In *Sidebottom* v *Kershaw, Leese* the articles were altered so as to give the directors power to direct a shareholder who was concerned with a competing business to transfer his shares. This was held to be a valid alteration. The company could properly come to the conclusion that it was in its interests that competitors be excluded from membership and there was no discrimination based on the number of shares owned. In *Brown v Abrasive Wheel Co.* the articles were altered to give 90% of the shareholders power to require the minority shareholders to sell their shares. In fact, the majority shareholders (who owned 98% of the shares) had good commercial reasons for wanting the alteration, but nevertheless the court held that the alteration was invalid. Although it was bona fide in the interests of 98% of the present shareholders it was not in the interests of the other 2%, nor nor was it necessarily in the interests of future shareholders and so it was discriminatory.

26.5.3.3 The hypothetical member

It is sometimes suggested that whether an alteration is bona fide in the interests of the company as a whole can be tested by reference to the interests of a 'hypothetical member'. This was first suggested in *Greenhalgh v Arderne Cinemas Ltd* [1951] Ch 286, where, during the course of a long and frequently litigated dispute within a company, the articles were altered to allow a member to transfer shares to any person with the sanction of an ordinary resolution. (The articles as originally drafted contained pre-emption rights in favour of the remaining shareholders.) The real purpose of the alteration was to allow the majority shareholders to sell out. The alteration was held to be valid on the rather casuistic argument that every shareholder who wished to transfer shares was given the same right to ask for an ordinary resolution allowing transfer free of the existing pre-emption rights. The fact that a majority shareholder was certain of success whilst a minority shareholder had practically no chance, did not reduce the legal value of the rights given to the latter when compared with those given to the former. During the course of his judgment Sir Raymond Evershed MR said '. . . "the company as a whole" . . . means the corporators as a general body. That is to say, the case may be taken of an individual hypothetical member . . .'.

It can be seen from the facts of *Greenhalgh v Arderne Cinemas* that the hypothetical member is neither specifically a majority shareholder nor a minority shareholder since both those groups must be treated equally. It is doubtful how useful the hypothetical member test is in deciding the validity of alterations in other circumstances. Is he, for example, to be assumed to be neither specifically a unit trust manager nor a non-unit trust manager, so as to explain the *Australian Fixed Trust Pty Ltd v Clyde Industries* case? Is he to be assumed not to be in competition with the company so as to explain the *Sidebottom v Kershaw, Leese* case?

Probably it is safer to ignore the hypothetical member and to concentrate on the two basic rules which seem to have evolved from the cases:

  (a) The members may generally decide themselves whether an alteration is bona fide in the interests of the company as a whole.
  (b) The court will interfere with their decision where the members could not properly come to that decision because it discriminates between groups of members.

26.5.3.4 *Clemens v Clemens*

Although the case of *Clemens v Clemens Brothers Ltd* [1976] 2 All ER 268, was not concerned with alteration of the articles (see **9.3**), the general principles stated there are especially appropriate to alteration of the articles. Discrimination is not, therefore, the only ground on which an alteration may be held to be invalid. It may be that *Clemens v Clemens* marks a watershed or it may be limited 'to its own particular facts', but any move away from the rigidity and narrowness of the decision on alteration of articles is to be welcomed.

TWENTY SEVEN

A DEBENTURE DOCUMENT

27.1 Introduction

In this chapter we will look briefly at some of the terms which might be found in a debenture document. Before reading this chapter you will find it useful to read **Chapter 10** again.

Debentures vary enormously. In this chapter we will be looking at one type of debenture only, that is, a debenture which is given by a company in return for a loan by a bank. This type of debenture will contain different provisions from a debenture which is designed to secure a long term loan from people who want to invest money in a company but who prefer a fixed return rather than the possibility of a variable dividend which would be produced by an issue of shares.

A debenture is likely to contain clauses dealing with the following matters:

    (a) the amount of the loan (which may be fixed or variable);
    (b) a promise by the company that it will repay the loan on a fixed date and/or on the happening of certain events;
    (c) a promise by the company that it will pay interest at a fixed or variable rate;
    (d) a charge or charges over some or all of the company's assets, this may include floating as well as fixed charges;
    (e) clauses designed to protect the position of the lender (e.g., by giving the lender power to appoint a receiver).

In the rest of this chapter we have given examples of the sort of clauses which may be found in debentures of this type. They are not taken from the debenture of any particular bank. They are provided for the purposes of illustration only so that students may get an idea of what the different clauses in the debenture are for. In practice those who draft debentures for banks will (quite rightly) wish to cover every possible contingency in their debentures. The clauses which they draft are, therefore, usually much fuller than the illustrations given below.

27.2 Terms Relating to Repayment and Interest

The debenture will include a promise by the company that it will repay to the bank the amount which is lent to it. Frequently the debenture will relate to any money which the company owes to the bank. In this case the debenture is mainly designed to secure the repayment of an overdraft by the company. The repayment clause will then refer to something along the lines of 'all monies or other liabilities actual or contingent now or in the future owed by the company to the bank on any account or for which the company may for any reason be or become liable to the bank now or in the future'. Usually provision is made for payment 'on demand', i.e., as soon as the bank asks for it.

If none of the money secured by the debenture consists of a long term loan (so that the sums secured all relate to variable amounts such as overdraft, interest and bank charges) there will often be a promise to pay a fixed small amount. The clause might, for example, include a term under which the company 'covenants to pay to the bank the sum of one pound (£1) on demand'. Such a provision ensures that the agreement between the company and the bank is not discharged if the company temporarily pays off its overdraft so that the bank temporarily is owed nothing.

There will be a promise to pay interest. In the case of the type of loan we are considering (i.e., a loan by a bank) this will usually be a promise to pay a variable rate of interest on any money outstanding from time to time. This clause could refer to a particular way in which interest is to be calculated (e.g., that it should be a certain number of percentage points above the bank's base rate from time to time). However, the more usual provision is to say that the interest is to be calculated 'in accordance with the bank's usual practice'. Provision may also be made for the rate to be agreed between the parties if possible. Such provisions might at first sight seem rather vague. However, the practice of banks in relation to various classes of loans can be determined objectively if it becomes necessary to do so. The bank is also protected by the fact that if the company does not pay the interest which it is asked to pay, the bank can always call in the whole loan. The company also has the right to redeem the loan by paying the bank, if it can afford to do so.

27.3 Terms Relating to Security

It is possible to have an unsecured debenture. However, the type of bank debenture which we are examining in this chapter is pointless unless security is given by the borrowing company to the bank. Before it will lend or allow an overdraft the bank will wish to be satisfied that the company is and is likely to remain solvent. Before it will lend or allow an overdraft the bank will also wish (in most cases) to be satisfied that the company's assets are sufficient security for the loan. This will require the bank to consider two matters:

(a) what is the value of the assets offered as security?
(b) is the company free to give security over the assets?

Valuation is a question of fact. As far as security is concerned the bank will wish to know what other charges the company has already created over its assets. This information will be available from a company search (see the requirements as to registration in **Chapter 10** and as to searches in **Chapter 29**).

27.3.1 FIXED CHARGES

The first type of security which the bank will wish to consider is fixed charges over the valuable assets of the company. A fixed charge in the form of a legal mortgage of any land which the company may own, is likely to be viewed as the best security which the bank can take in most cases. It is usual for the debenture to give such a charge to the bank over the land owned by the company at the date of the mortgage. This charge will be supplemented by a charge over later acquired land (freehold and leasehold) which the company may acquire. This charge will be an equitable charge as a legal mortgage of land to be acquired in the future is not possible. The debenture will often also say that the bank can insist on the company executing a legal mortgage of any future acquired land once it is acquired and that the title deeds are to be deposited with the bank in the mean time. For most purposes a specific equitable charge is as good as a legal mortgage so this adds little to the bank's security.

The debenture will also usually provide for security by way of fixed charge over any shares which the company owns in other companies.

The debenture will also frequently contain a fixed charge over the company's goodwill. This is not necessarily a very valuable security as the goodwill is itself often of rather questionable value especially as the security is only likely to be enforced if the company is in financial difficulties.

Modern debentures often contain a fixed charge over 'the book debts and other debts of the company'. Book debts are the sums owed to the company by, for example, its customers. In effect the fixed charge over book debts says that the bank is entitled to collect the money due to the company in order to discharge the company's own debt to the bank. The law recognises that such a charge is possible but there are technical problems with regarding the charge as a fixed charge as the company is usually free to deal with its book debts as it wishes. The debenture will, therefore, provide that when payment of the debts is received by the company the money must be paid into the company's account at the bank and that the company is not to be free to assign or otherwise deal with its debts.

The mortgage will require the company to insure the property and to keep it in a good state of repair.

27.3.2 FLOATING CHARGES

As we saw in **Chapter 10** a company can create a floating charge over any of its assets. This is a charge which allows the company to deal with the assets even though they are the subject of the charge. This has the benefit of giving the company flexibility while at the same time giving the bank some sort of security. The problem from the bank's point of view is that the charge is of uncertain value until the security crystallises. In order to reduce this problem it is usual to provide that the company is not free to sell the whole of its undertaking without the consent of the bank. There will also be provision stating that the bank can give notice of crystallisation. This is a clause which says that the bank may 'give notice to the company converting the floating security into a fixed charge in relation to any assets specified in the notice'.

The company is also usually prohibited from creating any later charge ranking in priority to the floating charge. Such a provision is necesssary as without it the company is free to charge the floating charge assets by way of specific charge. This does not invalidate the floating charge but clearly if the assets are now subject to a fixed charge which will take priority, the value of the floating charge as a security is greatly reduced.

The company will usually also be required to insure the floating charge property.

27.4 Clauses Designed to Give the Lender Further Protection

27.4.1 PERSONAL GUARANTEES

If the bank is not satisfied with the security which the company can provide, it may well require personal guarantees from the directors of the company in addition to the security given by the company.

27.4.2 APPOINTMENT OF A RECEIVER

One of the clauses which will be contained in the debenture will allow the bank to appoint a receiver. Where the debenture includes a floating charge the receiver will normally satisfy the definition of an administrative receiver and so will have all the powers of such a receiver (see **Chapter 23** for the powers and duties of an administrative receiver). The function of the receiver is to realise assets for the bank, pay them off and then return the company to the directors. In practice the company may well be wound up after the receivership as the receiver will have withdrawn many of the assets of the company. The powers and duties of a receiver are dealt with in **Chapter 23**.

Debentures vary somewhat as to the circumstances in which a receiver may be appointed. The following are likely to be among those which are included:

(a) The bank demands payment of the principal, interest or any other obligation of the company and the company fails to pay within a specified period of time (usually this will be a small number of days).

(b) A petition for an administration order is presented. As we saw in **Chapter 23** the power to appoint an administrative receiver is lost if an administration order is made. However, a person with power to appoint an administrative receiver has power to veto an administration order by appointing an administrative receiver in most circumstances.

TWENTY EIGHT

SHAREHOLDERS' AGREEMENTS

28.1 Introduction

In this chapter we will look at shareholders' agreements. These are agreements between shareholders about how their company should be run. The company is also sometimes joined as a party in the agreement so that it too will be bound by the terms (the company cannot, however, override its statutory powers in this way). In particular they are likely to contain terms under which the shareholders agree how they will vote on various issues which may be raised at company meetings. For example, each shareholder might agree to support the re-election of the other shareholders as directors.

Shareholders' agreements are only likely to be effective in the case of companies with a small number of shareholders. If an agreement about how members will vote is to be effective it must usually be made by at least enough members of the company to ensure that a majority of the votes at any meeting will be cast in accordance with the agreement. If there are many members it will be difficult to get a large number of them to enter into a contract. Remember also that the contract (like any other contract) is only enforceable by and against those who are parties to it, so the effectiveness of the agreement is much reduced if a large number of members are not party to it.

28.2 The Advantages of a Shareholders' Agreement

28.2.1 SECRECY

The agreement, unlike the articles, is not open to inspection by the public.

28.2.2 PROTECTION OF INTERESTS

A shareholders' agreement can protect the interests of some of the members in ways which cannot be easily achieved by the articles. In particular, unless the company provides for different classes of shares, all the shareholders have to be treated alike. If this is not what is desired then it may be much simpler to give one shareholder exceptional rights in a shareholders' agreement. For example, it may be intended that one person (perhaps the founder of the company) should remain a director throughout his life. This is quite difficult to achieve in the articles because the shareholders have a statutory right to remove a director from office. Added voting rights may effectively give a director an invulnerable position (see, for example, *Bushell* v *Faith* at **8.10**) but these rights will be attached to the shares and so will pass to the director's successors in title unless very cumbersome arrangements are made. A shareholders' agreement can achieve this very simply if the shareholders agree to vote for X each time his re-election as a director is in issue and to vote against any resolution to remove him from office.

28.2.3 DIFFICULTIES OF ENFORCING ARTICLES

Although the articles of a company are deemed to be a contract between the company and its members, many cases have decided that this does not mean that each individual member is entitled to enforce compliance with every term of the articles. Generally only those terms which relate to the membership rights of the shareholder can be enforced. If the terms are included in a shareholders' agreement then any party to the agreement can enforce it in full. Furthermore a shareholders' agreement can be enforced simply by means of an action by one shareholder against another. If a shareholder seeks to enforce a term in the articles he will normally have to sue in a representative capacity.

28.2.4 VETO

A shareholders' agreement may give each individual party to it a veto over any proposal which is contrary to the terms of the agreement. In this way a shareholder may be protected even though he only has a small number of shares. However, such agreements should not be lightly entered into. Each shareholder will wish to have a veto against any decisions which he thinks are inappropriate, but he should remember that the other parties will also have the same veto powers (unless he is able to negotiate them for himself alone).

28.3 Drafting a Shareholders' Agreement

The uses to which shareholders' agreements are put and consequently the clauses which are included in them vary greatly depending on the circumstances which lead to the particular agreement. In this paragraph we will examine some of the main types of provision which may be included.

28.3.1 APPOINTMENT OF DIRECTORS AND SERVICE CONTRACTS

The agreement will frequently require all the parties to the agreement to vote in favour of any resolution which reappoints any of them to be a director of the company. It should then also include a term requiring each party to the agreement to vote against any resolution for the removal of any of the parties from the office of director. If it is decided to include such terms, then it may also be appropriate to consider whether there should be any time limit; for example, it might be for a fixed period of time, or it might only apply until each director reaches a specified age.

This clause might also provide for remuneration of the directors and approval of their service contracts for specified or indefinite periods exceeding five years.

28.3.2 APPROVAL FOR POLICY DECISIONS

The articles of almost all companies including those (the vast majority) which use Table A as the basis of their articles, provide that business decisions are to be taken by the directors. It would usually be quite inappropriate for articles to provide that the shareholders are to have power to run the company's business. However, if there are particular issues which the shareholders have agreed to as matters of policy, these could be included in a shareholders' agreement. The agreement might, for example, require the agreement of the parties before any new ventures could be undertaken by the company, or before the company could expand the area of its operation. This would be reinforced by an agreement that the parties would vote against any attempt to circumvent such an agreement, and would take whatever steps they could to prevent these things from happening without such approval.

28.3.3 ISSUE OF SHARES AND PROTECTION OF VOTING RIGHTS

One of the main purposes for which a shareholders' agreement may be used is to protect the shareholders from 'watering' of their interests. This occurs where new shares are issued and a shareholder does not get some of the shares. For example if a shareholder now has 40 per cent of the 1,000 shares which have been issued, he has enough shares to block a special resolution. If a further

1,000 shares were issued and he got none of them then his interest would be reduced to 20 per cent and so (unless the voting rights were changed) he would lose the power to block a special resolution. To prevent this from happening pre-emption rights may be included in the shareholders' agreement.

The considerations here are similar to those in relation to pre-emption rights contained in the articles of a company which we considered in **Chapter 26** (and remember that there are also statutory pre-emption rights in limited circumstances; see **10.2.2**). In some cases it may be more appropriate to include pre-emption rights in a shareholders' agreement. This would be so, for example, if the shareholders wished to keep the existence of the pre-emption rights secret or if they were to apply only to some of the shareholders.

An issue of debentures or other borrowing by the company will not affect the powers of the shareholders to vote in respect of their shares. However, the effect of borrowing will be to reduce the amount of profit available for potential dividend payments to the shareholders. It may, therefore, be appropriate for the clause to require the approval of the parties for borrowing above a certain figure.

A clause in a shareholders' agreement could be drafted so as to require approval of the parties to the agreement for any issue of shares or other reorganisation of capital. This would go further than a simple pre-emption right as it would effectively give the parties a right to veto issue of shares, not just a right to insist on taking some of the shares themselves. Alternatively the clause could provide that the existing shareholders would be bound to make further investment in certain circumstances specified in the clause. Obviously a shareholder should not undertake such an obligation lightly in case he does not have the resources to meet his obligation when it arises.

28.3.4 WITHDRAWAL FROM THE COMPANY

One of the principal features of company law is that a shareholder (unlike a partner in a partnership) is not normally allowed to withdraw his investment. This is the idea of maintenance of capital which we saw in **Chapter 10** (we also saw the limited exceptions in **Chapter 11** under which a company can redeem or buy back its own shares). A shareholders' agreement can be used to allow a shareholder an opportunity to leave the company and to take out his capital. For example, the agreement will often include a clause requiring a shareholder to offer his shares to the other members pro rata if he wishes to sell. As in the case of a pre-emption right on transfer contained in the articles (see **Chapter 26**), this clause will contain valuation provisions which will be designed to ensure fairness to both the selling member and the buying member.

A simple pre-emption right will not, however, ensure that the shareholder can sell his shares. He must offer them to the other members but they may not wish to buy. In this case the member is unlikely to be able to sell to an outsider, as there is likely to be a restriction on the right to transfer either in the articles or in the shareholders' agreement. It is possible to include a term whereby the shareholder who wishes to get out of the company has a right to insist that the other members of the company will buy his shares. Such a clause should only be entered into if the finances of the potential purchasers are likely to be strong enough to be able to comply with the agreement.

28.3.5 PAYMENT OF DIVIDENDS

Although it is not likely to be one of the commonest clauses to be found in a shareholders' agreement, it is possible to include a term which will either require the payment of dividends or which will restrict the payment of dividends. A clause which purported to require payment of dividends other than out of accumulated realised profits (after deduction of accumulated realised losses) would be unenforceable as such payments would be illegal.

28.3.6 RESTRICTIVE COVENANTS

Restrictive covenants may be included in a shareholders' agreement. This sort of term might be appropriate where a shareholder has brought particular expertise to the company and the other shareholders wish to preserve that expertise for the company. If such a clause is included it is likely also to appear in any service contract which the shareholder has with the company (for example where he is a director as well as a shareholder). Restrictive covenants are void on grounds of public policy unless they are reasonable in area and time.

28.3.7 AN ARBITRATION CLAUSE

Like many commercial agreements the shareholders' agreement will often include an arbitration clause so that any disputes which arise out of it can be resolved without the need for action in the courts.

28.4 Legal Limits on the use of Shareholders' Agreements

28.4.1 POWER TO ALTER THE ARTICLES

A company has a statutory power to alter its articles by special resolution. A shareholders' agreement cannot take this right away. However, it can provide that members are personally in breach of contract if they vote in favour of an alteration which is contrary to the terms of the agreement.

28.4.2 DIRECTORS' DUTIES

The directors of a company have a fiduciary duty to the company. A shareholders' agreement could not lawfully permit the directors to breach this fiduciary duty. Furthermore directors have a number of duties which are of a public nature (particularly in relation to insolvent companies). A shareholders' agreement could not authorise or direct the directors as to how they are to perform their functions. For example, a director would be liable for failure to make statutory returns to the Registrar of Companies even if his shareholders' agreement purported to require this. Similarly a director could not absolve himself from liability for wrongful trading on the basis of a shareholders' agreement.

28.5 Enforcing the Agreement

A shareholders' agreement is a contract. Each party provides consideration by agreeing to abide by the terms of the agreement. It follows from this that if the agreement is broken, the other parties can claim damages. The agreement can also be enforced by an injunction which requires a shareholder who is a party to it not to vote in a way contrary to the terms of the agreement. It may also be enforced by a positive injunction requiring a shareholder who is a party to it to vote in accordance with its provisions.

TWENTY NINE

MAKING AND INTERPRETING A COMPANY SEARCH AND COMPANY ACCOUNTS

29.1 Introduction

One of the core concepts of company law is that information about a company, its 'constitution' and financial status should be made available to the public. The purpose of this policy of 'openness' is to enable anyone interested in the affairs of a company (whether they are current or prospetive shareholders in the company or its creditors) to have access to the information they need to make an informed judgment on the company's financial affairs and the abilities of the company's management. They will also be able to determine whether the company has the necessary authority and powers to enter into the transaction which, for example, a third party creditor may be considering.

This information will be made available by the company:

    (a)   keeping at its registered office records and registers available for inspection by its members and the public;

    (b)   disclosing financial information to its members through the annual directors' report and annual audited accounts;

    (c)   delivering to the Registrar of Companies documents which the Registrar in turn makes available to the public for inspection; and

    (d)   the publication of certain information about the company in the *London Gazette*.

In this chapter, we will look at the information which will be made public in the *London Gazette* as well as the information which can be found through making a search at the Companies' Registry. At the end of the chapter, we will look at the rules with which the company must comply in relation to its account, as well as giving some guidance on how to interpret the published accounts of a company.

29.2 Official Notification

Section 711 CA 1985 requires the Registrar of Companies to advertise the issue by him or receipt by him (as the case may be) of certain documents in the *London Gazette*. This is called official notification and applies to the following in relation to any company.

    (a)   the issue of any certificate of incorporation;

    (b)   the receipt of any document making or evidencing an alteration to the memorandum or articles;

    (c)   the receipt of a notification of any change of directors;

    (d)   the receipt of the company's accounts;

    (e)   the receipt of a notification of the change of the address of the company's registered office;

    (f)   the receipt of a copy of a winding up order;

    (g)   the receipt of a copy of a dissolution order after winding up;

    (h)   the receipt of a return by the liquidator following a final meeting; or

    (i)   the receipt of certain other documents in relation to public companies only.

In the case of the making of a winding up order, alteration to the memorandum and articles, or a change in the directors, the company cannot rely on the happening of the event against another person until the notice is put in the *Gazette* unless the other person actually knew about it. The company cannot rely on the event for 15 days after it is put in the *Gazette* if the other person is unavoidably prevented from knowing about the event. The same rule applies to a change in the address of the registered office as regards service of any document on the company (i.e., service is effective at the old registered office until the change is gazetted), and also to the appointment of a liquidator in a voluntary winding up (in this case, the notice is put in the *Gazette* by the liquidator, not by the Registrar).

In addition to the file kept by the Registrar, certain information about a company is available for inspection at the company's registered office (see **7.4.3**).

29.3   Company Searches

29.3.1   GENERAL

While information about a company can be obtained from advertisements in the *London Gazette* or from inspecting the records and registers maintained by the company at its registered office, a great deal of information about a company can be discovered from making a search at the Companies' Registry. The Registrar of Companies keeps copies of the information supplied to him by the company and this is available for public inspection. In this section of the chapter we will look at the information which a company must supply to the Registrar and then look at the procedure for making a company search.

29.3.2   THE INFORMATION AVAILABLE FOR INSPECTION

The information available for inspection at the Companies' Registry includes the following:

    (a)   the company's memorandum and articles of association (changes to be registered within 15 days);

    (b)   particulars of directors and secretary (giving details both of the original directors and secretary as well as subsequent changes);

    (c)   particulars of the issue of shares;

    (d)   particulars of (most) charges (within 21 days);

    (e)   particulars of all special, elective and extraordinary resolutions (no particular form is required — copy resolution to be delivered within 15 days);

    (f)   the notice of the accounting reference date;

    (g)   the notice of any increase of capital (within 15 days of the change);

    (h)   resolutions under s. 80 CA 1985 (a copy of resolution to be delivered within 15 days);

    (i)   particulars of the address of the registered office (both the first address and subsequent changes);

    (j)   the annual return; and

    (k)   the accounts.

Of this list, the last two items merit further consideration (see **29.4** below for the rules relating to the accounts which the company must file). So far as the 'annual return' is concerned, s. 363 CA 1985 requires every company to make an annual return to the Registrar on Form 363 once in every year (a fee of £25 is payable). The company is required to file returns signed by a director or the secretary made up to the company's return date which must be within 12 months of the date of the previous return or, in the case of a new company, the date of incorporation. The return must be filed with the Registrar within 28 days of the return date. The return must set out details of:

(a)   the address of the registered office of the company;

(b)   the company's principal business activities;

(c)   the location of the register of members if it is not kept at the registered office;

(d)   the location of the company's register of debenture holders if it is not kept at the company's registered office;

(e)   the company's type (that is to say, public limited company, private company limited by shares or whatever);

(f)   the name and address of the company secretary;

(g)   the name and address of every director plus nationality, date of birth, business occupation and the particulars required for the register of directors;

(h)   details of the company's issued share capital (stating for each class of share, the nature of the class and the total number and aggregate number of issued shares of that class as at the date of the return);

(i)   names and addresses of the members of the company on the date on which the return is made up plus the persons who have ceased to be members since the last return;

(j)   details of the shares held by member; and

(k)   a statement that the company has elected to dispense with the holding of annual general meetings, or with the laying of accounts in general meetings, if it has.

The Registrar of Companies will not keep documents in relation to a company at the Registry indefinitely. At any time after the expiration of two years from the date of the dissolution of any company, the Registrar may direct that any records in his custody relating to that company be removed to the Public Record Office. Furthermore, the Registrar is only obliged to keep originals of documents for 10 years. Once that period has expired, the documents may be destroyed.

29.3.3   THE PROCEDURE FOR MAKING A COMPANY SEARCH

The wide range of information which companies are required to file with the Registrar of Companies is filed by the Registrar by reference to each company's unique company number. With the company's number (and on payment of the fee), it is possible to obtain a copy of the company's file. Rather than be presented with a bulky file of hard copies of the documents which the company has filed, the searcher will be given the company's file on 'microfiches' (which are, in effect, a collection of reduced photographic negatives of every page of information which the company has filed with the Registrar). The microfiches will contain, in date order, all the information which the company has filed with the Registrar so that the number of pages on the microfiches can be considerable in the case of long-established companies.

29.3.3.1   Where searches can be made

Searches can be made at the Companies' Registry in Cardiff or at the 'branch' offices in London, Leeds, Manchester and Birmingham. A full public search service is available both in Cardiff and London (although the hard copies of the documents filed with the Registrar are kept at Cardiff). The smaller 'branch' offices (in Leeds, Manchester and Birmingham) offer a more limited service but they do have public search facilities available. All the branch offices have access, through their computer equipment, to all the information filed in respect of registered companies.

29.3.3.2   Types of searches

A company search can be carried out in person but it is also possible to apply for a company search by telephone, post, fax or even through the Registry's on-line service, CHORUS. Personal public searches can be carried out at each of the branches of the Registry but only those in Cardiff and London provide a 'same day' service. When a request for a search is made in Cardiff and London (on payment of the fee of £3), the microfiche is usually available within one hour. However, if the information is required urgently, on payment of a higher fee (of £20) the microfiche can be made available within 20 minutes. If the public search is made but one of the other branches of the Registry (Leeds, Manchester or Birmingham), the microfiches will be available the next day since they have to be sent to the branch office by the main office in Cardiff.

29.3.3.3 Making a personal search

The first step when making a search (whether in person or otherwise) is to find the company's registered name and number. This can be found on all of the company's business letters and order forms. This information can also be found in the public index of companies which can be scanned on the computers at each branch of the Registry. There is a main index which lists all existing companies and subsidiary indexes which give the numbers of dissolved companies and details of any companies which have changed their names. It will, therefore, be possible to find the current name of a company if the searcher only has the old company name.

Once the searcher has the correct name and number for the company, the searcher will pay the appropriate fee for the search and the microfiche will be delivered to him.

The microfiche will be a complete record of all documents which the company has filed and it can be read on the microfiche readers provided at every branch of the Registry. The microfiches are not returnable and so the searcher can, provided he has access to a microfiche reader, take the microfiches away to study later.

29.3.3.4 Reading a company search

The microfiches for each company will be divided into three categories which are:

(a) the general documents giving information on the company's incorporation, constitution, structure and management (marked with the suffix 'G' or 'GEN');
(b) the financial and other information contained in the company's audited accounts and annual returns (marked with the suffix 'A', 'AC' or 'AR'); and
(c) information on the mortgages and charges which the company has created, including notice of the appointment of a receiver or liquidator (marked with the suffix 'MD' or 'MR').

The documents on the microfiches for each of the three categories will appear on the microfiches in chronological order and therefore if the searcher is merely looking for the most recent information falling into one of the three categories, he should find the latest annual return and work forwards from that. (The system of keeping records of returns by companies began before the microfiche system was introduced. Therefore, in the case of older companies, some early documents will not appear on the microfiches. The originals of the documents which have not been put onto the microfiches are available for inspection on application.)

Even if the company complies with its obligations with regard to the time limits for filing documents with the Registrar, there can be an interval between the happening of the relevant event and the filing of the return, with the result that the information shown on the search is always potentially out of date. The company may have charged its property, or a receiver or a liquidator may have been appointed, without these events being apparent from an inspection. There is no system of priorities to protect a person who makes a search, as there is with searches at the Land Registry and the Land Charges Department. However, if the return has been received by the Registrar (but not yet put onto the microfiches), 'warning microfiches' are included in the microfiches the searcher will be given. These warning microfiches can indicate that the Registrar has received details of a mortgage, charge, liquidation, receivership or administration order and the searcher will be given details of these documents on request.

29.3.3.5 Failure to file returns

The effectiveness of the system requiring companies to make information about themselves public depends on the companies making the information available whether in their own records and registers or by filing the information with the Registrar of Companies. Section 713 CA 1985 enables the court to make an order directing a company and its officers to provide information when they are in default. The application to the court can be made by a member of the company, a creditor of the company or by the registrar of companies. Failure to comply with an order under s. 713 can lead to the company and its officers being charged with contempt of court and so subject to a fine and imprisonment. Furthermore, under s. 652 CA 1985, the Registrar of Companies can strike from the register the name of the company in default in relation to delivering information, but only if the Registrar has reasonable cause to believe that the company is not carrying on business or is not in operation.

29.4   The Duty to Submit Accounts

Limited companies are required, by law, to prepare a set of 'final accounts'. These consist of a profit and loss account and a balance sheet. The accounts will usually be prepared by accountants, but the duty to ensure that they are prepared is placed on the directors of the company by s. 266 CA 1985. Once they have been prepared the final accounts are laid before the company in general meeting (s. 241). This means that a general meeting of the company will be held at which the accounts will be placed before the shareholders for their consideration. This meeting is called the accounts meeting. It may be either the annual general meeting of the company or an extraordinary general meeting. However, the company can dispense with the need to hold an accounts meeting if it passes an elective resolution to that effect.

In addition to presenting the accounts to the shareholders at a general meeting, the company is also required to send copies of the accounts to the shareholders (if an accounts meeting is held this must be done before the meeting). This must be done within seven months after the end of the company's financial year in the case of a public company and within ten months in the case of a private company.

Subject to what is said below about small and medium sized companies, all companies must also send copies of their accounts to the Registrar of Companies. Failure to deliver accounts on time leads to an automatic penalty. These accounts are then a matter of public record and anyone who pays to do a company search will get a microfiche copy of the accounts (s. 241(3)).

29.5   Small and Medium Sized Companies

If a private company comes within the definition of a small or medium sized company for a particular financial year, its duty to deliver accounts to the Registrar of Companies is modified. A company is small if at least two of the following criteria are satisfied:

(a)   the company's turnover does not exceed £2,800,000;
(b)   its balance sheet total does not exceed £1,400,000;
(c)   the average number of employees does not exceed 50 people.

A small company does not need to submit a profit and loss account and the information required in its balance sheet is reduced.

A medium sized company is one which satisfies at least two of the following criteria:

(a)   its turnover does not exceed £11,200,000;
(b)   its balance sheet total does not exceed £5,600,000;
(c)   the average number of employees does not exceed 250.

A medium sized company must submit both a balance sheet and a profit and loss account, but the profit and loss account is in an abbreviated form.

In the above definitions 'turnover' broadly speaking means the sums earned by the company in selling goods or services before deducting expenses. The balance sheet total is broadly speaking the value of the company's assets without deducting any liabilities except short term liabilities.

The exemptions from reporting available to small and medium sized companies mean that they can keep their affairs secret from the public to a greater extent than public companies, or companies which do not satisfy these definitions. However, small and medium sized companies are not exempt from the requirement to produce full accounts nor from the requirement to present the accounts to their own shareholders. The duty to have the accounts independently audited remains but the auditors need not make a full report.

29.6   Profit and Loss Account

A profit and loss account is an account which shows what income the company has received in a particular period of time and what expenses have been incurred by the company in producing that income. Once the expenses are deducted from the income the resulting figure is a profit (or a loss if the expenses are more than the income). The profit and loss account is strictly speaking only designed to show income profits. If a company makes a capital profit (for example, if it sells its factory for a profit) this may be shown as an addition to the profit and loss account. It will then usually be labelled as an 'exceptional item' as opposed to the ordinary income profit.

Profit and loss accounts are almost always prepared for 12 month periods (the company may wish to produce forecasts or full accounts for its own internal purposes on a more regular basis). The period covered by the accounts ends with the accounting reference date which the company can choose for itself. Companies are not required to prepare accounts for a calendar year (although some companies do choose 31 December as their accounting reference date in which case the accounts will be for a calendar year).

A very simple traditional profit and loss account might look like the following:

XYZ Ltd
Profit and Loss Account
Year ending 28 February 1993

	£	£
INCOME		
Sales		200,000
Opening stock	80,000	
Purchases	90,000	
	170,000	
Less closing stock	70,000	
		100,000
Gross profit from sales		100,000
Interest received		8,000
		108,000
EXPENDITURE		
Wages	55,000	
Miscellaneous	10,000	
		65,000
PROFIT BEFORE TAX		43,000
DEDUCT TAX		12,000
TRANSFERRED TO RESERVE		31,000

Notice the following points in relation to it:

(a) The account is divided into three parts. The first shows the income of the business. The second shows the expenditure which is incurred in earning that income and the third shows what has happened to the income (this third part is strictly speaking the appropriation section rather than part of the profit and loss account itself. If any dividends were paid they would be shown as a deduction in this section).

(b) In the income section the opening and closing stock are shown. Unless stock is taken into account it is impossible to work out the profit. If a company has a storeroom full of goods left over from last year which it sells this year, it cannot calculate its profit unless it takes into account the fact that it paid for that stock.

(c) The figure which is labelled transferred to reserve is what is left of the profit after the tax has been paid. It is in effect profit which has been retained in the business. An explanation of the term 'reserve' in this context is given in **29.7** below.

29.7 Balance Sheet

A balance sheet shows the assets and liabilities of the company. An asset is something of value or potential value. The factory which a company owns is an asset, so is any money which it has in the bank. Sometimes the balance sheet will also show much more intangible things such as goodwill. Goodwill is the difference between the real assets of a company and its overall value to a purchaser. For example, a company running a business in a shop might own the following assets:

	£
The shop	100,000
Fixtures (shelves etc.)	10,000
Stock (the goods for sale)	5,000
Cash	2,000

If the company decided to sell the business it would be likely to want more than £117,000 for it. The real value of the business includes the fact that it has a loyal group of customers, or it is situated in a good location for running this type of business (or both). The difference between the assets value and what the shop could be sold for is the goodwill of the business.

The liabilities part of the balance sheet includes liabilities due to outsiders (such as bills owed by the shop), money owed to the bank or other lenders. The money which would be paid to the shareholders if the company were wound up is also shown as a liability because, at least in theory, it will be paid out to the shareholders one day.

MAKING AND INTERPRETING A COMPANY SEARCH AND ACCOUNTS

A simple traditional balance sheet might look like this:

Balance Sheet of XYZ Ltd
28 February 1993

	£	£
FIXED ASSETS		
Premises		400,000
Fixtures (shelves etc.)		10,000
		410,000
CURRENT ASSETS		
Stock (the goods for sale)	5,000	
Cash	2,000	
	7,000	
LESS CURRENT LIABILITIES		
Electricity bill	4,500	
		2,500
		412,500
CAPITAL		
Share capital		200,000
Share premium account		160,000
Bank loan		10,000
Reserves		42,500
		412,500

Notice the following points in relation to it:

(a)   The totals balance i.e., they are the same figures in each half of the balance sheet. This is not a coincidence. It happens because of the way in which accountants record transactions in the company's records. It also reflects the fact that everything which the company owns will, or may, one day be paid to someone else — either to the creditors (people owed money by the company) or to the shareholders if the company is wound up.

(b)   A distinction is made between fixed assets and current assets. Fixed assets are assets which are likely to be held by the company for a considerable period of time. Current assets are those which are likely to be used up by the company in the course of its business.

(c)   Current liabilities (that is sums owed by the company which are likely to be paid within a year) are shown as a deduction from current assets. They are accordingly not in the same part of the account as the long term liabilities.

(d)   The second half of the balance sheet is labelled 'capital'. Although in common parlance the word capital often means money or wealth, to an accountant it is a liability which is owed to someone with a proprietary or other long term interest in the business. The money owed to the bank is included in capital on the assumption that it is a long term loan and so is something like an investment in the business. If the same money was owed to the bank on an overdraft it would be shown as a short term liability like the electricity bill.

(e)   The other sums shown under the heading of capital are all sums due to the shareholders of the company. The share capital is the liability which arises from the fact that the shareholders paid the nominal value of their shares to the company at some time in the past. The share premium is the liability which arises from the fact that when the shares were issued the shareholders paid more than the nominal value for them. The difference between these two sums is theoretical only. Remember that a company cannot generally return the sums invested by the shareholders until the company is wound up.

(f)   The item referred to as reserves is in a way a balancing item. If the company was wound up its assets would realise £417,000. This would be used to pay the bank and the outstanding bill. This would then leave £402,500 for the shareholders. They would be repaid their original investment of £360,000 (shown in share capital and share premium). This would then leave £42,500. The reserve is in effect a liability owed to shareholders which results from the fact that the company has made profits over the years.

(g)   The balance sheet is dated 28 February. Businesses constantly acquire and dispose of assets, pay bills and incur new liabilities. A balance sheet is, therefore, always relevant to a particular moment in time, not to the whole of a period of time (in which respect contrast the profit and loss account).

(h)   The company has a surplus of short term assets over short term liabilities. The resulting surplus is called net current assets (confusingly it is also often called 'working capital' even though it is an asset). This figure is particularly important as it is a strong indication of the solvency of the company.

29.8   Format of Accounts

Schedule 4 to the Companies Act 1985 contains formats for both profit and loss accounts and balance sheets. These are templates which all companies must choose from in presenting their accounts for each financial year. They set out the order in which all the different items in the accounts must appear. For the purposes of illustration we have not adhered exactly to any of the formats in the very brief examples given above.

Companies' published accounts are often difficult for beginners to follow because much of the information is given in the form of notes. Indeed the published profit and loss account is likely to contain very little information about the company's income and expenditure unless close attention is paid to the notes as well as to the account itself.

29.9   Interpretation of Accounts

29.9.1   INTRODUCTION

In this paragraph we will look at some ideas about interpretation of accounts. Interpretation is a process whereby information is extracted from the accounts for two main purposes:

(a)   to assess the company's present financial position in relation to profitability and solvency;
(b)   to predict the future prospects of the company.

Neither of these processes is an exact science. Interpretation of accounts will not always produce a 'right answer' but rather an opinion about the company.

29.9.2   REASONS FOR INTERPRETATION AND SOURCES OF INFORMATION

Interpretation of accounts is likely to be undertaken by or for a variety of people for a variety of reasons. In particular the management of the company may wish to know how efficient the business is. Investors or potential investors in a quoted company will want to know whether the company is over or under valued (in their opinion) at the present price of the shares. Creditors will be particularly concerned to investigate the company's solvency.

The most obvious source of information about the accounts of the company is the published accounts of the company. It should be noted, however, that these accounts will not provide as much information as the interpreter might ideally like. The management of the company will have more detailed accounts than the published accounts in the form of what are usually called management accounts. These are not available to the public (not even to the shareholders) as a matter of right, but sometimes the management may be willing to show them to others such as potential lenders or purchasers of the business.

If the information which is available to the particular investigator is limited to published accounts, then he will usually do well to look at the accounts for several years. In interpreting the performance of a business the trend over a period of time is very important. Past results are not necessarily a guide to the future, but nevertheless they may give some indication of the likely progress of the company in the future. An investor, for example, is likely to be more interested in a company which shows a long record of growth than one which has been merely holding its own.

29.9.3   WHAT ARE THE LIMITS INHERENT IN ACCOUNTS?

The most obvious limit is the possibility of outright fraud. If the accounts are a work of fiction they will tell you nothing useful. The process of auditing accounts ensures that fraud is unusual.

Published accounts are produced once a year and, as we have seen, may be submitted to the Registrar up to seven months after the end of the accounting period (ten months if the company is private). This means that the accounts may be quite considerably out of date. The balance sheet date should be checked both to see how out of date the accounts are and also to see how typical that date might be. The balance sheet of a resort hotel business may tell a very different story if it is drawn up just after the end of the season (when there will be an unusually large amount of cash or an unusually small overdraft), than if it is produced at the end of the winter.

The notes to the accounts should be examined carefully to see what the company's policy is in relation to valuation of assets. In particular, have the fixed assets been revalued recently so that the figures approximate to market value? If not, then the fixed assets may be shown at historic cost (i.e., what was paid for them) in which case they, and so the company, may be worth much more than shown.

Another important factor to look for is how debtors have been dealt with in the accounts. The figure described as debtors shows the amount of money owed to the company. Almost all businesses suffer some degree of bad debts. That is, some of the people who owe them money cannot or will not pay what they owe to the company. Bad debts and an estimate of potential bad debts ('provision for bad debts') should be deducted in computing the profits, and from the current assets of the company, otherwise the accounts will be misleading.

Often the accounts will include some special feature which is relevant to the accounts in a particular year only. These are usually called exceptional items. For example, in a particular year a company may have sold a fixed asset or issued shares. In both of these cases it will have received a large amount of cash. If it has not yet spent the cash then the net current assets figure may be unusually high. Will the company still have enough cash to pay its creditors if it replaces the fixed asset which it sold?

29.10   Solvency

A company is solvent if it is able to pay its debts as they fall due. It is important to realise that solvency is not the same thing as profitability. A company may make profits and yet be insolvent. For example, the profits may arise from the fact that the company has supplied goods or services for which it has not yet been paid. This company will be insolvent if it has to pay its own creditors before it collects from its debtors. Similarly a company may be unprofitable and yet solvent for a very long time. For example, a company may be making losses and yet can keep itself going by selling fixed assets.

In judging the solvency of a company it is desirable to work out certain solvency ratios. These are calculations made from the information given in the accounts.

The first of the ratios is the 'current ratio': this is a test of the company's liquidity. Liquidity is the ability of a company to pay its debts in the short term. The current ratio is the ratio of current assets to current liabilities. In the example in **29.7** above, the current assets were £7,000 and the current liabilities were £4,500. This gives a ratio of 7:4.5 or 1.55:1. This would generally be regarded as a satisfactory figure as it means that for every pound which the company will have to pay in the short term, it has, or will soon receive, £1.55. However, this does assume that the stock will be easy to sell at the value shown in the balance sheet (in the case of stock the value will normally be the lower of purchase price or current value).

Because stock cannot always be sold in a hurry the liquidity ratio (also known as the acid test) is often preferred to the current ratio. This compares liquid assets (i.e., cash and things as good as cash) with current liabilities. Applying this ratio to our figures we get a ratio of 2:4.5 or .44:1. This is much less satisfactory. It means that for every pound that the company will have to pay, it only has ready access to 44p. This is not necessarily as dangerous as it may seem at first sight, however. If the company can rely on selling a lot of stock quickly it will be able to pay the electricity bill. Similarly the company may have an arrangement with its bank for an overdraft which will see it through the temporary crisis of the payment of the electricity bill.

A company which is in the position of the one illustrated here is in danger of overtrading. This occurs where the company has insufficient working capital (i.e., net current assets). As it pays its bills it may be unable to replace its stock which obviously means that it cannot continue to be profitable and solvent in the future. The solution to this problem may be for the company to acquire more working capital, either by retaining more profits in the business, by acquiring further investment or by increasing the size of its long term borrowing (the last of these is likely to be a real possibility in view of the large amount of fixed assets and the small amount of borrowing). The fact that not all companies can in practice do any of these things is the reason for a very high proportion of business failures.

29.11 Profitability

The bottom line profit figure is found in the profit and loss account. In our example the profit is £43,000 before tax and £31,000 after. The proprietor of the business will want to know whether this figure is satisfactory or not. There is no simple answer to this, not least because different people have different expectations and so are more or less easily satisfied. The most important step to take may be to compare with previous years and to compare with other similar business (this is more easily done with large companies as the published accounts of small and medium sized companies give much less information). However, ratios can help here as with solvency.

29.11.1 INVESTMENT

An investor or potential investor will be interested in the whole of the company's financial situation. He will be particularly interested in what return on capital he can expect (i.e., in how much income will be generated by his investment). One simple calculation which may assist in judging this is the 'return on capital employed'. This is the net profit (before tax, dividends and any interest paid) expressed as a percentage of the company capital (including debentures and other long term loans), in our example this is 43,000/412,500 × 100 = 10.42%. This figure should be judged against previous year's profits and is possible against other similar companies. If the shareholders are also directors of the company, they might wish to treat any directors' fees as part of the return on capital if they exceed what the directors regard as a fair return for their labour.

An alternative to the return on capital calculation is to calculate earnings per share. In our example assume that there are 10,000 shares, the earnings per share would then be 31,000/10,000 = £3.1 per share (it is usual to deduct tax in this calculation). This information is often given in relation to companies quoted on the stock exchange. Similarly in relation to such companies a price/earnings (or P/E) ratio can be calculated. This compares the market price of the share (on the stock exchange) with the earnings per share. A high P/E ratio shows that the stock market has confidence in the company as its shares are valuable despite low earnings. It is not possible to calculate a P/E ratio for a private or unquoted public company as there is no market price for their shares.

29.11.2   EFFICIENCY RATIOS

These are ratios which are mainly calculated so that the management of the company and other interested parties can calculate how efficient the profit making process of the company is. The return on capital employed (see **29.11.1** above) is a good indicator of the company's general efficiency in making money.

Another useful ratio is the net profit percentage. This expresses trading profit (before deduction of tax and interest payments) as a percentage of sales. In our example this is $43,000/200,000 \times 100 = 21.5\%$. This should be compared with other businesses and with previous years. Whether 21.5% is a good profit margin depends on the nature of the business in question.

THIRTY

SALE OF A BUSINESS TO A COMPANY

30.1　Introduction

A sole trader or partnership may decide, for a variety of reasons, to incorporate the business. If this step is taken, although the business will remain unchanged, the incorporation will give rise to a number of tax and other problems. In this chapter we will consider these problems and how they can be avoided, or at least mitigated. As we shall see, the tax rules are the most important in this area, since if they are not appreciated the payment of an unexpected tax bill can cause very serious cash flow problems. As an aid to understanding these problems, it is helpful to bear in mind that when the trader (which for these purposes includes partnerships) incorporates the business, it is transferred to a separate legal entity, the company. This means that the trader ceases to trade as an unincorporated business and disposes of the business and its assets to the company. The fact that the former proprietor or proprietors own the company and operate the business in exactly the same way as before is immaterial since the members of the company are distinct legal entities (*Salomon* v *A. Salomon & Co. Ltd* [1897] AC 22).

It may therefore come as a surprise to many traders who incorporate their businesses to discover that incorporation can lead to the payment of income tax, capital gains tax and stamp duty. In this chapter these tax liabilities will be considered in turn.

30.2　Income Tax

30.2.1　THE CLOSING YEARS RULES

Of the possible tax liabilities which can arise, the one which may cause the most difficulties, if it is not provided for, is the liability to income tax. Transferring the business to the company means that the unincorporated trader has permanently stopped trading, with the result that the closing years rules of assessment set out in s. 63 ICTA 1988 will apply. To recapitulate, the effect of s. 63 is as follows:

(a)　In the tax year in which the business is sold to the company, the trader pays tax on the profits made from 6 April to the date of discontinuance, that is, the date the business is transferred to the company. If the trader has no accounts which cover this period, the profits made in the final accounting period will be apportioned on a time basis.

(b)　In the penultimate and pre-penultimate tax years, the preceding year basis will apply, so that the trader will be assessed on the profits made in the accounting period which ended in the tax year immediately preceding the relevant year. The Inland Revenue have a right to tax both the penultimate and the pre-penultimate tax years on an actual or current year basis (that is, the profits from 6 April to the following 5 April) if the profits for those periods are higher.

The problems that can result from these rules are best illustrated by applying the rules to a set of facts. If a trader makes up his accounts to 5 July each year and transfers his business to a company on 6 July 1994, the profits on which he will be assessed, if the Revenue do not make their election, are as follows:

(a) Final tax year (1994/95) — profits made from 6 April 1994 to 5 July 1994. As he has no accounts covering this three-month period he will pay tax on ¼ of the profits made in the final accounting period which ends on 5 July 1994.

(b) Penultimate tax year (1993/94) — profits made to 5 July 1992, since the preceding year basis is applicable.

(c) Pre-penultimate tax year (1992/93) — profits made to 5 July 1991 (since, again, the preceding year basis applies).

This shows that there is a 'tax-free' gap from 6 July 1992 to 5 April 1994. Clearly, were it is not for the Revenue's right to elect to tax the trader on the actual basis for the penultimate and pre-penultimate tax years, the sensible trader would ensure that he completed as much work as possible (assuming he is assessed on the earnings basis) during the accounting period ending on 5 July 1993, since the profits arising would fall into this 'tax-free gap'. If the trader's profits are higher during these two tax years the Revenue will make their election, which means the profits on which he will be assessed are as follows:

(a) Final tax year — as above.

(b) Penultimate tax year — profits made between 6 April 1993 and 5 April 1994, apportioning accounts for the appropriate accounting periods on a time basis.

(c) Pre-penultimate tax year — profits made between 6 April 1992 and 5 April 1993, again apportioning the accounts.

The election has the effect of wiping out the 'tax-free gap' from July 1992 to April 1994, but since the tax year before the pre-penultimate one (1991/1992) is assessed on the preceding year basis, so attracting tax on the profits made to July 1990, the 'tax-free gap' merely appears earlier in the accounts. Now, no tax will be paid based on the profits made between 6 July 1990 to 5 April 1992.

The end result is that whether or not the Revenue make their election, a tax-free gap of between 12 and nearly 24 months (depending on the date the accounts are made up to) will appear somewhere in the accounts of the last four years of the business.

30.2.2 THE ADDITIONAL TAX LIABILITY

While the 'tax-free' gap may be a considerable advantage, the closing years rules as a whole can lead to a serious cash flow problem when the Revenue do elect to tax the trader on the actual basis (which they will do if his profits have been increasing). The problem stems from the dates for payment of tax, which for Schedule D Cases I and II taxpayers are 1 January in the relevant tax year and the immediately following 1 July.

Since the Revenue's right to elect relates, in the illustration, to the tax years 1992/93 and 1993/94, by the date of transfer (6 July 1994) the dates for payment of tax in respect of both these years will already have passed. The result of this is that any extra tax is immediately payable, subject only to the time it takes for the Revenue to consider the accounts for these periods and to produce a revised assessment for the two tax years. (It should be remembered that the Revenue will already have calculated, and probably have received, the tax payable for these two years on the preceding year basis, so that only the difference between the tax already assessed and the tax liability that has arisen on the actual basis will now be payable.) If the profits have been rising sharply, or if the rates of tax have increased, the extra amount that is now payable could be a considerable burden, especially if provision has not been made to meet it.

30.2.3 FUNDS USED TO PAY ADDITIONAL TAX LIABILITY

If steps have not been taken to guard against this eventuality and the trader has transferred all the assets of the business to the company, he faces serious problems trying to raise the money to pay this tax. If he tries to borrow money from a bank, he will have to pay interest charges and he will not be able to borrow money from the new company since he will, presumably, be a director and loans to directors are generally forbidden. If he is merely a shareholder in the company it could lend him the money, but since it will almost certainly be a close company, it will have to pay a sum equivalent to ACT until the loan is repaid and should it be written off, the trader will have to pay income tax on the amount of the loan grossed up at basic rate.

Since the company cannot simply pay the tax liability on the trader's behalf, the only other method of receiving money from the company is in the form of either directors' fees or dividends. Since these are themselves taxable as income receipts, he would have to bear income tax on them so he would need to receive sufficiently large fees or dividends to leave him, after tax, with enough to live on and to meet the additional tax liability. Such a payment could place an intolerable burden on the new company.

If these methods were unavailable to the trader, his only alternative would be to sell his personal assets, which would include the shares in the new company. Thus a lack of foresight could lead to the trader having to sell all his shares, or at least introduce an unwanted 'partner' and, to add insult to injury, possibly having to pay capital gains tax on the sale of these personal assets.

The problems outlined above can be avoided by, for example, the trader retaining any cash that he set aside out of the business profits as a tax provision or the book debts of the business. However, when considering this, care must be taken to ensure that retaining such sums or assets does not deny the trader relief from other taxes. As will be seen later (**30.3.2** below), retaining cash has no effect on the trader's entitlement to capital gains tax roll-over relief, but retaining an asset such as the book debts can cause the trader to lose this relief altogether (although it will save stamp duty; see **30.6.5** below).

30.2.4 LOSS RELIEF

If a loss was made in the final 12 months' trading, it could be carried across against other income under s. 380 ICTA 1988, and any unabsorbed loss carried back and set against the profits of the three tax years immediately preceding the year of incorporation, taking later years before earlier ones (s. 388 ICTA 1988). This would have the effect of reducing, if not wiping out, the profits, made during the last months of the unincorporated business's life and would almost certainly prevent the Revenue making their election. If, having made use of both provisions, there is still an unabsorbed loss, it cannot be used by the company. However, s. 386 permits the former proprietors, provided they sold the business in exchange wholly or mainly for shares in the new company, to set the remaining loss against income received from the company while they continue to own the shares. They must reduce earned income (such as directors' fees) before investment income (such as dividends).

Although it may appear strange that a loss-making business should be incorporated there may be sound reasons for doing so. For example, the business may be entering a temporary period of recession and the trader may want to protect himself from personal liability for future debts, or the loss may have been deliberately created by claiming capital allowances in respect of items of plant and machinery bought shortly before incorporation.

30.2.5 CAPITAL ALLOWANCES

Whether or not the purchase of an item attracting capital allowances has created the final year loss, the trader's capital allowance position is the remaining income tax point which needs to be considered. The rules relating to capital allowances have already been considered (see **Chapter 17**). The important point to be considered in the context of incorporating a trader's business, is that the transfer to the company, even if the purchase price is to be paid in shares, will be a disposal. If the capital allowances claimed exceed the amount by which the assets have depreciated in value, the Revenue have a right to levy a balancing charge under Schedule D Case VI. This means the Revenue recovers the tax lost as a result of the over-deduction of allowances. Thus there can be another additional income tax bill arising on the incorporation. However, if the company buys the assets for more than their written-down value, the transfer of plant and machinery is not to be regarded as a discontinuance of the trade for the purposes of capital allowances provided:

(a) the trader and persons connected with him (which includes partners) are the majority shareholders in the new company; and

(b) an election is made to the effect that if there is no discontinuance, there is no disposal and the balancing charge does not arise. The result is that the new company takes over the trader's capital allowance position and makes the appropriate claims for writing-down allowances in respect of the, as yet, unallowed expenditure.

30.3 Capital Gains Tax

30.3.1 THE DISPOSAL

The incorporation of the old business not only means there is a discontinuance for income tax purposes, but that there is also a disposal for CGT purposes. This disposal arises because the business, its assets and connections (i.e., goodwill) are being *sold* to the company in exchange for shares. This is a chargeable disposal within the Taxation of Chargeable Gains Act (TCGA) 1992 and the trader will be liable for any gain that is realised.

The gain is calculated in the normal way by deducting the allowable expenditure from the market value of the assets transferred. Allowable expenditure includes the expenses incurred in acquiring, improving and disposing of the assets. Any indexation allowance which is available is also deducted. This liability cannot be avoided by the company issuing shares of a purely nominal value in exchange for the assets, as the Revenue have a right to substitute the market value of the assets in such circumstances. This gain could be considerable, especially if the business is successful and was set up several years previously. However, relief is available to the trader if the requirements of s. 162 TCGA 1992 are satisfied.

30.3.2 RELIEF UNDER s. 162 TCGA 1992

30.3.2.1 The basic rule

Section 162 TCGA 1992 applies where a person (not being a company) 'transfers to a company a business as a going concern, together with the whole assets of the business, or together with the whole of those assets other than cash, and the business is transferred wholly or partly in exchange for shares issued by the company to the person transferring the business'. The section permits a deduction to be made from the gain arising when the business and its assets are disposed of. Section 162(4) provides that this deduction is the gain reduced by the fraction A/B, where A is the 'cost of the new assets' (that is, the value of the shares issued to the former owner), and B is the whole of the consideration received by the former owner in exchange for the business. Thus, if the former owner transfers a business with assets worth £100,000 to the new company and receives £90,000 worth of shares and £10,000 worth of debentures in exchange, his gain will be reduced by the fraction £90,000/(£90,000 + £10,000), i.e., $^9/_{10}$ths. This means that the former owner only pays tax on $^1/_{10}$th of the gain realised on the disposal of the business; the remaining $^9/_{10}$ths are, however, taxable when he disposes of the shares at some time in the future. If he only receives shares, the whole of the tax liability on the gain would be postponed in this way, or 'rolled-over' as the Act describes it.

It should be noted that the relief only applies to the former owner and his tax liability. The company's acquisition price of the assets will be their full market value at the date of the disposal.

30.3.2.2 The assets transferred to the company

Although these rules may appear complex at first sight, two simple requirements can be extracted from them. Firstly, to claim the relief at all, the whole of the assets of the business (other than cash) at the date of incorporation must be transferred to the company, and secondly, the relief may only be claimed in full if the consideration received was entirely in the form of shares. Provided these conditions are satisfied, the effect of s. 162 is that the former owner acquires the shares at a value equal to his original acquisition price of the assets that have just been transferred to the company, so tax is only paid when they are later sold or given away (by which time he may qualify for retirement relief). Since s. 162 relief can be obtained so easily by following these rules, it may seem strange that a number of traders choose not to follow them. There are, however, two good reasons for this:

(a) To provide a fund from which the extra income tax liability, arising as a result of the Revenue's election under the closing years rules, can be paid. The section itself envisages the retention of a cash fund but other assets, such as book debts owed to the business at the date of transfer, might be kept by the former owner and would perform the same function as such a fund. Furthermore, the retention of non-cash assets can lead to a stamp duty saving (see **30.6.5** below).

(b) To avoid the 'double capital gains tax charge', which is a problem where companies own appreciating assets, such as land or buildings. If a company owns such an asset and disposes of it realising a gain, the company will pay corporation tax on that gain. The post-tax gain will then increase the value of the company's assets, which in turn has the effect of increasing the value of the shares. This will result in the shareholder making an increased gain, and so paying more capital gains tax, on a later disposal of the shares. Retaining the asset in the former owner's hands ensures that there is only one capital gains tax charge if the asset is disposed of. It may also produce a stamp duty saving (see **30.6.5** below). However, this is at the cost of the potential loss, or at least reduction, of certain capital tax reliefs (retirement relief and business property relief; see **30.5.2** and **30.5.3** below).

For either of these reasons, therefore, the former owner may retain assets even though, prima facie, this means the loss of the s. 162 relief. However, if the trader is sufficiently careful, it may be possible to retain assets without forfeiting the relief.

Section 162 relief is lost if all of the assets in the business *at the date of transfer* are not transferred, but there is nothing to prevent the trader transferring assets out of the business prior to incorporation and the company receiving all that is left. Provided the assets retained did not prevent the business being transferred as a 'going concern', the only stumbling block is convincing the Revenue that the assets no longer form part of the business. One method would be to make appropriate entries in the business's books, by debiting the trader's capital account with the value of the assets involved, but this would not amount to conclusive evidence that the asset had become 'private' property. Such conclusive evidence would be provided by transferring the assets to someone else, but unless an exemption was available, a tax charge would arise as a result of that transfer. An exemption is, of course, available if the assets are transferred to the former owner's spouse. However, the decision in *W. T. Ramsey v IRC* [1981] 2 WLR 449, which created a form of 'associated operations' for capital gains tax, might lead the court to decide that the transaction was made simply with a view to avoiding tax, thereby denying the former owner the right to take advantage of s. 162.

30.3.2.3 Method of payment for assets

Even if the Revenue are convinced that all the assets comprised in the business have been transferred, the relief can only be claimed in full if the company 'pays' for the assets in shares. As has already been explained, if the consideration is wholly or partly in debentures and/or cash the roll-over relief is wholly or partly denied to the former owner. Despite this, a trader might want to be paid either in cash or debentures for the following reasons. The advantage of receiving cash is that it provides a fund from which the former owner can pay the extra income tax liability arising on discontinuance. Since s. 162 permits cash to be retained without loss of the relief, this form of payment will only be necessary if the business had insufficient cash at the date of transfer to meet the tax liability, but was able to raise cash (for example, by collecting debts) shortly after incorporation.

It is much more common for the former owner to be paid in shares and debentures. Debentures have advantages for both the holder (in the form of security of both capital and income) and the company (in the form of a pre-tax deduction in respect of the interest payments), and these advantages may compensate the former owner for partial loss of capital gains tax relief. It should be remembered that receiving part of the consideration in debentures means only a proportionate part of the gain is taxable, and the taxable gain could be reduced or wiped out by the annual £5,800 exemption. This has the attraction of reducing any future taxable gain and also of ensuring that he does not lose the benefit of the annual exemption for the year of incorporation.

30.3.3 RELIEF FOR GIFTS OF BUSINESS ASSETS (s. 165 TCGA 1992)

Section 165 gives 'hold-over' relief where an asset used by the trader in his trade, profession or vocation is transferred to a company, provided the transaction is not a bargain at arm's length. This means that if the asset is 'sold' at an under-value, or even given to the company, the trader and the company can elect that the company acquires the asset for a consideration equal to the trader's acquisition cost (if there is an outright gift) or the sale price (if there is a sale at an under-value). The effect of the relief is to postpone the payment of tax until the asset is disposed of, when the *company* will be liable to pay the tax, not the trader.

30.4 VAT

If the trader is registered for VAT, VAT may be chargeable on the transfer of the assets unless the business is transferred as a going concern (s. 33 Value Added Tax Act 1983).

30.5 Capital Tax Relief and Retained Assets

Retaining business assets can have the immediate disadvantage of denying the former owner the relief given by s. 162 and it can also have the long-term disadvantage of affecting his entitlement to both capital gains tax and inheritance tax reliefs. There are three such reliefs that the retention puts at risk.

30.5.1 ROLL-OVER RELIEF (s. 152 TCGA 1992)

Firstly, it will be remembered that s. 152 TCGA 1992 gives traders, be they companies or individuals, the right to roll over any gain made on the disposal of specified business assets into replacement assets. Obviously, if the company receives the asset and deals with it in this way, relief can be obtained and the payment of tax postponed. However, the former owner may retain an asset (perhaps to avoid the double capital gains tax charge) intending to let the company make use of it. A problem may arise if he wishes to replace it with another. To obtain the roll-over relief an additional requirement must be satisfied.

The tax can be postponed only if the asset is disposed of by him and it was used in a business carried on by his 'personal company' (see **Chapter 18**) which will cause no problems if the former owner was a sole proprietor of the business, but the former partners need to be aware of the necessity to acquire a minimum holding (of at least 5%).

30.5.2 RETIREMENT RELIEF (ss. 163-164, Sch. 6 TCGA 1992)

A more serious problem arises in relation to retirement relief. Relief is available to an individual who disposes by sale or gift of the whole or part of a business or shares or securities of a company, having reached the age of at least 55, or who retires through ill-health below that age (see **Chapter 18**). Obviously if assets are retained there will be no disposal and so the relief will not be available.

30.5.3 BUSINESS PROPERTY RELIEF (ss. 103-114 IHTA 1984)

The third, and final, capital tax relief that is affected, is the relief for business property from capital transfer tax. This enables the transferor to claim a 100% reduction in the value transferred if shares forming part of a controlling holding are given away. While the value transferred will reflect not only the value of the underlying assets, but also the value of the controlling interest, the reduction will, in effect, be a 100% reduction in the asset's value. However, if the asset given away has been kept out of the company, a 50% reduction in the value transferred is all that can be claimed and only then if the transferor controls the company that used the asset. The retention therefore means that, in effect, the trader will face a liability to IHT on an additional 50% of the value of the asset. This could lead to a considerable tax liability.

Therefore, when deciding whether or not to retain assets, the trader must weigh up the advantage of avoiding the double capital gains tax charge against the loss of s. 162 relief and the payment of additional capital transfer tax when the asset is given away at some time in the future.

30.6 Stamp Duty

30.6.1 INTRODUCTION

So far we have considered the tax liabilities of the trader personally; now we will consider the liabilities of the company to stamp duty. When a business is incorporated sufficient provision must be made to enable the company to meet this liability. In this section we do not intend to consider the duty in great detail, but will look at the particular points relevant on the incorporation of an existing business.

30.6.2 THE CHARGE TO TAX AND s. 59 OF THE STAMP ACT 1891

When dealing with stamp duty it is necessary to decide whether the assets transferred attract the duty at all, whether duty is paid on the contract or the conveyance, and finally, what the rate of duty should be.

Stamp duty is only payable if a transaction is evidenced by written instrument. Thus, oral contracts do not attract the duty, neither do transactions where ownership of the asset passes by delivery. Where a written instrument is used, stamp duty is payable, by s. 54 of the Stamp Act 1891, on the conveyance on sale but not on a mere contract to convey. Since a binding contract transfers the equitable title, if a purchaser is satisfied with the equitable title, it is prima facie possible to avoid stamp duty by never executing the conveyance. Normally a purchaser will not be satisfied with such title, but where a business is being incorporated, the new company may be prepared to accept this. To prevent the loss of revenue that would result from this situation, s. 59(1) of the Stamp Act 1891 provides that the purchaser shall pay duty on the contract for the sale of any equitable interest or interest in any property or for the sale of any estate or interest in any property, except (*inter alia*) land, goods, wares or merchandise, or marketable securities or any ship or vessel, as if it were an actual conveyance on sale of the estate, interest, or property contracted or agreed to be sold.

The effect of the section is to levy duty on any contract to sell many of the assets that are likely to be transferred when incorporating an existing business (for example, goodwill, book debts, patents, 'know-how', the benefit of pending contracts, tenants' fixtures on *leasehold* property, *equitable* interests in freehold property and cash on deposit). If there is a subsequent conveyance no further duty is payable on that conveyance but if the duty was not paid on the contract no penalty becomes payable (other than one for late stamping), provided a conveyance or transfer is presented for stamping within six months of its execution (or within such longer period as the Commissioners of Inland Revenue may think reasonable in the circumstances of the case).

30.6.3 TREATMENT OF ITEMS OUTSIDE THE s. 59 CHARGE

Of the items excepted by s. 59, those falling into the category 'goods, wares or merchandise' are totally exempt from the charge provided title in them passes by delivery. This will be so in relation to stock-in-trade, plant and machinery, cash in hand and cash in a current bank account, but only if they are not specifically dealt with in the later conveyance (s. 34(4) Finance Act 1958). With regard to the cash, the exemption only applies to cash in hand or in a current account, since the Revenue regards such money as not being 'property' within the meaning of s. 59(1). However, cash on deposit is a debt to the customer by the bank (*Foley* v *Hill* (1848) 2 HL 28) and so is caught by the section.

Where a legal estate in land (which includes fixtures on freehold property), marketable securities or ships is transferred, duty is paid, but on the conveyance or transfer, if there is one, and not the contract, so that it is theoretically possible to avoid stamp duty in respect of these items, although in practice a conveyance will normally be required.

Once the items that are subject to the duty have been valued, all the values are aggregated to calculate the rate of duty that is payable. If the business has liabilities that the new company is taking over, s. 57 of the Stamp Act 1891 requires duty to be paid on the total value of the dutiable assets being transferred without the deduction of the liabilities. This is because the agreement to pay the debts is part of the consideration given in exchange for receiving the assets (one practical point, unrelated to stamp duty, is that in such a case the agreement of the creditor will have to be obtained).

30.6.4 THE STAMP DUTY RATES

The full rate of tax is £1 per £100 or part thereof of the value of dutiable items being transferred. However, if the instrument contains a certificate of value certifying that the value of the dutiable items does not exceed £30,000 no duty is payable. The usual wording for the certificate is:

> It is hereby certified that the transaction hereby effected does not form part of a larger transaction or of a series of transactions in respect of which the amount or value or the aggregate amount or value of the consideration exceeds £30,000.

It is important to note that the certificate of value relates to the total value passing under the transaction as a whole, so that where some assets pass under the contract and others under a conveyance, the values of property passing under both the contract and the conveyance must be aggregated. The calculation of the duty paid on the contract is made by apportioning the total consideration on the form 'Stamps 22'.

30.6.5 SAVING STAMP DUTY

Stamp duty can be saved in two ways: either by not transferring dutiable items to the company, or by converting ones that attract the duty into ones that do not. Thus the trader can retain book debts to provide a source of money to meet his additional income tax liability or to pay his existing trade creditors. Another possible way of saving stamp duty is to transfer cash on deposit into a current account. This need only be done for the day of the transfer.

30.7 Subsidiary Matters

The tax matters already dealt with will, of course, be important to the former owner but there are a number of other points that must not be overlooked.

30.7.1 THE TRANSFER AND EMPLOYMENT LAW

Firstly, the effect of the transfer on the business' employees. The general rule used to be that the transfer of the business terminated the contracts of employment of all the employees and, if common law and statutory claims were to be avoided, the employees had to be notified of the transfer and offered employment with the new company on the same, or suitable, terms before the transfer took place. However, as a result of the Transfer of Undertakings (Protection of Employment) Regulations 1981 (SI 1981 No. 1794), this is no longer the case, since regulation 5(1) provides that a 'relevant transfer' shall not terminate a person's contract of employment and the contract shall have the effect after the transfer as if it had originally been made between the employee and the transferee. (A 'relevant transfer' is defined in regulation 3(1) as being 'a transfer from one person to another of an undertaking situated immediately before the transfer in the United Kingdom or of a part of one which is so situated'.) Thus, if a business is transferred to a company, the employees are treated as if their contracts had originally been made with the new company, which takes over all the trader's rights, powers, duties and liabilities under the employment contracts. Therefore the employee's period of continuous employment is preserved as are any pre-existing rights against the old employer for breach of contract, or duty. As a result, the new employer could be faced with liability for a constructive dismissal arising from the old employer's breach, for example, and should obtain suitable indemnities.

While these regulations do not prevent an employee bringing a claim against the trader if there is a substantial change made in his working conditions, no action can be brought simply because the identity of the employer has changed, unless the employee shows the change to be significant and to his detriment.

Regulation 5 does not enable the fact of the transfer to be kept from the employees. Regulation 10 imposes an obligation on the transferor to inform and consult with trade union representatives.

30.7.2 THE TRANSFER AND COMPANY LAW

In addition to the matters that always arise on the formation of a new company, one special problem particularly relevant to this kind of transfer must be considered. On the assumption that the transferor of the business is to be made a director of the new company, the consent of the members in general meeting will almost certainly be needed to the purchase by the company of the assets. Section 320 CA 1985 requires such consent to be obtained if a director sells to (or buys from) the company a non-cash asset or assets of the 'requisite value', which means assets worth £50,000 or representing at least 10% of the company's assets (subject to a minimum value of £1,000). If the consent is not obtained, the transaction is voidable at the instance of the company and the director will have to account to the company for any profit made and indemnify it for any loss or damages arising. In order to obtain the necessary consent, a general meeting of the company will have to be held immediately after incorporation and before the transfer takes place.

Furthermore, the transferor must make sure that the new company's name appears on all letters, cheques and order forms as required by s. 348 CA 1985, and that the letters have printed on them the information required by ss. 305 and 351 CA 1985.

30.7.3 THE TRANSFER AND OTHER MISCELLANEOUS MATTERS

Further practical points to be dealt with include:

(a) The local inspector of taxes must be notified that there is a new employer for PAYE purposes as well as there being a new company liable to corporation tax.

(b) If the business's turnover exceeds the threshold for VAT registration, its VAT registration must be cancelled and the company must apply to have itself registered. In order to ensure there is no gap in the VAT registration it is advisable to cancel the old one after the company's registration has been confirmed.

(c) The consent of a landlord to the assignment of a lease must be obtained. If the new company is taking over responsibility for hire-purchase contracts, the consent of the finance house must be obtained.

(d)   The former owner can bring his personal liability to existing creditors to an end by entering into a contract of 'novation'. However, the consent of the creditors is required.

(e)   The company must take out appropriate insurance cover and have any vehicles transferred into its own name.

THIRTY ONE

CHOICE OF BUSINESS MEDIUM

31.1 Introduction

The purpose of this chapter is to make a comparison between companies, on the one hand, and partnerships or sole traders on the other, with a view to explaining the various factors which ought to be taken into account when a choice is made between the two business media.

This choice will first be made when a new business is set up, but should be kept under review as circumstances (and the law) change. For the sake of clarity, the differences between companies and partnerships are considered under various headings. It is important to realise that in making a choice each factor should be taken into account. In particular cases one factor may outweigh all the others, but generally each medium has some advantages and some disadvantages so that often the choice will be a difficult one.

31.2 Risk of Capital

All business involves a risk of capital. The degree of risk obviously varies considerably depending on the nature of the business, the economic climate and the skill of the people running the business. The amount of capital which is at risk also varies considerably — some types of business require a great deal of capital, others very little.

One advantage of a company over a partnership is that a company can be formed with limited liability. This means that the shareholders must contribute the amount unpaid on their shares, but no more, if the company goes into liquidation when it is insolvent. In the vast majority of cases the shares will be fully paid, so that no contribution towards the company's debts has to be made. However, the shareholders will lose their shares when the company fails so that, realistically, the limit to their liability is what they have invested in the company. A shareholder who is also a director will also lose his livelihood. A director (including a shadow director) may also become personally liable in certain circumstances when the company is wound up (see **Chapter 23**).

If a partnership becomes insolvent, each of the partners is jointly and severally liable for all the debts of the partnership. This means that he stands to lose not only what he has invested in the business but also any other property which he owns. The liability of partners is, therefore, unlimited in amount. The partnership agreement may make provision as to how losses are to be shared between the partners but this does not prevent creditors claiming in full from a rich partner whose poor partners are unable to pay their share of the loss.

At first sight limited liability would seem to be an enormous advantage to the proprietors of a business in every case. However, there are at least two circumstances where limited liability is not very significant:

(a) *Where there is little risk of substantial loss of capital* — The clearest example of this is a business involving the giving of advice, such as a consultancy. The proprietor expects to make profits by providing expertise in return for payment; comparatively little is required in the way of capital expenditure on equipment and the running costs of the business will be small. In many cases the biggest potential loss will be claims for damages if bad advice is given to clients and this can be covered by insurance.

(b) *Where the proprietor risks everything he owns in the business* — If the proprietor's only assets are what he has invested in the business, he will effectively lose everything when the business fails whether it is a company or partnership. (This is, of course, only true while all the capital remains in the business, so that limited liability will become relevant once the proprietor starts to take profits out of the business on a large scale.)

Sometimes limited liability would be very desirable but cannot realistically be achieved because credit is needed but cannot be obtained without a personal guarantee. Many businesses rely on borrowed money. A bank lending to a small company will often require a personal guarantee from the directors or shareholders, so that if the company cannot repay the loan the bank has further security. This may wipe out the advantage of limited liability to a large extent.

Limited liability is most significant (and can realistically be achieved) where there is a substantial risk of loss of capital invested and the proprietor (or one of the proprietors) has private wealth not invested in the business. In such cases limited liability may be so desirable that it far outweighs any other consideration, and therefore the business must be run as a company.

31.3 Expense

Certain expenses must inevitably be incurred when a company is formed. These include the Registrar's fee of on incorporation and the cost of preparing the memorandum and articles. If a partnership is formed these expenses need not be incurred since there are no registration requirements. However, in most cases the partners will want a properly drawn up partnership agreement and will wish to instruct a solicitor to draw it up for them.

It is difficult to make any general comparison between costs of formation, since they will depend largely on the complexity of the proposed memorandum and articles or partnership agreement. The legal fees payable for formation are about the same in both cases where the documents have to be drafted by a solicitor. Where a company is bought 'off-the-peg' from a law stationer the costs are likely to be in the region of £150 (including the Registrar's fee), which is likely to be less than the cost of drawing up a partnership agreement of similar complexity.

In addition to legal advice, the proprietors of a new business will often wish to seek advice from accountants. Again, the amount payable for the advice will depend on the complexity of the advice given rather than the business medium used. Similarly, certain printing costs will be incurred for business letter paper. These expenses are only *necessary* in the case of a company (which must comply with the provisions of the Companies Act relating to the name, number and address of the company), but in the case of a partnership printed letter paper will normally be used even though it is not required by law.

With both media, formation expenses are likely to be fairly substantial (for a small business, hundreds rather than thousands of pounds) but are unlikely to influence the *choice* of business medium.

After formation the major administrative costs of a business will again depend on the complexity of the business. However, in respect of accounts a company is at a disadvantage when compared with a partnership. All types of business will wish to keep accounts and prepare final accounts annually. Nearly all businesses will wish to pay a qualified accountant to draw up these accounts (if only so as to make sure that advantage is taken of tax reliefs and exemptions). A company, however, must draw up the accounts in a particular way. This means that the accounts must in some respects show more information than the accounts of a partnership and for a small business this may involve considerable extra cost. (It should be remembered that the partial exemption of 'small' companies from accounting requirements applies only to the published accounts — full accounts must be prepared for the members.) Furthermore, once the accounts have been produced they must be audited by an independent qualified accountant. This means that a company must incur two lots of accountants' fees annually, whereas a partnership need only incur one.

A company is also required to prepare an annual return and to pay a fee on filing it with the Registrar. The Companies Act also requires many other returns to be filed from time to time (e.g., particulars of directors, charges and address of registered office); although fees are not payable on the filing of these returns, their preparation will add to the running costs of the business if it is a company. Many company directors will not feel able to deal with these matters themselves and so will have to hire a qualified company secretary or take legal advice.

The running costs of a company will be more than those of a partnership although the difference is not likely to be great enough to be significant except in the case of small businesses.

31.4 Management

The Companies Act lays down certain rules as to the management structure of companies. A company is, for example, required to have at least one director and a secretary. Certain obligations are imposed on these officials in relation to filing returns. However, a company is entitled to lay down in its articles rules as to management of whatever type it chooses. A partnership may also establish its own rules for management of the business. The Partnership Act 1890 lays down certain presumptions (e.g., that, in the absence of contrary agreement, decisions are taken by a majority vote of the partners except in a limited number of cases where unanimity is required). The partners are free to vary these presumptions by agreement or by a course of dealings. Both types of business medium are, therefore, entitled to choose a management structure which is suitable for the particular case.

31.4.1   INTERNAL FLEXIBILITY

After a suitable management structure has been chosen it may need to be changed because of changed circumstances. In the case of a company, changes to the articles require a special resolution (i.e., a 75% majority of the shareholders). However, many changes of management structure can be made without a change in the articles. Thus if the articles are in the usual form, the maximum number of directors can be increased and new appointments can be made to the board by an ordinary resolution (simple majority of shareholders) and a managing director can be appointed by the board. The board may also decide on its own procedures for taking decisions and may delegate decision making powers as and when necessary. If it is considered that the structure is too flexible, the articles may provide for special resolutions in circumstances where an ordinary resolution would otherwise be sufficient (except in the case of removal of directors from office, where an ordinary resolution is always sufficient (s. 303 CA 1985)). The articles may also restrict the powers of the board and require the approval of the members in general meeting for major decisions. An extreme degree of inflexibility can be achieved, if desired, by including in the memorandum provisions which could have been included in the articles and by making these provisions unalterable.

In the case of a partnership, the agreement between the partners can be altered. This normally requires the approval of all the partners so that the 'constitution' of a partnership is more rigid than that of a company. However, if, when the partnership agreement is drawn up, it is decided that a greater degree of flexibility is required, the agreement can provide for alteration by a majority (without unanimous agreement), either in general or in particular cases.

It is, therefore, possible for either business medium to have a very flexible or a very rigid management structure, as the proprietors wish.

31.4.2 SECURITY OF TENURE

Just as the profits of a partnership are divided between the partners so, in the case of most small companies, the profits will be divided between the directors. Security of tenure as a partner or director is, therefore, of vital concern to the proprietors of a business.

A director is always subject to removal by an ordinary resolution of the members. However, a director who has the majority of votes (or a majority of votes on a resolution for his removal — see *Bushell* v *Faith* [1970] AC 1099, at **8.10.3.2**) is effectively irremovable. A director who does not have a majority of votes but who has a service agreement may be entitled to substantial compensation if removed from office, and so to that extent may be protected. If the company is a 'quasi-partnership' (see **8.10.3.2**), removal of a director from office may also lead to liquidation of the company.

In the case of a partnership, removal of a partner will, subject to contrary agreement, involve the dissolution of the partnership. At first sight this would seem to put a partner in a stronger position than a director. However, in practice, this is not necessarily so. In some cases it will be possible for some of the partners to get rid of one of their colleagues and then set up a 'new' business after the dissolution, which will in effect be a continuation of the old business. This will be possible particularly if those who remain own the premises where the business is carried on. The position of a junior partner is not, therefore, necessarily stronger than that of a director who is not in control of the company.

The practical reality of the situation is that if a director or partner is vital to the business he cannot be removed without bringing the business to an end. However, where a director or partner is really no more than a senior employee, he can be removed on payment of any compensation provided for in his service contract or in the partnership agreement. A director, but not a partner, may also be entitled to compensation for unfair dismissal or redundancy.

31.4.3 SUCCESSION TO THE BUSINESS

The articles of a company may restrict the right to transfer shares, thus preventing a shareholder from selling out or giving away shares to anyone he pleases. Such restrictions may be coupled with pre-emption rights given to the other shareholders. Alternatively, shares may be freely transferable. It is, therefore, possible to make provision for succession in advance, provided that sufficient thought is given to the problem at the time when the articles are drafted. Similarly, a partnership agreement may make provision for bringing in new partners and for payment to the existing partners on leaving. If no other provision is made, unanimity is required for the admission of a new partner. Since the partners have to be able to work together in running the business, it is unlikely that they would be willing to allow admission of new partners without such agreement.

It is, therefore, possible to lay down rules for succession with either type of business medium. In practical terms the problem of succession is one which can only be solved if suitable purchasers can be found or if suitable donees willing to carry on the business are available. It is generally easier to achieve succession in the case of a company, since the sale of a majority shareholding passes control to the purchaser. The majority shareholder will usually be free to sell out since he is in control of the board who will, therefore, approve any transfer of his shares unless there are any pre-emption rights.

31.4.4 LEGAL STATUS OF BUSINESS MEDIA

There are a number of ways in which the legal status of a company differs from that of a partnership, for example:

(a) A company is a separate legal person whereas a partnership is not.
(b) Only companies can create floating charges.

(c) A company is bound by the ultra vires doctrine (although following the enactment of the Companies Act 1989 this doctrine has been greatly modified in its effect) whereas a partnership is not, so that a partnership is free to change the nature of its business (unanimous agreement of the partners is required but outsiders will not be affected by the absence of such agreement).

(d) An unlimited number of persons may be members of a company at any time whereas partnerships (other than in certain professions) are limited to 20 members.

None of these differences is likely to affect the choice of business medium in most cases.

31.5 Publicity

A company is required to make a considerable amount of information, including annual accounts, available to the public. A partnership is not required to make such information available. A desire to keep the affairs of the business secret may influence some businessmen to prefer a partnership to a company, but it is not likely to be a major factor in most cases, especially since the partners will, in practice, be required to show their accounts to any prospective lender.

31.6 Taxation — Trading Profits

The reader is advised to re-read **Chapters 13-19** before reading the rest of this section. A company has a choice as to how to use its profits — they may be used to pay dividends, interest, or directors' fees, or they may be retained in the business. Each of these four possibilities has different tax consequences. Generally speaking, the payment of directors' fees is the most tax-efficient use of profits, and for a small private company most of the profits will normally be used for this purpose for non-tax reasons anyway. This is because the directors must be compensated for the work that they do for the business and often little profit will be left over for other purposes.

Where profits are sufficiently large, however, a company can be used as a means of tax planning by deciding to retain profits or pay dividends. Retained profits are liable to corporation tax at 25% or 35% (depending on the size of the profit). The rate can be kept down to 25% if sufficient is paid in directors' fees to keep the profits below the threshold for the higher rate of corporation tax. This rate of tax may be somewhat less than the shareholder's rate of income tax (which may be 40%). However, the future consequences of capital taxes must also be taken into account. The accumulated profits will be reflected in the value of the shares in the company so that on a disposal of shares CGT (in rare cases income tax where the company buys back its own shares or under s. 703 ICTA 1988) and/or IHT may be payable, thus reducing the effectiveness of the income tax saving resulting from retention of the profits.

A decision to pay dividends may be taken for non-tax reasons, since it is the only way to provide a shareholder who is not also a director with a return on his investment. However, a dividend may be tax-inefficient in the case of a company where profits are high.

A partnership offers less scope for tax planning in relation to income profits than a company. All the income profits are taxed as income of the partners whether they are actually paid to them or are retained in the business (unless a capital allowance is available). To the extent that profits are withdrawn from the business a partner is in the same position as a director receiving directors' fees — both pay income tax on the sums that are received.

It should be noted, however, that partners pay tax on the preceding year basis, that is, in each tax year they pay tax on the profits of the accounting period ending in the preceding year of assessment. A director pays tax on his fees under the PAYE scheme immediately, so that there is a cash flow advantage in paying tax on partnership income rather than on directors' fees.

To the extent that profits are retained in the business, a partner pays the same tax as if the profits had been withdrawn. This will be an advantage when compared with a company where the partner's rate of tax is less than the rate of corporation tax, and a disadvantage when it is more.

It is, unfortunately, not possible to come to any general conclusions about which business medium is the more suitable from the point of view of income taxation. Probably in most circumstances there is now little to choose between the two. This is partly the result of the fact that relatively small differences now exist between the rates of tax applying to individuals and companies. In any case, in most businesses, substantially all the profits will be used to pay directors' fees or will be withdrawn by the partners. Where profits are sufficiently large that there is a real possibility of tax planning, the greater flexibility provided by the system of company taxation may be advantageous.

31.7   Interest Relief

A payment of interest must generally be paid out of taxed income. However, in some cases interest paid may be deducted from income before it is assessed to tax as a 'charge on income' (so that tax relief is available on the interest payment). This relief is available where money is borrowed to buy an interest in a partnership. Relief is also available where money is borrowed to buy shares in a close company provided that either:

(a)   the shares give the borrower a 'material interest' (i.e., more than 5% of ordinary share capital or a right to more than 5% of the income); or
(b)   the borrower owns some shares and, from the time when he used the loan until the time when the interest was paid, he was working for the greater part of his time in the management or conduct of the company.

31.8   Capital Gains

A company pays corporation tax at the rate of 25% or 35% of any capital gain which it makes. The disposal of assets by a partnership gives rise to tax at the appropriate rate or rates of the partners (which may be 25% or 40%). However, a company and its proprietors suffer two disadvantages in respect of capital gains. Firstly, the profit made on the disposal of a capital asset (after payment of tax) will be reflected in the value of the shares in the company and further capital gains tax will be payable on disposal of those shares. (For example, an asset is purchased for £10,000 and sold for £20,000. Tax of (say) £2,500 will be paid, leaving a net profit of £7,500. This profit will be reflected in the value of the shares so that if they are disposed of, a further gain of £7,500 will be taxed. This extra charge to tax can be avoided if the disposal of the shares is tax-free (e.g., because they are given away on the death of the shareholder).) Secondly, a company is not entitled to an annual exemption, whereas in the case of a partnership each partner is entitled to an annual exemption for the first £5,000 worth of gains during each tax year.

There are also differences between companies and partnerships in respect of various capital gains tax exemptions; thus:

(a)   Retirement relief is usually available to a partner who disposes of an interest in a partnership when he is over 55. Similar relief is available in the case of a disposal of shares, but only if the company is a trading company and a personal company and the disposal is by a full-time working director.
(b)   Roll-over relief is available on the disposal and replacement of certain types of business asset (including land, goodwill and fixed plant and machinery). When such assets are disposed of the gain is not taxed (if the disposer so elects) but instead the gain is deducted from the allowable expenditure on the replacement assets (so that when they are disposed of both gains are taxed). The relief is available to a partner and to a company.

31.9   Inheritance Tax

A company cannot normally be used as a means of avoiding IHT, since gifts by a close company are attributed to the shareholders in the company (s. 94 IHTA 1984). Nearly all small companies come within the definition of a close company. Similarly, gifts of partnership assets will be liable to tax as gifts of the individual partners. Inheritance tax is, therefore, generally a neutral factor in the choice of business medium.

There are, however, a number of differences between the ways in which IHT business property relief operates in respect of a company and a partnership. The relief operates as a reduction in the value transferred of 100% in the case of a gift of shares giving control of the company. One hundred per cent relief is also available on a gift of an 'interest in a business', which includes a partner's share of partnership assets. However, relief is available at a rate of only 50% in the case of a minority shareholding. A minority shareholder is, therefore, less favourably treated than a partner (who is entitled to the 100% relief however small his interest in the partnership). There is also a difference in the relief given where an asset is owned by an individual partner or shareholder but used by the partnership or company. A partner whose private property is used by his partnership is entitled to relief of 50% when he gives the property away. Similar relief is available to a shareholder but only if he owns shares which give control of the company.

Business property relief is, therefore, neutral as between a partner and a *majority* shareholder, but treats a partner more favourably than a *minority* shareholder.

31.10   Pensions and Social Security

There are a number of ways in which businessmen may provide for their retirement (see **Chapter 19**). The most favourable method from the tax point of view is an 'exempt approved pension scheme'. Such a scheme affords generous tax relief on contributions by both employers and employees and further relief from capital taxes to the managers of the scheme. Its purpose is to provide a pension and, in some cases, a lump sum on retirement. Such schemes are not available to the self-employed (such as partners). Partners are able to get the relief by means of a personal pension. Contributions are deductible from taxable income up to a certain percentage of relevant earnings depending on the age of the contributor. However, the relief is limited to the appropriate percentage of £75,000 in the case of partners whose income exceeds this figure.

Social security also operates differently in respect of employees and the self-employed. Contributions must be made by both employer and employee in respect of an employed person; a self-employed person must contribute at a rate higher than the employee's contribution but lower than the employer's and employee's contributions combined. The benefits to which an employed person is entitled are correspondingly higher than those to which a self-employed person is entitled. The overall effect of the differences between the two schemes is controversial but many consider that the self-employed are at a disadvantage.

31.11   Conclusion

It is not possible to lay down any hard and fast rule as to which business medium is the more beneficial since there are too many variables. In a significant number of cases the desirability of limited liability will indicate company formation as the only real possibility. Where limited liability is not of great importance, the tax factors will be more significant. Generally speaking, a company will be more likely to be required where profits are large and a partnership where they are small, but really the only sound advice is that each case must be determined according to the particular circumstances.

THIRTY TWO

PUBLIC COMPANIES

32.1 Introduction

Under s. 1(2) of the Companies Act 1985 it is possible to create three different types of company:

(a) a company limited by shares;
(b) a company limited by guarantee; and
(c) an unlimited company.

We considered the key elements of these three different types of company in **6.5**. It is possible to incorporate all three types of company as a 'private company' but only companies limited by shares can be 'public companies'. We considered in outline the key differences between public and private companies in **6.6.2**.

Throughout the rest of the book we have not drawn any distinction between public and private companies as the majority of the rules to which companies are subject apply to both types of company limited by shares. However, the differences between the two types of company are important and we will consider them in this chapter. In addition, we will look briefly at the rules for re-registering a private company as a public company and vice versa, as well as the procedure by which a public company can gain a listing on the Stock Exchange.

Although the most well known companies in the country will (with very few exceptions) be public companies with a Stock Exchange listing, in terms of numbers they represent a tiny minority of the total number of companies registered at the Companies' Registry. Furthermore, being a public company does not necessarily mean the company has a Stock Exchange listing as it is possible to be an unlisted public company.

32.2 The Distinguishing Features of a Public Company

32.2.1 DEFINITION

A public company is defined by s. 1 CA 1985 as:

A company limited by shares . . . being a company:

(a) the memorandum of which states that the company is to be a public company; and
(b) in relation to which the provisions of [the Companies Act] as to the registration or re-registration of a company as a public company had been complied with . . .

32.2.2 THE DIFFERENCES BETWEEN PUBLIC AND PRIVATE COMPANIES

These were outlined in **6.6**. For the sake of completeness, these differences are repeated here but with some additional detail.

32.2.2.1 Name

The name of a public company must end with the words 'Public Limited Company' or its equivalent. Equivalent for this purpose includes 'PLC' (although there is no requirement that these letters be capitalised) and, for Welsh companies, Cwmni Cyfyngedig Cyhoeddus (or CCC). The company will be a Welsh company if the company states in its memorandum that its registered office is to be in Wales.

32.2.2.2 The company's memorandum

The memorandum which the company registers with the Companies' Registry must be in the form specified for a public company by the Companies (Tables A to F) Regulations 1985, or be as close to that form as is possible in the circumstances. If the company is to be a public company limited by shares, the form with which it has to comply is contained in Table F. The main difference between the form of memorandum specified for public companies and for private companies is that the form for a public company requires its memorandum to include an additional clause stating that the company is to be a public company.

32.2.2.3 The nominal value of the share capital

The nominal value of the public company's allotted share capital must not be less than the 'authorised minimum' which is currently £50,000 (although this figure can be changed by Statutory Instrument). When a public company allots shares, while it can make a part call when seeking payment, it is under an obligation to ensure that at least 25% of the nominal value of the shares (plus the whole amount of any premium on the shares) is paid on allotment. It will be recalled from **6.6.2** that a private company can issue shares without requiring any immediate payment for them.

32.2.2.4 Number of members and directors

Public companies, like private companies, need only two members (in the past they needed seven members) but public companies must have at least two directors whereas private companies need have only one.

32.2.2.5 The issue of shares or debentures

The principal advantage which a public company had over a private company used to be that public companies could offer shares or debentures to the public (for cash or other consideration) and to allot those shares or debentures with a view to them being offered for sale to the public (s. 81 CA 1985). This provision has now been replaced by s. 170 Financial Services Act 1986 (amended by s. 199 CA 1989) under which only a public limited company (subject to certain exceptions) is permitted to issue an advertisement offering securities which that company will issue.

32.2.2.6 Registration requirements

Subject to the points on the contents of the documents set out above, the procedure followed and documents required to register a public company are the same as for a private company. Once the Registrar of Companies is satisfied that the documents comply with the registration requirements, a certificate of incorporation will be issued. However, before the public company can do business or borrow money, the company must obtain from the Registrar a further certificate which will only be issued if the Registrar is satisfied that the company's share capital is adequate. The procedure which the company must go through to get this additional certificate involves a director or the company secretary filing a statutory declaration (on Form 117) with the Registrar. The declaration will state that the nominal value of the company's allotted share capital is at least equal to the authorised minimum (of £50,000). The company must also supply on Form 117 details of:

(a) the amount paid up on the allotted share capital (which must exceed the minimum referred to in **32.2.2.3** above);
(b) the amount of the preliminary expenses and details of who will meet them; and
(c) any amount or benefit paid to the company's promoters.

A company which does not obtain this additional certificate before it commences business can face some severe consequences. If the company fails to meet its obligations in connection with a transaction entered into at a time when it does not have the additional certificate, the directors will be jointly and separately liable to indemnify the other parties to the transaction for any loss. Furthermore, both the company and its offices will be liable to a fine and if the company fails to obtain this certificate within one year of its registration, the court can wind the company up (s. 122 Insolvency Act 1986).

32.2.3 SPECIAL RULES APPLICABLE TO PUBLIC COMPANIES

We saw in **32.2.2.5** above that a public company can solicit investment in itself from the public. This can give the company a much wider source of potential investors than is the case with the private company but, in order to protect the public, public companies are subject to a number of restrictions which do not apply to private companies. We will consider them in this section.

32.2.3.1 Payment for share capital

(a) The original subscribers to a public company's memorandum are required to pay cash for their shares.
(b) At least 25% of the nominal value and the whole of any premium on shares in a public company must be paid on allotment.
(c) A public company cannot accept an undertaking to do work or perform services as consideration for the allotment of shares.
(d) A public company can accept the transfer of assets to the company as full or part (subject to the 25% limit) payment for the allotment of shares but any undertaking to transfer those assets to the company must be performed within five years of the allotment. In addition, the company must take steps to satisfy itself that the value of the assets transferred to the company is accurate by obtaining an expert's valuation and report.

32.2.3.2 Pre-emption rights on the allotment of shares

A public company, unlike a private company, cannot exclude the statutory pre-emption rights (set out in ss. 89-96 CA 1985) by a provision in its memorandum or articles. However, a public company (like a private company) can prevent the pre-emption rights applying by giving the directors the authority to allot shares in accordance with s. 80 CA 1985.

32.2.3.3 Maintenance of capital

The directors of a public company are under an obligation to convene an extraordinary general meeting (EGM) if the company's net assets are 50% or less of its called up share capital. The meeting must be convened within 28 days of one of the directors becoming aware of this fact and it must be held within 56 days. Obviously, the purpose of the meeting is for the problem to be considered but the governing provision (s. 142 CA 1985) does not require the directors to take any definite steps to remedy the position.

32.2.3.4 Purchase by a public company of its own shares

Public companies, like private companies, can buy back their own shares and issue redeemable shares. However, public companies cannot (unlike private companies) use capital to purchase or redeem shares; a public company can only use its profits for these purposes. (In addition, the tax rules which, if the various conditions are complied with, allow the shareholder whose shares have been bought by the company to treat the purchase as a disposal for capital gains tax purposes, rather than the receipt of a distribution attracting income tax liability, only apply to the shares in *unquoted* companies. It should, however, be remembered that a public company will not necessarily have a listing on the Stock Exchange.)

32.2.3.5 Financial assistance for the acquisition of shares and loans to directors

The rules prohibiting companies from providing financial assistance for the purchase of their own shares are more stringent in the case of public companies than in the case of private companies (see ss. 151 and 155-158 CA 1985). Similarly, the rules dealing with loans to directors are more stringent in the case of loans to directors of public companies (see s. 330 CA 1985).

32.2.3.6 Distribution of profits

In addition to the general rules restricting the funds from which companies can make distributions, public companies are only permitted to make a distribution if their net assets are not, as a result of the distribution, reduced below the combined total of their called up share capital and 'undistributable reserves'.

32.2.3.7 Accounting requirements

The provisions which permit 'small' and 'medium sized' companies to file less detailed accounts with the Registrar of Companies do not apply to public companies. They also cannot qualify as 'dormant' companies (which would lead them to be able to dispense with auditors).

32.2.3.8 Age of directors

The directors of public companies must retire at age 70.

32.2.3.9 Written resolutions

Section 381A Companies Act 1985, under which the members of private companies can take decisions by written resolutions rather than passing resolutions at general meetings, does not apply to public companies.

32.2.4 RE-REGISTRATION OF A PRIVATE COMPANY TO A PUBLIC COMPANY AND VICE VERSA

Given the various special rules to which public companies are subject, promoters of a company are unlikely to want to incorporate the company as a public company unless they intend to issue securities in the company to the public within the foreseeable future. However, many companies start life as private companies and are then converted into public companies so that they can be floated on the Stock Exchange. The reasons why a company might be floated are explained in **32.3.2** below. Equally, although perhaps less frequently, the shareholders and/or directors of a public company may decide to convert the company into a private company. They may do so for a variety of reasons, for example, where they have decided to cancel the company's listing on the Stock Exchange and no longer intend to make the company's securities available to the general public.

32.2.4.1 Re-registration of a private company to a public company

The procedure which the private company will have to go through in order to re-register as a public company is set out in ss. 42-47 CA 1985. The company cannot be re-registered unless it satisfies the various requirements in relation to share capital to which public companies are subject. These were referred to in **32.2.2** and **32.2.3** above and include the requirement that the company's allotted share capital must not be less than the authorised minimum of, currently, £50,000 and that not less than 25% of the nominal value of shares allotted plus the whole of the new premium on the shares must be paid up.

Provided the requirements with regard to share capital are satisfied, the company must pass a special or written resolution (a copy of which must be sent to the Registrar of Companies within 15 days of it being passed) which:

(a) states that the company should be re-registered as a public company;

(b) alters the company's memorandum by adding a clause stating that the company is to be a public company and making other consequential amendments to the memorandum (for example, changing the company's name to show that it is a 'public limited company'); and

(c) alters the company's articles to meet the company's new circumstances (by, for example, removing restrictions on transferability).

Once the resolution has been passed, a director or the company secretary must sign the application for re-registration and submit it to the Registrar of Companies with:

(a) a printed copy of the company's memorandum and articles in their altered form;

(b) a copy of a statement in writing by the company's auditors confirming that the company's net assets are not less than the combined total of its called up share capital and distributable reserves (this written statement should relate to a balance sheet prepared for a date not more than seven months before the date the company has made its application for re-registration);

(c) a copy of the balance sheet on which the auditors based their written statement referred to in (b) above together with an unqualified report on the balance sheet by the company's auditors;

(d) certain reports and statutory declarations where shares have been allotted for non-cash consideration since the date of the balance sheet.

Once the Registrar of Companies is satisfied with these papers, a certificate will be issued confirming that the company has been re-registered as a public limited company.

32.2.4.2 Re-registration of a public company as a private company

It is easier for a public company to be re-registered as a private company than the other way round. A company must pass a special resolution by which it:

(a) resolves to re-register as a private company;

(b) removes the words 'public limited company' (or their equivalent) from its name and replaces them with 'limited'; and

(c) makes any other alterations to the memorandum and articles of the company to suit its new circumstances.

The special resolution must be filed within 15 days will normally be filed with the application (on Form 53) signed by a director or the company secretary seeking the re-registration (which will be accompanied by a printed copy of the altered memorandum and articles).

One consequence of a public company re-registering as a private company is that its securities may be less easily transferred. Therefore, protection has to be given to minority shareholders in case they object to this change in the status of the company. In any event, the Registrar of Companies will not normally issue a certificate confirming the re-registration until 28 days after the passing of the special resolution. This ties in with the provisions contained in CA 1985 giving minority shareholders a right to apply to the court within the 28 day period to have the resolution cancelled. Such an application for cancellation can only be made by (in the case of shareholders in companies limited by shares):

(a) shareholders holding not less than 5% of the nominal value of the company's issued share capital (or for any class of the share capital, if there is more than one); or

(b) not less than 50 of the company's members.

The application for cancellation can only be made by a person who has not consented to or voted in favour of the resolution and the court can make an order either cancelling or confirming the resolution on such terms and conditions as it thinks fit (which could, for example, include ordering that the company should buy the shares of the dissentient member or members).

Re-registering a private company as a public company is always a voluntary act. However, in two circumstances, a public company can be compulsorily re-registered as a private company:

(a) If the court makes an order confirming a reduction of capital of a public company which results in the nominal value of the company's allotted share capital falling below the authorised minimum (currently £50,000) the company ceases to be a public company. In these circumstances, the court can make an order to the effect that the company will be re-registered as a private company (making consequential amendments to the memorandum and articles of the company) which will avoid the necessity for the company to pass a special resolution to re-register.

(b) The cancellation by a public company of shares will lead to the company having to apply to be re-registered as a private company if the cancellation reduces the company's allotted share capital below the authorised minimum (currently £50,000).

32.3   Seeking and Maintaining a Stock Exchange Listing

32.3.1   INTRODUCTION

In this section we will look in outline at the advantages and disadvantages of obtaining a Stock Exchange listing and the requirements for seeking and maintaining that listing. It is not our intention to go into this area in detail, we will merely outline the key issues.

32.3.2   THE ADVANTAGES AND DISADVANTAGES OF A STOCK EXCHANGE LISTING

It will take a great deal of time by the officers of the company (and their advisers) to seek and maintain a listing which is, therefore, an expensive exercise. While there may be a number of advantages to the company in being listed, the company will have to accept the imposition of restrictions over and above those imposed on it by the Companies Acts and other legislation which affects listed companies. The key to understanding the need for these restrictions to be imposed is to appreciate that the principal advantage to a company of being listed is that its shares are more easily marketed. Therefore, the company has the obligation to make public information relating to its current performance and future prospects. This will give the company's current and potential future shareholders adequate information on which to base their decisions on how to deal in the company's shares.

While improved marketability (in the sense that all the shares, including minority holdings, will be freely tradable on a market which is open to a wide range of potential investors) is the principal advantage of the company being listed, it is not the only advantage. The mere fact of being a listed company may improve the status of the company within the market in which it operates. Having quoted shares may open to the company a future source of finance in the sense that it can issue new shares to raise additional funds rather than incur the expense of borrowing money from a bank (although the issue of new shares will itself give rise to some expense). Should the company wish to grow by means of acquisitions, it may find that its ability to offer its quoted shares as full or part payment of the purchase price for the company it is acquiring, is an attractive and cost efficient alternative to borrowing money or using its own cash reserves.

While a listing can be attractive to an acquisitive company, it can also create problems for a company which could be the target of a take-over itself. Such a company could find that a potential bidder is able to acquire a stake in it through the open market, although there are a number of mechanisms in place to ensure that a company is aware if it is the target for a potential bid. Another potential disadvantage, particularly if the company seeking the listing has traditionally been run by a small group of directors/shareholders, is that they will find their activities become the subject of much closer scrutiny by both their shareholders and other interested parties (both potential investors and the press) following the listing. Since the price of a company's shares will depend on the market's view of their value, the price can fluctuate, sometimes dramatically, in response to both good and bad news about the company. To prevent people with inside information about the company's activities taking advantage of that knowledge, there are various prohibitions in place to prevent 'insiders' using information for their own benefit which is not freely available.

32.3.3   THE EUROPEAN DIMENSION

The EC has introduced a number of directives designed to harmonise the requirements for the listing and public offering of securities across the Community. The ultimate aim of the directives is to create a single European market in securities although that aim is unlikely to be achieved for some time.

It is beyond the scope of this book to go into the detail of the directives but we have listed the relevant directives, all of which have been implemented by the UK:

(a)   the Admission Directives (Directive 79/279/EEC);
(b)   the Listing Particulars Directive (Directive 80/390/EEC);
(c)   the Interim Reports Directive (Directive 82/121/EEC);
(d)   the Mutual Recognition Directive (Directive 87/345/EEC);
(e)   the Prospectus Directive (Directive 89/298/EEC); and
(f)   the Second Mutual Recognition Directive (Directive 90/211/EEC).

32.3.4   THE ADMISSION AND LISTING PARTICULARS REQUIREMENTS

When a company wishes to seek a listing on the Stock Exchange, it must firstly satisfy the 'admission requirements' and secondly provide information which satisfies the 'listing particulars' requirements which are governed by the rules laid down in the London Stock Exchange's publication 'Admission of Securities to Listing' (commonly known as the 'Yellow Book'). Provided the company satisfies these requirements, it can be admitted to the Senior Equity Market in London which is known as the Official List. At the time of writing, the Stock Exchange announced that a new Yellow Book would be available in September 1993 but the text was not available. It was understood that the new Yellow Book will make the listing rules easier to follow without changing the essential substance of the existing rules. This section should, therefore, be read in the light of this 'health warning'.

There is a secondary market, open to smaller companies, called the Unlisted Securities Market, which is subject to the requirements set out in the 'Green Book'. In December 1992, the Stock Exchange proposed that the USM should be closed with no new companies being allowed to join after 30 June 1993. However, the life of the USM has been extended since the Stock Exchange has decided that the USM will not be closed before the end of 1996 and new companies will be allowed to join until the end of 1994. A working party is currently looking at alternatives to the USM. We will not look further at the rules relating to companies quoted on the Unlisted Securities Market.

To be admitted to the Official List, the company must be registered as a public company and it must intend to place on the market shares which are expected to have a market value of £700,000 or more. The company will not be admitted (save in exceptional circumstances) to the Official List if it has not published or filed accounts covering the three years preceding the application for listing, and the company must have arranged for a report prepared by independent accountants covering the three preceding years to be produced (which will be included in the Listing Particulars).

The directors must obviously consider that the company is financially viable and therefore a further condition for admission is that they must be satisfied that the company's working capital is sufficient. This admission requirement is satisfied by the 'sponsor' to the issue (usually a merchant bank or stockbroker with overall responsibility for arranging the issue) sending a letter to the Stock Exchange stating that the directors have made careful enquiries to satisfy themselves and the sponsor that the working capital is indeed adequate. The final principal admission requirement is that it must be intended that at least 25% of any class of shares will be in the hands of the public.

If the company can satisfy the admission requirements, it must then also satisfy the listing particulars requirements. This obligation involves the company publishing listing particulars which comply with section 3 of the *Yellow Book* (which in turn satisfies the Listing Particulars Directive — see **32.3.3** above). The range of information which must be published includes information on the shares which are to be listed, on the company and its share or loan capital, on the company's principal activities, place of business and employees, on the company's finances (in the form of balance sheet and profit and loss accounts for the last three years) and management and on trends in the company's business. The listing particulars need to include a statement that the annual accounts of the company have been audited for the last three financial years, and the people responsible for the listing particulars need to make a declaration to the effect that 'to the best of their knowledge, the information given in that part of the listing particulars for which they are responsible is in accordance with the facts and contains no admissions likely to affect the import of the listing particulars'. There are a variety of additional detailed rules (relating to such information as details of options, tax clearances, and the terms of the directors' service contracts) which are beyond the scope of this book.

Should information in the listing particulars prove to be misleading, false or deceptive, both civil and criminal liability can arise under the Financial Services Act 1986. The detail of this civil and criminal liability is beyond the scope of this book.

32.3.5 METHODS OF LISTING

All applicants for listing must be represented by a 'sponsor' (see **32.3.4** above) and they must appoint a stockbroker. The sponsor's principal responsibility is to check that the company is suitable for listing and the stockbroker deals with the marketing of the company's shares.

If the securities do not need to be marketed, the company can get on to the Official List by way of an 'introduction'. However, if the shares need to be marketed, the entry onto the Official List will be by an 'initial public offering' which can be made in one of three ways, depending on its size:

(a) An offer for sale (for large public offerings where the company is trying to raise over £30 million) under which the securities are offered to the public at large. This will entail making application forms available to the public who will complete and return them, paying the specified fixed price for the shares. It is, however, possible for the offer merely to fix a minimum price and require the applicants of the shares to tender a higher price, with the shares going to the highest bidder.

(b) A placing (where the company is trying to raise up to £15 million). In this case, the company's shares will not be offered to the public generally, rather they will be offered to clients of the sponsor.

(c) Where the company is trying to raise between £15 million and £30 million, the lesser of 75% or £15 million can be raised by a placing. The balance must be dealt with either by an offer for sale or an 'intermediaries' offer. An intermediaries offer involves securities being allocated to 'intermediaries' (for example, the Stock Exchange member firms) who will in turn allocate the securities to their own clients.

32.3.6 CONTINUING OBLIGATIONS AFTER A LISTING HAS BEEN ACHIEVED

Section 5 of the *Yellow Book* sets out a variety of continuing obligations to which companies on the Official List are subject. These include obligations to avoid a false market in the company's shares; to give notice of the date of a board meeting at which the directors will decide on payment of dividends (and details of their decision); to announce preliminary profits and losses for the year once the board has given approval for the figures; to publish information about certain acquisitions and realisations of assets (including the purchase by the company of its own shares); to comply with the detailed provisions of the *Yellow Book* as to the content of the company's annual report and accounts (which includes the obligation to prepare half yearly accounts) and to give details of any change in the board of directors, as well as adopting rules on dealings by the directors in the companies' shares which are no less strict than those contained in the Model Code on directors' share dealings issued by the London Stock Exchange.

THIRTY THREE

BUSINESS CONTRACTS — DISTRIBUTORSHIP OR MARKETING AGREEMENTS

33.1 Introduction

It is in the very nature of running a trade or business, whether it is run as a partnership or through a company, that the proprietors of the business will deal with 'outsiders'. The most important group of 'outsiders' are the customers of the business who buy its goods or services. They are not, however, the only 'outsiders' with whom the business must deal.

Most businesses require premises of some description (whether offices and/or factories) and so the proprietors will have to deal with the landlords or vendors of such premises. Those premises may have to be adapted to suit the particular needs of the business and so the proprietors will have to deal with builders. Once the shell of the premises is ready for occupation, they will have to be equipped in whatever way is necessary to suit the needs of the business. This may include the acquisition of plant and machinery for a factory or office equipment for office premises. Whatever the nature of the business and its premises, it will need to arrange for a supply of such public utilities as water, electricity, gas and telephones. Once the infrastructure of the business is ready, the proprietors of the business (depending on the nature and size of the operation) may need to recruit employees ('outsiders' in the sense that they will not be the proprietors even if the proprietors may be 'employees' as directors of the company). The proprietors will also, of course, need to enter into contracts to acquire the raw materials or stock in trade which they will use in the course of their business activities.

While many businesses will deal direct with their customers (particularly businesses which involve supplying services directly to the customers), some businesses enter into contracts with intermediaries to whom they supply goods which the intermediaries sell on to the ultimate purchasers.

Of all the wide range of contracts businesses can enter into, the ones which we will look at in this chapter are the contracts with intermediaries. Depending on the nature of the arrangement with the intermediary, the contract may be either an agency or a distributorship (or marketing) agreement.

Before we look at these agreements in more detail, it is worth considering why a business might enter into such arrangements. At first sight, it might appear to make more financial sense for the supplying business to deal directly with its ultimate customers rather than through an intermediary who will, obviously, be looking to make a profit on the transaction. The reasons why it would in fact make commercial sense to use the intermediary will depend on the nature of the supplier's business and its reasons for considering using an intermediary. For example, a manufacturer of goods may not have the finance to support, or the expertise to run the retail outlets it needs to sell its goods to the general public. Alternatively, a supplier may have decided that there is a wider market for its goods, but that it lacks the necessary knowledge of the new market to be able to exploit the opportunity. In these types of circumstances the most sensible way for the supplier to reach its ultimate customer, or to expand its business, is to use an intermediary with the necessary facilities or expertise.

33.2 An Agent or a Distributor?

When setting up the relationship with the intermediary, the supplier will need to decide whether he wishes to appoint an agent or a distributor. So what is the difference between an agent and a distributor?

It is not our intention to look at the laws of agency in any detail (for that the reader is referred to one of the standard contract textbooks) but, in brief, the agent will represent the supplier when seeking, negotiating and concluding contracts with the ultimate purchaser of the goods. Even though the ultimate purchaser may deal principally (or even exclusively) with the agent, the contract created will be between the supplier and the ultimate purchaser (assuming that the supplier is fully disclosed as the principal of the agent). In this circumstance, the agent will usually take a fee for each contract concluded and the risks, financial and commercial, will be borne by the supplier.

Conversely, a distributor will buy the goods from the supplier and then re-sell them to the distributor's own customers, with the return the distributor seeks from the arrangement represented by whatever profit he can make on the re-sale. Given that the distributor will be bearing the financial and commercial risk involved in finding the ultimate purchaser, the profit margin the distributor adds when re-selling the goods may be greater than the commission which an agent would charge. This will have the effect of increasing the ultimate sale price of the supplier's goods. This in turn may have an adverse affect on the marketability of those goods if a supplier's principal rivals in the particular market are able to sell at lower prices (because, for example, they have the necessary resources or expertise to be able to sell directly to the ultimate purchaser). Where a distributor is involved, the supplier will have no direct contractual relationship with the purchaser (since the contractual relationship will be between the distributor and the ultimate purchaser), but this will not necessarily protect the supplier from liability for defective goods.

Whichever type of intermediary arrangement the supplier decides to opt for, it is sensible to set out the terms of the arrangement in a written agreement. The written agency agreement will define the authority and duties of the agent and set out the agent's rights as against the supplier. The structure of a distribution agreement will be different to reflect the fact that the distributor buys the goods outright from the supplier. Perhaps the key provisions in a distributorship agreement relate to the restrictions on competition which each party to the agreement wishes to impose on the other.

On the assumption that the circumstances are such as to make the use of an intermediary appropriate (for example, where the supplier is selling products which require little or no direct contact with the ultimate purchaser), the distributorship arrangement will be attractive where the supplier is trying to break into a new market, because the agreement can impose an obligation on the distributor to make an agreed volume of purchases, thus, in effect, guaranteeing the supplier a market. In return, the distributor will be given rights to resell the supplier's goods. Whether those rights are exclusive or not will depend on the nature of the distributorship agreement but, obviously, an exclusive right to resell a highly valued product could be extremely valuable to the distributor.

One problem with distributorship agreements is that by their very nature they can restrict competition. The national and EC competition rules, therefore, may have an impact on the terms of the agreement into which the supplier and the distributor can enter.

In the rest of this chapter, we will concentrate on the provisions relating to distributorship agreements, looking firstly at the different types of distributorship agreements, then at the competition rules and finally at some common provisions to be found in distributorship agreements.

33.3 Types of Distributorship Agreement

33.3.1 EXCLUSIVE DISTRIBUTORSHIP AGREEMENTS

The distinguishing feature of such agreements is that they give the distributor the exclusive right to sell the product in the territory covered by the distributorship agreement. The supplier will be prevented from selling the goods in the relevant area either on his own account or through agents or other distributors.

The Office of Fair Trading in the UK and the European Commission favour this form of distributorship agreement for a variety of reasons. Exclusive distributorship arrangements are considered to encourage competition between different brands of the same type of goods. This is because knowing that he is the only source of a particular brand of goods within his territory will encourage the distributor to market those goods heavily and the supplier's wish to establish itself within that area will encourage it to maintain the continuity of supply. Furthermore, appointing an exclusive distributor means that the supplier of each brand of goods only has to deal with one entity in the region and thus avoid the necessity for maintaining a potentially expensive network of dealers. Exclusive distributorship arrangements will usually mean that there are a number of brands of the same product competing vigorously against each other. The effect of this will be to benefit members of the public who will have access to a wider choice of goods at more competitive prices.

33.3.2 SOLE DISTRIBUTORSHIP AGREEMENTS

The key difference between a sole distributorship agreement (although the term 'sole' is not a term of art here) and an exclusive one is that while the distributor under a sole distributorship agreement will be the only distributor with whom the supplier will deal in a particular territory, the supplier is *not* prevented from continuing to sell its products in the territory on its own account. In return, the distributor will commonly agree to regard the supplier as his sole supplier of the type of goods which are the subject of the agreement.

The economic benefits of an exclusive distributorship agreement do not apply to a sole distributorship agreement and so these types of agreements are not so favourably treated by the Office of Fair Trading and the European Commission.

33.3.3 NON-EXCLUSIVE DISTRIBUTORSHIP AGREEMENTS

Under such an arrangement, the distributor merely takes the supplier's products. The distributor has no exclusive rights to those products, so that the supplier can appoint other distributors in the same territory, nor is the supplier prohibited from selling its own products on its own accounts in the territory.

Again, the economic benefits of exclusive distributorship agreements do not apply to non-exclusive ones, and so the Office of Fair Trading and the EC Commission do not look upon them as favourably as exclusive arrangements.

33.3.4 SELECTIVE DISTRIBUTORSHIP AGREEMENTS

The distinguishing feature of such an arrangement is that the supplier limits the number of distributors he will appoint in a particular territory so that the distributors who enter into such an agreement will not be given exclusive rights to deal with the supplier's goods.

A selective distributorship arrangement may not encourage as much inter-brand competition as an exclusive distributorship arrangement, and so they are less favourably treated by the UK and EC competition authorities than are exclusive arrangements. Nevertheless, they will be permitted, subject to satisfying certain conditions which are set out in **33.4.2** below.

In **33.4** below we will look at the competition issues, both from the UK and European perspectives in relation to exclusive and selective distribution agreements.

33.4 The Competition Issues

33.4.1 THE UK RULES

33.4.1.1 General

The UK has introduced a variety of controls which will apply to agreements or practices which are potentially anti-competitive. In this section we will look, in outline, at the provisions of the three statutes which regulate these agreements or practices, but it must be remembered that in addition to our own national legislation, the arrangements may also be subject to the European regulations which are considered in **33.4.2** below.

33.4.1.2 Restrictive Trade Practices Act 1976 (RTPA)

This applies to any agreement between two or more persons who carry on business in the UK under which two or more parties accept restrictions in respect of the matters specified by the Act. The 'matters specified' cover many of the issues dealt with by distributorship agreements, including the volume of goods which the distributor agrees to buy and the territory which the agreement will cover. An important point to note is that the RTPA will not apply if only one party accepts restrictions. The nature of an exclusive distributorship agreement (see **33.3.1** above) is such that they will almost certainly be caught by the RTPA. If the terms of an agreement impose restrictions which will bring it within the scope of the RTPA, unless an exemption applies, the agreement will be regarded as a registrable agreement. Particulars of its provisions will then have to be submitted to the Director General of Fair Trading within the time limits prescribed by the Act. The Director General will enter those particulars on a public register. (If the agreement is not registered within the time limits set out by the Act, the restrictions in the agreement will be rendered unenforceable.)

Once the agreement has been registered, it can be investigated by the Restrictive Practices Court unless the Director General gets confirmation from the Secretary of State for Trade and Industry that the Secretary of State considers the restrictions which the agreement imposes are insignificant. Once the agreement has been referred to the Restrictive Practices Court, the presumption is that the restrictions which the agreement imposes are contrary to the public interest. Assuming that view is upheld, the Restrictive Practices Court has a wide range of remedies available to it, which can include requiring the parties to the agreement to change the agreement's terms.

The agreement will not need to be registered (and so will not run the risk of being investigated by the Restrictive Practices Court) if an exemption applies. These include:

(a) the exports exemption which will be available if the restrictions only apply to exports or overseas trade; and

(b) the exclusive dealing exemption which applies to two party agreements (provided neither party is a trade association) and the only restrictions to which the parties are subject are a restriction on the supplier, relating to the persons to whom the supplier will supply goods of the same description, and a restriction on the distributor as to the sale or acquisition of other goods of the same description. Careful drafting can ensure that this exemption does apply to an exclusive distributorship agreement.

33.4.1.3 Resale Prices Act 1976

This Act will render void a provision preventing a distributor from reselling the goods which are the subject of the arrangement below a specified price. Again, careful drafting will prevent this Act applying to the agreement in question.

33.4.1.4 Competition Act 1980

The provisions of this Act will be relevant where parties which control a significant share of a particular market enter into some form of long term arrangement which can be regarded as having economic significance. In these circumstances, the Act empowers the Director General of Fair Trading to investigate the arrangements and, if any 'anti-competitive practices' in relation to a particular market are identified, refer the issue to the Monopolies and Mergers Commission. (An 'anti-competitive practice' is one where a person pursues a course of conduct which has or is intended to have or is likely to have the effect of restricting, distorting or preventing competition.)

While the provisions of this Act must always be borne in mind when considering a distributorship agreement, the nature of most distributorship agreements is such that they will not run the risk of an investigation by the Office of Fair Trading. In any event, the Competition Act provides exemptions for export contracts and for contracts which involve only a relatively minor anti-competitive element. The latter exemption would be available provided the entity who is considered to be engaging in an anti-competitive practice has a turn-over in the UK of less than £5 million and products subject to the practice represent less than 25% of the market in those types of goods.

33.4.2 THE EC RULES

33.4.2.1 General

In **Chapter 21** we looked at Article 85 of the Treaty of Rome which (with Article 86) governs the competition policy of the European Community.

It will be remembered from that chapter that Article 85(1) prohibits 'all agreements between undertakings, decisions by associations of undertakings and concerted practices which may affect trade between member States which have as their object or effect the prevention, restriction or distortion of competition within the common market'. The controls imposed by reason of Article 85 have direct affect in the UK and so that article must be borne in mind when considering distributorship agreements (even where both parties to it are based in the UK) in addition to the national rules.

If a distributorship agreement falls within Article 85(1) it is automatically void and the parties to it can be subject to substantial fines. However, there are various ways of ensuring that Article 85 does not apply to particular distributorship agreements and these are considered in this section.

Article 86 of the Treaty of Rome is intended to prevent companies with a dominant market position from abusing that position. This was covered in **21.3** and the provisions of that article are not considered further in this chapter.

33.4.2.2 Notification of the agreement for negative clearance

Parties to the agreement can apply to the European Commission for a certificate to the effect that the Commission has no grounds for action under either Article 85 or 86. Obviously, this will depend on the facts of a particular case.

33.4.2.3 Notification of the agreement for exemption

Parties can apply to the European Commission for a decision that the arrangement is suitable for exemption under Article 85(3), even though the agreement does in fact fall within the scope of Article 85(1). (See **21.2.3** for the details of Article 85(3).)

33.4.2.4 Informal clearance by a comfort letter

The parties to the distributorship agreement can provide the European Commission with details of the arrangement which they are entering into and ask the Commission to confirm that Article 85 does not apply. This approach avoids the parties going to the time and expense of seeking a formal decision from the Commission. However, all they will get in return is a 'comfort letter' recording an administrative decision from the Commission confirming that the arrangements, as described to the Commission, are not within Article 85. This 'comfort letter' will not prevent the national courts of the parties reaching the conclusion that the agreement is anti-competitive (and so void) but with most distributorship agreements it is considered to be protection enough.

33.4.2.5 Commission Notice on agreements of minor importance

The European Commission has issued a Notice informally recognising that agreements whose potential effect on inter-state trade is insignificant are not caught by Article 85. For an agreement to be within the scope of the Notice two conditions need to be satisfied:

(a) the products or goods which are the subject matter of the distributorship agreement do not represent more than 5% of the total market for such products in the area of the common market affected by the agreement; and

(b) the aggregate annual turn-over of the participating undertakings does not exceed 200 million ECU.

33.4.2.6 The EC block exemptions

Certain specified types of agreements have been declared by the European Commission to be outside the scope of Article 85. One of these 'block exemptions' applies to exclusive distributorship agreements provided certain approved clauses (the 'white list clauses') are included and the disapproved clauses (the 'black list clauses') are excluded.

To be within the scope of the block exemption, the exclusive distributorship agreement must impose a restriction on the supplier not to supply goods to other distributors in the territory. However, no other restrictions on competition can be imposed on the supplier. If they are, the exemption will not apply.

The block exemption allows certain restrictions on competition to be imposed on the distributor and also allows the agreement to impose on the distributor certain obligations. These restrictions and obligations are as follows:

(a) *Restrictions* The distributor can have imposed on him obligations not to:
    (i) manufacture or distribute competing goods;
    (ii) obtain the goods which are the subject matter of the agreement from anyone other than the supplier; and
    (iii) seek customers, establish a branch or maintain a distribution depot in relation to the goods which are the subject matter of the agreement outside the territory covered by the distribution agreement.

(b) *Obligations* The block exemption permits the distributor to accept obligations to:
    (i) buy complete ranges of products or buy minimum quantities of them;
    (ii) sell goods under trademarks or in packaging determined by the supplier; and
    (iii) promote sales for the goods by taking steps to advertise, maintain stocks, provide backup services and so on.

These conditions relating to restrictions and obligations from the 'white list clauses'. The 'black list clauses' which must not be present if the block exemption is to apply are aimed at preventing a variety of potential abuses. The exemption will not apply to reciprocal exclusive distributorship agreements entered into by manufacturers of goods which can be regarded as being identical or at least equivalent.

This is designed to prevent the situation where manufacturers of competing goods, in effect, agree that each shall have exclusive rights to market the product in particular territories. (Even if the agreement is not reciprocal, the block exemption will still not apply unless the total annual turn-over of one or more of the manufacturers does not exceed 100 million ECU.) Given that this area of regulation is aimed at ensuring there is proper competition, hardly surprisingly the block exemption will not apply if the effect of entering into the exclusive distributorship agreement means that there is a single supplier of the products which are the subject matter of the agreement in the territory in question. It should be emphasised that the block exemption only applies to *exclusive* distributorship agreements. Therefore, if the distributorship agreement which the parties enter into is either a 'sole' or a 'non-exclusive' agreement, the block exemption will not apply, and if the agreement is caught by Article 85 the parties will have to decide whether they can use the points described in **33.4.2.2** to **33.4.2.5** above to give them protection from Article 85.

33.4.3 SELECTIVE DISTRIBUTION AGREEMENTS AND COMPETITION ISSUES

As we explained in **33.3.4** above, a selective distribution agreement will limit the number of distributors of a supplier's goods in a particular territory. The anti-competition rules contained in Article 85 and/or Article 86 of the Treaty of Rome and in the UK's Competition Act 1980 can apply where the supplier uses the selective distributorship arrangements to maintain prices (by, for example, terminating a distribution agreement with a distributor who wishes to reduce the sale price of the goods which are the subject matter of the arrangement).

A supplier wishing to enter into selective distribution arrangements will not fall foul of the anti-competition rules if he uses objective criteria for deciding with which entities to enter into the selective distribution arrangements. The objective criteria can relate to the distributor's technical and financial resources, but the supplier must take care to ensure that the criteria are applied in the same way to all the potential distributors and that there is no discrimination against one or more of the potential distributors.

Apart from making sure that there are no provisions which offend the general UK or EC competition rules, the supplier must be sure that the goods which would be the subject matter of the selective distributive arrangements are suitable for that kind of distributorship scheme. High value consumer goods are suitable, while food is probably not. The criteria which the supplier applies must not be more rigorous than is necessary to ensure the distributorship scheme works efficiently. This means that requiring the distributor to provide repair facilities at central locations within each region of the territory covered by the arrangement is probably acceptable, whereas a provision requiring repair facilities to be available at each retail outlet of the distributor probably is not.

33.5 The Provisions of Exclusive Distribution Agreements

In this section we will look, in outline, at the key provisions which could be included in such agreements.

33.5.1 EXCLUSIVITY

The very nature of such agreements are that they should grant exclusive rights to the products to the distributor, and the rights and obligations imposed on both sides of the agreement must be clearly stated. Care should be taken when drafting these provisions to ensure that the block exemption for exclusive distributive agreements applies (see **33.4.2.6** above).

33.5.2 TERM

If a supplier is using the exclusive distributorship agreement as a way of establishing its products in a new territory, it will obviously want to ensure that the distributor he chooses is encouraged to put in the necessary marketing effort to achieve the supplier's aim. Accordingly, the supplier will probably want to offer the distributor a long term contract while reserving for himself the right to terminate the agreement if, for example, there is a major structural or financial change to the distributor adversely affecting the promotion of the supplier's goods. The distributor will probably also be keen to enter into a long term arrangement with the supplier as it will ensure continuity of supply of the goods. However, from the distributor's viewpoint, such long term arrangements can have their problems, for example if the supplier tries to impose an obligation of a heavy 'minimum purchase commitment' on the distributor. Furthermore, should the agreement be for a fixed term the distributor will probably want to include a provision giving him the right to extend the term provided the arrangements specified by the agreement are working satisfactorily. He will want to do this as a way of protecting his investment if he has spent time and money promoting the supplier's goods. The distributor will not want to face the risk of the supplier switching the distributorship arrangement to another, cheaper distributor after the initial effort of establishing the product in the territory has been made.

33.5.3 MINIMUM PURCHASE COMMITMENT

A distributorship agreement can be a way of guaranteeing a market for some at least of the supplier's products and many exclusive distributorship agreements contain a provision to this effect (whether setting a minimum purchase requirement for each year of the agreement or over the whole term of the agreement). Such a requirement can be unattractive to a distributor who will not only have to lay out funds to promote the goods, but may also have to lay out funds to buy stocks before the market in the goods has been properly established.

33.5.4 TERRITORY

The area which the agreement will cover should be specified and obviously should be realistic given the resources and expertise of the distributor.

33.5.5 PRICE, PAYMENT, TITLE AND DELIVERY

Most agreements will provide for an agreed price for the goods to be supplied at the start of the term of the agreement but the supplier will usually reserve the right to increase the price subsequently to cover increased manufacturing costs and the like. If this right to increase the price is entirely at the discretion of the supplier, the distributor can find himself in an extremely difficult financial position, especially where he is subject to a minimum purchase commitment. Therefore, distributors try to limit the rights of the supplier to increase prices to inflation-linked rises, or increases in the cost of production, as well as trying to ensure that the prices can only be increased at fixed intervals (say, annually).

Whatever the price agreed may be, the supplier will want to ensure he receives payment before he loses control of the goods. One device which is often incorporated into these agreements is a provision permitting the supplier to retain title of the goods until full payment has been received.

From the distributor's point of view, he will need to ensure that the goods are delivered on time to mesh in with his own distribution schedules. The distributor will usually try to include in the agreement a provision enabling him to claim damages from the supplier for late delivery.

33.5.6 TRADE MARK AND PATENTS

The agreement should include provisions dealing with whether the distributor must sell on the goods using the supplier's trade mark or whether the distributor can re-brand them. Similarly, there must be protections built into the agreement to cover the situation where there is any allegation of an intellectual property right infringement (usually in the form of an indemnity given by the supplier to the distributor in such circumstances).

33.5.7 RESTRICTIVE COVENANTS, WARRANTIES AND EXCLUSION CLAUSES

The supplier will often want to protect himself from the distributor taking advantage of any knowledge acquired in the course of the distributorship agreement. The nature of the restrictive covenants which the supplier will want to impose will depend on the circumstances, but might include preventing the distributor acting as a distributor for competing goods produced by a rival supplier (but whether such a provision will be enforceable will depend on the nature of the restriction).

The distributor may be willing to rely on the warranties given by the Sale of Goods Act 1979 but the supplier will usually give express warranties (subject to exclusion clauses usually limiting or excluding altogether a supplier's liability for any loss of profits the distributor suffers).

33.5.8 OTHER CLAUSES

There may be a variety of other clauses which the parties will want to consider, such as obligations imposed on the distributor in relation to marketing, reporting, providing adequate technical backup, taking out appropriate insurance, seeking any necessary approvals, dealing with assignment of the benefit of the contract and disputes.

33.5.9 OTHER TYPES OF DISTRIBUTORSHIP AGREEMENTS

The terms of the other types of distributorship agreements (see **33.3** above) will often be broadly similar to those found in exclusive distributorship agreements, save that the terms creating the exclusive nature of the arrangement will, obviously, not apply.

INDEX

Accounts
  balance sheet   245-7
  duty to submit   243
  format of   247
  inherent limits in   248
  interpretation of
    reasons for   247-8
    sources of information   247-8
  profit and loss   244-5, 249
  public companies   272
  small and medium-sized companies   243-4
Agency
  partnership and   15-18
Articles of association
  amendment of   47, 77
  Form G10   47-8
  Form G12   48
  form of, choice of   47
  off-the-peg companies   51
  private companies, of *see* private company
  shelf companies   51
  special voting rights   64
  Table A   36, 47, 51, 55, 57, 78, 105, 225
  Table G   47

Bankrupt
  discharge of   197
  estate of, assets in   194-6
    distribution of
      order of priority for payment of
        debts   196-7
      procedure   196
Bankruptcy
  duration of   197
  order
    effect on bankrupt personally   194
    making 191
      procedure following   192
  petition
    consequences of presenting   191
    creditor's   190-1
    debtor's own   191

Bankruptcy — *continued*
  DPP, by   191
  voluntary scheme
    person bound by, by   191
    supervisor of, by   191
  trustee in
    appointment
      court, by   192
      creditors, by   192
      Secretary of State, by   193
    extension of title to bankrupt's property
      194-6
    functions of   193
    powers of   193
    property not available to   194
    removal of   193
    resignation of   193
    vesting assets in   194
  see also liquidation; winding up
Board meetings
  directors' decisions at   58
Borrowing powers
  exercise of   88
  express and implied   87-8
  ultra vires borrowing   88
Business
  contracts *see* contracts
  incorporation of
    capital gains tax   254-6
    capital tax relief and retained assets
      business property relief   257
      retirement relief   256
      roll over relief   256
    company law and   259
    employment law and   258-9
    income tax
      additional tax liability   252
        funds used to pay   253
      capital allowances   253-5
      closing years rules   251-2
      loss relief   253
    stamp duty   257-8

Business — *continued*
  VAT   256
  medium, choice of
    management
      expense   262-3
      internal flexibility   263-4
      legal status of business media   264-5
      security of tenure   264
      succession to business   264
    pensions and social security   267
    publicity   265
    risk of capital   261-2
    taxation
      capital gains   266
      inheritance tax   267
      interest relief   266
      trading profits   265-6

Capital
  increase of   95-6
  power to alter   95
  reduction of   96
  risk of   261-2
Capital allowances   157-60
  industrial buildings
    the allowance   159-60
    definition   159
  plant and machinery
    definition   157-8
    special rules on   159
    writing down allowances   158-9
Capital gains tax
  business assets, on   161-7
    companies, retirement relief   165-6
    partnerships   164-5
    purchase by company of its own shares
      166-7
    roll over relief on re-investment   166
  business medium, choice of, and   266
  partners
    death of   131
    new   133
    retirement of   126-30
  partnerships, dissolution of   124-5
  sale of business to company and   254-6
Charges
  avoidance of   93
  discharge of   92
  fixed   92-3
  floating   89, 93, 217
    advantages and disadvantages   89
    crystallisation of   91
    over land   92
    priority of   93
  over land   92
  priority of   92-3

Charges — *continued*
  registration of
    company's register of charges   92
    process   90
    requirements, consequences of failure to
      comply with   90-1
Close company   38
  corporation tax and   139
Companies *see* limited companies
Company law
  sources of   35-6
Company searches
  failure to file returns   242-3
  information available for inspection   240-1
  personal search, making   242
  procedure for making   241-3
  reading   242
  types of   241-2
  where can be made   241
Company secretary   67
Contracts
  agent   280
  competition issues
    EC rules   283-5
      see also European Community
    selective distribution agreements   285
    UK rules   282-3
  distributor   280
  distributorship agreement, types of
    281-2, 287
  exclusive distribution agreements   281
    exclusion clauses   287
    exclusivity   285
    minimum purchase commitment   286
    price, payment, title and delivery   286
    restrictive covenants   287
    term   285-6
    territory   286
    trade marks and patents   286
    warranties   287
  non-exclusive distributorship agreement   281
  pre-incorporation   52
  selective distributorship agreement   281-2
  sole distributorship agreement   281
Corporation tax
  advance   142-3, 144
    set-off of   143
  assessment
    basis of   136
    rates of tax   136-7
  calculation of profits
    capital allowances   136
    capital gains   136
    income   135
      charges on   135
  close companies   139

Corporation tax — *continued*
  loss relief 137-8
  retained profits 151
Corporations 35

Debenture
  document
    lender, protection of
      personal guarantees 233
      receiver, appointment of 233-4
    terms in
      interest 231-2
      repayment 231-2
      security
        fixed charges 232-3
        floating charges 233
  holders of
    position of 94
    receiver, appointment of 94
    remedies of
      application to court 93-4
      express and implied powers 93
  interest on 144-5
  public companies 270
Directors
  agency
    actual authority 66
    estoppel, by 66
    general position 66
    liability of agency to third party 66
    ratification 66
  alternate 57
  appointment of 55-6
  board meetings, decisions at 58
  contracts made by, irregular 64-5
  decisions
    board meetings, at 58
    written resolution, by way of 58
  disqualification 56-7
  duties of
    care and skill 60
    fiduciary 58-60, 74, 238
    shareholders agreement, in 238
    statutory 60
    third parties, to 60
  fees, taxation of
    employee's perspective 147-51
    employing company's perspective 145-6
  freedom of contract, restrictions on 61-2
  information, disclosure of 60-1
  interests of
    contracts in, disclosure of 61
    register of 61
  loans to 61
  managing *see* managing directors
  names of, publicity as to 61

Directors — *continued*
  outsiders, protection of
    agency 66
    Royal British Bank v *Turquand*, rule in 65
    statutory protection 64-5
  powers of 57-8, 59
  private companies, of 38, 228
  property transactions 62
  public companies, of 38
  register of 60-1
  removal of 56-7, 63-4
    compensation, right to 63-4
    ordinary resolution, by 63
      procedure 63
  retirement by rotation 56
  retirement provision *see* retirement provision
  secret profits and 58-9
  service contracts 61, 62, 73
  shadow 57
  statutory provisions concerning 60-2
Dissolution of company 213-14
Distributions
  definition 142
  franked investment income 144
  recipient, taxation of 143-4
  tax consequences on company of 142-3
Dividends *see* shareholders

Elective regime companies 38
European Community
  competition issues
    agreements
      block exemptions 284-5
      informal clearance by comfort letter 284
      minor importance, of, Commission
        Notice on 284
      notification for exemption 283
      notification for negative clearance 283
  establishment, right of 181-2
    limitations on 182
  services, provision of 181-2
    limitations on 182
  see also Treaty of Rome

General meetings
  accounts, presentation of 243
  annual (AGM) 103
  calling 105
  extraordinary (EGM) 103
  minutes 107
  notice of 106
  resolutions *see* resolutions
  returns 107
  statutory rules 105
  Table A 105
  types of 103
  see also meetings

Income tax
  assessment 117
  closing years of trade 116-17
  early years of trade 114-16
  income profits
    accounting bases 112-13
    deductible expenditure 112
    income, definition of 112
    stock, valuation of 113-14
    tax schedules 111-12
    work-in-hand, valuation of 113-14
  losses 118-19
  partners
    death of 131
    new 133
    retirement of 125-6
  partnerships
    dissolution of 123-4
    liability of 119
  preceding year basis 114
  sale of business to company and 251-5
Inheritance tax
  business assets, on 167-71
    companies 170-1
    partnerships 170
  business medium, choice of, and 267
  partner
    death of 132
    new 134
    retirement of 130-1
  partnerships, dissolution of 125
Insolvency
  administration, voluntary arrangements,
    relationship between 206
  company insolvency proceedings
    administration orders 201
      administration and other remedies 205
      administration process 204-5
      consequences of 203
      petition for
        application and grounds 202-3
        consequences of 203
    administrative receivership 201, 205
    liquidation 201-2
  liabilities arising from
    floating charges 217
    preference 215, 216
    relevant time requirement 216
    transaction with connected person 216
    transactions at an undervalue 215, 216
    transactions defrauding creditors 216
    wrongful trading 215
  voluntary arrangements
    administration, relationship between 206
    companies 201

Insolvency — *continued*
    creditors' meeting, challenging
      decision of 199
    debtor's proposals
      consideration of 198
      effect of accepting 198-9
    implementation of approved scheme by
      supervisor 206
    interim order 198
      procedure following making of 198
    meetings of members and creditors 206
    proposals and nominee's report 205-6

Land, charges over 92
Lender
  company, to 94-5
    partner distinguished 10-11
Limited companies
  accounts
    duty to submit 243
    group 40
    see also accounts
  agents for shareholders, as 40
  articles of association *see* articles of association
  books
    inspection of 50
    statutory 50
  business assets, of
    capital gains tax 165-7
    inheritance tax 170-1
  certificate of incorporation 48
  charges *see* charges
  close 38
    corporation tax and 139
  company searches *see* company searches
  contracts, pre-incorporation 52
  corporations 35
  dissolution of 213-14
  distributions *see* distributions
  documents kept by 48, 50
  elective regime 38
  formation of 43-53
  fraudulent trading 40
  group accounts 40
  incorporation
    methods of 50-2
    steps leading to 43-8
  insolvency *see* insolvency
  legal obligations, attempts to avoid 40
  limited by guarantee 37
  limited by shares 36-7
    partnership compared 37
  memorandum of association *see* memorandum
    of association
  name
    change of
      notification 52

Limited companies — *continued*
    procedure 52
    choice of 53
    company stationery 49
    letters and order forms 49
    liability of officers 49
    memorandum of association, in 44-5
    publication of 49
  objects
    change of 53
    ultra vires doctrine 45-6, 74
  off-the-peg *see* off-the-peg companies
  partnership limited companies 38
  pre-incorporation contracts 52
  private *see* private companies
  profitability *see* profitability
  public *see* public companies
  quoted 38
  registered, types of 36-7
  registered office 45, 47-8
  registers kept by 48
  seal 48
  separate legal personality 39
  shelf *see* shelf companies
  small and medium-sized *see* small and
    medium-sized companies
  solvency of 248-9
  tailor-made 50-1
  trustees for shareholders, as 40
  unlimited 37
  veil of incorporation, lifting 39-40
    courts 40
    tax legislation 40-1
  wrongful trading 40
Liquidation
  assets
    collection and distribution of 211-12
    order of entitlement to 212-13
  compulsory 210
  functions of liquidators 210-11
  proceedings against company 211
  voluntary
    creditors' 210
    members' 210
  see also bankruptcy; winding up
Loans
  lender to a company, steps to be taken by
    94-5
  raising funds to invest in company 152
  secured
    fixed charges 88-9
    floating charges 89
      advantages and disadvantages 89
    types of security 88

Managing director
  appointment of 62-3
  powers of 63
  service contract of 63, 73
Meetings
  agenda 107
  dispensing with 107
  general *see* general meetings
  notice
    contents of 106-7
    length of 106
    service of 106
  proceedings at 107
  quorum 107
  voting 107
Memorandum of association
  alteration of 77
  capital clause 46
    alteration to 95-6
  liability clause 46
  name
    change of 45
    choice of 44-5
    passing off 45
  objects and ultra vires doctrine 45-6
  registered office 45

Off-the-peg companies
  advantages and disadvantages 52
  articles of association 51
  business name 51
  company name 51

Partners
  accounts, right to inspect 8
  admission of 223-4
    tax consequences of
      capital gains tax 133
      generally 132
      income tax 133
      inheritance tax 134
  authority of
    apparent 16-17
      examples 17-18
    express and implied 16
  capital 10
    interest on 12
    sharing of 11
  death of 223-4
    estate, rights of 31-2
    liability for debts 32
    partnership agreement, provision in 32
    tax consequences 131-2
  decisions of 7-8

Partners — *continued*
  expulsion of 22
  good faith, duty of 8-10
  information, duty to disclose 9
  legal relationship between 7-8
  lenders distinguished 10-11
  liability
    debts, for 32
    outsiders, to 15-19
      nature of 15
      new partners 18
      persons held out as partners 18
      tort, in 18-19
  loans, interest on 12
  losses, sharing of 12
  majority, restrictions on 8
  number of 4
  profits
    competing business, from 9-10
    division of 11-13
    drawings 13
    secret, duty to account for 9
    sharing of 11
  remuneration of 12-13
  retirement of 29-31, 223-4
    change of name following 31
    debts incurred
      after 29-31
      before 29
    financial arrangements 31
    legal consequences of 29-31
    tax consequences of
      capital gains tax 126-30
      income tax 125-6
      inheritance tax 130-1
  retirement provision for *see* retirement
    provision
  suing or being sued 19
Partnership
  accounts 8
  agency and 15-18
  agreement *see* Partnership agreement
  business assets, of
    capital gains tax 164-5
    inheritance tax 170
  capacity 4
  capital of 222
  characteristics of 3-6
  death of partner *see* partners
  definition of 3-4
  disputes 21-3, 223
    arbitration 22
    expulsion of partner 22-3
  dissolution of 25-9, 223-4
    agreement, by 26
    automatic 26

Partnership — *continued*
    court, by 26-7
      breach of partnership agreement 21-2
      conduct prejudicial to business 21
      just and equitable dissolution 22
    legal consequences of 27-9
    notice, by 25-6
    notification of 28-9
    partnership property
      application of 28
      realisation of 27-8
    tax consequences of 123-5
      capital gains tax 124-5
      death, where
        capital gains tax 131
        income tax 131
        inheritance tax 132
      income tax 123-4
      inheritance tax 125
    winding up and 27
  duration of 4-5
  expulsion from, tax consequences of 132
  finances of
    partners' capital 10
    sources 10
  good faith, duty of 8-10
  income of 222
  income tax liablity of 119-21
  interest, payment of 13
  joining, tax consequences of 123-34
  leaving, tax consequences of 123-34
  limited company compared 37
  majority, restrictions on 8
  management of 7, 223
  name 5, 222
    approval of 5
    automatically permitted 5
    change of, retirement of partner,
      following 31
    disclosure requirements 5-6
  nature of 4
  number of partners 4
  partners *see* partners
  property of 13-14, 223
  publicity of information 5-6
  receiver, appointment of 22
  relevant law 3
  retirement of partner *see* partners
  see also partners; partnership agreement
Partnership agreement
  clauses of
    admission of partners 223-4
    capital of 222
    commencement date and term of
      partnership 222
    death 223-4

Partnership agreement — *continued*
  disputes 223
  dissolution 223-4
  income 222
  management 223
  name 222
  nature of business 222
  parties 222
  prolonged absence, effect of 223
  property 223
  restrictions 223
  retirement 223-4
  issues for incoming partner 224
  written 221
Partnership company 38, 47
Passing off 45
Private company
  articles of
    alteration of
      benefit of company, to be for 229-30
      power to alter 228
      registration 228-9
    directors 228
    provision in 38
    share capital 226
    shareholders' meetings 228
    shares
      issue of 226
      transfer of 226-7
    Table A 225
  definition 37
  public company
    compared 37-8, 270-1
    re-registered as 272, 273-4
  re-registration to public company 272, 273
  shares, purchase of own 101
Profitability
  efficiency ratios 250
  generally 249
  investment 249
Pubilc company
  accounting requirements 272
  capital, maintenance of 271
  company memorandum 270
  debentures, issue of 270
  definition 37, 269
  directors
    age of 272
    loans to 272
    number of 270
  distinguishing features of 269-74
  members, numbers of 270
  name 270
  private company
    compared 37-8, 270-1
    re-registered as 272, 273

Public company — *continued*
  profits, distribution of 272
  re-registration to private company 272, 273-4
  registration requirements 270-1
  share capital
    nominal value of 270
    payment for 271
  shares
    allotment of, pre-emption rights on 271
    issue of 270
    purchase of own 272
      financial assistance for 272
  special rules applicable to 271-2
  stock exchange listing
    admission requirements 275-6
    advantages and disadvantages 274-5
    continuing obligations following 277
    European Community and 275
    listing particulars requirements 275-6
    methods of listing 276
    seeking and maintaining 274-7
  written resolutions 272

Quoted companies 38

Receiver
  administrative
    definition 206-7
    powers and duties 207-8
  appointment of
    debenture holders, protection of 94, 233-4
    partnership, dissolution of 22
Receivership
  choice of remedy 208
  nature of 206
Registrar of Companies 36, 47
  fee 48
  official notification 239-40
Resolutions
  elective 104-5
  extraordinary 104
  ordinary 104
  special 104
Retained profits
  corporation tax 151
  future taxation of 151-2
Retirement provision
  capital gains tax 165-6, 256
  directors and employees, for
    fees paid to non-executive directors 174-5
    private occupational pension schemes 173-4
    retirement annuity schemes 174
    state pension 175
  sole proprietors and partners
    appointment as consultant 176
    partnership annuities 176

Retirement provision — *continued*
    personal pensions 175-6
      retirement annuity contracts 175
    state pension 176-7

Secret profits
  directors duties and 58-9
  duty to account for 9
Share capital
  private companies 226
Shareholders
  accounts, presentation to 243
  actions by 75
  agreements
    advantages of
      difficulties of enforcing articles 236
      protection of interests 235
      secrecy 235
      veto 236
    arbitration clause 238
    directors
      appointment of 236
      service contracts 236
    dividends, payment of 237
    drafting 236-8
    enforcing 238
    implied contracts and 73
    legal limits on use of 238
    policy decisions, approval for 236
    restrictive covenants 237-8
    shares, issue of 236-7
    voting rights, protection of 236-7
    withdrawal from company 237
  company as own 86
  contract
    members, between 72
    members and company, between 72
  court, powers of, purchase of petitioners
    shares 77
  directors, appointment and removal of 63
  distributions *see* distributions
  dividends
    legal entitlement to 79
    procedure for declaring and paying 78-9
    sources of, restrictions on
      basic rule 79
      profits available 79-81
      relevant accounts 81
    unlawful distributions, consequences 81
  duties of 71-2
  Foss v *Harbottle*, rule in 73-5
    exceptions to 74-5
  internal disputes 72
  majority rule 74-5
  meetings of 228
    presentation of accounts 243

Shareholders — *continued*
  membership rights 73
  powers of
    control, of 71
    sources of 71
  profits and 77-8
  register of membership
    contents of 70
    rectification of 70-1
    trusts 70
  rights 73
    membership 73
  special voting rights 64
  unfair prejudice 75-6
    court, powers of 76-7
Shares
  buy-back of 86-7, 100
    financing 87
  classes of 87
  disposal of 97-101
  issue of 38, 83-5, 236-7
    powers 84-5
    private companies 226
    public companies 270
    public, to 85
  legal nature of 83
  payment for 37
    consideration 85
    premium 85
  public and private companies compared 37-8
  purchase of own 86-7
    capital gains tax 166-7
    financial assistance by company for
      87, 100, 272
      general prohibition on 100-1
        general exception for all
          companies 101
        specific exception for private companies
          101
  redeemable 86
  redemption 100
    financing 87
  return as to allotments 85
  rights attaching to 83-4
  share capital
    authorised minimum 37
    company as member of itself 86
    maintenance of capital 85-6
    public companies 271
    share premium account 86
  transfer of
    contract for sale 97
    pre-emption rights 99-100
    private companies 226-7
    procedure on 97
    restrictions on 98-9

Shares — *continued*
    stock transfer form   97-8
    transmission by operation of law   100
    value of   84
Shelf companies
    advantages and disadvantages   52
    articles of association   51
    business name   51
    company name   51
    documentation   51
Small and medium-sized companies   38
    accounts   243-4
Sole proprietors
    retirement provision for *see* retirement
      provision
Solvency   248-9
Stamp duty   257-8

Taxation *see* capital allowances; corporation
    tax; income tax; inheritance tax
Treaty of Rome
  Article 85   183-5
    agreements of minor importance   184
    Article 85(3)   184

Treaty of Rome — *continued*
    block exemptions   185, 284-5
    horizontal agreements   184
    vertical agreements   184
  Article 86   185
  competition policy
    enforcement of
      Commission, by   186
      direct effect   185-6
  UK competition law and   186
  see also European Community

Unlimited companies   37

Winding up
  administration orders and   205
  compulsory
    court's discretion to refuse order   209
    grounds   208-9
    locus standi   209
  just and equitable   77
  partnership, dissolution of   27
  types of   208
  voluntary   209-10
  see also bankruptcy; liquidation